HISTORY
OF THE RISE, PROGRESS
AND TERMINATION OF THE
AMERICAN REVOLUTION

A Liberty Classics Edition

MERCY OTIS WARREN

HISTORY
OF THE RISE, PROGRESS
AND TERMINATION OF THE
AMERICAN REVOLUTION

interspersed with Biographical,

Political and Moral

Observations

IN TWO VOLUMES

by Mrs. Mercy Otis Warren

EDITED AND ANNOTATED

BY LESTER H. COHEN

VOLUME II

Liberty Fund

Indianapolis
1989

WITHDRAWN

Liberty*Classics* is a publishing imprint of Liberty Fund, Inc., a foundation established to encourage study of the ideal of a society of free and responsible individuals.

The cuneiform inscription that serves as the design motif for our end-papers is the earliest-known written appearance of the word "freedom" (*ama-gi*), or "liberty." It is taken from a clay document written about 2300 B.C. in the Sumerian city-state of Lagash.

Frontispiece portrait of Mercy Otis Warren by J. S. Copley. Courtesy of the Museum of Fine Arts, Boston, Massachusetts.

Facsimile title and index pages of the 1805 Manning and Loring edition courtesy of the Lilly Library, Indiana University, Bloomington, Indiana.

Cover art courtesy of the New York Public Library. Volume I, engraving by Paul Revere. Volume II, Painting by J. Trumbull.

Library of Congress Cataloging-in-Publication Data

Warren, Mercy Otis, 1728–1814.
    History of the rise, progress, and termination of the American Revolution.

    Reprint. Originally published: Boston : Printed by Manning and Loring.
for E. Larkin, 1805.
    Bibliography: v. 1, p.
    Includes indexes.
    1. United States—History—Revolution, 1775–1783.
I. Cohen, Lester H., 1944–   .   II. Title.
E208.W29   1988   973.3   87-26243

ISBN 0-86597-066-1 (set)
ISBN 0-86597-067-x (v. 1)
ISBN 0-86597-068-8 (v. 2)

ISBN 0-86597-069-6 (pbk.: set)
ISBN 0-86597-070-x (pbk.: v. 1)
ISBN 0-86597-071-8 (pbk.: v. 2)

10 9 8 7 6 5 4 3 2

Contents

VOLUME ONE

[VOLUME ONE OF THE 1805 EDITION]

VOLUME TWO

HISTORY
OF THE RISE, PROGRESS
AND TERMINATION OF THE
AMERICAN REVOLUTION

CHAPTER XVII

Distressed Situation of the Army and the Country, from various Causes • General Gates sent to the Southward—Surprised and defeated at Camden by Lord Cornwallis—Superseded • General Greene appointed to the Command in the Carolinas • Major Ferguson's Defeat • Sir Henry Clinton makes a Diversion in the Chesapeake, in favor of Lord Cornwallis • General Arnold sent there • His Defection and Character • Detection, Trial, and Death of Major Andre • Disposition of the Dutch Republic with regard to America • Governor Trumbull's Character, and Correspondence with the Baron Van der Capellen • Mr. Laurens appointed to negociate with the Dutch Republic

[227] The year one thousand seven hundred and eighty, was a year of incident, expectation, and event; a period pregnant with future consequences, interesting in the highest degree to the political happiness of the nations, and perhaps ultimately to the civil institutions of a great part of mankind. We left England in the preceding chapter, in a very perturbed state, arising both from their own internal dissensions, and the dread of foreign combinations, relative to their own island and its former dependencies.

At the same time, neither the pen of the historian, or the imagination of the poet, can fully [228] describe the embarrassments suffered by congress, by the commander in chief, and by men of firmness and principle in the several legislative bodies, through this and the beginning of the next year. The scarcity of specie, the rapid depreciation of paper, which at once sunk the property and corrupted the morals of the people; which destroyed all confidence in public bodies, reduced the old army to the extremes of misery, and seemed to preclude all possibility of raising a new one, sufficient for all the departments; were evils, which neither the wisdom or vigilance of congress could remedy.

CHAP. XVII   At such a crisis, more penetration and firmness, more judgment,

1 7 8 0   impartiality, and moderation, were requisite in the commander in
chief of the American armies, than usually fall within the compass of
the genius or ability of man. In the neighbourhood of a potent army,
general Washington had to guard with a very inadequate force, not
only against the arms of his enemies, but the machinations of British
emissaries, continually attempting to corrupt the fidelity both of his
officers and his troops.

Perhaps no one but himself can describe the complicated sources
of anxiety, that at this period pervaded the breast of the first military
officer, whose honor, whose life, whose country, hung suspended,
not on a single point only, but [229] on many events that quivered
in the winds of fortune, chance, or the more uncertain determinations
of men. Happy is it to reflect, that these are all under the destination
of an unerring hand, that works in secret, ultimately to complete the
beneficent designs of Providence.

Some extracts from his own pen, very naturally express the agitations
of the mind of general Washington, in the preceding as well as the
present year. In one of his letters to a friend* he observed,

> Our conflict is not likely to cease so soon as every good man would wish.
> The measure of iniquity is not yet filled; and unless we can return a little
> more to first principles, and act a little more upon patriotic ground, I do
> not know when it will—or—what may be the issue of the contest.
> Speculation—peculation—engrossing—forestalling—with all their concom-
> itants, afford too many melancholy proofs of the decay of public virtue;
> and too glaring instances of its being the interest and desire of too many,
> who would wish to be thought friends, to continue the war.

> [230] Nothing, I am convinced, but the depreciation of our currency,
> proceeding in a great measure from the foregoing causes, aided by stock-
> jobbing and party dissensions, has fed the hopes of the enemy, and kept
> the arms of Britain in America until now. They do not scruple to declare
> this themselves; and add, that we shall be our own conquerors. Cannot
> our common country (America) possess virtue enough to disappoint them?
> With you, sir, I think, that the consideration of a little dirty pelf to
> individuals, is not to be placed in competition with the essential rights
> and liberties of the present generation, and of millions yet unborn.

---

* This original letter was to James Warren, esquire, speaker of the assembly of
Massachusetts, March the thirty-first, one thousand seven hundred and seventy-
nine. [George Washington to James Warren, March 31, 1779, in John C. Fitzpatrick,
ed., *The Writings of George Washington* (39 Vols.; Washington, 1931–1944), 14: 311–
314. Also reprinted in WAL, II: 97–100.]

Shall a few designing men, for their own aggrandizement, and to gratify
their own avarice, overset the goodly fabric we have been rearing at the
expense of so much time, blood, and treasure?—and shall we at last
become the victims of our own abominable lust of gain?—Forbid it
Heaven!—forbid it all, and every state in the union! by enacting and
enforcing efficacious laws for checking the growth of these monstrous evils,
and restoring matters in some degree, to the pristine state they were in at
the commencement of the war.

Our cause is noble,—it is the cause of mankind; and the danger to it
springs from ourselves. [231] Shall we slumber and sleep then, when we
should be punishing those miscreants who have brought these troubles
upon us, and who are aiming to continue us in them? while we should be
striving to fill our battalions, and devising ways and means to appreciate
the currency, on the credit of which every thing depends?—I hope not.

                *   *   *

Let vigorous measures be adopted to punish speculators—forestallers—
and extortioners;—and above all—to sink the money by heavy taxes—to
promote public and private economy—encourage manufactures, &c.

Measures of this sort gone heartily into by the several states, will strike
at once at the root of all our misfortunes, and give the *coup de grace* to
British hope of subjugating this great continent, either by their arms or
their arts. The first, as I have before observed, they acknowledge unequal
to the task; the latter I am sure will be so, if we are not lost to every thing
that is good and virtuous.

A little time now, must unfold in some degree, the enemy's designs.
Whether the state of affairs in Europe will permit them to augment their
army, with more than recruits for the regiments now in America, and
therewith attempt an active and vigorous campaign,—or whether with their
Canadian [232] and Florida force, they will aid and abet the Indians in
ravaging our western frontier, while their shipping with detachments harass,
(and if they mean to prosecute the predatory war threatened by administration through their commissioners,) burn, and destroy our sea-coast,—or
whether, contrary to expectation, they are more disposed to negociate than
to either, is more than I can determine. The latter will depend very much
on their apprehensions of Spain, and their own foreign alliances. At present,
we seem to be in a chaos, but this cannot last long, as I presume the
ultimate determinations of the British court will be developed at the
meeting of parliament, after the holidays.

An extract of another letter from general Washington to the governor
of Pennsylvania, dated August the twentieth, one thousand seven
hundred and eighty, discovers the same anxiety for the fate of the
contest, as the above. In this he said,

To me it will appear miraculous if our affairs can maintain themselves much longer, in their present train. If either the temper or the resources of the country will not admit of an alteration, we may soon expect to be reduced to the humiliating condition, of seeing the cause of America held up in America by foreign arms. The discontents of the troops have been gradually nurtured to a dangerous extremity. Something [233] satisfactory must be done, or the army must cease to exist at the end of the campaign; or it will exhibit an example of more virtue, fortitude, self-denial, and perseverance, than has perhaps ever been paralleled in the history of human enthusiasm.

While thus impressed with these apprehensions of the depreciation of public virtue, general Washington had to balance the parties, and to meliorate the distresses of the inhabitants, alternately ravaged by all descriptions of soldiers, in the vicinity of both armies. It was impossible for him to strike any capital blow, without money even for daily expenses, without a naval force sufficient to cover any exertions; his battalions incomplete, his army clamorous and discontented, and on the point of mutiny, from the deficiencies in their pay, and the immediate want of every necessary of life.

At the same time, the legislatures of the several states were in the utmost anxiety, to devise ways and means to supply the requisitions of congress, who had recently laid a tax of many millions on the states, in order to sink the enormous quantity of old paper money. The calls of an army, naked, hungry, and turbulent, even to the discovery of symptoms of revolt, were indeed alarming. The pressing necessities of the [234] army, and the critical exigencies of the times, crowded upon them in every department, and required the utmost wisdom, vigilance, and fortitude.

Nothing depictures the characters, the sentiments, and the feelings of men, more strongly than their private letters at the time. Perhaps this may be evinced, by giving the reader a paragraph of a letter from the speaker* of the house of representatives of Massachusetts, to a private friend, at this critical area of embarrassment and perplexity.

> Our public affairs wear a most disagreeable aspect. Embarrassments increase from every quarter. My contemplations are engrossed by day and by night, for the salvation of my country. If we succeed, I shall have pleasure which a fortune cannot give; if we fail, I shall feel consolations that those who are intent only on making fortunes, must envy. In a country abounding with men and provisions, it would torture a Sully to raise and

---

* The honorable James Warren, esquire, to [Source not identified].

support an army in the field. Every thing is resolved into money: but the great question is, how to get it?—Taxes, though so great, and often repeated, do not bring it in fast enough; we cannot borrow, because no one will lend: while the army is in danger of [235] starving or disbanding. If we lay more taxes, the very people who have been used to tender the one half of their property, or even their all, for the service of their country, will now revolt at the idea of paying a two-hundredth part; and it might perhaps create uneasiness that might break the union. On the other hand, if we do not lay more taxes, for aught I see, there must be an end of the contest. All these difficulties are increased by the successes of the enemy, which clog our measures by dispiriting the army and the people. But I do not despair. One vigorous and grand campaign may yet put a glorious period to the war. All depends on proper exertions. We have to choose glory, honor, and happiness, or infamy, disgrace, and misery.

The complicated difficulties already depictured, clearly prove, that such a spirit of avarice and peculation had crept into the public departments, and taken deep hold of the majority of the people, as Americans a few years before, were thought incapable of. The careful observer of human conduct will readily perceive, that a variety of concurring causes led to this sudden change of character. The opulent, who had been used to ease, independence, and generosity, were reduced, dispirited, and deprived of the ability of rendering pecuniary service to their country, by the unavoidable failure of public faith. Great part of the fortunes of the [236] widow, the orphan, and the aged, were sunk in the public funds; so that the nominal income of a year, would scarcely supply the necessities of a day.

The depreciation of paper had been so rapid, that at this time,* one hundred and twenty dollars of the paper currency was not an equivalent to one in silver or gold: while at the same time, a sudden accumulation of property by privateering, by speculation, by accident, or fraud, placed many in the lap of affluence, who were without a principle, education, or family. These, from a thoughtless ignorance,

---

* See scale of depreciation. [The rapid and nearly catastrophic depreciation of state and continental currencies was widely discussed between 1777 and 1781. In September 1779 Congress issued a Circular Letter to the states in which it rejected any suggestion that paper money should be officially discounted. By March 1780 it resolved upon exactly such a scheme. See JCC, XV: 1051–1064 (September 13, 1779); XVI: 205–207 (February 26, 1780), 216–217 (February 28, 1780), 262–267 (March 18, 1780). The best contemporary historical discussion of financial chaos is David Ramsay, *The History of the Revolution of South-Carolina* (2 vols.; Trenton, 1785), II: 68–100, 410–431.]

and the novelty of splendor to which they had been total strangers,
suddenly plunged into every kind of dissipation, and grafted the
extravagancies and follies of foreigners, on their own passion for
squandering what by them had been so easily acquired.

Thus, avarice without frugality, and profusion without taste, were
indulged, and soon banished the simplicity and elegance that had
formerly reigned: instead of which, there was spread in America
among the rising generation, a thirst for the accumulation of wealth,
unknown to their ancestors. A class who had not had the advantages
of the best education, and who had paid little attention to the
principles [237] of the revolution, took the lead in manners. Sanctioned
by the breach of public faith, the private obligations of justice seemed
to be little regarded, and the sacred idea of equity in private contracts
was annihilated for a time, by the example of public deficiency.

The infantile state of government, the inexperience of its leaders,
and the necessity of substituting a medium with only an imaginary
value, brought an impeachment on congress, without voluntary deviations from probity, or willing breaches of faith. Perhaps nothing is
more true, than an observation of a member of that body, that "*the
necessity of affairs had often obliged them to depart from the purity of their
first principles.*" The complaint that the foundation was corrupt, was
artfully diffused: however that might be, the streams were undoubtedly
tainted, and contamination, with few exceptions, seemed to run
through the whole body of the people; and a declension of morals
was equally rapid with the depreciation of their currency.

But a superintending Providence, that overrules the designs, and
defeats the projects of men, remarkably upheld the spirit of the
Americans; and caused events that had for a time a very unfavorable
aspect, to operate in favor of independence and peace, and to make
a new nation [238] of the recent emigrants from the old and proud
empire of Britain.

But they had yet many difficulties to struggle with, which will be
sufficiently evinced as we follow the *route* of the British army, and
detail the transactions in the Carolinas. The embarrassments and
distresses, the battles, skirmishes, and disappointments, the alternate
successes and defeats, flight and pursuit, that took place between the
contending parties there, must be more copiously related, previous
to the manoeuvers through the state of Virginia, that led to the last
capital stroke, which finished with glory and renown the grand contest
between Great Britain and her colonies, and sealed the independence
of America.

Indeed a considerable time had elapsed, before the distresses of CHAP. XVII the country; the situation of the army, naked, hungry, and clamorous; 1 7 8 0 the pressing importunity of general Washington; the addresses and declarations of congress; and the remonstrances of the several legislative bodies, could arouse from the pursuit of private interest, those who thought themselves secure from immediate danger.

Though from many untoward circumstances, a cloud for a time had seemed to hover over the minds of many, the people again awaked, both from the dream of secure enjoyment in [239] some, and the dread apprehensions in others of falling under the British yoke. The patriotic exertions and unshaken firmness of the few in every state, again had their influence on the many, and all seemed ready to suffer any thing, but a subjugation to the crown of Britain.

Not the loss of Charleston, a captured army, the destruction of their marine, the sinking state of their medium, the internal ravages of their country, and their sea-coast blazing under the fire of their enemies, had the smallest tendency to bend the Americans to a dereliction of their claim to independence. A confidence in their own good fortune, or rather in that Providence, whose fiat points out the rise and marks the boundaries of empire, supported the more thoughtful; while a constitutional hardiness, warmed by enthusiasm, and whetted by innumerable and recent injuries, still buoyed up the hopes of the soldier, the statesman, the legislator, and the people at large, even in the darkest moments.

Immediately after the news reached congress, that general Lincoln had surrendered Charleston, and that himself and his army were prisoners to the British commander, the baron de Kalb, a brave and experienced Prussian officer, who had been some time in the American service, was ordered to Virginia, with sanguine [240] hopes of checking the further progress of the British arms. Though the baron de Kalb was an officer of great military merit, his command at the southward was only temporary.

General Gates, the successful conqueror in the northern, was vested with the chief command in the southern department. It was an appointment of great responsibility: this might be a reason, in addition to the great respect which this foreign nobleman had for general Gates, that led him to express in all his letters to his friends, the peculiar satisfaction he felt on his arrival to take the chief command. An officer of his name and experience, at once emboldened the friends of their country, and intimidated the wavering and disaffected. The renowned soldier who had captured one proud British general and his

army, was at this time viewed with particular awe and respect by
another.

Nor was it long before most of the British commanders were
convinced of the delusory nature of those assurances they had received
from the loyalists, that a general disgust to the authority of congress
prevailed; that the defection, more particularly in North Carolina,
was such, that the people were ready to renounce all *American
usurpations*, as soon as the royal standard should be erected among
them. [241] But experiment soon convinced them of the futility of
such expectations.

The baron de Kalb had been sent on earlier from head-quarters:
he had with him a detachment of fourteen hundred men. He stayed
only a few weeks in Virginia, and moved from thence to Carolina,
where he soon after met general Gates. After the junction of general
Gates and the baron de Kalb, they, with unexampled patience and
fatigue, marched an army of several thousand men through a barren
country, that afforded no subsistence except green fruits, and other
unwholesome aliments. They reached the borders of South Carolina,
and encamped at Clermont the thirteenth of August.

On his arrival in the vicinity of the British headquarters, general
Gates published a proclamation, inviting the patriotic inhabitants of
South Carolina, "to join heartily in rescuing themselves and their
country, from the oppression of a government imposed on them by
the ruffian hand of power." In this proclamation he promised forgiveness and perfect security, to such of the unfortunate citizens of the
state, as had been induced by the terror of sanguinary punishments,
and the arbitrary measures of military domination, apparently to
acquiesce under the British government.

[242] He observed,

> that they had been obliged to make a forced declaration of allegiance and
> support to a tyranny, which the indignant souls of citizens resolved on
> freedom, inwardly revolted at with horror and detestation: that they might
> rest satisfied, that the genuine motive which has given energy to the
> present exertions, is the hope of rescuing them from the iron rod of
> oppression, and restoring to them those blessings of freedom and inde-
> pendence, which it is the duty and interest of the citizens of these United
> States, jointly and reciprocally to support and confirm.

The situation of general Gates at Clermont was not very advantageous, but his design was not to continue long there, but by a sudden
move to fall unexpectedly on lord Rawdon, who had fixed his head-

quarters at Camden. This place was about thirteen miles distant from
Clermont, on the borders of the river Santee, from whence the
communication was easy to the internal parts of the country.

Lord Cornwallis had gained early intelligence of the movements of
the American army, and had arrived at Camden himself, with a similar
design, by an unexpected blow, to surprise general Gates and defeat
his arrangements. His lordship effected his purpose with a facility
beyond his own expectations. The two armies [243] met in the night
of the fifteenth of August, one thousand seven hundred and eighty.
Mutually surprised by the sudden necessity of action, a loose skirmish
was kept up until the morning, when a general engagement commenced.

The British troops were not equal in numbers to those of the
Americans, including the militia, while the renowned character of
general Gates heightened the ideas of their strength. But the onset
on both sides began with equal spirit and bravery, and was continued
with valor equally honorary to both parties, until the militia intimidated, particularly those from Virginia and North Carolina, gave
ground, threw down their arms, and fled with great precipitation. The
order of the army was immediately broken, and fortune no longer
favorable, forsook the American veteran, at the moment his reputation
courted, and depended on her smiles. His troops were totally routed,
and the general himself fled, rather than retreated, in a manner that
was thought for a time, in some measure to sully the laurels of
Saratoga.

The baron de Kalb, an officer of great military talents and reputation,
was mortally wounded in this action. He died rejoicing in the services
he had rendered America in her noble struggles for liberty, and gloried
with his [244] last breath, in the honor of dying in defence of the
rights of man. Before his death he dictated a letter to a friend,
expressive of the warmest affection for the Americans, containing the
highest encomiums on the valor of the continental troops, of which
he had been so recent a witness, and declaring the satisfaction which
he then felt, in having been a partaker of their fortune, and having
fallen in their cause.*

* When lord Cornwallis was informed of the rank and merits of the baron de Kalb,
he directed that his remains should be respectfully interred. He was buried near
the village of Camden; but no memorial of the deposite of this distinguished hero
has been preserved, though congress some time afterwards directed a monument
should be erected to his memory. Nothing was however done, except planting an
ornamental tree at the head of his grave.

CHAP. XVII   The proportion of slain among the Americans, was much greater
1 7 8 0   than that of the British. Brigadier general Gregory was killed, with
several other brave officers: Rutherford and others were wounded and
captured. The total *rout* of the Americans was completed, by the
pursuit and destruction of a corps at some distance from the scene of
the late action, commanded by colonel Sumpter. He was advancing
with a strong body to the aid of general Gates, but meeting the news
of his defeat, he endeavoured to retreat, and being unfortunately
overtaken by colonel Tarleton, his whole party was dispersed or cut
off.

[245] Censure for a time fell very heavily on general Gates, for the
precipitation and distance of his retreat. He scarcely halted until he
reached Hillsborough, an hundred miles from the field of battle. Yet
neither the courage nor the fidelity of the bold and long-tried veteran
could be called in question: the strongest human fortitude has
frequently suffered a momentary eclipse from that panic-struck influence, under which the mind of man sometimes unaccountably falls,
when there is no real or obvious cause of despair. This has been
exemplified in the greatest military characters; the duke of Parma*
and others; and even the celebrated royal hero of Prussia has retreated
before them as in a fright, but recovered himself, defied and conquered
his enemies.

General Gates, though he had lost the day in the unfortunate action
at Camden, lost no part of his courage, vigilance, or firmness. After
he reached Hillsborough, he made several efforts to collect a force
sufficient again to meet lord Cornwallis in the field: but the public
opinion bore hard upon his reputation: he was immediately superseded,
and a court-martial appointed to inquire into his conduct. He was
indeed [246] fully justified by the result of this military investigation,
and treated with the utmost respect by the army, and by the inhabitants
on his return to Virginia. Yet the tide of *fame* ebbed fast before him:

* The masterly retreat of the duke of Parma before the king of France, was indeed a
hasty flight; but he soon recovered himself, and asked the king by a trumpet, "what
he thought of his retreat?" The king was so much out of humor, that he could not
help saying, "he had no skill in retreating; and that in his opinion, the best retreat
in the world was little better than a flight." The duke however gained, rather than
lost reputation thereby. He resumed his high rank, as a commander of the first
abilities, and lived and died crowned with military fame and applause.

SIEGE OF ROUEN . . . *Mod. Univ. History.*
[*Modern Universal History*, XXIV: 249.]

but the impression made by his valor and military glory could never
be erased.

The most exalted minds may, however, be clouded by misfortunes. Chagrined by his defeat, and the consequences attending it, the climax of his affliction was completed by the death of an amiable wife, and the loss of his only son, a very hopeful youth, who died about the same time. This honest republican, whose determined spirit, uncorruptible integrity, and military merits, had been so eminently useful to America in many critical emergencies, retired to *Traveller's Rest*, his seat in Virginia, where he continued until the temporary prejudice against him had subsided, when he again resumed his rank in the army.

After a little time had dissipated the sudden impression made by his ill success and retreat, it was allowed by almost every one, that general Gates was not treated by congress with all [247] the delicacy, or indeed gratitude, that was due to an officer of his acknowledged merit. He however received the orders for supersedure and suspension, and resigned the command to general Greene with becoming dignity.

With a generosity and candor characteristic of himself, general Greene, who succeeded in the southern command, on all occasions vindicated the reputation of general Gates, who was fully restored to the good opinion of his countrymen; and continued to act an honorable part till the conclusion of the war. General Greene invariably asserted, that if there was any mistake in the conduct of Gates, it was in hazarding an action at all against such superior forces, not in his retreating after the battle was irretrievably lost. There was a large class, who from various motives, after the misfortunes of general Gates, endeavoured to vilify his name, and detract from his character.

It may be observed in this, as in innumerable instances in the life of man, that virtue and talents do not always hold their rank in the public esteem. Malice, intrigue, envy, and other adventitious circumstances, frequently cast a shade over the most meritorious characters; and fortune, more than real worth, not seldom establishes the reputation of her favorites, in the opinion of the undiscerning multitude and hands them down to posterity with laurels on their brow, which perhaps they never earned, [248] while characters of more intrinsic excellence, are vilified or forgotten. General Gates however, had the consolation at all times to reflect on the just and universal plaudits he received, for the glorious termination of his northern campaign, and

CHAP. XVII the many advantages which accrued to America, from the complete
1 7 8 0 conquest of such a formidable body of her foes.

Lord Cornwallis did not reap all the advantages he had expected from his victory at Camden. His severity did not aid his designs, though he sanctioned by proclamations the most summary executions of the unhappy sufferers, who had by compulsion borne arms in the British service, and were afterwards found enlisted under the banners of their country, in opposition to royal authority. Many of this description suffered immediate death, in consequence of the order of the commander in chief, while their houses were burned, and their families obliged to fly naked to the wilderness to seek some miserable shelter. Indeed little less severity could have been expected, from circumstances not favorable to the character of a British nobleman.

Whether stimulated by resentment, aroused by fear, or prompted by a wish to depopulate a country they despaired of conquering, is uncertain; it is true, however, that some of the British commanders when coming to action, observed in general orders, that they *wanted no* [249] *prisoners:* and it was said, that even lord Cornwallis had sometimes given the same cruel intimation, to troops too much disposed to barbarity, without the countenance of their superiors. The outrages of Tarleton and other British partisans, who cruelly and successfully ravaged the Carolinas, exemplified in too many instances, that the account of this disposition is not exaggerated. Their licentiousness was for several weeks indulged, without any check to their wanton barbarities. But the people daily more and more alienated from the royal cause, by a series of unthought of miseries, inflicted and suffered in consequence of its success; the inhabitants of the state of North Carolina, as well as of South Carolina and Georgia, and indeed the settlers on the more distant borders, were, in a few weeks after the battle of Camden, every where in motion, to stop the progress of British depredation and power. For a time these fierce people were without connected system, regular discipline or subordination, and had scarcely any knowledge of each other's designs. Small parties collected under any officer who had the courage to lead them on, and many such they found, ready to sacrifice every thing to the liberty they had enjoyed, and that independence they wished to maintain.

From the desultory movements of the British after the battle of Camden, and the continual [250] resistance and unceasing activity of

the Americans, attack and defeat, surprise and escape, plunder, CHAP. XVII
burning, and devastation, pervaded the whole country, when the 1 7 8 0
aged, the helpless, the women, and the children, alternately fell the
prey of opposite partisans. But the defeat of major Ferguson, a brave
and favorite officer, early in autumn, was a blow that discovered at
once the spirit of the people, and opened to lord Cornwallis the
general disaffection of that part of the country, where he had been
led to place the most confidence.

Major Ferguson had for several weeks taken post in Tryon county,
not far distant from the western mountains. He had there collected a
body of royalists, who united with his regular detachments, spread
terror and dismay through all the adjacent country. This aroused to
action all who were capable of bearing arms, in opposition to his
designs. A body of militia collected in and about the highlands of
North Carolina: a party of Hunter's riflemen, a number of the steady
yeomanry of the country, in short, a numerous and resolute band, in
defiance of danger and fatigue, determined to drive him from his
strong *position* on a spot called King's Mountain. Under various
commanders who had little knowledge of each other, they seemed
all to unite in the design of hunting down this useful prop of British
authority, in that part of the country.

[251] These hardy partisans effected their purpose; and though the
British commander exhibited the valor of a brave and magnanimous
officer, and his troops acquitted themselves with vigor and spirit, the
Americans, who in great numbers surrounded them, won the day.
Major Ferguson, with an hundred and fifty of his men, fell in the
action, and seven hundred were made prisoners, from whom were
selected a few, who, from motives of public zeal or private revenge,
were immediately executed. This summary infliction was imposed by
order of some of those fierce and uncivilized chieftains, who had spent
most of their lives in the mountains and forests, amidst the slaughter
of wild animals, which was necessary to their daily subsistence.

Perhaps the local situation of the huntsman or savage, may lessen
their horror at the sight of blood, where streams are continually pouring
down before them, from the gasping victim slain by their own hands;
and this may lead them, with fewer marks of compassion to immolate
their own species, when either interest or resentment stimulates. In
addition to this, all compassionate sensations might be totally deadened
by the example of the British, who seemed to estimate the life of a
man, on the same grade with that of the animal of the forest.

[252] The order for executing ten of the prisoners* immediately on their capture, was directed, as previously threatened, by a colonel Cleveland, who with Williams, Sevier, Shelby, and Campbell, were the principal officers who formed and conducted the enterprise against Ferguson.

After this victory, most of the adherents to the royal cause in the interior parts of the Carolinas, either changed sides or sunk into obscurity. Lord Cornwallis himself, in a letter to sir Henry Clinton about this time, complained, that

> it was in the militia of the northern frontier alone, that he could place the smallest dependence; and that they were so totally dispirited by Ferguson's defeat, that in the whole district he could not assemble an hundred men, and even in them he could not now place the smallest confidence.†

[253] There had been repeated assurances given by the loyalists in North Carolina, that their numbers and their zeal would facilitate the restoration of his majesty's government in that province; but it appears by many circumstances, that these promises were considered as very futile, in the opinion of several of the principal officers of the British army, as well as to the chief commander.

Soon after the affair with Ferguson, lord Cornwallis's health was so far impaired, that he directed lord Rawdon to make communications to sir Henry Clinton, and to give him a full statement of the perplexed and perilous situation of his majesty's forces in the Carolinas. After stating many circumstances of the deception of the loyalists, the difficulty of obtaining subsistence in such a barren country, and other particulars of their situation, lord Rawdon observed in his letter to general Clinton, that they were greatly surprised that no information had been given them of the advance of general Gates's army; and "no less grieved, that no information whatever of its movements, was conveyed to us by persons so deeply interested in the event, as the North Carolina loyalists."

After the defeat of general Gates, and the dispersion of his army,

---

* This step was justly complained of in a letter to general Smallwood from lord Cornwallis. He particularly regretted the death of a colonel Mills, a gentleman of a fair and uniform character; also a captain Oates, and others, who were charged with no crime but that of royalism.

† Sir Henry Clinton observed on this occasion, that "the fatal catastrophe of Ferguson's defeat, had lost lord Cornwallis the whole militia of Ninety-Six, amounting to four thousand men; and even threw South Carolina into a state of confusion and rebellion." [Stevens, *Campaign*, I: 186–189.]

the loyalists were informed, that the moment had arrived when they
[254] ought immediately to stand forth, and

exert themselves to prevent the re-union of the scattered enemy. Instant support was in that case promised them. Not a single man however, attempted to improve the favorable opportunity, or obeyed that summons for which they had before been so impatient. It was hoped that our approach might get the better of their timidity: yet, during a long period, whilst we were waiting at Charlotteburgh for our stores and convalescents, they did not even furnish us with the least information respecting the force collecting against us. In short, sir, we may have a powerful body of friends in North Carolina, and indeed we have cause to be convinced, that many of the inhabitants wish well to his majesty's arms; but they have not given evidence enough, either of their numbers or their activity, *to justify the stake of this province, for the uncertain advantages that might attend immediate junction with them.* There is reason to believe, that such must have been the risk.

Whilst this army lay at Charlotteburgh, Georgetown was taken from the militia by the rebels; and the whole country to the east of the Santee, gave such proofs of general defection, that even the militia of the High-Hills could not be prevailed upon to join a party of troops, who were sent to protect the boats upon the river. The defeat of major Ferguson [255] had so far dispirited this part of the country, and indeed the loyal subjects were so wearied by the long continuance of the campaign, that lieutenant colonel Cruger (commanding at Ninety-Six) sent information to earl Cornwallis, that the whole district had determined to submit, as soon as the rebels should enter it.*

While lord Cornwallis lay ill of a fever, lord Rawdon wrote to major general Leslie, in terms of disappointment and despondence. He observed,

that events had unfortunately taken place very different from expectation: that the first rumor of an advancing army under general Gates, had unveiled a spirit of disaffection, of which they could have formed no idea; and even the dispersion of that force did not extinguish the ferment which the hope of its support had raised. This hour, the majority of the inhabitants of that tract between the Pedee and the Santee, are in arms against us; and when we last heard from Charleston, they were in possession of Georgetown, from which they had dislodged our militia.†

* Lord Rawdon's letter to general Clinton, October the twenty-ninth, one thousand
  seven hundred and eighty. [Rawdon to Clinton in Stevens, *Campaign*, I: 277–280.]
† See printed correspondence of the generals Clinton, Cornwallis, Rawdon, &c.,
  published in London, one thousand seven hundred and eighty-three. [Rawdon to
  Leslie, October 24, 1780 in Stevens, *Campaign*, I: 271–276.]

[256] While lord Cornwallis was thus embarrassed and disappointed by various unsuccessful attempts, and the defeat of many of his military operations in the Carolinas this year, sir Henry Clinton made a diversion in the Chesapeake, in favor of his lordship's designs. A body of about three thousand men was sent on, under the command of general Leslie. He was under the orders of lord Cornwallis; but not hearing from his lordship for some time after his arrival, he was totally at a loss in what manner to proceed. But some time in the month of October, he received letters from lord Cornwallis, directing him to repair with all possible expedition to Charleston, to assist with all his forces in the complete subjugation of the Carolinas.

Sir Henry Clinton, from an idea that Cornwallis's prime object was the reduction of the Carolinas, and sensible of the necessity, at the same time, of *solid* operations in Virginia, paid all proper attention to the expedition into the Chesapeake. After general Leslie, in obedience to the orders of lord Cornwallis, had marched to the southward, the command of the armament in Virginia was given to general Arnold, who now acted under the orders of sir Henry Clinton. In consequence of his defection, he had been advanced to the rank of a brigadier general in the British army.

[257] General Arnold had recently deserted the American cause, sold himself to the enemies of his country, and engaged in their service. He was a man without principle from the beginning; and before his defection was discovered, he had sunk a character raised by impetuous valor, and some occasional strokes of bravery, attended with success, without being the possessor of any intrinsic merit.

He had accumulated a fortune by great crimes, and squandered it without reputation, long before he formed the plan to betray his country, and sacrifice a cause disgraced by the appointment of a man like himself, to such important trusts. Proud of the trappings of office, and ambitious of an ostentatious display of wealth and greatness, (the certain mark of a narrow mind,) he had wasted the plunder acquired at Montreal, where his conduct had been remarkably reprehensible; and had dissipated the rich harvest of peculation he had reaped at Philadelphia, where his rapacity had no bounds.

Montreal he had plundered in haste; but in Philadelphia, he sat himself down deliberately to seize every thing he could lay hands on in the city, to which he could affix an idea that it had been the property of the disaffected party, [258] and converted it to his own

use.* Not satisfied with the unjust accumulation of wealth, he had CHAP. XVII
entered into contracts for speculating and privateering, and at the 1 7 8 0
same time made exorbitant demands on congress, in compensation of
public services. In the one he was disappointed by the common failure
of such adventures; in the other he was rebuffed and mortified by
the commissioners appointed to examine his accounts, who curtailed
a great part of his demands as unjust, unfounded, and for which he
deserved severe reprehension, instead of a liquidation of the accounts
he had exhibited.

Involved by extravagance, and reproached by his creditors, his
resentment wrought him up to a determination of revenge for public
ignominy, at the expense of his country, and the sacrifice of the small
remains of reputation left, after the perpetration of so many crimes.

The command of the very important post at West Point, was vested
in general Arnold. No one suspected, notwithstanding the censures
which had fallen upon him, that he had a heart base enough
treacherously to betray his military trust. Who made the first advances
to negociation [259] is uncertain; but it appeared on a scrutiny, that
Arnold had made overtures to general Clinton, characteristic of his
own turpitude, and not very honorary to the British commander, if
viewed abstractedly from the usages of war, which too frequently
sanctions the blackest crimes, and enters into stipulations to justify
the treason, while generosity despises the traitor, and revolts at the
villany of the patricide. Thus his treacherous proposals were listened
to, and sir Henry Clinton authorised major Andre, his adjutant general,
a young gentleman of great integrity and worth, to hold a personal
and secret conference with the guilty Arnold.

A British sloop of war had been stationed for some time, at a
convenient place to facilitate the design: it was also said, that Andre

---

* See resolutions of the governor and council at Philadelphia, February the third, one
  thousand seven hundred and seventy-nine, relative to Arnold's conduct in that city.
  [Pennsylvania's charges against Arnold were published in a broadside which is
  reprinted in LDC, 12: 27. See Samuel Hazard, ed., *Pennsylvania Archives*, VII: 337–
  338 (Joseph Reed to George Washington, April 24, 1779); 347–350 (Joseph Reed to
  President of Congress, April 27, 1779); 351–355 (Washington to Reed, April 27,
  1779); 377–383 (Reed to Washington, May 8, 1779). Reed's attitude toward Arnold
  was surprisingly lenient. Reed was also deeply concerned that the military court
  martial, based in part on a complaint against Arnold made by a state (Pennsylvania),
  was both a usurpation of state jurisdiction and a denial of due process to the
  defendant Arnold.]

CHAP. XVII and Arnold had kept up a friendly correspondence on some trivial
1 7 8 0 matters, previous to their personal interview, which took place on the
twenty-first of September, one thousand seven hundred and eighty.
Major Andre was landed in the night, on a beach without the military
boundaries of either army. He there met Arnold, who communicated
to him the state of the army and garrison at West Point, the number
of men considered as necessary for its defence, a return of the
ordnance, and the disposition of the artillery corps in case of an attack
or alarm. The accounts he gave in writing, with drafts of all the works.
These papers [260] were afterwards found in the boot of the unfortunate Andre.

The conference continued so long, that it did not finish timely for
the safe retreat of major Andre. He was conducted, though without
his knowledge or consent, within the American posts, where he was
obliged to conceal himself in company with Arnold, until the ensuing
morning. It was then found impracticable for Clinton's agent to make
his escape by the way he had advanced. The Vulture sloop of war,
from whence he had been landed, had shifted her station while he
was on shore, and lay so much exposed to the fire of the Americans,
that the boatmen whom Arnold had bribed to bring his new friend to
the conference, refused to venture a second time on board. This
circumstance rendered it impossible for major Andre to return to New
York by water; he was therefore impelled, by the advice of Arnold,
to a circuitous *route*, as the only alternative to escape the danger into
which he was indiscreetly betrayed.

Thus was this young officer, whose former character undoubtedly
rendered him worthy of a better fate, reduced to the necessity of
hurrying as a disguised criminal, through the posts of his enemies, in
fallacious hopes of again recovering the camp of his friends. In this
painful state of mind, he had nearly reached the [261] British, when
he was suddenly arrested within the American lines, by three private
soldiers. His reflections may be more easily imagined than described—
taken in the night, detected in a disguised habit, under a fictitious
name, with a plan of the works at West Point, the situation, the
numbers, and the strength of the American army, with a pass under
the hand of general Arnold in his pocket-book.

He urged for a few moments, the man who first seized his horse's
bridle, to let him pass on; told him that his name was John Anderson;
that his business was important; and that he could not be detained:
but two other soldiers coming up, and in a peremptory manner saluting

him as their prisoner, after challenging him as a spy, he attempted
no farther equivocation, but presented a purse of gold, an elegant
watch, and offered other very tempting rewards, if he might be
permitted to pass unmolested to New York. Generously rejecting all
pecuniary rewards, the disinterested privates who seized the unfortunate Andre, had the fidelity to convey their prisoner as speedily as
possible, to the head-quarters of the American army.

Such instances of fidelity, and such contempt for private interest,
when united with duty and obligation to the public, are so rare among
the common classes of mankind, that the names of [262] *John Paulding,
David Williams,* and *Isaac Vanvert,** ought never to be forgotten.
General Washington immediately informed congress of the whole
business, and appointed a court-martial, consisting of the principal
officers of the army, to inquire into the circumstances and criminality
of this interesting affair.

The day after major Andre was taken, he wrote to general Washington with a frankness becoming a gentleman, and a man of honor
and principle. He observed, that what he had as yet said of himself,
was in the justifiable attempt to extricate him from threatened danger;
but that, too little accustomed to duplicity, he had not succeeded.
He intimated, that the temper of his mind was equal; and that no
apprehensions of personal safety had induced him to address the
commander in chief; but that it was to secure himself from the
imputation of having assumed a mean character, for treacherous
purposes or self-interest, a conduct which he declared incompatible
with the principles which had ever actuated him, as well as with his
condition in former life.

In this letter he added:—"It is to vindicate my fame that I speak;
not to solicit security. The person in your possession, is major John
[263] Andre, adjutant general to the British army." He then detailed
the whole transaction, from his going up the Hudson in the Vulture
sloop of war, until seized at Tarry-town, without his uniform, and, as
himself expressed, "betrayed into the vile condition of an enemy
within your posts." He requested his excellency that he might be
treated as a man of honor; and urged, that

in any rigor policy might dictate, I pray that a decency of conduct towards
me may mark, that though unfortunate, I am branded with nothing

---

* These were the names of the three soldiers who detected and secured major Andre.

dishonorable, as no motive could be mine, but the service of my king; and that I was involuntarily an impostor.

After a thorough investigation, the result of the trial of major Andre, was an unanimous opinion of the court-martial, that his accusation was just. They reported,

> that major Andre, adjutant general to the British army, ought to be considered as a *spy* from the enemy: that he came on shore from the Vulture sloop of war, in the night of the twenty-first of September, on an interview with general Arnold, in a private and secret manner; that he changed his dress within our lines, and under a feigned name, and in a disguised habit, passed our works at Stoney and Verplank's Points; that he was taken in a disguised habit on his way to New York; that he had in his possession several papers, which [264] contained intelligence for the enemy; and that agreeable to the laws and usages of nations, it is their opinion he ought to suffer death.*

Great interest was made in favor of this young gentleman, whose life had been unimpeached, and whose character promised a distinguished rank in society, both as a man of letters and a soldier. He was elegant in person, amiable in manners, polite, sensible, and brave: but from a misguided zeal for the service of his king, he descended to an assumed and disgraceful character; and by accident and mistake in himself, and the indiscretion and baseness of his untried friend, he found himself ranked with a class held infamous among all civilized nations.

The character of a spy has ever been held mean and disgraceful by all classes of men: yet the most celebrated commanders of all nations, have frequently employed some of their bravest and most confidential officers to wear a guise, in which if detected, they are at once subjected to infamy and to the halter. Doubtless, the generals Clinton and Washington were equally culpable, in selecting an Andre and a Hale to hazard all the hopes of youth and talents, on [265] the precarious die of executing with success, a business to which so much deception and baseness is attached.

But the fate of Andre was lamented by the enemies of his nation: his sufferings were soothed by the politeness and generosity of the

---

* The court consisted of fourteen very respectable officers, of whom general Greene was president. See trial of major Andre. [*Proceedings of a Board of General Officers, Held by Order of His Excellency Gen. Washington . . . Respecting Major Andre, Adjutant General of the British Army. September 29, 1780* (Philadelphia, 1780).]

commander in chief, and the officers of the American army. The CHAP. XVII
gloom of imprisonment was cheered in part, and the terrors of death 1 7 8 0
mitigated, by the friendly intercourse and converse of benevolent
minds; and the tear of compassion was drawn from every pitying eye,
that beheld this accomplished youth a victim to the usages of war.
While the unfortunate Hale, detected in the effort of gaining intelligence of the designs of the enemies of his country, in the same
clandestine manner, had been hanged in the city of New York, without
a day lent to pause on the awful transition from time to eternity.*

This event took place soon after the action on Long Island. The
dilemma to which he was reduced, and the situation of his army,
rendered it expedient for general Washington to endeavour to gain
some intelligence of the designs, [266] and subsequent operations of
sir William Howe, and the army under his command. This being
intimated by colonel Smallwood to captain Hale, a young gentleman
of unimpeachable character and rising hopes, he generously offered
to risk his life for the service of his country, in the perilous experiment.
He ventured into the city, was detected, and with the same frankness
and liberality of mind that marked the character of Andre, acknowledged that he was employed in a business that could not be forgiven
by his enemies; and, without the smallest trait of compassion from
any one, he was cruelly insulted, and executed with disgraceful rigor.
Nor was he permitted to bid a melancholy adieu to his friends, by
conveying letters to inform them of the fatal catastrophe, that
prematurely robbed them of a beloved son.

The lives of two such valuable young officers, thus cut off in the
morning of expectation, were similar in every thing but the treatment
they received from the hands of their enemies. The reader will draw
the parallel, or the contrast, between the conduct of the British and
the Americans, on an occasion that demanded equal humanity and
tenderness from every beholder, and make his own comment.

A personal interview, at the request of sir Henry Clinton, took
place between the generals Robertson and Greene; and every thing
in the [267] power of ingenuity, humanity, or affection, was proposed
by general Robertson to prevent the fate of the unhappy Andre. It
was urged that he went from the Vulture under the sanction of a flag;

* See an account of captain Hale's execution, in the British Remembrancer, and other
historical records. [Hale's execution was not reported in the *Remembrancer*, 1776 or
1777. For an exhaustive account of Hale, see George Dudley Seymour, *Documentary
Life of Nathan Hale* (New Haven, 1941).]

and that general Arnold had, as he had a right to do, admitted him within the American lines. But major Andre had too much sincerity to make use of any subterfuge not founded in truth: in the course of his examination, he with the utmost candor acknowledged, that "it was impossible for him to suppose he came on shore under the sanction of a flag."

The propriety and dignity with which he had written to general Washington, on his first becoming a prisoner; acknowledgment of his rank and condition in life, the manner of his detection, the accident of his being betrayed within the American posts; and indeed such was his whole deportment, that the feelings of humanity forbade a wish for the operation of the rigorous maxims of war.

It was thought necessary, that he should be adjudged the victim of policy; but resentment towards him was never harbored in any bosom. He gratefully acknowledged the kindness and civilities he received from the American officers; but he wished some amelioration of some part of his sentence; his sensibility was wounded by the manner in which he was doomed to die.

[268] He wrote general Washington the day before his execution, that

> Buoyed above the terror of death, by the consciousness of a life devoted to honorable pursuits, stained with no action that can give me remorse, I trust that the request I make to your excellency at this severe period, and which is to soften my last moments, will not be rejected.
>
> Sympathy towards a soldier, will surely induce you to adapt the mode of my death to the feelings of a man of honor.
>
> Let me hope, sir, that if aught in my character impresses you with esteem towards me; if aught in my misfortunes marks me the victim of policy, not of resentment; I shall experience the operation of those feelings in your breast, by being informed, I am not to die on a gibbet.

This his last and pathetic request, to die as a soldier and a man of honor, not as a criminal, the severity of military rules pronounced inadmissible, and this gallant and amiable young officer fell as a traitor, amidst the armies of America, but without a personal enemy: every tongue acceded to the justice of his sentence, yet every eye dropped a tear at the necessity of its execution. Many persons, from the impulse of humanity, thought that general Washington might, consistently with his character as [269] a soldier and a patriot, have meliorated the sentence of death so far, as to have saved, at his own earnest request, this amiable young man from the ignominy of a

gallows, by permitting him to die in a mode more consonant to the
ideas of the brave, the honorable, and the virtuous.

When general Arnold was first apprised of the detection of major Andre, and that he was conducted to head-quarters, he was struck with astonishment and terror, and in the agitation and agonies of a mad man, he called for a horse, mounted instantly, and rode down a craggy steep, never before explored on horseback. He took a barge, and under a flag he passed Verplank's Point, and soon found himself safe beneath the guns of the Vulture sloop of war. Before he took leave of the bargemen, he made them very generous offers if they would act as dishonorably as he had done: he promised them higher and better wages, if they would desert their country and enlist in the service of Britain; but they spurned at the offer, and were permitted to return. Perhaps, had these American watermen been apprised of the full extent of Arnold's criminality, they would have acted with as much resolution as the *trio* who seized major Andre, and have secured Arnold, when he might have suffered the punishment he deserved.

[270] After Arnold had got safe to New York, he wrote to general Washington in behalf of his wife; endeavoured to justify his own conduct, and his appointment and conference with Andre; claimed his right to send a flag to the enemy for any purposes he might think proper, while he held a respectable command in the American army; and urged the release of major Andre with art, insolence, and address. He did not stop here, but on the seventh of October, five days after the execution of Andre, he sent out an address to the people of America, fabricated under the auspices of his new masters, and couched in very insolent and overbearing language. He cast many indecent reflections on congress, on his countrymen, on the French nation, and on the alliance between America and France.

Soon after his arrival in New York, he received the price of his fidelity, ten thousand pounds sterling, in cash,—and of his honor, in a new commission under the crown of Great Britain.

The generals Clinton and Robertson did every thing to save the life of their favorite Andre, except delivering up the traitor Arnold. To this exchange, general Washington would readily have acceded; but a proposal of this nature could not be admitted; for, however beloved or esteemed the individual may be, personal [271] regards must yield to political exigencies. Thus while the accomplished Andre was permitted to die by the hand of the common executioner, the infamous Arnold was caressed, rewarded, and promoted to high rank in the British army.

The American government was not remiss in all proper encouragement to signal instances of faithful attachment to the interest and
service of their country. Congress ordered, that the three private
soldiers who had rejected the offers of Andre on his detection, should
each of them be presented with a silver medal, two hundred dollars
annually during life, and the thanks of congress, acknowledging the
high sense they retained of the virtuous conduct of *Paulding, Williams,*
and *Vanvert.*

Sir Henry Clinton had so high an opinion of general Arnold's military
abilities, and placed such entire confidence in this infamous traitor to
his country, that he vested him with commands of high trust and
importance; and for a time placed his sole dependence on him for
the ravage of the borders of Virginia. He had now the sole command
in the Chesapeake; and by his rapacity he was qualified to surprise
and plunder: his talents for prosecuting hostilities by unexpected
attack and massacre, were well known in both armies. But affairs in
Virginia beginning to wear a more serious aspect, general [272] Clinton
thought it not proper to leave general Arnold to his own discretion
for any length of time, without the support and assistance of officers
of more respectable character, who we shall see were appointed, and
sent forward the beginning of the next year.

We leave the operations of the British commanders in their several
departments, for the present, and again advert to some interesting
circumstances, and new disappointments, that took place towards the
close of the present year, and filled the mind of every true American
with the utmost concern. There had yet been no treaty or public
stipulations between the United States and any foreign nation, except
France; but circumstances had been ripening to bring forward immediate negociations with the Dutch republic.

Holland was at this period in a more delicate situation than almost
any other European power. Great Britain claimed her as an ally, and
held up the obligations of patronage and protection in strong language:
but the nature of the dispute between Great Britain and her trans-
atlantic domains, as well as the commercial views of the Belgian
provinces, interested the merchants, the burgomasters, and the
pensioners of Holland, in favor of America; while the partiality of the
stadtholder, his family, and the court connexions, were altogether
British; or at [273] least, the motives of interest, affection, or fear,
held them up in that light.

In the intermediate time, the clandestine assistance given by the

Dutch merchants was very advantageous to America; and the private
encouragement of some of the magistrates of the United Netherlands,
that a treaty of alliance and the strictest amity might in time be
accomplished between the two republics, heightened the expectations
of the American congress. None of the principal characters among the
Batavians, were more zealously interested in the success of the
American struggle for independence, than *Robert Jasper Van der
Capellen, lord of Marsch.*

This worthy Dutchman, as early as the seventh of December, one
thousand seven hundred and seventy-eight, had solicited a correspondence with several of the most prominent characters in America. A
more correct and judicious correspondent he could not have selected,
than governor Trumbull of Connecticut, whose merits as a man, a
patriot, and a christian, cannot be too highly appreciated. This
gentleman was distinguished in each line of this triple character: as a
man, his abilities were conspicuous, his comprehension clear, and his
judgment correct. The sedateness of his mind qualified him [274] for
the patriot, and the friend of a young and growing country, whose
manufactures had been checked, her commerce cramped, and their
liberties (for the enjoyment of which they had fled to a distant world)
curtailed; and in no instance did he ever deviate from the principles
of the revolution. His uniform conduct as a christian, was not less
signal; his integrity and uprightness, his benevolence and piety, and
the purity and simplicity of his manners, through a long life, approached
as near the example of the primitive patterns of a sublime religion,
as that of any one raised to eminence of office, who, by the flatteries
of their fellow-men, are too often led to forget themselves, their
country, and their God.

The baron Van der Capellen was a zealous supporter of the
Americans in their claim to independence, and pre-disposed many of
his countrymen to unite cordially with them, and enter into treaties
of amity and commerce, previous to the arrival of a minister at the
Hague, to negociate on that subject.

In one of his letters to governor Trumbull he had observed,

> that among other causes of distrust, in relation to the credit of America,
> was the false intelligence which the English incessantly circulate, the
> effects of which the friends of the Americans cannot destroy, for the want
> of information: that it was of the last importance [275] to enable them by
> authentic relations, which should contain nothing but what was *precisely*
> true, and in which even the disadvantages inseparable from the chances

of war, should not be concealed; in order to enable them from time to time, to give an idea of the actual state of things, and of what is really passing on the other side of the ocean.

He added:

> If you choose, sir, to honor me with such a correspondence, be assured that I shall make a proper use of it. Communications apparently in confidence, have a much stronger influence than those which appear in public.

He observed, that

> a description of the present state and advantages of United America; of the forms of government in its different republics; of the facility with which strangers there may establish themselves, and find a subsistence; of the price of lands, both cultivated and unimproved, of cattle, provisions, &c.; with a succinct history of the present war, and the cruelties committed by the English,—would excite astonishment in a country, where America is known but through the medium of the gazettes.

Governor Trumbull had not hesitated to comply with this request: he had detailed a succinct narrative of past and present circumstances, [276] and the future prospects of America; for a part of which the reader is referred to the Appendix.* The baron Capellen observes on the above letter of this gentleman, that "it was to be regretted that so handsome, so energetic a defence of the American cause, should be shut up in the port-folio of an individual: that he had communicated it with discretion in Amsterdam; and that it had made a very strong impression on all who had read it."

These favorable dispositions among many persons of high consideration in the United Netherlands, whose ancestors had suffered so much to secure their own liberties, led congress to expect their aid and support, in a contest so interesting to republican opinion, and the general freedom of mankind. It forbade any farther delay in the councils of America. Congress were convinced no time was to be lost; but that a minister with proper credentials, should immediately appear in a public character at the Hague; or if that should be found inadmissible, that he should have instructions to regulate any private negociations, according to the dictates of judgment, discretion, or necessity.

Accordingly, early in the present year, the honorable Henry Laurens

---

* See Appendix, Note No. IX.

of South Carolina, late president of the continental congress, was
[277] vested with this important commission. Perhaps a more judicious
choice of a public minister could not have been made throughout the
states. From his prudence, probity, politeness, and knowledge of the
world, Mr. Laurens was competent to the trust, and well qualified
for the execution thereof: but he was unfortunately captured on his
way by admiral Edwards, carried to Newfoundland and from thence
sent to England, where he experienced all the rigors of severity
usually inflicted on state criminals.

Before Mr. Laurens left the foggy atmosphere of Newfoundland,
an apparent instance of the deep-rooted jealousy harbored in the
breasts of the British officers, against all Americans who fell into their
hands, was discovered by the refusal of admiral Edwards to permit,
at Mr. Laurens's request, Mr. Winslow Warren to accompany him to
Europe, in the frigate in which he sailed.

This youth was the son of a gentleman who had been vested with
some of the first and most respectable offices of trust and importance
in America; he was captured on his way to Europe, a few weeks
before Mr. Laurens, to whom he had introductory letters from some
of the first characters in America, to be delivered on his arrival at the
Hague: their unfortunate meeting as prisoners on this dreary spot,
gave him an early opportunity to present them. No cartel had yet
been settled for the exchange of [278] prisoners; and sensibly touched
with compassion for their sufferings, Mr. Warren voluntarily engaged
to remain as an hostage till that arrangement might take place. The
admiral consented to send a great number of Americans to Boston,
on Mr. Warren's word of honor, that an equal number of British
prisoners would be returned.

Mr. Laurens wished to anticipate his release, from the generous
feelings of his own mind, as well as from the delicacy of sentiment
and the accomplished manners of Mr. Warren; and though they were
both treated with the utmost politeness by admiral Edwards, he
refused to gratify these gentlemen in their mutual wishes to be fellow-
passengers, as they were fellow-prisoners: but the admiral permitted
Mr. Warren, within three or four days after Mr. Laurens's departure,
to take passage in another frigate, bound directly to England.

Mr. Laurens took an affectionate leave of Mr. Warren, and requested
him to write his friends, or to tell them if he reached America before
him, that "though he was an old man, who had recently lost all his
estates in Charleston by the capture of that city, and had now lost his

liberty, that he was still the same; firm, cheerful, and unruffled by the shocks of fortune.''

[279] When Mr. Laurens arrived in England, he was committed to the tower, confined to very narrow apartments, and denied all intercourse with his friends. There Mr. Warren saw him when he arrived in England, near enough to exchange a salute, but they were not permitted to speak to each other.

It is observable that the defection of general Arnold, and the capture of Mr. Laurens, took place within a few days of each other. These two circumstances operated on the passions of men in a contrasted point of view. The treachery of Arnold was beheld with irritation and disdain, by his former military associates, and with the utmost disgust and abhorrence through all America. The fate of Mr. Laurens awakened the better feelings of the human heart. As an individual of the highest respectability, all who knew him were pained with apprehensions, lest he should be subjected to personal danger or sufferings. As a diplomatic officer, the first public character that had been sent to the Batavian provinces, it was feared, his captivity and detention might have an unfavorable effect on the foreign relations of America, and particularly on their connexion with Holland. Indeed a variety of circumstances that took place through the summer and autumn of this, did not augur the most propitious promises, relative to the operations of the next year.

C H A P T E R   X V I I I

Revolt of the Pennsylvania Line—Discontents in other Parts of the Army • Paper Medium sunk • Some active Movements of Don Bernard de Galvez in America • War between Great Britain and Spain opened in Europe by the Siege of Gibraltar • Short View of Diplomatic Transactions between America and several European Powers • Empress of Russia refuses to treat with the American States

[280] We have already seen the double disappointment experienced by the United States, occasioned by the capture of one army in South Carolina under general Lincoln, and the defeat of another commanded by general Gates in North Carolina, who was sent forward with the highest expectations of retrieving affairs in that quarter. . . . We have seen the complicated embarrassments of the United States, relative to raising, paying, and supporting a permanent army. . . . We have seen the pernicious effects of a depreciating currency, and the beginning of a spirit of peculation and regard to private interest, that was not expected from the former habits and professions of Americans. . . . We have seen the disappointments and delay relative to foreign negociations. . . . We have seen both the patient sufferings of the American army under the greatest necessity, and the rising restlessness [281] that soon pervaded nearly the whole body of the soldiery; and we have also seen the desertion of a general officer, in whom confidence had been placed as a man of courage: we left Arnold stigmatized as a traitor, and in all the pride and insolence of a British general, newly vested with command in reward of villany, beginning under the British standard, his career of ravage and depredation in Virginia.

In addition to the alarming circumstances already recapitulated, at the close of the preceding year, the most dangerous symptoms were exhibited in the conduct of a part of the army, which broke out in revolt; and the secession of the whole Pennsylvania line spread a temporary dismay.

On the first of January, one thousand seven hundred and eighty-one, upwards of a thousand men belonging to that line, marched in a body from the camp; others, equally disaffected, soon followed them. They took an advantageous ground, chose for their leader a serjeant major, a British deserter, and saluted him as their major general. On the third day of their revolt, a message was sent from the officers of the American camp: this they refused to receive; but to a flag which followed, requesting to know their complaints and intentions; they [282] replied, that "they had served three years; that they had engaged to serve no longer; nor would they return, or disperse, until their grievances were redressed, and their arrearages paid."

General Wayne, who commanded the line, had been greatly beloved and respected by the soldiery, nor did he at first himself doubt, but that his influence would soon bring them back to their duty. He did every thing in the power of a spirited and judicious officer, to dissipate their murmurs, and to quiet their clamors, in the beginning of the insurrection: but many of them pointed their bayonets at his breast; told him to be on his guard; that they were determined to march to congress to obtain a redress of grievances; and that, though they respected him as an officer, and loved his person, yet, if he attempted to fire on them, "he was a dead man."

Sir Henry Clinton soon gained intelligence of the confusion and danger into which the Americans were plunged. He improved the advantageous moment, and made the revolters every tempting offer, to increase and fix their defection. He sent several persons to offer, in his name, a pardon for all past offences, an immediate payment of their full demands on congress, and protection from the British government. He desired them to send proper persons [283] to Amboy, to treat farther, and engaged that a body of British troops was ready for their escort.*

How far the conduct of sir Henry Clinton is to be justified by the laws of war, we leave to the decision of military characters; but to the impartial spectator, though so often practised by officers of consideration and name, it appears an underhand interference, beneath the character of a brave and generous commander, to stimulate by those

---

* See sir Henry Clinton's letter to lord George Germaine, January, one thousand seven hundred and eighty-one. [See Lord George Germaine to Sir Henry Clinton, March 7, 1781, in Stevens, *Campaign*, I: 334.]

secret methods, a discontented class of soldiers, to turn the points of
their swords against their country and their former friends.

But the intrigues of the British officers, and the measures of their commander in chief, had not the smallest influence: the revolted line, though dissatisfied and disgusted, appeared to have no inclination to join the British army. They declared with one general voice, that was there an immediate necessity to call out the American forces, they would still fight under the orders of the congressional officers. Several British spies were detected, busily employed in endeavouring to increase the ferment, who were tried and executed with little ceremony.

[284] The prudent conduct of the commander in chief, and the disposition which appeared in government to do justice to their troops, subdued the spirit of mutiny. A respectable committee was sent from congress to hear their complaints, and as far as possible to relieve their sufferings. Those whose term of enlistment was expired, were paid off and discharged; the reasonable demands of others satisfied; and a general pardon granted to the offenders, who returned cheerfully to their duty.

The discontented and mutinous spirit of the troops was not, however, entirely eradicated: the sources of disquietude in an army situated like the present, were too many to suppress at once. They were without pay, without clothing sufficient for the calls of nature; and not satisfied with the assurances of future compensation, their murmurs were too general, and their complaints loud and pressing.

The contagion of the mutinous example of the Pennsylvania line, had spread in some degree its dangerous influence over other parts of the army: it operated more particularly on a part of the Jersey troops, soon after the pacification of the disorderly Pennsylvania soldiers, though not with equal success and impunity to themselves. They were unexpectedly surrounded by a detachment from the main body of the army, and ordered to parade without their [285] arms: on discovering some reluctance to obey, colonel Sprout, of the Massachusetts division, was directed to advance with a party, and demand their compliance within five minutes. As their numbers were not sufficient for resistance, they submitted without opposition. A few of the principal leaders of the revolt, were tried by a court-martial and adjudged guilty: as a second general pardon, without any penal inflictions, would have had a fatal effect on the army, two of them suffered death for their mutinous conduct.

This example of severity put a period to every symptom of open

CHAP. XVIII revolt, though not to the silent murmurs of the American army. They
1 7 8 1 still felt heavily the immediate inconveniences of the deficiency of
almost every article necessary to life: they had little subsistence, and
seldom any covering, except what was forced from the adjacent
inhabitants by military power. These circumstances were aggravated
by the little prospect there still appeared of filling their battalions,
and establishing a permanent army. Every evil had been enhanced,
and every pleasing anticipation darkened, by the general stagnation
of paper money, previous to the absolute death of such a ruinous
medium of intercourse between man and man. It had created suspicion
and apprehension in every mind, and led every one reluctantly to
part with their [286] specie, before they knew the fate of a currency,
agonizing in the last pangs of dissolution.

The successes at the northward had indeed given a spring to
expectation and action; but the gloomy appearances of affairs at the
southward, the ineffective movements in the central states, and the
perseverance of the king and parliament of Britain, in their measures
against the colonies, notwithstanding their recent connexion with a
potent foreign power, wrapt in the clouds of uncertainty, the final
termination of the present conflict.

These were discouragements that in theory might be thought
insurmountable: but *American Independence* was an object of too great
magnitude, to sink under the temporary evils, or the adventitious
circumstances of war.

That great source of moral turpitude, the circulating paper, which
had languished the last year until without sinew or nerve for any
effective purpose, died of itself in the present, without any visible
wound, except from the immense quantity counterfeited in New
York, and elsewhere under British influence. In a confidential letter
to lord George Germaine about this time, general Clinton observed,
that

> the experiments suggested by your lordship have been tried; no assistances
> that could be drawn from the power of gold, or the *arts* of [287]
> counterfeiting, have been left unattempted: but still the currency, like the
> widow's cruise of oil, has not failed.

It is true, indeed, that the currency answered most of the purposes
of congress, for some time after the date of the letter from which the
above extract is taken. When the paper ceased to circulate, no one
mourned or seemed to feel its loss; nor was it succeeded by any

stagnation of business, or derangement of order. Every one rejoiced
at the annihilation of such a deceptive medium, in full hope that
confidence between neighbour and neighbour, which this had destroyed, would again be restored.

The immense heaps of paper trash, denominated money, which
had been ushered into existence from necessity, were from equal
necessity locked up in darkness, there to wait some renovating day
to re-instamp some degree of value, on what had deceived many into
an ideal opinion that they possessed property. It was not long after
this paper intercourse ceased, before silver and gold appeared in
circulation, sufficient for a medium of trade and other purposes of
life. Much of it was brought from the hoarded bags of the miser, who
had concealed it in vaults instead of lending it to his distressed
countrymen; and much more of the precious metals were put into
circulation, by [288] the sums sent from Europe to support a British
army in captivity, and for the pay of the fleets and troops of France,
which were sent forward to the assistance of the Americans.

Notwithstanding all the baneful evils of a currency of only a nominal
value, that fluctuates from day to day, it would have been impossible
for the colonies to have carried on a war, in opposition to the power
of Great Britain, without this paper substitute for real specie. They
were not opulent, though a competence had generally followed their
industry. There were few among themselves wealthy enough to loan
money for public purposes: foreigners were long shy; and appeared
evidently reluctant at the idea of depositing their monies in the hands
of a government, with whom they had but recently commenced an
acquaintance.

France indeed, after the declaration of independence, generously
lent of her treasures, to support the claims of liberty and of the United
States, against the strong hand of Britain; but Spain kept her fingers
on the strings of her purse, though as observed above, America had
sent several agents to the court of Madrid, to solicit aid: nor was it
until the year one thousand seven hundred and eighty-two, that even
Holland opened her's to any effective purpose, for the pecuniary calls
that accumulated beneath [289] the waste of war, in which their sister
republic was involved.

A few observations on the eventful transactions which took place
among the nations of Europe this year, may here be properly
introduced, before a farther continuance of the narrative of the war.
This is necessary to give a clearer idea of the connexion brought

forward between America and several foreign nations, besides France and Spain, before the pride of Great Britain could condescend to acknowledge the independence of the United States.

Previous to lord Cornwallis's last campaign in America, most of the belligerent powers in Europe had stood aloof, in a posture of expectation, rather than immediate action, as waiting the events of time, to avail themselves of cooperation when convenient, with that side that might offer the greatest advantage, when weighed in the political scale by which the interest of all nations is generally balanced.

France had long since acknowledged the independence of America; and the whole house of Bourbon now supported the claim of the United States, though there had yet been no direct treaty between America and Spain. It had been the general expectation for some time [290] before it took place, that Spain would finally unite with France in support of the American cause. From this expectation, the Spaniards in South America had prepared themselves for a rupture, a considerable time before any formal declaration of war had taken place, between the courts of Madrid and St. James. They were in readiness to take the earliest advantage of such an event. They had accordingly seized Pensacola in West Florida, and several British posts on the Mississippi, before the troops stationed there had any intimation that hostilities were denounced in the usual style, between the crowns of England and Spain.

Don Bernard de Galvez, governor of Louisiana, had proclaimed the independence of America at New Orleans, at the head of all the forces he could collect, as early as the nineteenth of August, one thousand seven hundred and seventy-nine, and had proceeded immediately to surprise and conquer wherever he could, the unguarded settlements claimed by the crown of Britain. The British navy, generally masters of the ocean, had, early after hostilities commenced, beaten some of the Spanish ships, intercepted the convoys, and captured or destroyed several of the homeward bound fleets of merchantmen. But by the time we are upon, the arms of Spain had been successful in several enterprises by sea: at the Bay of Honduras and [291] in the West Indies, they also soon after gained several other advantages of some moment.

Don Bernard de Galvez had concerted a plan with the governor of the Havannah, to surprise Mobille. He encountered storms, dangers, disappointments, and difficulties, almost innumerable. This enterprising Spaniard recovered however, in some measure, his losses; and

receiving a reinforcement from the Havannah, with a part of the
regiment of Navarre, and some other auxiliaries, he repaired to, and
landed near Mobille. He summoned the garrison to surrender, who,
after a short defence, hung out a white flag, and a capitulation took
place, by which the English garrison surrendered themselves prisoners
of war.

In Europe, the war had been opened on the side of Spain, by the
siege of Gibraltar. This strong fortress had been closely invested by
a powerful fleet and army, for some time. The piratical states of
Barbary, who, to the disgrace of Europe, were permitted to war upon,
or to make tributary all the nations, had been recently disgusted with
Great Britain; and such a defection had taken place, that no relief
could be expected from that quarter, or any supplies of provisions
obtained from them for the garrison, which was reduced to such
distress, that they were several weeks without bread, except a few
worm-eaten biscuits, sold at an enormous [292] price: a guinea was
refused for a calf's head, a chicken sold for nine shillings sterling,
and every thing else proportionately scarce and dear; until the hardy
British veterans found they could subsist on the scanty allowance of
a jill or two of rice per day.

But by the unexampled intrepidity of general Elliot, and the equal
bravery of Boyd, the second in command; by the courage and
perseverance of many gallant British officers, and the spirit and
constitutional valor of their troops, the garrison was enabled to resist,
and to hold out amidst the distresses of famine, and against the most
tremendous attack and bombardment that perhaps ever took place.
A prodigious number of cannon of the heaviest size, and a vast
apparatus of mortars, at once spouted their torrents of fire and brimstone
on that barren rock. With equal horror and sublimity, the blaze was
poured back by the besieged, with little intermission.

The sheets of flame were spread over the adjacent seas and the
shipping for three or four weeks; when the magnanimous officers in
the garrison, who had been for four days together without provisions
of any kind, except a few kernels of rice, and a small quantity of
mouldy bread, were relieved by the arrival of admiral Rodney, on his
way to the West Indies. He was accompanied by a British fleet under
the [293] command of admiral Digby, who continued there with a
number of ships sufficient for defence, and for the security of a large
number of Spanish prizes taken by admiral Rodney. He had fallen in
with a fleet of eleven heavy ships of the line, commanded by don

Juan Langara, who, after being dangerously wounded, and his ship reduced to a wreck, yielded to the superiority of the British flag, as did the San Julien, commanded by the marquis Modena, and indeed nearly the whole of the Spanish fleet.

Notwithstanding the reduction of Gibraltar was suspended, we shall see the object was not relinquished. More formidable exertions were made the next year by the combined forces of France and Spain, for the completion of this favorite project.

It was indeed some time after the accession of Spain, before any other European power explicitly acknowledged the independence of the United States: but Mr. Izard, who was sent to Tuscany, and Mr. William Lee to the court of Vienna, in one thousand seven hundred and seventy-eight, inspired with that lively assurance which is sometimes the pledge of success, had met with no discouraging circumstances.

Holland had a still more difficult part to act, than France, Spain, or perhaps any other European power, who actually had adhered to, or appeared [294] inclined to favor, the cause of America. Her embarrassments arose in part from existing treaties with Great Britain, by which the latter claimed the Dutch republic as their ally, reproached her with ingratitude, and intimated that by former engagements, that republic was bound in all cases, to act offensively and defensively with the court of Great Britain. Thus the measures of the Batavian provinces were long impeded, by the intrigues of the British minister and the English faction at the Hague, before their high mightinesses acceded to the acknowledgement of American independence.

We have seen above, that the friendly disposition of the Batavians towards America was such, as to render it at once rational and expedient, for the American congress to send a public minister to reside at the Hague. Mr. Laurens, as already related, was appointed, sent forward, captured on his way, and detained for some time in Newfoundland. The unfortunate capture of the American envoy, prevented for a time all public negociations with Holland. He had been vested with discretionary powers, and had suitable instructions given him, to enter into private contracts and negociations, as exigencies might offer, for the interest of his country, until events were ripened for his full admission as ambassador from the United States of America.

[295] Mr. Laurens was captured at some leagues distance from Newfoundland. When he found his own fate was inevitable, he

neglected no precaution to prevent the public papers in his possession,
from falling into the hands of his enemies. The British commander
knew not the rank of his prisoner, until the packages seasonably
thrown overboard by Mr. Laurens, were recovered by a British sailor,
who had the courage to plunge into the sea with so much celerity as
to prevent them from sinking.

By these papers a full discovery was made, not only of the nature
of Mr. Laurens's commission, but of the dispositions of the Batavians
to aid the exertions beyond the Atlantic, for the liberties of mankind.
Their own freedom was a prize for which their ancestors had struggled
for more than seventy years, against the strong hand of despotism,
before they obtained the independence of their country.

In Mr. Laurens's trunk, thus recovered, was found a plan of a
treaty of alliance between the States of Holland and the United States
of America; also, letters from the pensioner of Amsterdam, with many
communications and letters from the principal gentlemen and merchants in that and many other cities in the Dutch provinces.

[296] Admiral Edwards considered the capture of Mr. Laurens as
so important, that he immediately ordered a frigate to England for
the conveyance of this gentleman, and the evidences of the commission
on which he had been sent out. These important papers received in
England, sir Joseph Yorke, the British minister resident at the Hague,
was directed by the king his master, to lay the whole of these
transactions before their high mightinesses the states-general of the
United Provinces.

The British minister complained loudly, and in terms of high
resentment, of the injuries and insults offered to Great Britain, by
the ungrateful conduct of the republic of Holland. He urged, that
secretly supplying the *rebellious colonies* with the accoutrements for
war, was a step not to be forgiven: that what had been suspected
before, now appeared clearly; and that he had the evidences in his
hand, and the names of the principal conspirators: that the Belgic
provinces were countenancing public negociations, and on the point
of executing treaties of amity and commerce with the *revolted Americans*.
He informed the states-general, that the king of England demanded
prompt satisfaction for these offences: that as a proof of their disavowal
of these measures, he required immediate and exemplary punishment
to be inflicted on the pensioner Van Berkel, and his accomplices,
[297] as disturbers of the public peace, and violaters of the law of
nations.

Notwithstanding the resentment of the British envoy, the conduct of the Dutch court remained for some time so equivocal, that neither Great Britain or America was fully satisfied with their determinations. It is true, a treaty with the United States was for some time postponed; but the answer of their high mightinesses to the memorial and remonstrances of sir Joseph Yorke, not being sufficiently condescending and decided, his disgust daily increased. He informed his court in very disadvantageous terms, of the effect of his repeated memorials, of the conduct of their high mightinesses, and of that of the principal characters of the Batavian provinces at large.

Great Britain soon after, in the recess of parliament, amidst all her other difficulties, at war with France, Spain, and America, and left alone by all the other powers of Europe, to decide her own quarrels, announced hostilities against the Netherlands; and a long manifesto from the king was sent abroad in the latter part of December, one thousand seven hundred and eighty.

A declaration of war against the republic of Holland, by the king of Great Britain, was very [298] unpleasing to most of the northern powers. The baron Nolken, the Swedish ambassador resident at the court of London, remonstrated against it in a state paper, in which he observed,

> that the flame of war, kindled in another hemisphere, had communicated to Europe; but the king of Sweden still flattered himself, that this conflagration would not extend beyond its first bounds; and particularly that a nation entirely commercial, which had made neutrality the invariable foundation of its conduct, would not have been enveloped in it: and yet, nevertheless, this has happened, almost in the very moment when that power had entered into the most inoffensive engagements, with the king and his two northern allies.

> If the most exact impartiality that was ever observed, could not exempt the king from immediately feeling the inconveniences of war, by the considerable losses sustained by his commercial subjects, he had much greater reason to apprehend the consequences, when those troubles were going to be extended; when an open war between Great Britain and the republic of Holland multiplied them; and to conclude, when neutral commerce was about to endure new shackles, by the hostilities committed between those two powers.

He added:

> The king could not but wish sincerely, that the measures taken by the empress [299] of Russia, for extinguishing this new war in its beginning, might be crowned with the most perfect success.

But, indifferent to the remonstrances and memorials of the potentates of Europe, Great Britain, hostile, wealthy, powerful, and proud,
appeared regardless of their resentment, and ready to bid defiance,
and spread the waste of war among all nations.

The capture of Mr. Laurens was however no small embarrassment
to the British ministry. Their pride would not suffer them to recognise
his public character; they dared not condemn him as a rebel; the
independence of America was too far advanced, and there were too
many captured noblemen and officers in the United States to think
of such a step, lest immediate retaliation should be made; and his
business was found too consequential to admit of his release. He was
confined in the tower, forbidden the use of pen, ink, and paper, and
all social intercourse with any one; and was even interdicted any
converse with a young son, who had been several years in England
for his education.

There he suffered a long imprisonment at his own expense, until
many months had elapsed, and many unexpected events had taken
place, that made it expedient to offer him his liberty without any
equivalent. This he refused to accept, [300] from the feelings of
honor, as congress at that time, had offered general Burgoyne in
exchange for Mr. Laurens.

The integrity of Mr. Laurens could not be warped either by flatteries
or menaces, though his health was much impaired by his severe and
incommodious confinement. It was intimated to him at a certain
period of his imprisonment, that it might operate in his favor, if he
would advise his son, colonel John Laurens, to withdraw himself from
the court of France, where he was then executing with success, a
commission from congress to negociate a loan of money, and solicit
farther aid both by sea and land, in behalf of the American States.

The firmness of Mr. Laurens was not shaken by the proposal. He
replied with equal confidence, both in the affection of his son and
the delicacy of his honor. He observed, that

> such was the filial regard of his son, that he knew he would not hesitate
> to forfeit his life for his father; but that no consideration would induce
> colonel Laurens to relinquish his honor, even were it possible for any
> circumstance to prevail on his father to make the improper request.

Immediately after the news of Mr. Laurens's capture, imprisonment,
and detention in England, the American congress directed [301] *John
Adams*, esquire, who had a second time been sent to Europe in a
public character, to leave France and repair to Holland, there to

CHAP. XVIII transact affairs with the states-general, which had before been en-
1 7 8 1 trusted to the fidelity of Mr. Laurens. Mr. Adams's commission was
enlarged: from a confidence in his talents and integrity, he was vested
with ample powers for negociation, for the forming treaties of alliance,
commerce, or the loan of monies, for the United States of America.
Not fettered by instructions, we shall see he exercised his discretionary
powers with judgment and ability.

Thus in strict amity with France and Spain, on the point of a treaty
of alliance with the Batavian republic, Sweden and Denmark balancing,
and nearly determined on a connexion with America, her foreign
relations in general wore a very favorable aspect.

The empress of Russia only, among the European nations where
an intercourse was opened, refused peremptorily to receive any
minister at her court, under the authority of the congress of the United
States of America. Overtures were made to the haughty sovereign of
the Russian empire, early enough to evince the high consideration in
which her arms and her character were viewed in America, as well as
in Europe; but without the least shadow of success. Determined to
maintain her independent [302] dignity, and hold the neutral position
she had chosen, she did not even deign to see the person sent on by
congress, to act as agent at the court of Petersburgh: but she concluded
the business with the policy of the statesman, the address of her sex,
and the superiority of the empress Catharine.

It was indeed doubted by many at the time, whether Mr. Dana
was qualified to act as envoy at the court of Russia, and to negociate
with such a potent state. He was undoubtedly a man of understanding,
with due share of professional knowledge, having been for several
years an attorney of eminence. But it was thought that he had not
either the address, the penetration, the knowledge of courts, or of
the human character, necessary for a negociator at the court of a
despotic female, at the head of a nation of machines, under the
absolute control of herself and her favorites.

It requires equanimity of temper, as well as true greatness of soul,
to command or retain the respect of great statesmen and politicians.
Distinguished talents and a pleasing address, were peculiarly necessary
for a negociator at the court of Russia, both from the character of the
nation and the monarch. The Russians were sanguine and revengeful,
and ready by their precipitate counsels to aid their arbitrary mistress,
in her bold designs and despotic mandates; [303] while she, as the
dictatress of Europe, determined the ruin of princes, and the annihilation of kingdoms.

On the earliest notice of an application from the congress of the
United States, the empress, after several expressions of civility,
containing a respectful regard to the interests of the American states,
made all proper acknowledgments to them for the attention paid to
herself. She had before granted them the free navigation of the Baltic,
in spite of the remonstrances of the British minister resident at
Petersburgh, against it.

She, however, ordered her minister to inform the American envoy,
that

> as mediatrix with the emperor of Germany and the king of Prussia, relative
> to the disputes subsisting between France, Spain, and Great Britain, she
> thought it improper for her to acknowledge the independence of America,
> until the result of the mediation was known; because the provisional
> articles depended on the definitive treaty.

That

> "when the latter was completed, she should be ready to proceed in the
> business: but that it would be highly improper for her to treat with America
> as an independent state, by virtue of powers or credentials issued previous
> to the acknowledgment of American independence, by the king of Great
> Britain.

That

> her delicacy was [304] a law to her, not to take before that time, a step
> which might not be considered as corresponding with those which have
> characterised her strict neutrality, during the course of the late war:
> notwithstanding which, the empress repeats, that you may enjoy, not only
> for your own honor, but also for your countrymen, who may come into her
> empire on commercial business, or otherwise, the most favorable reception,
> and the protection of the laws of nations.

This declaration placed the American agent in a very unpleasant
predicament: totally at a loss what further steps to take, not able to
obtain even an audience of the empress, he soon after returned to
America.*

The failure of this negociation might not be entirely owing to a
want of diplomatic skill or experience in the agent employed at the
court of Russia. Though the choice of the congressional minister was

---

* It was a singular circumstance at the court of the empress Catharine, for any foreign
minister or agent to be refused an interview with her majesty. She had always, from
pride, curiosity, or policy, condescended to converse herself, with strangers who
visited her court on public business.

perhaps, not so judicious as it might have been, many concurring circumstances prevented his success. The intrigues of [305] Britain, the arts of France, and the profound policy of the court of Petersburgh, probably all combined to defeat a measure, which, from the situation of some of the belligerent powers, and the known character of the empress, could not rationally have been expected, at that time, to meet the wishes of congress. It was also suggested, that the double-dealings of some Americans of consideration, had their weight in frustrating the negociation, and preventing a treaty between one of the most distinguished and influential powers in Europe, and the United States of America.

The above is a summary sketch of the views, the dispositions, and connexions, of the most important European powers, while the manœuvres in Virginia and the other southern states, were ripening events which brought forward accommodations, that not long after terminated in a general pacification, among the nations at war. The narration of naval transactions, connected with or influential on American affairs, both in the West Indies and in the European seas, is postponed to a subsequent part of this work; while we proceed to some further detail of military operations by land.

CHAPTER XIX

General Gates surrenders the Command of the Southern Army to General Greene, on his Arrival in South Carolina • Action between General Sumpter and Colonel Tarleton • General Morgan's Expedition—Meets and defeats Colonel Tarleton • Lord Cornwallis pursues General Morgan • Party of Americans cut off at the Catawba • Lord Cornwallis arrives at Hillsborough—Calls, by Proclamation, on all the Inhabitants of the State to join him • Battle of Guilford—Americans defeated • Lord Cornwallis marches towards Wilmington—General Greene pursues him—General Greene returns towards Camden • Action at Camden • Lord Rawdon evacuates Camden, and returns to Charleston • Barbarous State of Society among the Mountaineers, and in the back Settlements of the Carolinas • Attack on Ninety-Six—Repulse—General Greene again obliged to retreat • Execution of Colonel Hayne • Lord Rawdon leaves the State of South Carolina, and embarks for England • Action at the Eutaw Springs • General Greene retires to the High-Hills of Santee • Governor Rutledge returns to South Carolina, and resumes the Reins of Government

[306] After the misfortune and suspension of general Gates, immediate chap. xix steps were taken by congress and the commander in chief, to restore 1 7 8 1 the reputation of the American arms, to check the progress of the British, and defeat their sanguine hopes of speedily subduing the southern [307] colonies. Major general Greene was ordered on to take the command in that quarter. He arrived about the middle of autumn, one thousand seven hundred and eighty, at the headquarters of general Gates; soon after which, every thing seemed to wear a more favorable appearance, with regard to military arrangements and operations in the American army.

General Gates surrendered the command with a dignity and firmness becoming his own character, conscious that his disappointment and

CHAP. XIX
1 7 8 1

defeat did not originate in any want of courage or generalship, but from the unavoidable and complicated difficulties of existing circumstances. General Greene succeeded him, received the charge of the army, and took leave of general Gates, with a delicacy and propriety that evinced the high respect he felt for his predecessor.

All the prudence and magnanimity, valor and humanity, that adorned the character of general Greene, were necessary in the choice of difficulties that attended his new command. He had succeeded a brave, but unfortunate officer, whose troops were intimidated by recent defeat, dispirited by their naked and destitute situation, in a country unable to yield sufficient subsistence for one army, and which had for several months been ravaged by two.

[308] Lord Cornwallis's army was much superior in number and discipline, his troops were well clothed and regularly paid, and when general Greene first arrived, they were flushed by recent successes, particularly the defeat of general Gates. It is true, the death of major Ferguson and the *rout* of his party, was a serious disappointment, but not of sufficient consequence to check the designs and expectations of a British army, commanded by officers of the first military experience.

The inhabitants of the country were indeed divided in opinion; bitter, rancorous, and cruel, and many of them without any fixed political principles. Fluctuating and unstable, sometimes they were the partisans of Britain, and huzzaed for royalty; at others, they were the militia of the state in continental service, and professed themselves zealots for American independence. But general Greene, with remarkable coolness and intrepidity, checked their licentious conduct, and punished desertion and treachery by necessary examples of severity; and thus in a short time, he established a more regular discipline.

Skirmishing parties pervaded all parts of the country. No one was more active and busy in these scenes, than the vigilant Tarleton. An affray took place in the month of November, between him and general Sumpter. After victory [309] had several times seemed to change sides, the continental troops won the field without much loss. General Sumpter was wounded, but not dangerously. The British lost in wounded and killed, near two hundred.

The British troops had yet met with no check, which had in any degree damped their ardor, except the defeat of major Ferguson. The most important movement which took place for some time after this

affair, was an action between general Morgan on the one part, and CHAP. XIX
colonel Tarleton on the other, in the month of January, one thousand 1 7 8 1
seven hundred and eighty-one. General Morgan was an early volunteer
in the American warfare: he had marched from Virginia to Cambridge,
at the head of a body of riflemen, to the aid of general Washington,
in one thousand seven hundred and seventy-five. He continued to
stand ready to enter on the post of danger, in any part of the continent,
where the defence of his country required the assistance of the most
valorous leaders. General Greene, convinced that no man could more
effectually execute any command with which he was entrusted,
ordered general Morgan with a considerable force, to march to the
western parts of South Carolina.

Lord Cornwallis having gained intelligence of this movement,
dispatched colonel Tarleton in pursuit of general Morgan. In a few
days, [310] they met near the river Pacolet. General Morgan had
reason to expect, from the rapid advance of colonel Tarleton, that a
meeting would have taken place sooner; but by various manoeuvers
he kept his troops at a distance, until a moment of advantage might
present, for acting with decided success. The Americans had rather
kept up the appearance of retreat, until they reached a spot called
the Cow-pens: fortunately for them, Tarleton came up, and a resolute
engagement ensued; when, after a short conflict, to the great joy of
the Americans, the British were routed, and totally defeated.

Colonel Tarleton, as one of the most resolute and active of the
British partisans, was particularly selected by lord Cornwallis, and
ordered to march with eleven hundred men, to watch the motions of
Morgan, impede his designs, and keep in awe the district of Ninety-
Six, toward which he found a detachment of the American army was
moving. The unexpected defeat of Tarleton, for a time threw him
into the back ground in the opinion of many of the British officers;
nor was lord Cornwallis himself much better satisfied with his conduct.*

[311] The name of Tarleton and his successes, had so long been
the terror of one side, and the triumph of the other, that neither had
calculated on a derangement or defeat of his projects. But three
hundred of his men killed in the action at Cow-pens, five hundred
captured, and himself obliged to fly with precipitation, convinced the

* Sir Henry Clinton observed afterwards, "that the unfortunate action at the Cow-
pens, diminished lord Cornwallis's army nearly one fourth." If this was true, it must
have been by desertion, or by a sudden defection of the inhabitants of the state,
who had previously aided him.

people that he was no longer invincible. The militia of the country were inspirited, and many of them flocked to the American standard, who had heretofore been too much intimidated to rally around it.

Colonel Tarleton was severely censured by the British officers, for suffering himself to be defeated, with his advantages of discipline, numbers, and every thing else that in all human probability might have insured him victory. They did not tax him with a want of personal bravery; but some of them would not allow, that he had talents for any thing superior to the requisites for "a captain of dragoons, who might skirmish and defeat in detail." However, he had certainly been considered by most of them in a higher point of view, before this misfortune: but his flight, and the loss of his light troops, left a tarnish on his military character, [312] that could not be easily wiped off, or forgiven. The loss of these light troops, so peculiarly necessary in the present service, was felt through all the succeeding campaign. But Tarleton soon recovered himself, and returned from his flight: he appeared within a day or two, not far from the ground from which he had been beaten, and resumed his usual boldness and barbarity.

Tarleton's defeat was a blow entirely unexpected to lord Cornwallis, and induced him to march himself from Wynnesborough to the Yadkin, in pursuit of general Morgan, with the hope of overtaking him, and recovering the prisoners. The British troops endured this long and fatiguing march under every species of difficulty, over rivers, swamps, marshes, and creeks, with uncommon resolution and patience. What greatly enhanced their hardships and inconveniences, the path of their *route* was, as lord Cornwallis expressed it, "*through one of the most rebellious tracts in America.*"

General Greene, on hearing that his lordship was in pursuit of Morgan, left his post near the Pedee under the command of general Huger, and with great celerity marched with a small party of friends and domestics, one hundred and fifty miles, and joined general Morgan before lord Cornwallis arrived at the Catawba. In [313] this pursuit, lord Cornwallis cut off some of the small detachments, not in sufficient force for effectual opposition. It is true, general Davidson made an unsuccessful stand on the banks of the Catawba, with three or four hundred men; but the British fording the river unexpectedly, he was himself killed, and his troops dispersed; and the crossing the river by the British army, was no farther impeded.

General Greene had ordered the colonels Huger and Williams,

whom he had left some days before at the Pedee, to join him with
their troops: however it was but a very short time after this junction,
before general Greene had the highest reason to conclude, that the
safety of his troops lay only in retreat; nor was this accomplished but
with the utmost difficulty, as the way he was obliged to traverse, was
frequently interrupted by steep ascents and unfordable rivers. But he
remarkably escaped a pursuing and powerful army, whose progress
was, fortunately for the Americans, checked by the same impediments,
and at much less favorable moments of arrival. Though we do not
assert, a *miracle* was wrought on the occasion, it is certain from good
authority,* that the freshets [314] swelled, and retarded the passage
of the British, while they seemed at times, to suspend their rapidity
in favor to the Americans: and the piety of general Greene in several
of his letters, attributed his remarkable escapes, and the protection
of his little army, to the intervention of a superintending Providence.

Thus after a flight and a chace of fifteen or twenty days, supported
by the most determined spirit and perseverance on both sides, general
Greene reached Guilford about the middle of February, where he
ordered all the troops he had left near the Pedee, under officers on
whom he could depend, to repair immediately to him.

Lord Cornwallis at or near the same time, took post at Hillsborough,
and there erected the royal standard. General Leslie had according
to orders left Virginia, and marched further south. He had arrived at
Charleston about the middle of December. He without delay marched
with fifteen hundred men, and soon overtook and joined lord Cornwallis, in the extreme part of the state. He had found the British
commander immersed in cares, perplexity, and fatigue, endeavouring
with all his ability, to restore by force the authority of his master,
among a people, the majority of whom, he soon found to his
mortification, were totally averse to the government and authority of
Great Britain. General Leslie continued with [315] him until some
time after the battle of Guilford, and by his bravery and activity was
essentially serviceable to the royal cause.

At Hillsborough, lord Cornwallis, by proclamation, called upon all
the faithful votaries to the crown of Britain, to repair immediately to
his camp with ten days provisions, to assist in the full restoration of
constitutional government. Numbers from all parts of the country,

---

* See general Greene's own letters, and the letters of other officers. [See Greene to
Washington, February 9, 1781 and February 15, 1781, in Sparks, *Correspondence*,
III: 225–228, 233–236.]

listened anew to the invitations and threatenings of the British commander, and moved with all possible dispatch towards his camp. But many of them fell on their way, by the fatal mistake of misapprehending the characters and connexions of the partisans about them. It must be extremely difficult in a country rent in sunder by civil feuds, and in arms under different leaders of parties opposed to each other, to know at once, in the hurry and confusions of crossing and re-crossing to join their friends, whether they were not encircled by their enemies.

Tarleton himself had sometimes mistaken his own partisans for the friends of congress: thus many of the royalists, as they were hastening to take protection under the banners of their king, were cut down by the same hand that spread slaughter and desolation among the opposers of the monarch. Many unfortunate victims of the sword, drew destruction upon themselves by [316] similar mistakes. An instance of this, among others shocking to the feelings of humanity, was the massacre of three or four hundred of this description of persons, headed by a colonel Pyles. They accidentally fell in the way of a continental detachment, commanded by general Pickens. The royalists mistaking the republicans for Tarleton and his party, whom Pickens was pursuing, they acknowledged themselves the subjects of the crown, made a merit of their advance, and called on colonel Tarleton as their leader: nor were they undeceived but by the blow that deprived them of life. It is indeed to be much lamented, that they were treated with as little mercy, and all cut down with equal cruelty, to any that had been experienced by the Americans from the most remorseless of their foes.

While in this state of confusion and depredation through the whole country, general Greene and lord Cornwallis lay at no great distance from each other: but Greene kept his position as much as possible concealed, as he was not yet in a situation to venture a decisive action: and though he was obliged to move earlier towards the British encampment, no engagement took place until about the middle of March. In the mean time, by his ability and address, he eluded the vigilance of his enemies, and kept himself secure by a continual change of posts, until strengthened by fresh reinforcements of the [317] North Carolina and Virginia militia. The few continental troops he had with him, joined by these, and a number of volunteers from the interior mountainous tracts of the western wilderness, induced him to think he might risk a general action.

On the fifteenth of March, the two armies met at Guilford, and

seemed at first to engage with equal ardor; but as usual, the raw
militia were intimidated by the valor and discipline of British veterans.
Almost the whole corps of Carolinians threw down their arms and
fled, many of them without even once discharging their firelocks.
This of course deranged the American army; yet they supported the
action with great spirit and bravery for an hour and a half, when they
were entirely broken, and obliged to retreat with the utmost precipitation. Both armies suffered much by the loss of many gallant officers,
and a considerable number of men.

Lord Cornwallis kept the field, and claimed a complete victory;
but the subsequent transactions discovered, that the balance of real
advantage lay on the other side. His lordship, immediately after the
action at Guilford, proclaimed pardon and protection to all the
inhabitants of the country on proper submission: yet at the same time,
he found it necessary to quit his present ground. He had previously
taken [318] the determination, to try the success of the British arms
in North Carolina and Virginia. He formed this resolution early; and
would have prosecuted it immediately after Ferguson's defeat, in
October, one thousand seven hundred and eighty, had he not been
detained by sickness. After his recovery he pursued the design; and
for this purpose had ordered general Leslie to leave Virginia, who (as
has been observed) joined him with a large detachment of troops,
about mid-winter. His lordship however, thought proper still to
postpone his original design, with the hope of bringing general Greene
to a decided action, and thereby more firmly uniting the inhabitants
of the country to the royal cause.

After the action at Guilford, and the dispersion of the American
troops, lord Cornwallis found it difficult to procure forage and provisions
sufficient for the subsistence of his army. He left the late field of
action, and moved onwards a few miles, and halted at Bell's Mills,
where he staid two days, and gave the troops a small supply of
provisions. From thence he moved slowly on account of his sick and
wounded, to Cross-Creek.

[319] It appears by his own letter to lord George Germaine, that
he had intended to continue thereabouts for some short time; but a
variety of disappointments that occurred, induced him to alter his
resolution. In this letter he observes:

> From all my information, I intended to have halted at Cross-Creek, as a
> proper place to refresh and refit the troops: and I was much disappointed
> on my arrival there, to find it totally impossible. Provisions were scarce;
> not four days forage within twenty miles; and to us the navigation of the

Cape Fear river to Wilmington, impracticable, for the distance by water is upwards of one hundred miles. Under these circumstances, I was obligated to continue my march to this place.*

Lord Cornwallis having decamped from the neighbourhood of his late military operations, marched with all possible expedition toward the more eastern parts of North Carolina. He found many difficulties on his way, but pursued his route with great perseverance, as did his army; they cheerfully sustained the severest fatigue; but as they had frequently done before, they marked their way with the slaughter of the active, and the blood of the innocent inhabitants, through a territory of many hundred miles in extent from Charleston to York-Town. It was afterwards computed, that fourteen hundred [320] widows were made during this year's campaign, only in the single district of Ninety-Six.†

After the defeat at Guilford, general Greene availed himself of his religious opinions to obtain relief and assistance from the neighbouring country. He had been educated in the Quaker denomination of Christians, but not too scrupulously attached to their tenets to take arms in defence of American liberty. The inhabitants in the vicinity of both armies, generally belonged to that sect: in the distress of the retreating army, he called them out to the exercise of that benevolence and charity, of which they make the highest professions. He wrote and reminded them, that though they could not conscientiously, consistently with the principles they professed, gird on the sword for the usual operations of war, yet nothing could execute them from the

---

* See earl Cornwallis's letter to lord George Germaine, dated Wilmington, April eighteenth, one thousand seven hundred and eighty-one. [Stevens, *Campaign*, I: 414–416.]

† General Greene's letters authenticate this fact. [Greene wrote numerous letters from Ninety-Six during his tenure as commander of the southern army. No surviving letter provides the estimate of "fourteen hundred widows," yet David Ramsay also used the same estimate years later. "The single district of Ninety-Six has been computed by well informed persons residing therein, to contain within its limits fourteen hundred widows and orphans; made so by the war." *The History of South Carolina* (2 vols.; Charleston, 1809; rpt. Spartanburg, S.C. 1858), I:258. Greene did, however, write to his wife, Catharine, on June 23, 1781: "My dear you can have no idea of the horrors of the Southern war. Murders are as frequent here as petty disputes to the Northward. . . . The Gentlemen in this quarter think themselves extreme happy if they can get their wives and families into some place of safety." (Original, Princeton University; copy, Nathanael Greene Papers, Rhode Island Historical Society.)]

exercise of compassion and assistance to the sick and wounded; to
this they were exhorted by their principles; and an ample field was now displayed to evince their sincerity by every charitable act.

His letters were more influential on this mild and unoffending body of people, than the proclamations of lord Cornwallis. They united to take care of the sick, to dress the wounded, and make collections of provisions for the relief of [321] the flying army. This was a very essential advantage to general Greene, whose confidence in the simplicity and kindness of this body of people, relieved him from any anxiety and embarrassment, relative to the sick and wounded he was obliged to leave behind.

Their example probably had an influence on others of different denominations, and indeed on most of the people in the circumjacent villages, whom we shall soon see quitting the royal standard, and following the fortune of the routed commander and his army, notwithstanding the high hopes which had been entertained for a short time by the British, that this defeat would put an end to any other effective operations of the *rebel general Greene*, as they styled him in their letters.

In consequence of the action at Guilford, general Greene had to lament the loss of several valuable officers, among whom were the generals Stephens and Huger, dangerously wounded. But those who were faithful to the service, on principles of supporting the general liberties of their country, lost no part of their vigor or fortitude under the sharpest disappointments and misfortunes; but rallied anew, and set their hardy faces against the most adverse circumstances [322] that might arise in the dangerous and uncertain conflict.

This, general Greene attested in all his letters: yet the ignorance of the people in general, the little knowledge they had of the principles of the contest, the want of stable principles of any kind among the generality of the inhabitants, rendered dependence on their fidelity very uncertain, on both sides the question, and put it beyond the calculation on events, as neither the British or American commanders could make an accurate statement of numbers from day to day, that belonged to their own army. Self-preservation often led both parties to deception; and the danger of the moment, sometimes, more than the turpitude of the heart, prompted them to act under disguise.

The letters and accounts of all the general officers, on both sides of the question, portray these difficulties in a style and manner more descriptive, than can be done by any one, who did not feel the complicated miseries which involved both armies, and the inhabitants of the Carolinas, at this period. To them the reader is referred, while we yet follow the American commander through perplexity, embarrassment, and fatigue, too complex for description.

After the defeat at Guilford, general Greene was far from being discouraged or intimidated [323] by the victorious triumph of his enemies. He retreated with a steady step, and retired only ten or fifteen miles from the scene of the late action. He had every reason to expect a second rencounter with the British army, who boasted that their victory was complete, though it was acknowledged by lord Cornwallis, that the action at Guilford was the bloodiest that had taken place during the war.* Yet when lord Cornwallis withdrew from the late scene of action, it did not appear so much the result of a systematic design of an able general, as it did that of the retreat of a conquered army.

This, with other circumstances, induced general Greene, after he had collected most of his scattered troops, to follow his lordship rather than to fly further. The inhabitants of the country (singular as it may appear) from this time more generally flocked to the camp of the defeated, than to that of the conquering general. A more thorough disaffection to British government hourly appeared, and a more impressive alarm from the apprehensions of subjugation, seemed to discover itself from the day of the retreat at Guilford. Numbers from all quarters came forward; and general Greene soon found himself in a situation to pursue in his turn.

[324] He accordingly followed the British army through cross roads and difficult paths, for about ten days; when finding his lordship declined meeting him again, and that by the rapidity of his movements their distance widened, general Greene thought it best to halt, and not further attempt to impede the route of the British commander toward Wilmington; and prepared himself to prosecute his previous design of relieving the state of South Carolina, without farther delay.

Within a few days he began his march toward Camden, the headquarters of lord Rawdon, on whom the command had devolved, and who was there encamped with only nine hundred men. General Greene's approach was rather unexpected to Rawdon; but by a sudden

---

* See lord Cornwallis's letter to sir Henry Clinton, in Clinton's Narrative, page 9. [Cornwallis to Clinton, April 10, 1781, in Stevens, *Campaign*, I: 395–399; "Narrative," p. 9. Also see two letters of Cornwallis to Germaine, March 17, 1781, *Ibid.*, pp. 354–362 and 363–370.]

and judicious advance, he fell on the Americans before they were in
readiness for his reception. Notwithstanding this sudden attack, which
took place on the twenty-fifth of April, general Greene, always cool
and collected, sustained a severe conflict with his usual intrepidity;
but was again obliged to retreat, though his numbers were superior.
Yet he observed about this time, that he was not so amply supported
as he might have expected, by aids from Virginia, Maryland, or
elsewhere; and that in North Carolina, such was the fluctuation of
opinion, the operation of fear, and a too general want of principle,
that he could not place [325] the strongest confidence in many who
accompanied him.

Lord Rawdon attempted soon after to bring general Greene to a
second engagement; but he too well understood the advantages he
might gain by declining it. The consequences justified his conduct;
as lord Rawdon, in a few days after the action at Camden, burnt many
of the mills, adjacent private houses, and other buildings, and
evacuated the post and moved toward Charleston, where he judged
his presence was more immediately necessary. This sudden evacuation
of Camden inspirited the *Continentals*, and inspired them with a
dangerous enthusiasm, that for a time could not be resisted. The
banks of the rivers and the country were scoured by various partisans,
in pursuit of forage and provisions, which were generally secured by
the Americans, after skirmishing and fighting their way through small
parties of the enemy, too weak for successful opposition.

Sumpter, Marion, and other leaders, general Greene observed,
"have people who adhere to them, and appear closely attached; yet,
perhaps more from a desire, and the opportunity of plundering, than
from an inclination to promote the independence of the United
States." General Greene was attended and supported by many brave,
humane and valiant officers, in his peregrinations through the Carolinas, [326] but their followers were generally licentious beyond
description. This sometimes impelled him to severities that wounded
the feelings of the man, though necessary in the discipline of an
army.

A detail of all the smaller rencounters that took place in this hostile
period in both the Carolinas, might fatigue, more than it would gratify,
the humane or inquisitive mind. It is enough to observe, that the
Americans, under various leaders and some capital commanders, were
continually attacking, with alternate success and defeat, the chain of
British posts planted from Camden to Ninety-Six: and as general

Greene himself expressed his sentiments in their embarrassed situation,—"We fight, get beaten; rise, and fight again: the whole country
is one continued scene of slaughter and blood. This country may
struggle a little longer; but unless they have more effectual support,
they must fall."*

It is to be lamented, that very many in this day of general distress,
suffered themselves to be governed either by vindictive passions, or
their feelings of resentment for personal injuries. Many took advantage
of the public confusion, to gratify, if not to justify, their own private
revenge, a stronger stimulus with some, than [327] any public or
political principle. Besides these, there were numbers who seemed
to enlist under the banners of liberty, with no views but those of
rapine, assassination, and robbery; and after they had for a time rioted
in the indulgence of those infernal passions, they frequently deserted,
and repaired to the British camp, and renewed each scene of villany
against the party they had just left. They were indeed well calculated
to become instruments in the hands of the British officers, to perpetrate
the cruelties they were too much disposed to inflict on the steady
adherents to the American cause. Thus, whether they pretended to
be the partisans of the one side or the other, rapacity and violence
raged among a fierce people, little accustomed to the restraints of law
and subordination.

The manners of the mountaineers and borderers of the Carolinas,
exemplified too strongly the native ferocity of man. Though descended
from civilized ancestors, it cannot be denied, that when for a length
of time, a people have been used to the modes of savage life common
to the rude stages of society, not feeling themselves restrained by
penal laws, nor under the influence of reason or religion, nor yet
impressed by apprehensions of disgrace, they sink into the habits of
savages, and appear scarce a grade above the brutal race. Thus it
required a very severe military discipline, to reduce to order the rude
peasantry that poured down from the [328] mountains, and collected
from the most rough, uncultivated parts of the country.

Dissension, mutiny, robbery, and murder, spread to an alarming
degree. There were too many instances of villany and barbarity, to
render it necessary to adduce more than a single fact, that may convey

* General Greene's letter to the chevalier de la Luzerne. [Greene to the Chevalier
de la Luzerne, April 28, 1781 (Original, Clements Library, University of Michigan;
copy, Henry E. Huntington Library). Greene began a letter to George Washington,
May 1, 1781, in almost the same language. Sparks, *Correspondence*, III: 298–300.]

an idea of the hazard of life without the risk of battle. We mention CHAP. XIX
therefore only the death of a colonel Grierson, a distinguished loyalist, 1 7 8 1
because this circumstance is particularly noticed by the commanders
of both armies. This gentleman was shot by an unknown hand, after
he had surrendered his arms to the Americans. Great exertion was
made to discover the perpetrator of this cruel deed: general Greene
offered a reward of one hundred guineas for the detection of the
murderer, but without effect: private assassination had become too
familiar a crime in that hostile country, for the perpetrators to betray
each other.

Perhaps few officers could have extricated themselves, and recovered
from the unforeseen embarrassments that attended him through the
southern campaign, with the facility, judgment, and perseverance,
that marked the conduct of the American commander in the Carolinas.
His mind was replete with resources in the greatest difficulties, and
his resolution equal to the severest enterprise. While the humanity
of [329] his disposition led him to soften as much as possible the
horrors of war, the placidity of his manners engaged the affections of
his friends, and the esteem and respect of his enemies. Yet he was
obliged to make some severe examples of atrocious characters, and
to punish by death, several who were detected under the description
of deserters and assassins.

After the action at Camden, Marion, Pickens, and Lee, with their
partisans, attacked and carried a number of small forts in the district
of Ninety-Six, with little or no effectual opposition, until they crossed
the Santee, and attacked fort Cornwallis, commanded by colonel
Brown, who defended it with great spirit and gallantry. As the
Americans approached, the British garrison, for their own better
security, nearly covered themselves under ground. They obstinately
refused to surrender, until every man who attempted to fire upon the
besiegers, was instantly shot down; but after a siege of twelve or
fourteen days, the fort, with about three hundred men, was surrendered
by capitulation.

Brown had been so barbarous and ferocious a partisan, that he was
hourly apprehensive of meeting with summary vengeance from the
hands of some of those who had suffered, either in their persons or
their friends. Many he had [330] murdered in cold blood; others he
had cruelly delivered into the hands of the savages, to suffer longer
torture. But the victor, feeling compassion for individual suffering,
sent him under an escort for his better security, to Savannah. Without

this indulgence, he must have fallen an immediate sacrifice, as he had to pass through a long tract of country, where he had been active in perpetrating the severest cruelties, accompanied by a number of loyalists, between whom and the adherents to the American cause, there raged such an infernal spirit of bitterness, that extermination seemed to be equally the wish of both parties.

The leaders of the American partisans were frequently checked by the humane advice of general Greene. He exhorted them, that it was more their duty by their lenity to induce those in opposition, to unite with them in supporting the cause of freedom, than it was to aim at their extermination. In a letter to Pickens he observed, that "the principles of humanity as well as policy required, that proper measures should be immediately taken, to restrain abuses, heal differences, and unite the people as much as possible."

While these desultory excursions were kept up, general Greene was endeavouring to concentrate his forces for the prosecution of more important objects. Many occurrences had redounded [331] much to his honor, though some of them were unfortunate. But his misfortunes did not impair his military reputation; nor was his courage or ability called in question on his assault on Ninety-Six, though, it did not terminate agreeably to his hopes. The garrison was defended with the greatest spirit and ability by lieutenant colonel Cruger. They sustained a siege with almost unexampled bravery, from the twenty-fourth of May to the eighteenth of June.

Notwithstanding the valor of the British troops, and the fortitude of their commander, they were reduced to the point of surrender, when by the address of an American lady, prompted by a laudable affection for her husband, a British officer within the garrison, she found means to convey a letter to colonel Cruger, with the pleasing intelligence, that if they could hold out a short time longer, their deliverance might be certain: that reinforcements were at hand; that lord Rawdon was marching to their relief with two thousand fresh troops, who had arrived within seven days from Ireland.

It was happy for general Greene, that he obtained early information that this strong body was on their way, and was hourly expected by his antagonists; but it was very affecting to the feelings of honor, patriotism, or pride, to find [332] himself obliged to raise the siege, almost in the moment of victory, and to retreat with precipitation from a spot, where but a day before, he had reason to flatter himself he should reap the laurels of conquest. This unexpected turn of affairs

was truly distressing to the American commander. It was painful and
humiliating to be compelled again to fly before a pursuing enemy, to
the extreme parts of a country he had recently trodden over with so
much fatigue and peril.

Some of his associates were so much disheartened by the untoward
circumstances of the campaign, that they advised him to fly from
Carolina, and to endeavour to save himself and the remainder of his
troops, by retreating to Virginia. To this advice, general Greene
replied, in the laconic style of the Spartan, with the spirit of a Roman,
and the enthusiasm of an American,—"*I will recover this country, or
perish in the attempt.*" His subsequent conduct and success justified
his noble resolution. He soon collected the militia from the distant
parts of the state, called in his detachments, and inspirited his troops
so far, as to recover his usual confidence in them. This encouraged
him to offer battle to lord Rawdon on the twelfth of July.

His lordship, strongly posted at Orangeburgh, and strengthened by
additional troops from several [333] quarters, declined the challenge.
This was not because he did not think himself in sufficient force to
accept it: he had previously determined to return to Charleston, as
soon as circumstances would permit. His presence was there necessary,
not only on account of military arrangements, but from the confusion
and disorder of civil affairs, the animosities of the citizens of different
descriptions, the insolence of the loyalists, and the complaints of
those who had been compelled to a temporary submission.

When lord Rawdon withdrew from Orangeburgh, he left a sufficient
number of troops for its defence; and making due arrangements for
the security of other posts, he hastened to Charleston. On this, general
Greene detached a part of his own army to march towards the capital,
and returned himself with the remainder, and took post on the heights
near the Santee. From thence he continually harassed the British by
small parties, who alternately returned these aggressions. Skirmish
and defeat, plunder, slaughter, and devastation, were every where
displayed, from the extremity of the country to the environs of the
city. Several weeks elapsed before the operations of either army were
more concentrated.

While the military operations against the Americans were vigorously
pursued without, the devoted city of Charleston suffered misery [334]
beyond description within. Severity, cruelty, and despair, raged for a
time without check or control. A single instance of inhumanity, in
the sacrifice of one of the victims of their resentment, will be sufficient

to evince the rigor and impolicy of British measures. The execution of colonel Hayne will leave a stain on the character of lord Rawdon, without exhibiting any other proofs of barbarous severity.

This gentleman had been a distinguished and very active officer in the American service, previous to the subjugation of Charleston. When this event took place, he found himself called to a separation from his family, a dereliction of his property, a submission to the conqueror. In this situation he thought it his duty to become a voluntary prisoner, and take his parole. On surrendering himself, he offered to engage and stand bound on the principles of honor, to do nothing prejudicial to the British interest until he was exchanged; but his abilities and his services were of such consideration to his country, that he was refused a parole, and told he must become a British subject, or submit to close confinement.

His family was then in a distant part of the country, and in great distress by sickness, and from the ravages of the loyalists in their neighbourhood. Thus he seemed impelled to acknowledge himself the subject of a government [335] he had relinquished from the purest principles, or renounce his tenderest connexions, and leave them without a possibility of his assistance, and at a moment when he hourly expected to hear of the death of an affectionate wife, ill of the small-pox.

In this state of anxiety, he subscribed a declaration of his allegiance to the king of Great Britain, with this express exception, that he should never be required to *take arms against his country*. Notwithstanding this, he was soon and repeatedly called upon to arm in support of a government he detested, or to submit to the severest punishment. Brigadier general Patterson, commandant of the garrison, and the intendant of the British police, a Mr. Simpson, had both assured colonel Hayne, that no such thing would be required; and added "that when the royal army could not defend a country without the aid of its inhabitants, it would be time to quit it."*

---

* See a representation of colonel Hayne's case, laid before congress after his death. [Hayne's execution became a *cause celebre* both in America and in England, where Parliamentary opponents of the war used it as an example of the brutalization of a losing effort. See *Cobbett*, XXII: 963–984 (January 31, 1782); JCC, XXI: 917–918, 927–929; *Annual Register* (1782), "History of Europe," pp. 155–157. Isaac Hayne was a colonel in the South Carolina militia who was captured at Charleston, May 12, 1780. After being placed on parole to his farm he was ordered to join the British army. He took this to be a violation of his parole and rejoined active service with

Colonel Hayne considered a requisition to act in British service, CHAP. XIX after assurances that this would never be required, as a breach of 1 7 8 1 contract, and a release in the eye of conscience, from any obligation on his part. Accordingly he took the first opportunity of resuming his [336] arms as an American, assumed the command of his own regiment; and all fond of their former commander, colonel Hayne marched with a defensible body to the relief of his countrymen, then endeavouring to drive the British partisans, and keep them within the environs of Charleston. He very unfortunately in a short time fell into the hands of a strong British party, sent out for the recovery of a favorite officer,* who had left the American cause, and become a devotee to British government.

As soon as colonel Hayne was captured, he was closely imprisoned. This was on the twenty-sixth of July. He was notified the same day, that a court of officers would assemble the next day, to determine in what point of view he ought to be considered. On the twenty-ninth he was informed, that in consequence of a court of inquiry held the day before, lord Rawdon and lieutenant colonel Balfour had resolved upon his execution within two days.

His astonishment at these summary and illegal proceedings can scarcely be conceived. He wrote lord Rawdon, that he had no intimation of any thing more than a court of inquiry, to determine whether he should be considered as [337] an American or a British subject: if the first, he ought to be set at liberty on parole; if the last, he claimed a legal trial. He assured his lordship, that on a trial he had many things to urge in his defence; reasons that would be weighty in a court of equity; and concluded his letter with observing,—

> If, sir, I am refused this favor, which I cannot conceive from your justice or humanity, I earnestly entreat that my execution may be deferred; that I may at least take a last farewell of my children, and prepare for the solemn change.†

But his death predetermined, his enemies were deaf to the voice

---

the militia. He was subsequently captured again and, without trial, hanged for treason and espionage on August 4, 1781.]

* This was a general Williamson, captured within seven miles of the city, by a small reconnoitering party sent out by colonel Hayne.

† See a more full account of the treatment of colonel Hayne in his own papers, afterwards presented to congress.

CHAP. XIX
1 7 8 1

of compassion. The execution of his sentence was hastened, though the reputation and merits of this gentleman were such, that the whole city was zealous for his preservation. Not only the inhabitants in opposition to British government, but even lieutenant governor Bull at the head of the royalists, interceded for his life. The principal ladies of Charleston endeavoured, by their compassionate interference, to arrest or influence the relentless hand of power. They drew up and presented to lord Rawdon, a delicate and pathetic petition in his behalf. His near relations, [338] and his children, who had just performed the funeral rites over the grave of a tender mother, appeared on their bended knees, to implore the life of their father. But in spite of the supplications of children and friends, strangers and foes, the flinty heart of lord Rawdon remained untouched, amidst these scenes of sensibility and distress. No amelioration of the sentence could be obtained; and this affectionate father took a final leave of his children in a manner that pierced the souls of the beholders. To the eldest of them, a youth of but thirteen years of age, he delivered a transcript of his case, directed him to convey it to congress, and ordered him to see that his father's remains were deposited in a tomb of his ancestors.

Pinioned like a criminal, this worthy citizen walked with composure through crowds of admiring spectators, with the dignity of the philosopher, and the intrepidity of the christian. He suffered as a hero, and was hanged as a felon, amidst the tears of the multitude, and the curses of thousands, who execrated the perpetrators of this cruel deed.

Soon after this transaction, lord Rawdon, on account of the broken state of his health, obtained leave to repair to England. Captured on his passage by the count de Grasse, he was detained a short time; but soon after his arrival [339] on the shores of Great Britain, his singular treatment of colonel Hayne was the topic of every conversation; and was proved to have been so pointedly severe, as to be thought worthy of parliamentary discussion. The strictures of the duke of Richmond thereon were pointed with severity. He thought the dignity and humanity of the nation, called loudly for a court of inquiry on high-handed executions, without trial, or any opportunity given for legal defence.

This motion however, was productive of no consequences, except the ebullitions of lord Rawdon's resentment; who, it was observed, conducted more with the violence of a soldier of untutored manners,

than with the urbanity or the politeness of the gentleman. He wrote CHAP. XIX
to the noble duke in high and offensive language, little if any thing 1 7 8 1
short of a direct challenge; but his grace did not deign to think himself
accountable to an individual, for defending the principles of equity,
and the cause of the injured, in the freedom of parliamentary debate
and investigation.

After lord Rawdon had taken leave of America, and embarked for
England, the command of the British army in Charleston devolved
on colonel Balfour. This officer, though a brave man, was not
distinguished for his humanity; nor did he seem more disposed, on a
new acquisition [340] of power, to soften the rigors of war, than his
predecessors in command.

It had, previous to the present period, appeared by the letters of
colonel Balfour, that his apprehensions relative to the southern
campaign, and the termination of the war, had been clouded to a
considerable degree. He had written to sir Henry Clinton on the sixth
of May, that

> their situation was exceedingly distressing and dreadful, notwithstanding
> lord Rawdon's brilliant successes; that the enemy's parties were every
> where; that the communication with Savannah by land was every where
> cut off; that the colonels Brown, Cruger, and others, at different important
> posts, were in the most critical situation.

He added in the same letter:

> Indeed I should betray the duty I owe your excellency, did I not represent
> the defection of this province so universal, that I know of no mode, short
> of depopulation, to retain it. The spirit of revolt is kept up by the many
> officers, prisoners of war: I should therefore think it advisable to remove
> them, as well as to make some striking examples of such as had taken
> protections, yet snatch every occasion to rise in arms against us.

Whether colonel Balfour wished to be the executioner of this cruel
policy or not, he justified it in his answer to general Greene, who
[341] demanded the reason of Hayne's execution. Balfour replied,
that it took place by the joint orders of lord Rawdon and himself, in
consequence of lord Cornwallis's directions, to put every man to death
who might be found in arms, if he had been received as a subject of
Great Britain, after the capitulation of Charleston in one thousand
seven hundred and eighty.

General Greene threatened retaliation; but his humanity led him
to the suspension of such severities, though he felt wounded at the

CHAP. XIX treatment of a person of such real merit as colonel Hayne, and the
1 7 8 1 premature stroke that robbed his country and his family of this brave,
unfortunate man. He pointedly criminated the authors of his death,
as acting an unjust, inhuman, and an illegal part. In a letter to colonel
Balfour he observed, that he was happy for the honor of colonel
Hayne, that nothing could be found against him to warrant his
execution, but

> the order of lord Cornwallis, given in the hour of victory, when he
> considered the lives, liberties, and property of the people, prostrate at his
> feet. But I confess I cannot repress my astonishment, that you and lord
> Rawdon should give such an extraordinary example of severity, upon the
> authority of that order, under such a change of circumstances, so long after
> it had been remonstrated against by myself, in a letter to lord Cornwallis.
> I informed his lordship, that his orders were cruel and [342] unprecedented;
> and that he might expect retaliation from the friends of the unfortunate.*

Indeed it was the universal voice, that the conduct of Rawdon and
Balfour in this affair, could be justified by no law, civil or military,
and was totally repugnant to the spirit of humanity, or to divine
injunctions. General Greene declared in the most solemn manner,
that he had never authorised or countenanced executions on such
principles; that he had done all in his power to soften resentment, to
conciliate the inhabitants of different descriptions, and to prevent as
much as possible all private assassinations, which had too frequently
taken place, in spite of discipline or humanity; and that he sanctioned
no public executions, but for the crimes of desertion and murder;
crimes which by no construction could be charged on colonel Hayne.

But the death of this worthy man, the victim of resentment, was
not avenged by retaliation, as threatened. It was postponed from the
humanity and generosity of the American commander, as well as from
the uncertainty of all human events, and the impossibility of calculating
from [343] the chances of war, which party might be the greatest
sufferers, by a determined spirit of retaliation and execution on both
sides.

---

* General Greene's letters to lord Cornwallis and colonel Balfour, in his dispatches to
congress at the time. [Greene to Cornwallis, August 26, 1781 (British Public Record
Office); Greene to Balfour, August 26, 1781 (Clements Library, University of
Michigan); Balfour to Greene, September 3, 1781 (Colonial Williamsburg); Greene
to Balfour, September 19, 1781 (Clements Library, University of Michigan). Greene
was still seething over Hayne's execution in November. Greene to Washington,
November 21, 1781, Sparks, *Correspondence*, III: 447–449.]

Fierce rencounters were still kept up between the British detachments posted on advantageous heights, and on the banks of deep and
unfordable rivers which intersected each other, and the hardy chieftains
who led the Carolinian bands, over mountains, declivities, swamps,
and rivers, to the vicinity of the city. Thence they were often obliged
to retreat back from the borders of civilization and softer habitations,
again to seek safety in the dreary wilderness, to which they were
pursued by their enemies, who were sometimes repelled, at others
successful in cutting off the little parties of Americans; until the
British, wearied by the mutual interchange of hostilities without
decision, drew in their cantonments, and took post about the beginning
of September, at the Eutaw Springs, which were situated at the
distance of only fifty miles from Charleston.

General Greene had, when near the waters of the Congaree, while
they were separated at the distance of only fifteen miles, attempted
to bring them to a closer engagement; but there appeared at that time
no inclination in the British to meet him. He found they were about
to take a new position. This induced him to follow them by a circuitous
march of [344] seventy or eighty miles. Desultory skirmishes continued
during the month of August; but on the eighth of September, general
Greene again renewed his challenge, fought and obtained an advantage, that was an over-balance for the many successless rencounters,
that had long kept the public mind in suspense and apprehension,
and Greene's army in such a continual fluctuation, that there was no
calculating its numbers or its strength, from day to day.

General Greene advanced to the Springs, where the main body of
the British troops were collected. He had with him only about two
thousand men; but these were commanded by some of the best of
his officers. They attacked and routed the British encampment. The
action was severe. Great numbers of the British officers and soldiers
were either slain or captured. Yet the Americans suffered so much,
that colonel Stuart, the British commander, claimed the advantage.
Indeed, general Greene suffered the loss of many brave soldiers, and
some very valuable officers. A colonel Campbell of Virginia, fell
toward the termination of the action, and had time after the mortal
wound only to observe, that "as the British fled, he died contented."

Colonel Stuart wrote sir Henry Clinton a detail of the affair, in the
pompous style of victory: but notwithstanding he arrogated so [345]
much on the occasion, the action at the Eutaw Springs put a period
to all farther offensive operations in that quarter; and the British

CHAP. XIX   troops after this, seldom ventured far beyond the boundaries of
1 7 8 1   Charleston. Besides the numbers slain in this action, four or five
hundred of the British troops were made prisoners of war. The
Americans suffered equally, and perhaps in greater proportion to their
numbers, than the British: not less than five hundred men, and
upwards of sixty officers, were killed or captured, besides the wounded.
After this action, general Greene retired again for a time, to the
heights bordering on the river Santee.

A new face to affairs now soon appeared in the city. The royal
army had been so much reduced by the vigilance and activity of
general Greene, that what has been denominated by some writers, a
re-action of events, began to operate. The British adherents to
monarchy in Charleston, and the power and influence of royal
government, were in a short time brought very low. Consequently,
the sufferings of those who had triumphed in the depression and
subjugation of their own countrymen, were felt with almost equal
rigor and severity, to that which had been inflicted on the opposers
of British authority, when their commanders in all the insolence [346]
of conquest, contemplated the certainty of the subjugation of the
southern states.

Governor Rutledge had left the state of South Carolina and repaired
to Philadelphia, after the surrender of Charleston. He now returned,
and re-assumed the reins of government. Soon after his arrival in his
native state, the governor published a proclamation offering pardon,
on certain conditions, to all who had been aiding in British service,
except such as had signed addresses, and voluntarily taken commissions
to support the arms and authority of Great Britain.

The injunctions contained in this proclamation, dated the twenty-
seventh of September, were rigorously executed. All those who were
implicated as opposed either in principle or practice, to the interests
or to the arms of their own country, felt heavily the reverse of a
change of masters. The governor, feeling not only the miseries in
which his native state had been so long involved, but the highest
indignation at the treatment received by individuals, and the inflictions
imposed on many by the severity of Rawdon and Balfour, suffered
his resentment to fall indiscriminately on all the partisans of royalty.

Many who had reaped the sweets of changing with the times, by
availing themselves of [347] the property of those who had fled, were
now compelled by the governor to fly from their agreeable plantations.
This description of people had seized the *villas* of those who had

taken their standard under congressional protection, rather than
relinquish their independence, by becoming subjects of the king of
England.

They had occupied without the city, the best accommodated situations which had before belonged to the captured or exiled inhabitants, who had opposed the British invasion. This class of persons were now reduced to the necessity of removing into a town still occupied by foreign troops. Driven into the city, and shut up with their families in inconvenient huts, the reverse of the easy accommodations to which they had lately been used, and the affluence which some of them had formerly possessed, many of them fell a prey to sickness, and the concomitant miseries of war.

Nor less aggravated were the distresses of those inhabitants within the city, whose fidelity to their country could not be shaken, and whose connexions were in arms without. They suffered every kind of distress, yet with the most heroic firmness; and even the ladies, in many instances, gave a glorious example of female fortitude. They submitted patiently to inconveniences never before felt, to hardships they had never expected; and wept in secret [348] the miseries of their country, and their separation from their tenderest connexions, with whom they were forbidden all intercourse, and were not permitted the soft alleviation of the exchange of letters. With becoming dignity, they had secluded themselves from the gaieties of the city; and refused on all occasions, to partake of any amusements in company with British officers; while with a charitable hand, they visited and soothed, whenever possible, the miserable victims crowded on board prison ships, and thrust into jails.

Their conduct was resented by the officers of the army, who themselves affronted them, and exposed them to insults of every kind, instead of defending the tender and helpless sex, as is justly expected, and required by the laws of civilization and humanity. But the busy hand of time was ripening events, that put a period to their afflictions; at least, for such of them as lived through the perils and hardships of the siege, the capture of their city, the waste of their property, the exile from their families, and sufferings too many to recount, which are usually inflicted on the vanquished, by the conqueror.

Among those who lived to return from their banishment to St. Augustine, was the venerable Gadsden, who, through all the shocks of fortune, and the rotation of events which he experienced, [349] was never shaken in his principles. He had always deserved and retained the confidence of his country. A firm, uniform republican, he was chosen a member of the general congress which met at New York in one thousand seven hundred and sixty-five. He was a worthy delegate in the respected assembly which assumed and declared the independence of the United States, in one thousand seven hundred and seventy-six. He had no predilection in favor of kings, and was ever averse to monarchic institutions and usages. This was probably a reason why he suffered such particular severities from the British commander. Notwithstanding his long confinement in the castle of St. Augustine, and his own personal sufferings, he lived to exemplify his humanity and generosity, toward persons who had been accessary, if not principals, in instigating the British officers to cruelties toward him, which they would not otherwise have practised.

The general assembly of the state was called upon to meet at Jacksonborough, the beginning of the ensuing year. Their constitution required a rotation of office, which rendered Mr. Rutledge ineligible to serve longer as their first magistrate. In consequence of this, Mr. Gadsden was chosen governor; but his advanced age and declining health, induced him to refuse the laborious task. This was a period of peculiar difficulty, in the administration of the civil [350] affairs of the state. In the sessions at Jacksonborough, there was little lenity exercised toward that description of persons who had taken British protections, or had in any manner abetted their measures, either in the city or the field. Their property was confiscated, many of their persons condemned to banishment, and the most rigorous prosecutions commenced against all suspected persons.

Though Mr. Gadsden had declined acting as governor of the state, he did not sit down an inactive spectator of the infringements of humanity or justice in society, into which persons might be hurried by an over-heated zeal, or the want of a proper restraint on the prejudices and passions of men. He vigorously opposed the proceedings of the assembly, which cut off the loyalists from returning to their allegiance, even if they wished it, and sitting down quietly in the bosom of their country.

It is now time to leave for the present, the deranged state of their civil police, and the hostile confusion which still pervaded the two most southern colonies, South Carolina and Georgia, and pursue the narrative of the march of the British army through North Carolina. The slaughter that accompanied this route, through every stage of its

progress, is an unpleasant tale. There appeared few interludes of
humane and generous deportment toward the miserable, [351] from
the borders of South Carolina, until lord Cornwallis reached the
important stand in Virginia, which finished his career of military fame
and success, and again humbled the proud glory of the British arms,
beneath the standard of the Americans.

But before we follow the conqueror of Charleston, his pursuit of
new victories in the more central part of the union, we will just
observe, that no one of the thirteen United States felt more severely
the fatal consequences of revolutionary convulsions, than that of South
Carolina. Many of the best of its citizens perished in the conflict;
others, from independence and opulence were reduced to the lowest
grade of hopeless penury, while they beheld with astonishment, the
sudden accumulation of fortune by those whom they had viewed as
a subordinate class, now grown up to incalculable wealth, amidst confusion and depredation. The convenient situations for commerce which
they had formerly occupied, were soon after possessed by British
agents, sent on at the close of the war to reap the gleanings of
property, by the demands of a speedy liquidation of old British debts.

Those debts could not be discharged by men whose plantations
were ruined, their slaves enticed or stolen away, and every other
species of property wasted in the general pillage. Their [352] capital
had been held for a considerable time as a conquered city, by the
invaders of life, liberty, and property, sanctioned by the authority of
the king of England. It is obvious, that his patronage and protection
should forever have nurtured the peace, prosperity, and growth of
the American colonies. Both interest and policy dictated the wisdom
of this line of conduct, which would have prevented the irretrievable
blow, which rent in sunder the empire of Britain.

But as a *wounded limb*, pruned or bent downwards, yet not destroyed
by the hand of the rude invader, sometimes revives and flourishes
with new vigor, while the parent stock is weakened, and its decay
accelerated, by the exuberance of its former luxury and strength, so
may some future period behold the *United Colonies*, notwithstanding
their depression, and their energetic struggles for freedom, revivified,
and raised to a degree of political consideration, that may convince
the parent state of the importance of their loss. They may perhaps
be taught to dread any future rupture with a people grown strong by
oppression, and become respectable among all nations, for their manly
resistance to the tyrannous hand stretched out to enslave them.

CHAPTER XX

Lord Cornwallis marches to Wilmington • Marquis de la Fayette sent to Virginia • Death of General Phillips • Lord Cornwallis moves from Petersburgh to Williamsburgh—Dissonant Opinions between him and Sir Henry Clinton—Crosses James River—Takes Post at Portsmouth • Indecision of Sir Henry Clinton—Meditates an Attack on Philadelphia— The Project relinquished

[353] In the first moments of victory, the mind is generally elate with the expectation of applause, and the prospect of additional fame. This was exemplified in the conduct of lord Cornwallis, when the retreating Americans had turned their faces from the field at Guilford, and left him to publish proclamations, invitations, and pardon to the inhabitants of the south. The sceptre of mercy was held out to them, on condition that they were sufficiently humbled to become the obedient subjects of those, who had destroyed their liberty, their property, and the lives of their friends, to obtain inglorious conquest, and arbitrary dominion.

He was a man of understanding and sagacity, though not so thoroughly acquainted with the [354] natural feelings of mankind, as to escape a disappointment from the conduct of the Carolinians. They revolted at the idea of seeing one American state after another, subdued and laid low at the feet of foreign conquerors. Many, whose minds had been held in a neutral state, previous to this period, now repaired with great precipitation to the congressional officers, and enlisted under their banners, for the defence of their native country.

Lord Cornwallis, after the action at Guilford and the retreat of general Greene, lost no time in expediting his previous plans of military arrangements; and, consistently with his own character, he soon moved to endeavour to prosecute them with success. He had reason to calculate, that when he had finished a long and fatiguing

march which lay before him, that he should meet general Phillips in CHAP. XX
Virginia, with a large body of troops, and by their junction impede 1 7 8 1
all resistance, and re-establish the authority of their master in that
rebellious state. Instead of a completion of these expectations, he had
when he arrived there, only to witness a fresh instance of the
uncertainty of human hope, followed by a train of new disappointments.

The British commander immediately hastened by the most convenient route to Wilmington, and from thence to Petersburgh.
Innumerable difficulties had attended lord Cornwallis [355] and his
army, in his march from Guilford to Wilmington; but in his judgment,
the march was absolutely necessary. Such was the situation and distress
of the troops, and so great were the sufferings of the sick and wounded,
that he had no option left after they had decamped from the field of
battle, and moved to Cross-Creek. The army was obliged to pass a
long way through a perfect desert, where there were neither provisions
for their subsistence, nor water sufficient to carry the mills, even
could they have procured a supply of corn. At the same time, he had
reason to expect, that the whole country east of the Santee and Pedee
would be in arms against them, notwithstanding his previous proclamation and promise of pardon, on his leaving Guilford.

He wrote sir Henry Clinton after his arrival at Wilmington, that he
had reason to suppose, many who had taken part in the rebellion had
been convinced of their error, and were desirous to return to their
duty and allegiance:—That he had promised them pardon, with few
exceptions, on the surrendering of themselves, their arms, and
ammunition: and that they should be permitted to return home, on
giving a military parole:—That their persons and properties should
be protected from violence: and as soon as possible, that they should
be restored to all the privileges of legal and constitutional government.

[356] These specious promises had little effect on the alienated
inhabitants: no allurements could induce them to join heartily, in
assisting the British commander to subjugate their native land. Their
defection daily increased; and a more thorough aversion to the designs
and the authority of the British government, almost universally
appeared. This, his lordship himself attested. He observed afterwards
in a letter to sir Henry Clinton, that "after the complete victory at
Guilford, his numbers did not increase, though he had staid two days
near the field of action." His lordship acknowledged, that though he

had marched through the part of the country where he had reason to suppose he had the most friends, he found himself equally disappointed and mortified. He observed, that—

> Many of the inhabitants rode into camp, shook me by the hand, said they were glad to see me, and to hear that we had beaten Greene, and then rode home again; for I could not get an hundred men in all the *Regulators' country* to stay with me, even as militia.*

This must have been a very unpleasant prelude to his lordship's march through a forlorn wilderness, interspersed with deep rivers, which must greatly impede an army encumbered with sick [357] and wounded, who were many of them obliged to travel in waggons, while all were scantily provided with clothes, shoes, or provisions. But notwithstanding all impediments, they reached Wilmington the seventh of April.

There, the commander found new sources of anxiety: he felt his apprehensions increased on account of the situation of lord Rawdon, on whom the command had devolved, when lord Cornwallis left Guilford. He had left with him only nine hundred men: but whatever dangers his little army might be exposed to from the pursuit of general Greene, which was now ascertained, it was impossible for lord Cornwallis to tread back his steps to their assistance. These considerations determined his lordship to take the advantage of general Greene's having left the back part of Virginia open, to march immediately into that state.

As he had received express injunctions from sir Henry Clinton, to leave the Carolinas as soon as possible, and repair to Virginia to the aid of general Phillips, it was his opinion, that his own movements were not optional. This officer had been sent forward to the Chesapeake with a reinforcement, in order to support the measures sir Henry Clinton had, early in the preceding winter, adopted, and for a time had entrusted general Arnold to prosecute.

[358] Previous to lord Cornwallis's removal from Wilmington, he wrote general Phillips, that he was in great distress at the reflection, that general Greene had taken the advantage of his absence, and had marched towards South Carolina: that he had endeavoured to warn

---

* See lord Cornwallis's letter to sir Henry Clinton, April 10, 1780. [Cornwallis to Clinton, April 10, 1781, in Stevens, *Campaign*, I: 395–399.]

lord Rawdon of this danger; but that he had reason to think, his CHAP. XX
dispatches had been intercepted. He observed, that   1 7 8 1

> the mountaineers and militia had poured into the back parts of that
> province; and he much feared, that lord Rawdon's posts would be so
> distant from each other, and his troops so scattered, as to put him into the
> greatest danger of being beat in detail: and that the worst of consequences
> might happen to most of the troops out of Charleston. By a direct move
> towards Camden, I cannot get there time enough to relieve lord Rawdon;
> and should he have fallen, my army would be exposed to the utmost
> dangers, from the great rivers I should have to pass, the exhausted state
> of the country, the numerous militia, the almost universal spirit of revolt
> which prevails in South Carolina, and the strength of Greene's army,
> whose continentals alone are almost as numerous as I am.

His lordship seemed however determined to make a feint in favor
of lord Rawdon, by moving towards Hillsborough; yet he did not
seem to expect much advantage could result therefrom. His situation
was such, that he appeared [359] embarrassed in his decisions; nor
could he easily determine, under the difficulty of existing circumstances, what line of conduct would best promote the general cause
in which he was engaged. In lord Cornwallis's letter to general Phillips,
from which an extract is given above, dated Wilmington, April 24th,
1781, he informed him, that an attempt to march from thence to
Virginia was exceedingly hazardous; and that many unforeseen difficulties might render it totally impracticable; that he should however
endeavour to surmount them, and as soon as possible attempt to
march to the Roanoke. In the mean time, he cautioned general
Phillips to take no steps that might expose the army with him to ruin,
if in any event their junction should be retarded. He urged him to
transmit the earliest intelligence from time to time, until circumstances
should admit of his meeting him at Petersburgh.

General Washington, soon after Arnold's embarkation from New
York, had ordered a detachment of continental troops, under the
command of the marquis de la Fayette, to follow, to watch the
motions, and if possible to defeat the sanguinary purposes of this
newly converted agent, to execute the designs of their enemies, and
waste the blood of his countrymen.

A French squadron had lately arrived at Rhode Island, a part of
which it was expected [360] would soon repair to the Chesapeake,
under an able and experienced naval commander, the count de Barras.

CHAP. XX High expectations were formed by every class of Americans, that the
1 7 8 1   assistance of France this year, would be sufficient to enable the armies
of the United States to counteract, if not to defeat, the designs of the
British commanders in their several departments.

Sir Henry Clinton, apprised of these circumstances, and very
apprehensive for the safety of his friends in Virginia, judged it
necessary, there should be no further delay in sending a more
respectable force to that quarter, to strengthen the hands of general
Arnold. Arnold had, on his first arrival in Virginia, landed at Westover,
and marched to Richmond, destroying all before him, with little or
no opposition. He was assisted in his marauding exploits by colonel
Simcoe, who marched from Richmond to Westham, and there destroyed one of the finest founderies for cannon in all America. They
burnt, plundered, and destroyed every thing before them as they
moved. Yet sir Henry Clinton was convinced, that their numbers were
not sufficient to facilitate his wishes and subdue the state, without a
more strong and respectable force. In consequence of this determination, he had ordered major general Phillips, with four thousand
men, to repair immediately to Virginia to succor Arnold. [361] He
likewise had directed lord Cornwallis to form a junction with general
Phillips, as soon as the affairs of Carolina would admit of his transferring
his command there, and leaving that state. By some expressions in
the order, it seemed to be left discretionary with his lordship, to move
when and where he thought proper: yet in consequence of this call,
and the reasons annexed thereto, he thought himself obligated to
hasten his march to meet general Phillips, according to the directions
of sir Henry Clinton.

Lord Cornwallis, notwithstanding all the discouraging circumstances
which he had encountered, and which at times still seemed to increase
before him, did not lose sight of the objects of conquest, victory, and
glory, to be acquired in Virginia. So prone is man to anticipate the
completion of his own wishes, that he continues to cherish them,
even after probabilities cease to exist. Thus the confidence his lordship
had in the military abilities of lord Rawdon, the repeated defeat of
general Greene, and the broken state of his army, from the frequent
instances of flight and desertion, still flattered him with ideas, that
the Carolinas might yet be subdued.

These considerations induced him to hasten his march toward the
state of Virginia. His [362] troops were indeed in a miserable condition
for a march of three hundred miles, in a hostile country, where they

could not avail themselves of its produce, however necessary for their CHAP. XX
subsistence, without being impeded by skirmishing parties. Both the 1 7 8 1
cavalry and infantry were in a very destitute situation, with regard to
forage, provisions, and clothing; but these were not impediments
sufficient to stop the progress of veteran troops, with an able commander at their head. They began their march on the twenty-fifth of
April, and arrived at Petersburgh on the twentieth of May.

The route from Guilford to Wilmington, and from Wilmington to
Petersburgh, was attended with unusual fatigue and difficulty; yet
lord Cornwallis moved with cheerfulness and alacrity, supported by
the sanguine expectation and pleasing idea of triumph in the reduction
of Virginia, in addition to the conquest of the Carolinas. Groundless
as were these expectations, his lordship at that time flattered himself,
that the work of subduing the Carolinas was nearly finished, and that
they should soon only have to take measures, for retaining in obedience
those turbulent and refractory states. But when he had completed his
march, and arrived at the destined spot, that opened to his imagination
new scenes of glory and victory, he found on every side, embarrassments that he had not contemplated, and disappointments that [363]
wounded both his personal feelings as a friend, and his military pride
as an officer.

He met at Petersburgh the melancholy tidings of the death of
general Phillips, from whose acknowledged military talents and
experience, he had reason to expect advice and assistance in every
exigence. This brave and judicious officer, who had so often staked
his life in the field of battle, fell a victim to sickness. Lord Cornwallis
had no opinion of Arnold; he despised him as a man, or an officer,
and hated him as a traitor. He wrote sir Henry Clinton, that experience
had made him less sanguine; and that more arrangements were
necessary for so important an expedition as the present, than had ever
occurred to *general Arnold*. To this his lordship added many other
expressions of contempt and disgust, for this new favorite of the
British commander in chief.

It is not strange, that many officers among the gallant troops of
Great Britain, men of name and distinction, should be much chagrined
at the rank given to, and the confidence placed in, this unprincipled
minion.

Before his death it had appeared, that major general Phillips, who
had formerly suffered by the bravery of Arnold and his associates,
was manifestly piqued at the attention paid to his advice, and the

CHAP. XX anxiety shewn by sir Henry [364] Clinton for his safety. Phillips had
1 7 8 1 but recently obtained his liberty, after the convention of Saratoga:
exchanged for general Lincoln, this expedition to Virginia was his
first command, of any magnitude, after his release. He found in the
orders received from general Clinton, some mortifying expressions,
and a letter that accompanied them contained still more. Clinton had
indiscreetly intimated therein to general Phillips, that "the security
of Arnold and his troops, at Elizabeth River, was the principal object
of Phillips's expedition to Virginia." For this expression, general
Clinton found himself afterwards obliged to apologize. It was deemed
grossly affrontive to an high-spirited officer, of the rank, merits, and
military abilities, possessed by general Phillips.

From the circumstances already related, it appears clearly, that lord
Cornwallis's route from Charleston to Virginia, was long, hazardous,
and fatiguing. He had not traversed less than eleven or twelve hundred
miles, when he reached Cobham on James River, including the
necessary circuitous marches he was obliged to make, to avoid rivers,
rapids, mountains, and other impediments to ease or expedition in
travelling.

From this place he wrote some of his most desponding and
discontented letters to general Clinton. He found the British troops
scattered [365] in small detachments, and posted at a distance from
each other in various parts of the country. He observed to sir Henry
Clinton:

> One maxim appears to me to be absolutely necessary, for the safe and
> honorable conduct of this war—which is, that we should have as few posts
> as possible; and that wherever the king's troops are, they should be in
> respectable force. By the vigorous exertions of the present governors of
> America, large bodies of men are soon collected: and I have too often
> observed, that when a storm threatens, our friends disappear.

Before lord Cornwallis left Cobham, he observed in a letter to
general Clinton, that

> he wished to call his attention to the inutility of a stand at an offensive
> post, that could have no influence on the war that still existed in Carolina,
> and that only gave them a few acres of unhealthy swamp in Virginia, liable
> at any time to become a prey to the enemy, without any superiority of
> force.*

---

* Lord Cornwallis's letter from Cobham, James River. [Cornwallis to Clinton, July 8,
1781, Stevens, *Campaign*, II: 56–59.]

From his first arrival in Virginia, he had declined acting with general CHAP. XX
Arnold; but he was not long mortified with the fight or the society of 1 7 8 1
a man he so much detested. He did not reach Petersburgh till the
twentieth of May, [366] and in the beginning of June, he was relieved
from an associate so disagreeable to the feelings of a man of honor,
by Arnold's return to New York.

Sir Henry Clinton had various reasons for the recal of this officer:
these he did not announce: but he doubtless thought, that from his
constitutional boldness, and the desperate situation in which he would
be found if defeated by the Americans, that Arnold would be a useful
agent if New York should be seriously attacked. But the principal
design appeared soon after, to be that of employing him in a business
for which he was peculiarly calculated; the surprise, the plundering,
and burning the plantations and defenceless towns, on the sea-coast
of the state of Connecticut, and other places.

The unexpected and much lamented death of general Phillips, and
the recal of general Arnold, a man held odious by Cornwallis in every
point of view, left his lordship the sole responsibility for events in
Virginia: and perhaps the movements and termination of the campaign
there, were conducted with as much judgment, ability, and military
skill, as could have been exhibited by any officer, involved in similar
difficulties and embarrassments.

It was not many weeks after lord Cornwallis arrived in Virginia,
before the intelligence he [367] received from the southward, filled
him with the most serious and alarming apprehensions for the safety
of lord Rawdon. He found by the most authenticated accounts, that
general Greene had taken the advantage of his absence, and had
moved with all possible expedition toward the environs of Charleston;
that success had attended his manoeuvres in various instances; and
that lord Rawdon had as frequently been disappointed in his systems.
To return, and follow him, was impracticable; though in his opinion,
the Carolinas were in the utmost danger of being lost to Great Britain.
Yet the work assigned him in Virginia, required the talents and the
vigilance of the ablest commander.

On his arrival in that state, he found the Americans in high spirits,
and their troops strongly posted on the most convenient grounds. He
found that general Arnold had done little to facilitate the conquest of
Virginia. He had indeed burnt several houses, destroyed some stores,
and murdered many of the inhabitants: but no consistent plan of
conquest appeared to have been either arranged or executed. His

lordship also felt heavily the death of general Phillips, from whom he expected much information and advice, in the critical emergencies that opened upon him the farther he advanced.

[368] The orders of general Clinton were peremptory, and to Cornwallis appeared inscrutable: and in addition to the list of perplexities and disappointments that daily thickened upon him, he received orders from sir Henry Clinton, to send on a part of his troops for the defence of New York, which he still apprehended would soon be attacked by the combined armies of France and America.

Thus, embarrassed on every side, his own systems deranged, his judgment slighted, and his opinions disregarded by the commander in chief, his lordship was evidently chagrined; yet he lost not the vigilance or activity of an officer of distinguished valor; and soon made an effort to concentrate his troops, and to place the main body of his army in the posts he judged best calculated for defence. In this he differed widely in opinion from sir Henry Clinton; but finally took his stand at York-Town, in obedience to the orders of the commander in chief.

The marquis de la Fayette had not been idle before the arrival of lord Cornwallis; and afterwards aided by the judgment and experience of the baron de Steuben, who arrived in the month of June, he kept the British troops in play for some time. But the number of his troops was inconsiderable, and most of them militia-men: they were easily routed in detached [369] bodies, by the more experienced partisans who opposed them. Besides many officers of superior name and character, in the train of lord Cornwallis, he was attended with very many who had no higher description of talent, than what was necessary for sudden and bold invasion of the weak and defenceless, without any relentings, or compassionate feelings toward the victims who fell into their hands. In a war like the present, they had many opportunities of indulging their propensities, and exhibiting those talents.

The violent and cruel vigilance of colonel Tarleton is already too well known to require any comment. Among other British partisans of notoriety, was a colonel Hamilton, who had distinguished himself for his activity and his severity, from Georgia to Virginia. Not less active than either of the above, was a colonel Simcoe; more remarkable for intrigue, stratagem, and surprise, than for the cool operations of the commander of magnanimity. The courage which is accompanied by humanity, is a virtue; but bravery that pushes through all dangers to destroy, is barbarous, is savage, is brutal.

These were the principal officers at this time, that headed the

detachments in most of the [370] marauding parties that infested the
state of Virginia. Simcoe had distinguished himself in this way through
the Jersies, until taken prisoner by the Americans. When he recovered
his liberty, he pursued the game; and became so perfect in the art of
coup de main, that in one of his excursions in Virginia, he eluded even
the vigilance of the baron Steuben, so far as to oblige him to remove
with precipitation from an advantageous post, not without considerable
loss.

Lord Cornwallis himself detailed some of the heroic feats of this
trio, in a letter to sir Henry Clinton, dated Williamsburgh, June 30th.
The principal design of his lordship was by their movements to
prevent the junction of general Wayne, who was marching through
Maryland to the assistance of the marquis de la Fayette. He pushed
his light troops over a river in haste, in order to effect this if possible.
Finding it impracticable, and that in spite of all his efforts general
Wayne had made good his march, and reached his intended post, he
took the advantage of the marquis's passing the Rappahannock, and
detached lieutenant colonels Simcoe and Tarleton, to disturb the
assembly of the state, then sitting at Charlotteville. The result of this
excursion was the capture of several of the members of the assembly,
and the waste of the continental stores in that quarter. They destroyed
at Charlotteville, and on their return, [371] one thousand stand of
arms, five hundred barrels of powder, and a large quantity of other
military accoutrements and provisions.

The baron Steuben had his station at this time, at the point of
Fork: he was surprised and obliged to retreat, after a short rencounter.
Simcoe followed, and used every exertion to attack his rear guard:
not effecting this, he destroyed as usual all the continental stores
which lay in their way. There, and in the places adjacent, the
Americans lost three or four thousand stand of arms, and a large
quantity of powder and other stores. The baron had with him in this
affray about eight hundred men, mostly militia.

After this, lord Cornwallis moved himself to Williamsburgh. There
he gave fully and freely to sir Henry Clinton, his opinion of the only
mode of effecting the security of South, and the reduction of North
Carolina, which he found was expected from him both in England
and America. He observed, that, in his judgment,

> until Virginia was subdued, they could not reduce North Carolina, or have
> any certain hold of the back country of South Carolina; the want of
> navigation rendering it impossible to maintain a sufficient army in either
> of those provinces, at a considerable distance from the coast; and the men

and riches of Virginia furnishing ample supplies [372] to the rebel southern army. I will not say much in praise of the militia of the southern colonies; but the list of British officers and soldiers killed and wounded by them since last June, proves but too fatally, that they are not wholly contemptible.*

It appears from all the correspondence and conferences between sir Henry Clinton, general Phillips, and other officers, that the British commander in chief had seriously contemplated an excursion to Philadelphia. He intimated in one of his letters to general Phillips, not long before his death, that they probably had more friends who would co-operate with them in the state of Pennsylvania, than either in Maryland or Virginia. He seems to have been led to this opinion, by the representations of a colonel Rankin. He urged this as an experiment that would redound much to the advantage of lord Cornwallis's operations in Virginia. General Clinton clearly discovered that he had a predilection, himself, in favor of the project. He asked the advice of the generals Phillips and Arnold on the subject, after he had appeared to be predetermined to make the experiment.

When it was disclosed to lord Cornwallis, by general Phillips's letters falling into his hands, [373] he did not hesitate to remonstrate against drawing off four thousand men from Virginia, for service in the Delaware, in this critical exigence of affairs in all the more southern colonies. He observed in the same letter from which an extract is given above, that sir Henry Clinton being charged with the weight of the whole American war, his opinions of course were less partial, and were directed to all its parts; and that to those opinions it was his duty implicitly to submit.

He then adds, that—

> Being in the place of general Phillips, I thought myself called upon by you, to give my opinion on the attempt upon Philadelphia. Having experienced much disappointment on that head, I own I would cautiously engage in measures, depending materially for their success on the active assistance from the country: and I thought the attempt on Philadelphia would do more harm than good to the cause of Britain; because, supposing it practicable to get possession of the town, (which, besides other obstacles, if the redoubts are kept up, would not be easy) we could not hope to arrive without their having had sufficient warning of our approach, to

* See lord Cornwallis's letter to general Clinton, dated Williamsburgh, June 30, 1781. [Cornwallis to Clinton, June 30, 1781, Stevens, *Campaign*, II: 31–39.]

enable them to secure specie, and the greatest part of their valuable public stores, by means of their boats and shipping.

[374] The difficulty of discriminating friends from foes in Philadelphia, the improbability that they could continue long there if they succeeded, the stronger necessity for all the troops that could be spared from New York to act in Virginia, and the hazard that would attend an attack on Philadelphia, were circumstances, that induced lord Cornwallis very judiciously to portray them in his letters to sir Henry Clinton, as an object where the balance of the risk far outweighed any promise of advantage.

It may easily be supposed, that those free opinions and advice which he considered as obtruded, could not be very acceptable to the commander in chief at New York; more especially, as it was evident there had long existed heart-burnings and jealousies between sir Henry Clinton and lord Cornwallis. These were heightened by the warm altercations between them, with regard to the most convenient and advantageous posts for defence, as well as the arrangements for offensive operations.

The encampment of the marquis de la Fayette was at this time about eighteen or twenty miles from Williamsburgh. He had with him about two thousand men. This was a number far too short for any offensive movements against such a strong and forcible British army, as was then posted in Virginia. He was in impatient [375] expectation of reinforcements, which he had now reason to conclude as certain, from the junction of the American and French troops commanded by the count de Rochambeau. But the marquis was obliged to act again, before there was time for his relief by the arrival of his friends.

Lord Cornwallis endeavoured before the middle of July, to cross James River and pass his army to Portsmouth. The marquis de la Fayette sent forward the Pennsylvania line, with some other detachments, to impede their passage. This brought on a smart engagement, which terminated with considerable loss on both sides. The approach of evening, with other disadvantageous circumstances, obliged the Americans to retreat, leaving the few cannon they had with them behind: the darkness of the night prevented a pursuit. The next day the British passed the river; but not without some difficulty from its width, which was about three miles.

The marquis la Fayette, through the difficulties which he had to encounter in Virginia, had on all occasions conducted with more valor, caution, prudence, and judgment, than could have been expected from so young an officer. When the baron de Steuben joined him in the month of June, he had few men under his command, except the militia, whose numbers were indeterminate, [376] and the time of their continuance in service always uncertain. Yet much generalship and military address had been shewn on various occasions, both by the young hero and the aged veteran. They through all the summer, opposed the vigilance and superior force of lord Cornwallis, with great courage and dexterity.

Lord Cornwallis had made several judicious attempts to surprise the marquis with his little armament, consisting, as his lordship occasionally observed, "mostly of unarmed peasantry." But wary and brave, his ability and judgment had supplied the deficiencies, and balanced the weakness of his detachment; and before the arrival of the generals Washington and Rochambeau, the marquis de la Fayette had rendered very essential service to the American cause, by his valor and firmness in the state of Virginia.

Lord Cornwallis had been but a few days at Portsmouth, before he received a letter from sir Henry Clinton, censuring him in direct terms for attempting to pass James River, and taking his stand at Portsmouth, though he had before recommended this to general Phillips, as a convenient post. He observed, that he had flattered himself, until he had the honor to receive his lordship's letter of the 8th of July,

> that upon re-considering the general purport of our correspondence, and general Phillips's papers in your possession, you would at least have [377] waited for a line from me, in answer to your letter of the 30th ultimo, before you finally determined upon so serious and mortifying a move, as the repassing James River, and retiring with your army to Portsmouth. And I was the more induced to hope that this would have been the case, as we both seemed to agree in our opinion of the propriety of taking a healthy station on the neck between York and James Rivers, for the purpose of covering a proper harbor for our line of battle ships.

Through all his correspondencies, orders, commands, counter-mands, and indecision, during the present summer, no man ever appeared more embarrassed, or more totally at a loss how to arrange his military manoeuvres, than did general Clinton. He appeared at times to consider the reduction of Virginia as a primary object, and that it was of the highest importance that lord Cornwallis should be there strengthened and supported, both by sea and land: at other

periods, he treated the operations there in so light a manner, that his CHAP. XX
ideas could not be comprehended, even by so intelligent an officer 1 7 8 1
as lord Cornwallis.

It was not more than three or four weeks previous to the date of
the above letter, that [378] sir Henry Clinton had pressed his lordship,
as if in a sudden fright, to send him two thousand troops to aid in
the defence of New York: and, as if under some panic-struck influence,
he said,

> The sooner they are sent the better; unless your lordship may have adopted
> my plan to move to Baltimore, or the Delaware Neck, and put yourself in
> a way to co-operate with us; but even in that case, you can spare us
> something I suppose. From all the letters I have seen, I am of opinion, if
> circumstances of provisions, stores, &c., turn out as they wish, that the
> enemy will certainly attack this post. As for men for such an object, in
> this (circumstanced as they suppose it to be) it cannot be doubted that
> they can raise a sufficient number.

Sir Henry Clinton had found by an intercepted letter, that there
were eight thousand men collected at West Point, and that others
were coming in very fast. He informed Cornwallis, that he had certain
intelligence that admiral Barras had sailed from Rhode Island; that
many circumstances had put it beyond a doubt, that the design was
to form a junction between him and general Washington, and that
they meditated an attempt on the post at New York.

It is needless to detail much more of the correspondencies of the
British officers acting at [379] this time in America: their characters
are sufficiently elucidated, not only by their own letters but by
subsequent transactions. It is enough to observe, that by the correspondence of the general officers, afterwards published in England,
it clearly appears, that they did not harmonize in opinion: their
councils at this time were confused, and their plans indecisive.

Yet it is worthy of notice, that distrust, dissension, and vilification,
were kept up equally between some of the British naval commanders
and sir Henry Clinton. In one of his confidential letters he complained,
that "all opportunities of advantage were impeded or lost, by the
slowness and obstinacy of the admiral." He observed, that "his strange
conduct had, if possible, been more inscrutable than ever: at one
time, he declared he was immediately going home; at another, he
had sworn that he knew nothing of his recal."

In a secret and confidential letter to general Phillips, sir Henry
Clinton assured him, that "if he was not better satisfied by the next

CHAP. XX post, relative to the recal of admiral Graves, he should probably leave
1 7 8 1 the management of him solely to lord Cornwallis."* In this letter he
censured his lordship in direct terms, for leaving the Carolinas but
half subdued, to pursue the chimerical [380] project of doubtful
conquests in Virginia. He asserted, that his invitation, not his commands to his lordship, to come to the Chesapeake, was on the
supposition that every thing was settled in the Carolinas, agreeably
to the wishes of administration, and the designs of the government
of England.

Sure of the confidence of general Phillips, sir Henry Clinton
expressed the utmost astonishment, that

> with nine British battalions, a legion of infantry, a detachment of yaughers,
> five Hessian and several provincial battalions, some American light-horse,
> and large detachments of artillery and dragoons, that lord Cornwallis should
> yet pretend that he wanted forces sufficient for the most solid operations
> in Virginia.†

He sneered at his lordship's idea, that it was impossible to act with
his army in Carolina, without the assistance of *friends*. This reflection
alluded to a letter received by him, in which lord Cornwallis observed,
that the *royal cause* had few *friends* in that country, and that when a
storm threatened, even those few disappeared. An historian has
observed, that "Chosroes relinquished the Colchian war in [381] the
just persuasion, that it is impossible to hold a distant country, against
the wishes and efforts of its inhabitants."‡ His lordship might probably
be of the same opinion. This opinion was justified by his own
experience, in too many mortifying instances for the tranquillity of a
man of his sensibility.

It has been above observed, that by the sudden death of general
Phillips, all these letters fell into the hands of Lord Cornwallis, with
several others of the same style and tenor. This circumstance greatly
aggravated the dissension and disgust, between the commanding

---

* See general Clinton's vindicatory letters. [Most of Clinton's letters from late April
  forward are readily construed as "vindicatory." Similar to the quotation in the text
  is Clinton to Philips, April 30, 1781, in Stevens, *Campaign*, I: 450–455.]

† General Clinton's letter to major general Phillips, April, 1781, printed in England
  with his other letters. [Clinton to Philips, April 30, 1781, in Stevens, *Campaign*, I:
  450–455. Also see Clinton to Philips, April 26/30, 1781, *Ibid*.: 437–441.]

‡ Gibbon on the Decline and Fall of the Roman Empire. [Edward Gibbon, *The History
  of the Decline and Fall of the Roman Empire*, (6 vols.; London, 1776–1788), Vol. IV,
  Ch. XLII.]

officers in New York and Virginia. Yet notwithstanding the implied
censure or reproach which they contained, in most of sir Henry
Clinton's letters afterwards to lord Cornwallis, he had written with
great complaisance, and had expressed the highest confidence in his
lordship's abilities and judgment. But the breach became irreconcile-
able.

Through the whole business, lord Cornwallis constantly affirmed,
that his force was insufficient even for defensive operations. He took
the liberty to intimate to sir Henry Clinton, that notwithstanding
there had been a call for a part of his troops for the defence of New
York, that he had never been under any apprehensions [382] for the
safety of that city. With the same freedom, he remonstrated against
a plan that had been meditated by the commander in chief at New
York, for an attack on the city of Philadelphia.

His lordship asserted with some degree of warmth, that it appeared
to him highly imprudent, that any part of his army should be detached
for that or any other purpose. But he observed further, that in his
subordinate situation, unacquainted with the instructions of administration, ignorant of the forces under the command of his excellency
general Clinton, and without the power of making arrangements, he
could only offer his opinion: that plans of execution must come from
himself, who had the materials for forming, as well as the power of
executing.

These remonstrances had little weight with the British commander
in chief. It appears through all their correspondence that these
gentlemen differed very widely in opinion, with regard to the modes
of action, the numbers necessary for effective execution, the best
posts for defence, and indeed in the general plan of all their operations.
However, sir Henry Clinton still kept up the idea of supporting the
war in Virginia, and of aiding lord Cornwallis to the utmost, notwithstanding he had sent an order to draw off a part of his troops.

[383] After he was thoroughly alarmed at the hazardous situation
of the commander in Virginia, he relinquished his chimerical project
of attacking Philadelphia; he countermanded the orders for drawing
off a considerable part of the troops; and endeavoured to hasten on a
small squadron of British ships then lying at Sandy-Hook. He flattered
himself that a few ships under the flag of Britain, might intercept the
fleet, and interrupt the designs of admiral Barras, who had sailed from
Rhode Island; or retard a still more important object, the arrival of
the count de Grasse in the Chesapeake, where he was hourly expected.

He made some other ineffectual efforts for the relief of the British army, which was soon after cooped up by a large French fleet that arrived within the Capes.

The dissension, discord, and division of opinion, among the British officers, was not all that occasioned the fatal delay of strengthening lord Cornwallis in Virginia; it may be ascribed more to that atmosphere of doubt in which sir Henry Clinton was involved. Irresolute measures are ever the result of a confusion of ideas. The vast object of reducing such a wide extended country, and setting the wheels of operation in motion, so as to work with equal facility, from Georgia to Virginia, from Virginia to the north, and from Canada to the eastern extreme, [384] was of too wide an extent for the compass of his ability.

His mind seemed for a time to be plunged in a chaos, uncertain where to begin, in the complicated difficulties of his official duties, or where to set the strongest materials of his machinery to work in all its parts, in a manner that would produce a complete system of conquest through the United States. There was no deficiency of courage, ardor, or fidelity to their master, among the officers of the crown, however dissentient in opinion with regard to the modes of execution. But these dissensions prevented that ready co-operation in action, which is necessary both to defeat the designs of their enemies, and to complete their own systems by judicious and prompt decision, and the immediate execution of well digested plans.

The movements of the continental and French army, had alarmed sir Henry Clinton to such a degree, that he long persisted in his determination of recalling a part of the troops from Virginia, for the immediate defence of New York. He informed lord Cornwallis, that general Washington had with him eight or ten thousand men, besides the French battalions; and observed, that every one acquainted with the disposition of the inhabitants east of the Hudson, must be sensible in what manner their [385] appearance would affect the numerous and warlike militia of the New England states.

Sir Henry Clinton, doubtful of the farther success of lord Cornwallis, apprehensive of an immediate assault on New York, and reasonably calculating the numbers in array against him, as very far superior to his own, lost sight for a time, of the dangerous situation of lord Cornwallis and the army in Virginia. To complete the agitation of his mind, he was now trembling for his sinking reputation, which had been severely attacked in England. From these circumstances, his despondency was nearly equal to his irresolution. Yet, apparent necessity awakened his energy for the defence of the city of New

York; and every possible step was taken, to meet the combined troops
in a manner becoming a British veteran commander.

Lord Cornwallis, with very different ideas, was parrying the attacks of the Americans then in Virginia, and preparing, as far as possible, for the resistance of stronger bodies of enemies. He was persuaded, that general Washington and the count de Rochambeau, aided by a powerful French fleet, had deeper laid systems, and were on the point of disclosing designs of higher magnitude, and more important consequences, than had ever been apprehended by sir Henry Clinton.

[386] The variety of smaller skirmishes, retreats, reprisals, and unexpected rencounters, that took place on the different rivers and posts in Virginia, may at present be left, to advert more particularly to the difficulties lord Cornwallis had to contend with, and the dangers he had to combat, previous to the decision of his fortune in that quarter. He had for a time taken his stand at Portsmouth, but he left that station as soon as possible; and, according to orders from the commander in chief, concentrated his forces at York-Town and Gloucester, towards the close of summer, much against his own judgment.

We have seen, that by the indecision of general Clinton, the delay of reinforcements both by land and sea, and the general defection and disgust of the Virginians to any appearance of the authority of the crown of Britain, there were causes sufficient to discourage an officer who was ambitious to act with vigor and promptitude. But these were far from comprising the whole of the gloomy prospect which lay before lord Cornwallis. He had the highest reason to expect the approach of general Washington, accompanied by the experienced and renowned Rochambeau. At the same time, he had well-grounded expectations of a French fleet in the Chesapeake, to counteract any naval operations on the part of Britain. This combination of dangers, added to the inconvenient and indefensible [387] post his lordship was impelled to take, reduced him to the most perplexed and embarrassed state of mind. Yet he supported himself with firmness and magnanimity, until new and inextricable difficulties led him to despair of the success of the campaign. This was apparent by the tenor of his letters, as well as by his general deportment, for some time previous to the catastrophe of the fatal day, which reduced a nobleman of the first rank, an officer of the highest military fame and pride, to the condition of a prisoner.

END OF VOL. II.

HISTORY

OF THE

RISE, PROGRESS AND TERMINATION

OF THE

AMERICAN REVOLUTION.

INTERSPERSED WITH

Biographical, Political and Moral Observations.

IN THREE VOLUMES.

BY MRS. MERCY WARREN,

OF PLYMOUTH, (MASS.)

...........Troubled on every side..............
perplexed, but not in despair ; persecuted, but not forsaken ;
cast down, but not destroyed.   *ST. PAUL.*

O God ! thy arm was here.........
And not to us, but to thy arm alone,
Ascribe we all.   *SHAKESPEARE.*

VOL. III.

BOSTON :

PRINTED BY MANNING AND LORING,
FOR E. LARKIN, No. 47, CORNHILL.

1805.

CHAPTER XXI

A short View of the Forces of the contending Parties • The Generals Washington and Rochambeau meet at Weathersfield • Attack on New York contemplated—The Design relinquished • Combined Armies march toward Virginia • Count de Grasse arrives in the Chesapeake • Sir Samuel Hood arrives at New York—Sails to the Chesapeake • Naval Action • Lord Cornwallis attempts a Retreat—Disappointed—Offers Terms of Capitulation • Terms of Surrender agreed on • Lord Digby and Sir Henry Clinton arrive too late • Comparative View of the British Commanders • General Exchange of Prisoners

[1] The additional weight of maritime force that appeared in the American seas in the year one thousand seven hundred and eighty-one, was [2] serious and eventful. In the view of every sagacious eye, this appearance portended events of magnitude, that might hasten to a decision, the long disputed point between Great Britain and the United States. The European nations considered the present period a crisis of expectation, and that the exertions of this year would either extinguish American hopes, or establish their claims as an independent nation.

Before the arrival of admiral Barras, the naval power of Britain in the American waters was much superior to any thing that had yet arrived from abroad, that could give assistance to the United States. The acquisition of strength, by the arrival of a squadron under the command of sir Samuel Hood, might have given an irresistible preponderance to the British flag, had not the count de Grasse fortunately reached the Chesapeake a few days before him.

There was now just reason to expect the most violent naval concussions would take place, between the Bourbon fleets and the still more powerful squadrons of Britain. They were soon to meet near the American shores, where they were destined to dispute the

CHAP. XXI decision of an object, that, from the emulation of power, the long
1 7 8 1 existing jealousies between two potent sovereigns, and the prospect
of a new face of affairs from the resistance of America, equally
interested the kings of England and France.

[3] On the part of Britain, their armies were bold, their troops well
appointed, and the pride of conquest urged to prompt execution to
insure success. The Americans, inured to fatigue, became disciplined
from necessity: naturally sanguine and brave, conscious of the justice
of their cause, and persuaded of the favor of Heaven, they were ready
to engage in defence of their country and their lives, which they were
sure would be the certain forfeit if defeated. Both, determined and
valorous, and perhaps both equally weary of the contest, they might
equally wish for some capital stroke of military prowess, some
honorable action, which might lead to equitable and amicable decision.

In this attitude of expectation, hope, and uncertainty, of the two
original parties, now combined with the strangers and aliens of different
nations, who had adopted the ardor of conquest equal to their
employers, nothing less could be anticipated than new scenes of
carnage. The auxiliaries on the part of Britain, were the feudal vassals
of despotic lords, the mere *automatons* of German princes, who held
them as their hereditary property. The allies of America were *Frenchmen*, who had long felt the weight of the chains of *Le Grand Monarque:*
they were commanded by polite and erudite officers, who just beheld
the dawn of freedom rising on their native land.

[4] Thus the two armies finally met in the Virginian fields, the
germ of the new world, the first British plantation in America; a state
dignified for its uniform adherence to, and its early and firm defence
of, the natural rights of mankind. Here they were to decide the last
stake for the freedom of nations, a game which had been beheld with
interest and expectation, by many of the officers before they left
Europe, and which might eventually have an extensive influence, to
enlighten and free the more enthralled parts of the world.

Previous to the junction of the French and the American armies,
general Washington, the count de Rochambeau, and several other
distinguished officers, had met and held a conference at Weathersfield,
in Connecticut. In consequence of this interview, it was reported and
believed for a time, that the combined armies would immediately
attempt the reduction of New York. This was a favorite object with
the Americans, who generally viewed the dislodgement of the British
forces from that stand, as a measure that would expedite relief to

every other quarter invested or oppressed by their fleets and armies.
Accordingly, great preparations were made, and high expectations
indulged through most of the summer, that the army under the
immediate command of sir [5] Henry Clinton, weakened by detachments for the southern service, and no reinforcements yet arriving
from England, would soon be driven from the important post of New
York.

General Washington had neglected no argument to impress the
necessity of immediate and vigorous exertions in all the states, to
enable him to act with decision. He urged the expectation of the
allied army, commanded by officers of the first abilities, of the highest
military character, some of them of the prime nobility of France, and
all ambitious of glory and eager for action. The disappointment they
would feel if any languor appeared in the United States, was obvious;
and every consideration was urged and enforced, that might induce
the whole body of the people to aid in facilitating the measures
adopted by the military commanders, which could not be executed
without union and prompt decision in all the legislatures.

Preparations were accordingly made, and on the sixth of July, the
junction of the French and American armies took place at White
Plains. They soon after took a nearer position, with every preparation
for, and all the appearance of, a formidable attack on the city. But
notwithstanding the sanguine hopes of the Americans on this occasion,
and the well founded apprehensions [6] of the British commander in
chief, a combination of circumstances prevented an enterprise, which
both the army and the people thought was not only designed, but
had calculated that it would be effected without much difficulty.

Nor was this less expected by sir Henry Clinton, who had no idea
that any system had been formed for the combined armies to move
toward Virginia. He had taken every measure to obtain the most
correct information: in this he succeeded: the letters of general
Washington were intercepted. His dispatches taken by the agents
employed for the purpose, were conveyed to New York, by which
the British commander obtained intelligence which alarmed his
apprehensions for the safety of New York, and led him to forget all
danger in any other quarter.

While the mind of the British commander remained in this situation,
a sudden reverse took place on the part of America: their measures
were disconcerted, their operations slow; and for a time they appeared
as indecisive in their determinations, though not so divided in their

councils, as the commanders of the British troops. The energies of a few leading characters were not sufficient to control the [7] many in the several states, who in their present disconnected police must all be consulted.

In spite of the exertions and the zeal of individuals, the requisitions from the respective states came in for some time but slowly. Many of those which were sent on to complete the battalions, were very far from being strong, effective men. Some companies appeared to be a rabble of boys; others, very unfit for immediate service; and the numbers far short of the calculations in the British camp, where imagination had multiplied them almost to a Russian army.

In short, it was found that it was impossible to establish an army at a call, fit for duty at the moment of their entrance in the field. Nor was it less difficult, in the existing circumstances of the infant republic, to provide at once for the exigencies which the magnitude of military enterprise at this time required. The design, if it ever was really intended, of assaulting that post and reducing New York, was a second time relinquished. The apprehensions of sir Henry Clinton, that a similar enterprise would have been attempted the preceding winter, had not continued long, before other objects intervened, which opened new views to both the British and American commanders.

[8] A different system was adopted from that expected by both sides, on the opening of the summer campaign. This might probably have been owing in part to the information recently given by colonel Laurens, who had lately arrived from France. He had immediately repaired to the southward, and reached the headquarters of the combined army in the month of August. The most interesting part of this intelligence was, that an alliance had been renewed between the emperor of Germany and the king of Great Britain; that the emperor had sent out a considerable reinforcement to the aid of the British commanders in America, and that additional troops were to follow; that this had greatly encouraged the court of Britain, and was not a pleasing circumstance to France.

It yet remains doubtful, whether it was a stroke of generalship, or the necessity of taking new ground, that induced the count de Rochambeau and general Washington, secretly to draw off most of the continental and French troops, at a period when they momently expected orders for an attack on the city of New York. It is success oftener than judgment, that crowns the military character: and as fortune followed their footsteps, few, if any, doubted the superiority

of genius that dictated the measure. The movement was sudden, and CHAP. XXI
the march rapid. The combined army crossed the North River on the 1 7 8 1
twenty-fourth of August: [9] they moved on hastily to Philadelphia;
and by a difficult and fatiguing route, reached Williamsburg in Virginia
on the fourteenth of September.

Sir Henry Clinton, apprehensive only for New York, had not the
smallest suspicion of this manoeuvre. By the address of a few Americans
left behind for that purpose, every appearance of an attack on New
York was for a time kept up. The deception was so complete, and
the manoeuvres of the American commander so judicious, that the
British themselves acknowledged, their own was fairly *outgeneralled*.
The illusion was so well calculated for the purpose, that its effects
were fully adequate to the design: the British commander continued
his diligence in preparing for the reception of the combined armies.

The intelligence, at this time, of an alliance between his Britannic
majesty and the emperor of Germany, and the arrival of two or three
thousand German troops, gave an exhilaration of spirits to the city,
to the soldiers, and to the general, who, from the protraction of the
illusion without, had the highest reason to expect, the assault of their
works would not much longer be delayed by the Americans. Though
general Clinton had received intelligence that [10] the French squadron
had left Rhode Island, he did not yet dream that they were destined
to the Chesapeake, or that Washington and Rochambeau had adopted
a new system. It was long before he could be persuaded to believe,
that they were concentrating their forces, and moving southward, with
design effectually to defeat all farther attempts on Virginia, and stop
the progress of the British arms in the Carolinas.

It was indeed too long for the interest of the crown of Great Britain,
before sir Henry Clinton could prevail with himself to look beyond
the defence of New York. But when he found the allied armies had
in reality marched toward Virginia, he did not neglect his duty. He
countermanded the orders to lord Cornwallis, of sending a part of his
troops to New York, and made all possible preparations to support
him. He sent on a fresh detachment of troops, and made arrangements
to follow them himself, with a hope of being timely enough for the
relief of his lordship.

In the mean time, the fortunate arrival of the count de Grasse in
the Chesapeake, hastened the decision of important events. A short
passage from the West Indies transported the French fleet under his
command safely to the Capes of Virginia, where they arrived on the

thirtieth of August. No intelligence of his near approach [11] had reached the British quarters; nor could any thing have been more unexpected to the British naval commander, sir Samuel Hood, who arrived soon after in the Chesapeake, than to find a Gallic squadron of twenty-eight sail lying there in perfect security.

Commodore Hood, who arrived from the West Indies soon after the middle of August, with near twenty sail of the line, joined the squadron under admiral Graves before New York. He was solicitous to have sailed immediately to the Chesapeake, with all the naval strength that was not necessary to be left for the defence of New York. But an unaccountable delay took place, which in his opinion could not be justified; and however it counteracted his inclination, it was too late before he sailed. He did not reach the Chesapeake until the fifth of September, six days after the arrival there of the count de Grasse. The French fleet had not been discovered by the British commander, nor had he gained any intelligence that de Grasse was on the American coast, until the morning of the fifth of September, when the English observed them in full view within Cape Henry.

Nothing could have been more mortifying to a man of the spirit and enterprise of sir Samuel Hood, than to find so respectable a French fleet had arrived in the Chesapeake before him. The [12] national rivalry, prejudices, and hatred, of the British commanders, and the gallant English seamen, could not be suppressed on such an occasion. These were a strong stimulus to immediate action, which had their full effect. The pride and valor of a renowned British commander could not admit of the smallest delay; and the boldness of English seamen urged all with the utmost alacrity to prepare for an engagement.

The British maritime force that had now arrived, was nearly equal to the French squadron under the count de Grasse. Both fleets immediately moved, and a spirited action ensued: equal gallantry was exhibited, but neither side could boast of victory. The ships on both sides were considerably injured, and one British seventy-four rendered totally unfit for service; to this they set fire themselves. The loss of men was on the usual average of naval action. The English indeed were not beaten, but the French gained a double advantage; for while the count de Grasse remained at a distance, watched by the British navy, he secured the passage of the count de Barras from Rhode Island, and gained to himself the advantage of first blocking up the Chesapeake. The count de Barras brought with him the French troops

from Rhode Island, amounting to about three thousand men. These
joined the marquis la Fayette, whose numbers had been greatly
reduced. This reinforcement [13] enabled him to support himself by
defensive operations, until, in a short time, they were all happily
united under the command of the valiant Rochambeau.

The British fleet continued a few days in the Chesapeake. Their
ships were much injured; and in a council of war it was determined
to be necessary for the whole fleet to return to New York, to refit and
prepare for a second expedition. This they had reason to flatter
themselves would be more successful, as they were sure of a great
acquisition of strength on the arrival of lord Digby, who was hourly
expected with a reinforcement from England.

While sir Henry Clinton remained in suspense with regard to the
operations in the Chesapeake, his anxiety prompted him to endeavour
to obtain immediate intelligence. He had no suspicion that he should
receive this by the return of admiral Graves, and the respectable
squadron under his command; and before the untoward circumstances
which occasioned this had reached New York, his impatience had
urged him to send on a gallant officer with letters to lord Cornwallis.
Major Cochran executed this business at no small hazard. The British
fleet had left the Capes of Virginia before his arrival; but at every
risk, he ran through the whole French fleet in an open boat. He
landed safely, delivered his dispatches, and [14] immediately had his
head shot off by a cannonball. Thus this unfortunate officer had not
a moment to rejoice in the success of his bravery.

After the return of the fleet of New York, it might reasonably have
been expected, that sir Henry Clinton would have acted with more
decision and energy. Previous to this unfortunate transaction, it had
been determined in a council of war, to send five thousand men to
the aid of lord Cornwallis. But the spirit of delay still pervaded the
mind of the British commander: he thought proper yet further to
postpone this wise measure, from a motive which he doubtless
considered justifiable. This was, to wait a little longer for the arrival
of admiral Digby; whose junction with the forces already in New
York, he judged would insure victory over the combination of France
and America, both by sea and land.

Flattering letters were again sent on to lord Cornwallis; but promises
and distant expectations were far from being adequate to the relief
of a mind borne down by disappointment, and the failure of the
means of supporting his own military character. He was also sensible,

CHAP. XXI that the dignity of command, and the royal cause, were suffering by
1 7 8 1 delay, indecision, and, as he thought, from less justifiable motives.
He was exhorted to hold out till about the twelfth of October, when
sir Henry Clinton thought it [15] probable he might receive assistance,
if no unavoidable accident should take place; or at farthest by the
middle of November. At the same time, he intimated, that if his
lordship should be reduced to the utmost extremity, before the arrival
of reinforcements, he himself would endeavour to make a diversion
by an attack on Philadelphia, in order to draw off a part of Washington's
army.* These all appeared to lord Cornwallis, very indigested, absurd,
and inconsistent ideas. He immediately informed sir Henry Clinton,
that he saw no means of forming a junction with him, but by York
River, and that no meditated diversion toward Philadelphia, or any
where else, could be of any use.

Lord Digby however arrived at New York on the twenty-ninth of
September. One of the princes† of the blood had taken this opportunity
to visit America, probably with a view of sovereignty over a part, or
the whole of the conquered colonies. This was still anticipated at the
court of St. James: and perhaps, in the opinion of the royal parents,
an American establishment might be very convenient for one of their
numerous progeny.

[16] Lord Digby was several days detained at New York, before
arrangements were made for the embarkation of the troops to reinforce
lord Cornwallis, and for the sailing of the mighty naval armament for
the Chesapeake. In the mean time, sir Henry Clinton busied himself
in writing letters full of specious promises, as if artfully designed to
buoy up the hopes of lord Cornwallis, by strong assurances that no
time should be lost in sending forward a force sufficient for his relief.
He informed him, that a fleet under the command of lord Digby,
who had recently arrived at New York, would sail for the Chesapeake
by the fifth of October; that himself was nearly ready to embark with
a large body of troops; and in the most sanguine terms, exhorted his
lordship to endeavour to keep his opponents in play, and to hold out
against every discouragement, until he should receive the needful
assistance, which another British fleet, and the addition of a body of
troops headed by himself, would secure.

These flattering assurances and pressing entreaties from the commander in chief, induced lord Cornwallis to evade a general action.

---

* See sir Henry Clinton's letter to lord Cornwallis, dated Sept. 30, 1781. [Stevens,
  Campaign, II: 172–173.]

† This was prince Henry, the duke of Clarence.

It was his opinion, that when the combined troops arrived, he could
only attempt the defence of York-Town. He was posted there by
general Clinton's express orders, contrary to his own judgment. He
had always (as has been before observed) thought this an ineligible
situation, [17] and far from being long defensible, without much larger
reinforcements both by land and sea, than he had reason to expect
would arrive seasonably.

His situation had been for some time truly distressing. Embarrassed
between his own opinion and the orders of his superior in command,
flattered by the promise of timely relief, and that in such force as to
enable him to cope with the united armies of France and America,
he thought it his duty to wait the result, and not suffer himself to be
impelled by contingent circumstances, to risk his army beyond the
probability of success. This prevented any advance to action, at the
same time that it forbid his endeavouring to retreat from Virginia,
until too late, when he had only to wait suspended between hope
and fear, the uncertain chances of war. He acknowledged afterwards,
that had he seasonably retired toward Carolina, though the attempt
would have been difficult, he might have saved his army from their
impending fate.

Though the courage and the inclination of lord Cornwallis might
prompt him in his present circumstances, to lead out his troops and
hazard an engagement in the open field, yet his judgment or his
prudence could not justify the risk, while he had the smallest hopes,
that a few [18] days might place him in a situation to combat on more
equal terms. His destiny often marked by disappointment, he had at
the same time much reason to despair of a successful termination of
the campaign, even if the forces from New York should arrive in
season. Yet, he observed to sir Henry Clinton, that

> if he had no hopes of relief, he should rather risk a general action, than
> attempt to defend his half-finished works. But, as you say Digby is hourly
> expected, and promise every exertion to assist me, I do not think myself
> justified in putting the fate of the war on so desperate an attempt.

The British commander was fully apprised of the difficulties that
would attend his armament under existing circumstances, even if the
troops from New York should arrive before his fate was decided. The
mouth of the river was blocked up by a very large French fleet; the
American army in high health and spirits, strengthened by daily
recruits, led on by *Washington,* in whom they had the highest
confidence, in conjunction with a fine army of Gallicans, headed by

the count de Rochambeau, an officer of courage, experience, and ability, were making rapid advances. On the twenty-eighth of September they had left Williamsburgh, and on the sixth of October they opened their trenches before York-Town.

[19] His lordship determined however, notwithstanding the choice of difficulties that pressed upon him, to make the best possible defence. His army was worn down by sickness and fatigue, but there was no want of resolution or valor; his officers were intrepid, and his men brave. They acquitted themselves with spirit; and kept their ground from the sixth to the sixteenth of October; when they became convinced, that the abilities and the experience of the count de Rochambeau, the cool equanimity of general Washington, and the vigor and valor of their officers and troops, rendered the united army irresistible in the present situation of their opponents.

Lord Cornwallis had now only to choose between an immediate surrender or an effort to escape, and save a part of his army by flight. He contemplated either a retreat southward, or an endeavour to force his way through the states between Virginia and New York, to join general Clinton. But, equally hazardous, he determined on the last expedient. For this purpose, he with the utmost secrecy, passed in the night of the sixteenth, the greatest part of his army from York-Town to Gloucester, leaving only a detachment behind to capitulate for the town's people, the sick, and the wounded.

But fortune did not favor the enterprise. It is true the boats had an easy passage, but at the [20] critical moment of landing his men, his lordship observed, that

> the weather suddenly changed from moderate and calm, to a violent storm of rain and wind, that carried the boats down the river, with many of the troops who had not time to disembark. It was soon evident, that the intended passage was impracticable; and the absence of the boats rendered it equally impossible to bring back the troops that had passed, which I had ordered about two in the morning.*

Here the serious mind will naturally reflect, how often the providential interference of the elements defeat what appears to be the most judicious design of the short-sighted creature, man.

---

* Lord Cornwallis to general Clinton. [Cornwallis to Clinton, October 20, 1781, Stevens, *Campaign*, II: 205–216. Cornwallis wrote this letter after his capitulation at Yorktown and announced the surrender in the letter. The passage concerning the weather appears at p. 212.]

The state of lord Cornwallis's mind at this time, the insurmountable CHAP. XXI
difficulties of his situation previous to his surrender, and the subse- 1 7 8 1
quent consequences, may be seen at large in his letter to sir Henry
Clinton, dated October twenty-first, one thousand seven hundred and
eighty-one.*

In this letter he details the circumstances of his disappointment,
in the last mode adopted for the safety of his army. It has been
observed, that his troops were dispersed by the storm [21] by which
the boats were driven down the river, though some of them returned
to York-Town the ensuing day. Desperate as was the situation of the
British troops, a feint of resistance was still made, by an order to
lieutenant colonel Abercrombie, to sally out with four hundred men,
to advance, attack, and spike the cannon of two batteries which were
nearly finished. This excursion was executed with spirit and success,
but attended with no very important consequences.†

The combined armies of France and America had continued their
vigorous operations without the smallest intermission, until prepared
for the last assault on the town, which they began at the dawn of the
morning after the circumstances above related had taken place. In
this hopeless condition, his own works in ruins, most of his troops
sick, wounded, or fatigued, and without rational expectation of relief
from any quarter, the British commander found it necessary, in order
to escape the inevitable consequences [22] of further resistance, to
propose terms of submission.

Lord Cornwallis, confident of the humanity and politeness of his
antagonists, made proposals on the seventeenth to the commanders
of the combined army, for a cessation of hostilities for twenty-four
hours. This was granted: but toward the expiration of the term,
general Washington, in a letter to the British commander, acquainted
him, that desirous to spare the farther effusion of blood, he was ready
to listen to such terms of surrender as might be admissible; and that
he wished, previous to the meeting of any commissioners for that
purpose, to have his lordship's proposals in writing. At the same time

* Appendix, Note No. I.
† Several reconnoitering parties on both sides met and skirmished during the siege.
  In one of these, colonel Scammel, a brave American officer, who was respected and
  beloved for the excellence of his private character, was captured by some British
  partisans. He surrendered, and delivered his sword, the usual signal of submission,
  after which he was mortally wounded by one of the British. He expired after
  languishing a day or two.

he informed lord Cornwallis, that after the delivery of this letter, only two hours of suspension of hostilities would be granted for consideration.

The time limited being thus short, the British commander, without a detail of many particulars, proposed terms of capitulation in a very concise manner.

General Washington, equally perspicuous and decisive, in a few words intimated to his lordship the only terms that would be accepted: that if his proposals were rejected, hostilities would be re-commenced within two hours of the delivery of those terms.

[23] In consequence of these negociations between the commanders, commissioners were immediately appointed to prepare and digest the articles of capitulation. It is not easy to conceive or to relate the mortification his lordship must have felt, at seeing his troops conquered by superior prowess and good fortune, and laying down their arms at the feet of the victorious Washington. This chagrin was undoubtedly much heightened, by the necessity of submitting to terms imposed in conjunction with the servants of a rival power, whom the kings of Great Britain, and the nation they govern, had viewed for many centuries with hatred and detestation.

The gentlemen appointed on the part of America to draw up the articles of capitulation, were the count de Noailles, a French nobleman who had served as an officer in the defence of the United States for a considerable time, and colonel John Laurens, a distinguished character, a son of the unfortunate ambassador who had been deputed to negociate in behalf of America at the Hague, but at this time was confined in the tower of London, and very severely treated.

The singularity of some circumstances relative to this gentleman, cannot be passed over unnoticed in this place. He was suffering a rigorous imprisonment in England: he had presented a [24] petition for some amelioration of the severities exercised against him; this was rejected; his veracity disputed by the minister; and his detention justified by lord Mansfield, as legal, politic, and necessary, to prevent the accomplishment of his pernicious projects.*

By a strange concurrence of events, the earl Cornwallis, constable of the tower of London, was now on the point of becoming a prisoner, and submitting to articles of surrender for himself and his army, under

* See Parliamentary Debates. [Henry Laurens's petition to the House of Commons from the Tower of London appears in *Cobbett*, XXII: 877–878 (December 21, 1781), and in *Annual Register* (1781), "State Papers," pp. 322–323. Also see *Annual Register* (1781), "History of Europe," pp. 142–143.]

the dictation of the son of Mr. Laurens, the same gentleman heretofore CHAP. XXI
alluded to, when an attempt was made by the British administration, 1 7 8 1
to corrupt the integrity of both father and son. By the capitulation,
his lordship was reduced to the humiliating condition of a prisoner to
the American congress, while the father of colonel Laurens remained
shut up in the tower, a prisoner to the captured earl.

However, as soon as circumstances permitted, an interchange of
prisoners took place. The noble lord, who with his army fell into the
hands of the American commander, was restored to liberty by an
exchange for Mr. Laurens, who had long languished in the tower of
London. The court of Britain had before rejected [25] the proposal
that Mr. Laurens should be exchanged for general Burgoyne; but
they were soon after this glad to receive an officer of equal rank to
almost any in the nation, in exchange for the American minister.

A detail of the particular articles of capitulation may not be necessary;
for them the reader is referred to the Appendix:* it is enough to
observe at present, that the British army was permitted only the same
honors of war, that lord Cornwallis had granted the Americans on the
surrender of Charleston the preceding year. The officers were allowed
their side-arms, but the troops marched with their colors cased, and
made their submission to general Lincoln, precisely in the same
manner his army had done to the British commander, a few months
before.

Here we cannot but pause a moment, to reflect on the vicissitudes
of human life, the accidents of war, or rather the designations of
Providence, that one day lift to the pinnacle of human triumph, and
another, smite the laurel from the brow of the conqueror, and humble
the proud victor at the feet of his former prisoner.

[26] As general Lincoln had recently felt the mortification of yielding
himself and his troops into the hands of the royal army, he was
selected to conduct the military parade, and receive the submission
of the British veterans. This might be thought by some, to wear
rather too much the air of triumph; but it was judged a kind of
compensation for his own military misfortunes, while it might call
into exercise the feelings of benevolence. These ever operate more
strongly on the human character from the experience of sufferings,
except in such ferocious minds as are actuated only by the principles
of revenge.

This was far from being the spirit of Americans; their victories were

* Appendix, Note No. II.

CHAP. XXI generally accompanied with so much moderation, that even their
1 7 8 1 enemies acknowledged their generosity. General Burgoyne and others
had often done this; and lord Cornwallis now expressed both pleasure
and surprise, at the civility, kindness, and attention, shewn by the
victor to the vanquished foe. In a letter to sir Henry Clinton, after
mentioning the Americans in very handsome terms, his lordship
observed, that

> he could not describe the delicate sensibility of the French officers on this
> occasion; and that he hoped their conduct would make an impression in
> the breast of every British officer, when the fortune of war might again
> put any [27] prisoners, either American or French, in the power of that
> nation.

Thus terminated the efforts of administration to reduce the United
States, by first conquering the southern colonies. On the nineteenth
of October, one thousand seven hundred and eighty-one, a second
British army yielded themselves prisoners to the confederated states
of America. The humiliation of the present captured army, as above
observed, was enhanced by the circumstances that made it necessary
for the British battalions, to bow beneath the banners of their hereditary
enemies of France, in conjunction with the stars of America.* One
of these armies, before its capture, had ostentatiously anticipated the
conquest of the north; the other had enjoyed the cruel triumph of
devastation and spoil, through the warmer latitudes of the south.

With incredible fatigue and fortitude, and no less zeal and havoc,
had the British army, and the royal partisans belonging to the American
states who had joined them, harassed and spread terror and desolation
for many months, from the borders of Georgia to the extremities of
Virginia.

[28] Within five days after the surrender of all the posts that had
been held by lord Cornwallis, a British fleet from New York, under
the command of lord Digby, with sir Henry Clinton and seven
thousand troops on board, entered the bay of Chesapeake in full
confidence of success; but to their inexpressible mortification, they
had only to appear and retreat.

By the capitulation, all the shipping in the harbor was left to the
disposal of the count de Grasse, with the exception only of the Bonetta
sloop of war. This was granted to lord Cornwallis to carry his dispatches
to New York. It included the liberty of conveying as many of his

---

* The American standard at this time was ornamented with only thirteen stars.

troops as was convenient, to be exchanged for an equal number of chap. xxi
American prisoners. His humanity prompted him to avail himself of 1 7 8 1
this liberty, to ship off, instead of soldiers, the most obnoxious of the
loyalists, terrified beyond description at the idea of falling into the
hands of their countrymen, against whom they had made every
exertion, both by their influence and their arms. After the return of
the Bonetta, as stipulated, she also was to be delivered at the order
of the French admiral.

The delay of reinforcements both by sea and land, until lord
Cornwallis and his army were irretrievably lost, was a misfortune and
a neglect that could not easily be excused or forgiven, either by the
ministry, the nation, or the numerous [29] friends of this unfortunate
nobleman. Much altercation took place afterwards between sir Henry
Clinton and lord Cornwallis, with little satisfaction to the wounded
feelings of the last, and as little advantage to the sinking character of
the first.

The surrender of lord Cornwallis's army was an event that produced
more conviction in the minds of men, that the American colonies
could not be conquered by the arms of Great Britain, than any
circumstance that had previously taken place. It was asserted by some
British writers at the time, that

> this was an event which carried a kind of irresistible conviction with it,
> even to those who were the least inclined to the admission of so humiliating
> a truth. When it was seen, that the most distinguished and successful
> general that had engaged in the royal cause, was obliged to surrender
> himself and his whole army prisoners of war, the generality even of those
> who had been the most earnest for the subjugation of America, began now
> to be convinced, that it was totally impracticable. But those who had a
> sincere regard for the honor and interests of Great Britain, could not reflect
> but with the utmost regret, that nearly one hundred millions of money
> should have been expended, and so many thousand valuable lives lost, in
> this unhappy contest; in a contest which had produced nothing but the
> loss of [30] our American colonies, an accumulation of the public debt, an
> enormous load of taxes, and a great degree of national dishonor; and which
> had afforded too much ground for the triumph and exultation of our most
> inveterate enemies.*

---

* British Annual Register for one thousand seven hundred and eighty-one. [See *Annual
  Register* (1781), "History of Europe," pp. 119–136; "Humble Address of the Lord-
  mayor, Aldermen, and Livery of the City of London" to the King, "State Papers,"
  pp. 320–322.]

CHAP. XXI   The defence of York-Town and Gloucester had always appeared
1 7 8 1   chimerical to the British commander in Virginia; yet from the printed
correspondence afterwards in every hand, he appeared perfectly right
in his adherence to the orders of general Clinton, and justifiable in
his endeavours to support himself there, until the promised reinforcements should arrive.

No man ever appeared more embarrassed when dangers approached,
or more indecisive in many instances of his conduct, through the
course of his American command, than sir Henry Clinton. Yet he was
not deemed deficient in point of courage; though he never discovered,
either in design or execution, those traits of genius or capacity, that
mark the great man or the hero.

He had often been mistaken in his calculations, as had most of the
British commanders, with regard to the ability, vigor, and valor of
[31] American troops. But combined with an European army, commanded by officers of the first military knowledge and experience,
and the numbers that flocked with alacrity to the American standard,
as they moved southward, in the fullest confidence in the judgment
and abilities of general Washington, were circumstances sufficient to
have eradicated those opinions, and to have quickened the movements
of the commander at New York, in the same ratio that it awakened
the apprehensions of an officer of more judgment in Virginia.

But whatever impression a combination of French and American
troops might at that time make on the mind, yet the hereditary hatred
of the one, and the affected contempt of the other, had always led
the commanders of Albion armies, to hold the haughty language
characteristic of the national pride of Britain. After this period, the
defeat of their armies and their most renowned officers, taught them
a more humble deportment; and more just and modest accents were
dictated from the lip of their captured generals.

The comparative military merits of the distinguished British characters that figured and fell in America, may be left to the masters in
tactics to decide; but it may not be improper to observe, that the
tribute of applause, both for generalship and abilities, may be more
justly [32] attributed to lord Cornwallis than to sir Henry Clinton.
Notwithstanding the unfortunate conclusion of his lordship's southern
campaign, he was doubtless a man of understanding, discernment,
and military talents, better qualified to act from his own judgment,
than as subordinate to general Clinton.

Nothing of the kind could exceed the exhilaration of spirits that

appeared throughout America, on the defeat at York-Town and the
capture of the British army. The thanks of congress were given, and
recorded on their journals, to the count de Rochambeau, general
Washington, and the count de Grasse; expressive of the sense they
had of their merits, and the high esteem they felt for the services
they had rendered to the United States. Public rejoicings were every
where displayed by the usual popular exhibitions; thanksgivings were
offered at the sacred altars; and the truly religious daily poured out
their oraisons of praise, for the interposition of Divine Providence in
favor of the American states.

By other descriptions of persons, little less gratitude and devotion
was expressed toward Washington, Rochambeau, and the count de
Grasse. They were the subjects of their eulogies and their anthems;
the admiration of the brave, and the idols of the multitude: and in
the complimentary addresses of all, they were [33] designated the
instruments of their salvation, the deliverers from impending ruin,
and the protectors from the concomitant evils of protracted war.*

Among the horrors that attend the operations of hostile armies, the
situation of those unfortunate men captured by their enemies, is none
of the least. There has yet been no attempt in these annals, at a
particular description of the sufferings of those victims of misery. The
compassionate heart would rather draw a veil over those principles in
human nature, which too often prompt to aggravate, rather than to
relieve, the afflictions of the wretched, who are thrown into the hands
of their enemies by the uncertain chances of war.

In consequence of the capture of lord Cornwallis and his army, and
some other decided strokes of success in the southern states, a general
exchange of prisoners soon after took place between the hostile parties.
There were doubtless [34] many instances of individual cruelty and
unjustifiable rigor exercised toward prisoners who fell into American
hands. Impartiality forbids any extenuation of such conduct on either
side. It has been alleged by some, that instigated by the shocking
inhumanity inflicted on their countrymen, retaliation and summary
punishment was in some instances necessary; but this will not excuse
a deviation from the laws of benevolence, and is far from being a

---

* The Americans did not soon forget the merits or the services of the count de Grasse.
Their gratitude and respect for his memory was exhibited by congress, who generously
pensioned four of his hapless daughters, who arrived in the Massachusetts in extreme
poverty, after the ruin of their family in the general wreck of nobility, and the
destruction of monarchy in France.

sufficient plea for the victor to enhance the sufferings of the vanquished.

Yet it must be allowed, that the general treatment of this unhappy
class of men by the contending powers, will not bear a comparative
survey. Many of the captured Americans were sent to Great Britain,
where they were for a time treated with almost every severity short
of death. Some of them were transported to the East Indies; others
put to menial services on board their ships: but after some time had
elapsed, those in general who were conveyed to England, might be
deemed happy, when their sufferings were contrasted with those of
their countrymen who perished on board the prison ships in America,
under the eye of British commanders of renown, and who in many
respects were civilized and polite.

No time will wipe off the stigma that is left on the names of
Clinton and Howe, when posterity [35] look over the calculations,
and find that during six years of their command in New York, eleven
thousand Americans died on board the Jersey, a single prison ship,
stationed before that city for the reception of those victims of despair.
Nor was the proportion smaller of those who perished in their other
jails, dungeons, and prison hulks.

It is true that in England, the language of government held up all
the American prisoners as rebels, traitors, insurgents, and pirates; yet
this did not prevent the compassionate heart from the exercise of the
benign virtues of charity and brotherly kindness. The lenient hand
of many individuals was stretched out for their relief: subscriptions
were repeatedly set on foot, and very liberal donations made by
several characters of high rank; and many well disposed persons
exhibited the most generous proofs of compassion to the languid
prisoner.

This charitable deportment was not confined within the circle of
those, who had either secretly or openly avowed themselves the
friends, or had advocated the principles, of the American opposition.
For some time before peace took place, more lenient measures were
observed by government toward those who were captured and carried
to England. They were considered and treated as prisoners of war;
compassion was every where extended to the unfortunate [36] strangers;
and the liberal contributions of various classes ameliorated their
sufferings in a distant land, where no tender connexions could extend
the hand of pity. While their sorrows were thus softened, their
brethren in America, in the neighbourhood of parents, children, and

the most affectionate partners, not permitted to receive from them CHAP. XXI
the necessary relief, were dying by thousands, amidst famine, filth, 1 7 8 1
and disease.

Great efforts had been made for earlier relief to many of the sufferers
of every condition, but without effect. Not even general Burgoyne
had yet been exchanged: from the many difficulties that arose with
regard to the convention at Saratoga, he was still held on parole as a
prisoner. The various delays and equivocations relative to the detention
of this gentleman, and the refusal of the minister to exchange him
for Mr. Laurens, had induced congress to summon him to return to
America, agreeable to his parole. The ill state of health to which this
unfortunate officer was reduced, from his fatigue of body in long
military services, and his vexation of mind in consequence of the ill
treatment of his employers, prevented his compliance with this
requisition. General Clinton endeavoured, as far as in his power, to
procure his exchange; but as no officer of equal rank was then in the
hands of the Americans, it had been stipulated, that one thousand
and forty men should be [37] given for his ransom. This was humorously
said by a member of parliament,* to be a fair equivalent—"a quantity
of silver for a piece of gold."

General Burgoyne very justly thought himself highly injured by the
treatment of the ministry; but he observed himself in the house of
commons, in the beginning of the sessions of the ensuing winter, that
he had not complained, though every officer in the army, down to
the serjeants, had been exchanged. He said, however, that he acceded
to the propriety of this, because he had resigned his commission, and
thereby put himself into a situation, which rendered it impossible for
him to be of any service to his country in a military capacity. He also
observed, that he thought it more proper, that those should be first
exchanged, from whose exertions in the field the nation might receive
advantage. But, with the spirit of a man of honor and an officer of
resolution, he declared, that

> sooner than condescend either to seek or to receive the smallest favor,
> from the hands of men who had heaped the grossest injuries upon his
> head, he would even return to America, be locked up in the gloomiest
> dungeon which the congress might assign him, and devote himself as that
> sacrifice, which his [38] enemies had long endeavoured to offer up to their
> resentment.†

* Mr. Burke.
† Parliamentary Debates. [See *Cobbett*, XX: 780–803 (May 1779); Burgoyne, *Expedition*.]

General Burgoyne observed, that the circumstances of the *Cedars men,* which had been the subject of so much altercation, was well known to the ministry; and that he thought all who knew the resolution of congress on that subject, as well as himself, must be convinced, that the conduct of the ministry in this matter was very singular and extraordinary. The determined spirit of that body was so well known, that a second proposition to exchange the Cedars men for him, could be calculated only to delay or prevent his release. He added,

> that it was surely singularly hard, that he should be the only one of all the army that had surrendered at Saratoga, who had not been included in the exchange of prisoners, and restored to liberty. It was an injustice beyond all example, that every officer and every man in the army should have received the valuable privilege of freedom, and that he alone, who was commander in chief on that occasion, should still be continued a prisoner.

The dispute in point was concisely this: The British government insisted, that a party of Americans who, some time before the convention [39] at Saratoga, had been taken at a place called the Cedars, and had made their escape, should still be considered as their prisoners; and offered them as a part of the number stipulated for the exchange of general Burgoyne. This, congress peremptorily refused; and demanded the whole number agreed on, exclusive of the Cedars men, for the release of the British commander from his parole. They did not consider the party at the Cedars, who had been surprised, but not held in duress, as the description of men to be exchanged for a British general.

The mutual charges of breaches of the articles, between congress and the British commander, occasioned a long and grievous captivity to the convention troops. As each side justified their own conduct, and no compromise could be made in the state of things which had long existed, these unfortunate men had been removed by order of congress from Cambridge, and conducted to the interior parts of one of the southern states. There they remained until the auspicious events above related, returned them to the bosom of their country and friends, in lieu of an equal number of Americans, who had many of them languished for as long a period, in the dreary apartments assigned the prisoners in New York, Charleston, and wherever else British head-quarters were established, in any part of the United States.

[40] The American congress, in a few weeks after the termination

of the campaign in Virginia, resolved, that as a preliminary to the discharge of the convention troops, all accounts of expenditures for their support should be immediately settled and discharged. At the same time, they authorised general Washington to set lord Cornwallis at liberty, on condition of the complete liberation of Mr. Laurens. These several proposals and demands were made and received in England in the beginning of the winter, one thousand seven hundred and eighty-two.

On the offer of the congress of the United States, immediately to release lord Cornwallis on fair and honorable terms, Mr. Burke, with his usual dexterity of combining and bringing into view, objects the most striking and impressive on the passions of men, observed, that the British ministry had been brought to some sense of justice in a moment;

> warned by a star that had arisen, not in the east, but in the west, which had convinced them of the danger of longer persevering in their unmanly, revengeful, and rigid treatment of Mr. Laurens. This was no other than the news arriving, that the son of Mr. Laurens, a brave, worthy, and accomplished officer in the American service, had earl Cornwallis in his custody; and that his treatment of his noble prisoner, was directly the reverse of that experienced by Mr. Laurens's father, who was then locked up [41] in *that tower*, of which lord Cornwallis was the constable.

Mr. Burke, in a very pathetic style, detailed the variety of sufferings, hardships, and injustice, which had been inflicted on Mr. Laurens during his long imprisonment. This, with other instances of severe and injudicious treatment of prisoners, he made the ground-work of a proposed bill, to obviate the difficulties arising from the present mode of exchanging the American prisoners; a mode which, he remarked, was at once disgraceful and inconvenient to the government of the kingdom. He urged, that "motives of humanity, of sound policy, and of common sense, called loudly for a new law, establishing a regulation totally different from the present, which was fundamentally erroneous." However, Mr. Laurens obtained his release from the circumstances above mentioned, before any new regulation of the British code of laws, relative to prisoners or any other object, took place.

CHAPTER XXII

General Wayne sent to the Southward • Embarrassments of General Greene in that Quarter • Recovery of Georgia, and Evacuation of Savannah by the British • Death and Character of Colonel Laurens • Character of General Greene • Consequent Observations

[42] Immediately after the successful operations in Virginia, the count de Grasse took leave of his American friends, and conformably to orders received from his court before he left France, sailed for the West Indies. He left the continent in the beginning of November, one thousand seven hundred and eighty-one. He was accompanied with the gratitude and good wishes of almost every individual in the United States; nor was this more than justice required.

A most extraordinary reverse of fortune and prospects had taken place in America, after the arrival of this brave commander and the auxiliaries of his nation, who had come forward and lent their aid to the Americans. This assistance was received by the United States, at a period when her armies, and America herself, stood in the most serious and solemn point of her distress.

[43] Decorated with the laurels of military fame, several of the principal officers withdrew from Virginia, and repaired to other quarters. General Washington, laden with the splendid trophies of victory, went on to Philadelphia, where, by particular request of congress, he continued some time. There he received a personal and complimentary address from that body, and the applauses of all conditions of men, in a degree sufficient to stimulate the least ambitious mind to pursue the path of victory, until time should bring a period of rest to the pursuits of war.

The marquis la Fayette, desirous to revisit his native country, which had been several years involved in a war with Great Britain, embraced the present opportunity and returned to France. He was complimented

by congress with an advance of rank in the army, and the highest CHAP. XXII
expressions of esteem for his bravery and good conduct in their service. 1 7 8 1
With a strong attachment to the inhabitants, and the most friendly
disposition toward the United States, he promised to return again to
America with further aids, if it should be found necessary to try the
fortune of another campaign, before the contested object should be
completely obtained.

After the capture of the British army, the surrender of their shipping
in the Chesapeake, [44] and the restoration of tranquillity in the state
of Virginia, general Wayne was ordered on with the Pennsylvania
line, to march with the utmost dispatch to South Carolina, to the aid
of general Greene, who had yet many difficulties to encounter in that
quarter. The distance from the central states, and the long service at
the southward, had exposed the American commander, and the army
there, to sufferings indescribable.

After the action at the Eutaw Springs, we left general Greene on
the High-Hills of Santee, where he thought it necessary to repair, to
secure and recruit the remainder of his army, and to wait the exigencies
that might again call him forward to the more active scenes of the
field. He did not continue there long, before he thought proper to
move forwards toward Jacksonborough. There the light troops from
Virginia, that had been commanded by the colonels Laurens and Lee,
joined him: but the whole army was so destitute of ammunition, and
every other necessary for an advance to any action, that they had
scarcely the means of supporting themselves in a defensive condition:
of consequence, only some small skirmishes ensued, without much
advantage to either party. It was happy for the Americans, that their
enemies were now almost as much reduced in numbers as themselves.
Yet the variegated causes of [45] distress among this small remnant
of continental soldiers, were almost unnumerable.

They were in an unhealthy climate, always unfriendly to northern
constitutions. They were destitute of many of the necessaries for
carrying on war with advantage, and almost without the means of
supporting human life. In addition to this, the general had to combat
disaffection, discontent, and mutiny, in his own army. The Maryland
line particularly, had indulged a mutinous spirit to an alarming extreme,
which required all the address of the commander in chief to suppress.
At the same time, he had to encounter dangers of every kind from a
valiant enemy, stimulated to cruelty by many circumstances that let
them almost to despair of their own cause.

CHAP. XXII   On the other hand, the disaffection of most of the inhabitants of
1 7 8 1   Charleston, and the fickleness of the country on which he had
depended, had been indeed discouraging circumstances to lord Rawdon. Not willing to risk his constitution longer in that insalubrious
latitude, he had embarked for England in the summer, was captured
on his passage by the count de Grasse, but was soon after restored to
his native country. The troops he left behind were not in want of
food, clothing, or warlike stores; while the little American army under
general Greene, was naked to that extreme, that they [46] had scarcely
rags left to veil them from the most indecent appearances.*

In this wretched situation, general Greene and his little army
continued through the winter; and such was the severe and vigilant
duty of the officers, that for seven months the general himself was
not able to take off his clothes for a night. This is sufficient to prove
the assertion in one of his letters, that the army was so destitute of
every thing, that it was not able to make a march of a day.

General Leslie had again, by proclamation, called on all who had
still any remains of attachment to the British government, to adhere
firmly to the royal cause. He assured them of the strongest support
in his power, notwithstanding the acts of disfranchisement, confiscation, and banishment, which took place after governor Rutledge had
again resumed the administration of civil government. However,
Leslie did not receive any new additions of strength by his proclamations, or his letters of altercation with the governor who succeeded
Mr. Rutledge, relative to the civil police of the country. Nor (as
observed) was general Greene able to advance, or take a single step
further, to put a period to the power of the British arms in that [47]
state. But it was not long before general Leslie proposed a cessation
of arms. The citizens were sickly, the loyalists disheartened, and his
own troops reduced. Every circumstance, and every party, required
a respite from the distresses of war. As general Greene had not yet
been authorised by congress to accede to the proposal, he did not
immediately comply.

* General Greene's letters at this period to general Washington and others. [It is
impossible to know precisely which letter of Greene's Warren had in mind. Greene
was camped at the High Hills of Santee from September 14 to November 11, 1781.
Between July and November, 165 letters appeared over his signature dated at that
place. Greene's letter to George Washington, October 25, 1781, "Headquarters,
High Hills of Santee," Sparks, *Correspondence*, III: 429–431, is representative of
many discussing the deplorable condition of the troops.]

The advance of general Wayne with his detachment from the army CHAP. XXII
in Virginia, which reached South Carolina before the close of the 1 7 8 1
present year, was a necessary acquisition, and had been impatiently
expected. Without this, it would have been impossible for general
Greene to have held out much longer. Some provisions, clothing, and
other necessaries, reached the army in the ensuing spring. This
partially relieved the American commander from the complicated
distresses he had suffered the preceding winter. It restored more
order and satisfaction among his troops; the discontents and mutinous
disposition among some of them were dissipated; and he was able,
with truth, soon afterwards to observe in general orders, that

> It is his happiness that he has the honor to command an army, that has
> not been less distinguished for its patience, than bravery: and it will add
> no small lustre to your character to say, that you have rejected with
> abhorrence, the practice of plundering and the exercise of cruelty, although
> urged by your [48] necessities to the former, and by the example of your
> enemies to the last. United by principle, and connected by affection, you
> have exhibited to the world a proof, that elevated souls, and persevering
> tempers, can triumph over every difficulty.

General Wayne did not stay long in South Carolina, but marched
forward by order of general Greene, to cross the Savannah. He was
reinforced by a party from Augusta, sent forward to his aid. Though
the state of Georgia was considered by the British as completely
subjugated to their power, yet there was a considerable number of
the inhabitants who still co-operated with congress, and continued a
delegation of members to that body, through all the hostile movements
or changes, that had for several years been shifting the prospects of
the inhabitants, who had been generally the subjects of the British
crown, more in name than reality; and the greater their distance from
the centre of British operations, the less were they disposed to submit
to British authority. A few other troops besides those from the
neighbourhood of Augusta, who had been stationed at different posts,
but retained their attachment to the American cause, joined the troops
collected under the command of general Wayne.

Thus the state of Georgia was relieved at a time when they least
expected it. Animated [49] by the successes in Virginia, and ambitious
for the honor of relieving the state of Georgia, the advance of general
Wayne was rapid, and his arrival on the borders very unexpected to
general Clarke, who commanded at Savannah.

On the first rumor of the march of this party of victorious Americans,

CHAP. XXII

1 7 8 1

orders were given by general Clarke to the officers commanding the British out-posts, to burn and destroy every thing on the fertile banks of the river, and to retire with the troops, within the works in the suburbs of the town.

After this waste of property, and the destruction of their crops, the Georgians and the few American troops there to support them, had more to endure than at any period before, from hunger, fatigue, the attacks of British partisans, the irruptions of the Creek Indians, and other savages in British service. We have seen the sufferings of that state had been grievous for several years, from invasion, slaughter, and conquest. Their subsistence now totally destroyed in the conflagration of the borders, the inhabitants were reduced to despair, until the arrival in Georgia of Wayne's detachment.

This happy event revived their sinking spirits, and invigorated them to new exertions in defence [50] of their country. The inhabitants from every quarter repaired immediately to the assistance of general Wayne; who, soon after he had crossed the river, was attacked by colonel Brown, who had marched with a considerable party from Savannah. With this body of troops, he fell suddenly on and attacked general Wayne. They fought with great spirit and valor, but were soon defeated, and driven back by the Americans.

A few days after this, a very large body of the Creek Indians, accompanied by their principal warriors and chieftains, headed by a British officer, attempted in the night to surprise general Wayne in his quarters. He, ever vigilant, and defying all personal danger, was in greater readiness for their reception than was expected. The assailants gained little advantage by this sudden onset. The affray was fierce, but did not continue long, before the Indians were willing to retreat, having lost a number of their principal associates.

But the capture of lord Cornwallis and his army, the low state of British affairs in the Carolinas, and the advance of a body of American troops, were circumstances so discouraging, that the British did not think proper to make any vigorous resistance. A period was soon put to those hostilities that had for several years ravaged the state of Georgia, and destroyed or [51] driven away many of its former inhabitants.

General Wayne was an officer of high military reputation. His prudence and judgment had been conspicuous, in the trying scene which called out his talents in one thousand seven hundred and eighty, on the mutiny and secession of the Pennsylvania line, which he commanded. His valor had been signalized at Stoney Point and in

Virginia, as well as in many other places where decided action was CHAP. XXII
necessary. He now had the honor of terminating the war in the state 1 7 8 1
of Georgia.

On the expectation of the British leaving Savannah, some proposals
were made to general Wayne by the merchants and others, for the
security of their property; and every reasonable indulgence was
promised by him, to those who chose to remain there. He engaged,
that those merchants who did not owe allegiance to the United States,
should be permitted to remain there a reasonable time, to dispose of
their property and settle their affairs; and that they should be protected
by the military, until delivered into the hands of the civil authority.

Thus, in a few months after the events above mentioned, the whole
state of Georgia was evacuated by their formidable enemies. This
was early in the year one thousand seven hundred [52] and eighty-
two. Not a single British soldier was left in the pay of the king of
England, except such as were prisoners to the Americans. Much to
the honor of general Clarke, he quitted the post without any injury
to the town of Savannah, and left the works standing that had been
erected by the industry of the royal troops.

This defeat of the efforts of the British government to hold the
state of Georgia in subjection, fully justified the observations of lord
Maitland, who had served his country with ability and applause in
several parts of America. By his exertions, in conjunction with general
Prevost, the state of Georgia had been long retained, against the
combined force of an American army under general Lincoln, and a
French fleet commanded by the count de Estaing.

The sum of lord Maitland's speech in the British parliament, on
his return to England afterwards, was, that those men who had brought
the nation into its present state, had come into life at a time, when
the arms of their country were carried to an unprecedented height of
splendor and glory; when the empire was under the benefit of wise
councils, and of a vigorous system; great and respectable abroad,
opulent and happy at home; when her trade covered every sea, and
filled every port in the world; and when [53] her navy claimed and
enjoyed the proud and enviable dominion of the seas.

He observed, that

their predecessors had come into life with gay prospects, and with pleasing
hopes; but how different was the fate of himself, and those who entered
into public life at the present moment? They came upon the stage of
public action, at a time when their country was perhaps upon the eve of
dissolution; when it certainly was fallen from the high consideration in

which it stood a few years before, and when every prospect of grandeur was vanished; when every incitement to great and laudable ambition was extinguished, and when they had not even the consolation to believe, that the efforts of their youth could snatch their country from impending ruin.

His lordship added

> that the prosecution of the war against America was criminal and absurd beyond expression; and that nothing short of the immediate discontinuance of it, could save the nation from irretrievable destruction. It was, therefore, the duty of that house, to raise their sinking country, which lay prostrate at their feet, and sought, amidst the bitterest hours of calamity, their aid to snatch her from impending ruin.

Though the state of Georgia was now happily relieved from the oppression of its foreign [54] foes, South Carolina continued some time longer in a state of hostility. They remained several months exposed to the ravages of small parties of the British, sent out for various purposes; the most important of which was, to collect provisions for their own immediate necessities.

Among the most painful events which took place on these occasions, and which was justly regretted by all America, was the death of colonel John Laurens. No one acquainted with his merits, can forbear to drop a tear over the memory of so worthy an officer. His zeal for the interests of his country and the cause of freedom, had often been exhibited by his exertions in the field; nor was he less distinguished as an able negociator in France, where he had repaired in some of the darkest days of America. There he rendered his country the most essential service, by procuring a loan of money, and expediting by his address, the troops and the navy that came to its relief, in the year one thousand seven hundred and eighty.

Colonel Laurens was a gentleman, not only of great military talents and public virtues, but was endeared to every one by his affability of manners, his polite accomplishments, refined understanding, and the most amiable private character.

[55] Immediately after the capture of lord Cornwallis, colonel Laurens returned to the state of South Carolina, to exert his talents in emancipating his native state from the power and oppression of its enemies. His zeal and activity ever prompted him to go forward on smaller, as well as the greatest occasions that required his assistance. He met his premature fate in one of the many desultory skirmishes that took place not far from the environs of Charleston. General Leslie

had sent out a party to march toward the Combahee River, to secure
rice and other provisions, which his army greatly wanted. They were
followed by a detachment sent on by general Greene. In this party,
colonel Laurens was a volunteer. He was mortally wounded in a
severe rencounter, almost at the moment when victory declared in
favor of the party commanded by general Gist.

His death was universally lamented. The tears of his country were
but a just tribute due to his own merits; while grief was heightened
in every compassionate bosom, when reflecting on the sorrow this
premature stroke must occasion to his respected father, just released
from the calamities of a long imprisonment in England.

The work to be completed in the state of South Carolina was yet
arduous. The sufferings of general Greene and his little army have
[56] been already portrayed. A more ample detail of these may be
seen in his own letters, if curiosity is not sufficiently gratified. The
distressing accounts from his own hand, above referred to, were not
ameliorated, nor did his military conflicts cease, until the final
embarkation of the British troops from Charleston. Such had been
the deranged state of affairs there, and such the distance of South
Carolina from the central states, as had rendered it impossible for him
to procure support, supplies, and pay, for his own army. He was
obliged, in order to procure subsistence for them, to enter into large
contracts on his own private security: this embarrassed him the
remainder of his life.

As general Greene had now nearly finished his military drama, it
may not be improper to observe here, that this worthy officer survived
the war but a few years. He died in Georgia by a *coup de soleil*, or
sudden stroke of the sun, not unusual in the southern parts of America,
which instantly puts a period to human life. His property was afterwards
seized by his creditors, and his family, after his death, left to the
mercy of the public.

It would not be doing justice to his memory to pass unobserved,
that general Greene conducted the whole campaign at the southward
with the most consummate prudence, courage, and ability, notwithstanding the innumerable [57] difficulties that lay in his way. He
entered on the command under every disadvantage: he superseded a
brave, unfortunate, popular officer, just beaten from the field: the
country was divided in opinion, and intimidated by the power of
Britain. His troops unprovided, naked, and desponding, had to march
a long way through a barren and inhospitable country, stripped of its

CHAP. XXII small produce by the previous march of the British army. They had
1 7 8 1   to attack and retreat, to advance and to fly, over rivers, swamps, and
mountains, in opposition to a conquering foe, flushed with recent
success, who considered at that time, South Carolina and Georgia as
already subdued, and North Carolina on the point of submission to
royal authority.

Cities have often contended for the honor of giving birth to men
of eminence: and when a great degree of celebrity has been acquired,
it awakens a curiosity in every one to inquire after their origin. General
Greene was a native of the state of *Rhode Island*. He was a gentleman
of moderate fortune, who, previous to the American war, had lived
in the plain and sober habits in which he was educated, which were
in that simplicity of style that usually marks the manners of those
denominated Quakers.

[58] It is well known, that the religious tenets of that sect are averse
to all the operations of offensive war. The situation of America was
then such, that no man of principle could balance on the line of
conduct which duty impelled him to take. The natural and civil rights
of man invaded, and all the social enjoyments interrupted, he did not
think himself bound to sit a quiet spectator of the impending
distractions and distresses of his country. He viewed the opposition
to the oppressions of Great Britain, in the light of necessary and
defensive war.

On these rational principles, he early girded on the buckler and
the helmet; and with the purest intentions in his heart, and the sword
in his hand, he came forward; nor did he resheathe it, until he had,
without the smallest impeachment of reputation, passed through many
of the most active and arduous scenes, as already related, and in
conjunction with many others of the same patriotic and heroic feelings,
essentially aided in delivering his country from foreign domination.

His valor and magnanimity, humanity and probity, through all his
military career, need no other encomium than a just detail of his
transactions, to complete the character of a brave and accomplished
officer, formed for the command of armies, by the talents and resources
[59] of his own mind, which were discoverable in a variety of instances.

Beloved by the soldiery, esteemed by his country; a confidential
friend of the commander in chief; endowed by nature with a firmness
of mind that in great characters runs parallel with hazard and fatigue;
and possessing that *amor patriae* that bids defiance to danger and
death, when contrasted with the public safety; general Greene did

not leave the southern department, until the British troops were beaten from post to post, their proud designs of conquest and subjugation extinguished, the whole country recovered, and the inhabitants who survived the severe convulsion again restored to the quiet possession of their plantations. This was not finally completed until the latter part of the year one thousand seven hundred and eighty-two, when the last remnant of British troops in the southern states, embarked under the command of general Leslie. This finished the invasion of the Carolinas, and the inglorious ravage of so fair a part of America.

CHAP. XXII

1 7 8 1

Savannah and Charleston evacuated, the British troops driven from the Carolinas, and captured in Virginia; the southern states were restored to that kind of repose, which is felt after a frightful and turbulent dream, which exhausts the strength, and so far unnerves the system, that the energies of nature cannot be [60] immediately called into exercise. After such a total derangement of government, of civil order, and the usual course of business, it must require a considerable lapse of time to awake from a kind of torpor, the result of too much agitation, and from the languor which pervades the mind when former habits are interrupted, and the usual stimulants to action annihilated. They had to restore confidence and justice at home, to settle equitably the demands of creditors, and at the same time, to secure the debtor from oppression on each side of the Atlantic, where a long commercial intercourse had subsisted for so many years.

This variety of difficulties must be left to the arrangements which may take place, when the independence of America shall be acknowledged by foreign powers. We shall here only observe, that by the invasion of America, and the attempts of the British government to reduce the colonies by conquest, the narrow prejudices of national attachment were laid aside, and those ideas nearly obliterated, that by long habit had led America to view with peculiar respect the customs, manners, religion, and laws of the country whence she originated, and on whom she too partially leaned in the days of infantile weakness.

The American colonies from their first settlement, had little reason for this partial attachment [61] to the parent state. Their progress in arts and manufactures was continually checked. They were prohibited from working up many of the raw materials which the country produced, for their own necessary use. They were restricted from carrying wool from one colony to another, though the coldness of the

CHAP. XXII   climate in many parts of America, required the most ready means of
1 7 8 1   procuring and working it into clothing. In a country abounding with
iron ore, they were restrained by act of parliament, from erecting
slitting-mills to manufacture it for their own use. In instances too
innumerable to be again recapitulated, the British government had
endeavoured to cramp the growth of the young settlements, to keep
them in poverty and dependence, and to compel them to repair to
their stores for almost all the necessaries of life.

It was a cruel exercise of power, to endeavour to prohibit a great
people from making all the advantages they could of their own
produce, and employing their stock and industry in their own way.
This, as observed by a writer,

> is a manifest violation of the most sacred rights of mankind. Such
> prohibitions are only impertinent badges of slavery, imposed without
> sufficient reason, by groundless jealousies.

The same writer has observed,

> When the English colonies were established, and had become so consid-
> erable as to attract [62] the attention of the mother country, the first
> regulations which she made with regard to them, had always in view, to
> secure to herself the monopoly of their commerce; to confine their market,
> and to enlarge her own at their expense; and consequently, rather to damp
> and discourage, than to quicken and forward, the course of their industry. *

In what way therefore, it may be asked, has the policy of England
contributed, either to the first establishment, or the present grandeur
of America? Let the same writer reply.

> In one way, and in one way only, it has contributed much. *Magna virum
> mater!* It bred and formed the men who were capable of achieving such
> great expectations, and of laying the foundation of so great an empire: and
> there is no other quarter of the world of which the policy is capable of
> forming, or has ever actually and in fact, formed such men. The colonies
> owe to the policy of Europe, the education and great views of their active
> and enterprising founders; and some of the greatest and most important
> of them, so far as concerns their internal government, owe it to scarce any
> thing else.

---

* Smith's Wealth of Nations. [Adam Smith, *An Inquiry into the Nature and Causes of the
Wealth of Nations* (2 vols.; London, 1776), Book IV, Chapter VII, Part II. I have
used the authoritative Oxford University Press (1976) edition: Liberty*Classics*
(Indianapolis, 1981), II: 590.]

The folly and misguided policy of the government of England, has CHAP. XXII
dissevered the colonies [63] from them forever. Their oppressions, 1 7 8 1
their invasions, and aggressions, first taught America to view the island
of Great Britain, with an averted eye and an alienated mind. Their
alienation was completed, when the king of England sent out his
fleets and his armies, strengthened by subsidized strangers, to subjugate, and bend to servile submission, the inhabitants of a country
which has been emphatically styled, by one of the first statesmen and
patriots* of the nation,

> the promised land, the Eden of England, her seminary for seamen: that
> from thence England supplied the neighbouring nations with fish, tobacco,
> rice, and indigo; thence she draws all her naval stores; and that the
> command of the sea would give her the dominion of the land.

The happy termination of the melancholy events which had for a
series of years pervaded America, soon after the present period, raised
the United States to the zenith of their respectability. The world now
viewed with humane satisfaction, millions of people, by unexampled
sufferings and steady perseverance, emancipated from a foreign yoke.
This pleasure was heightened by the contemplation, that a more
universal spirit of liberality, and a more perfect knowledge of the
rights of man, might be disseminated by their struggles for freedom,
not only in the [64] colonies, but through a considerable part of the
civilized world.

The singular combination of events which effected a total separation,
and annihilated the former political relation, between Great Britain
and the colonies, may be held up by the philosopher or the statesman
in various points of view; while the reflective mind, which believes
and rejoices in the intervention of Divine Providence, keeps its eye
on that Superintending Power which governs the universe, and whose
finger points the rise and fall of empires. Nor dare a weak mortal to
suggest, amidst all the confusion of the present world, that they may
not be permitted in order finally to complete the beauty and harmony
of the divine system. The world has recently beheld an infant nation
at once arise to the vigor of manhood, and with the cool resolution of
maturity, opposing the intrigues and resisting the power of Britain.
In strictest amity with the hereditary foe of Britain, America has been
seen leading captive the armies, and smiling at the impotent threats
of the king of England, to hold her longer in bondage.

* Lord Chatham.

This liberation of the American colonies, was the wish of the first
statesmen and politicians of the world, exclusive of Englishmen; and
even among them America had many powerful friends. The great
lord Chatham, whose unshaken [65] patriotism, and incorruptible
integrity, had braved the storms of court faction and intrigue, until
the frowns of majesty, the fury of party, and the arts of ambitious
courtiers, had caused him to retire from the helm of state, stood at
the head of the distinguished list of nobles who advocated the American
cause. But though his humanity and justice led him to vindicate the
American opposition to ministerial measures, it was with the utmost
reluctance, that he contemplated the alienation of the colonies from
their dependence on the crown of Britain.

The commanding and comprehensive genius of a *Chatham*, viewed
the consequences of such a dismemberment of the empire, in a clearer
light, and with superior penetration, to most of the statesmen in
England. Yet he was among the most strenuous advocates for the
maintenance of the constitutional rights claimed by Americans; and
on many occasions had exerted his brilliant talents in opposition to
the ministerial measures relative to the colonies. He criminated the
war, its prosecution, and its effects, in the most glowing epithets
which ever marked his superior elocution. It is recorded,* that he
once in the house of lords, felt himself [66] so interested in the
American cause, and so warmed by the subject, that though he had
passed his grand climacteric, he, with the vigor of youth and the
strong language of maturity, expressed himself in his own peculiar
manner. He asserted, that as

> he saw the declining liberties of England, and the growing spirit of the
> colonies, were it not for invincible obstacles, he would infallibly retire
> from Britain, and spend the remainder of his days in that glorious asylum
> of liberty, of manliness, and of virtue.

Yet his patriotism with regard to Great Britain, and his just ideas
relative to the oppression of the colonies, and their laudable opposition
to ministerial measures, could never reconcile him for a moment to
the thoughts of a total separation, and the unqualified independence
of the United States. But his energies in their defence were called

---

* Life of Lord Chatham. [William Pitt, first Earl of Chatham, 1708–1778. Several
biographies of Chatham had appeared before Warren's *History*. It is impossible to
know which one she had in mind.]

forth to the latest period of his life, when he had nearly reached the
term allotted for the existence of man.

Though debilitated by pain and sickness, tortured by gout almost to the dislocation of his limbs, and from feebleness of body rendered unable to stand alone, at a critical period of national affairs, he caused himself to be supported and led into the house of lords by his friends; where the vigor of a great soul was exerted, and the oratory of Greece and Rome rivalled, [67] by the pathos, energy, and argument, which flowed from a lip quivering on the marge of eternity.

The sudden seizure of this noble patriot in the house of lords, while thunder rolled from his tongue, and the acumen of his arguments, like lightning, flashed conviction to the bosoms of the advocates of a continuance of war, has been told and repeated with so many affecting circumstances, that it is needless to say more in this place, than that the event of his death seemed for a time to palsy all parties, and make a pause in the prosecution of public measures.

No example in English story has exhibited a character more zealous to extricate his country, plunged in difficulties which were indeed irretrievable. To arise from the chamber of sickness and the bed of lassitude, while "every limb was a rebel to his will," and with the awakened energies of a most vigorous mind, and the marks of a "never ebbing spirit," is one among the singular efforts of the human soul, to continue the elevation hoped for in immortality, when the teguments of the brittle casement were on the verge of crumbling into dust. One of his biographers has observed, that those exertions of the intellectual powers, discoverable to the last, in the character of lord Chatham,

> were of all others the most unparalleled, in whatever view considered, and must be forever [68] admired. Those instances in which the soul bursts the bands of earth, and stands alone in confessed eternity, are the most beautiful, the most pathetic, the most sublime exhibitions, of which the mind of man is capable to conceive.

The death of this illustrious champion of freedom, a justly boasted ornament of the British nation, took place at a very interesting period. It was soon after the misfortunes, the defeat, and the capture, of general Burgoyne and his army, and before the nation had recovered from their deep consternation and dismay, on the unexpected intelligence of the failure of the northern expedition. In the last speech made by the illustrious character above mentioned, who will never

CHAP. XXII be passed over in silence in any historic record connected with the
1 7 8 1 affairs of Great Britain, he observed, when he adverted to the disaster
at Saratoga, that "the presiding deities of Great Britain appeared to
have abandoned her, and that Providence militated against her arms,
and spurned with indignation at her cause."

But though the most brilliant talents were displayed, and the firmest
opposition made by many of the best orators, and most enlightened
and disinterested patriots of the nation, against the continuance of a
ruinous war that produced [69] nothing but defeat and disgrace, yet
we have seen that only a short time elapsed, before the king and his
ministry were again ready to prosecute their hostile intentions, and
to continue desolation and carnage among the inhabitants of the
United States. Reiterated barbarities have been detailed, miseries
displayed, and the tragic tale continued, until the mortifying surrender
of a second British army. The bosom of humanity was lacerated in
the barbarous scenes of protracted war; yet the breast of his Britannic
majesty seemed rather hardened by the misfortunes of the nation;
and the flinty hearts of a majority in parliament still urged, that the
scourge of war might pursue those who claimed the just rights of
men, in whatever part of the globe there appeared any attempt to
defend them.

This was exhibited, not only in their determined coercion of the
American colonies, and their hostile dispositions toward the Batavian
republic, but even in their refusal of assistance to the little distressed
state of Geneva, when struggling against the encroachments of the
aristocratic branch of their government. The people of Geneva had
borne too much to continue longer silent under their oppressions.
They had complained, that the magistrates had encroached upon their
privileges further than their constitution authorised. These complaints
only drew upon themselves new severities from [70] an ambitious
aristocracy. The democratic party had required a new code of laws,
which should be a standard for the conduct of rulers, and also a clear
decision on the fundamental principles of their own constitution, that
they might thereby be excited to a prompt and willing obedience to
the laws, when the foundation which demanded it was more clearly
defined. Mutual confidence would have rested upon this basis of
public order and common security, had not the intrigues of the
aristocratic party defeated the salutary project.

The magistrates not only employed the most unjustifiable practices
for the support of their authority, but represented their internal

disputes in such exaggerated colors, and in such a favorable light for CHAP. XXII
themselves, that they successfully interested several foreign powers 1 7 8 1
to support their claims. The court of France interfered; the aristocratic
cantons of Zurich and Berne, and the king of Sardinia co-operated;
and brought forward a body of twelve thousand men, with whom they
blockaded the city of Geneva. The citizens were thus compelled to
admit these military mediators within their city. A code of laws was
prepared under the point of the bayonet, for the future regulation of
their government.

This was so inconsistent with the liberties of the people, or the
independence of their republic, [71] that vast numbers of the Genevese
abandoned the city, to seek an asylum in distant regions, where they
might again possess that freedom their ancestors had once enjoyed.
The deserted habitations of the citizens were converted into barracks,
and a great part of the city, once flourishing under the benign influence
of their liberal institutions, reduced to a desert. Thus, as observed,—

> It is a just subject of regret, that the ambition of some individuals, who
> aimed at a degree of power to which they had no just claim, should have
> thus put a period to the prosperity of a republic, which has been the abode
> of so much liberty and happiness.

Amidst the distresses of their state, the Genevese had applied to
the earl of Abingdon, once a resident among them, and a known
friend to the liberties of mankind in every part of the world, to employ
his influence in their favor with the court of Great Britain. In this his
lordship was successless. They had besought the noble earl to continue
his friendly disposition, and to urge his nation to watch over the
situation of a little state, now on the point of being sacrificed to the
principles of despotism, whole struggles must be interesting to all in
whom the fine feelings of humanity were not totally extinguished.
He replied, that it was with much regret, that he had not succeeded
in his application [72] to the British ministry to afford relief to the
oppressed state of Geneva, and that there was too much reason to
fear no assistance would be lent them.

He attributed this to the present situation of Great Britain, rent by
divisions at home, and surrounded by enemies abroad.* It is however

---

* See the earl of Abingdon's reply to the applications. [Source not identified.
Willoughby Bertie, fourth Earl of Abingdon, was an outspoken member of the
House of Lords from 1775 to his death in 1799. A Rockingham Whig, he was a
strong supporter of popular rights and a staunch opponent of war with America.]

probable, that their indifference might arise from the general spirit
of all monarchies, to discountenance every effort of the people in
favor of republicanism. It is not to be expected, there should be any
partial bias to those liberal principles of democratic government, where
a monarch sits enthroned with all the powers of despotism in his
hands, a parliament at command to enforce his mandates, and a people
ready to relinquish their own will to the caprice or the pride of a
sovereign.

His lordship had observed in answer to the Genevan application,
that

> there was a time when the fleets of England were the speaking trumpets
> to the whole world. At that period their grievances would have been
> listened to, and their redress would have been certain. But there was a
> sad reverse in the affairs of Great Britain, which was no longer [73] in a
> capacity to speak to the enemies of the liberties of mankind, in its wonted
> tone of authority.

In Ireland, the emigrants from the ruined state of Geneva met with
the most liberal encouragement, from the government, from the
nobility, and from the nation at large. In an assembly of delegates of
the province of Leinster, it was unanimously resolved,

> that the virtuous citizens of Geneva who wished for an asylum in that
> kingdom, from the hand of tyranny and oppression, deserved their highest
> commendation; and that such of them as had established themselves
> amongst them, should upon every occasion receive their utmost attention
> and support.

Sympathy for oppressed sufferers under the hand of despotic power,
had been taught the inhabitants of Ireland from similar afflictions,
under which they had long groaned, and against which they were still
struggling to rescue their prostrated rights and privileges, which were
invaded by the haughty and domineering spirit of a more potent sister
kingdom.

The history of Geneva displays a striking portrait of the means by
which most republics have been subverted. This is generally done by
the pride of a few families, the ambition of [74] individuals, and the
supineness of the people. Thus an undue authority is established by
a select number, more mortifying to the middling class of mankind,
and which has a tendency to render more abject and servile the mass
of the people, than the single arm of the most despotic individual.*

* The history of Geneva has very properly been recommended to the study of every
American citizen, by a political writer. [Source not identified.]

CHAPTER XXIII

General Observations on the Conduct of the British King and Parliament, after the Intelligence of the Capture of Lord Cornwallis and his Army • King's Speech • Address of Thanks opposed • Proposition by Sir Thomas Pitt to withhold Supplies from the Crown • Vote carried in Favor of granting Supplies • General Burgoyne defends the American Opposition to the Measures of the Court • Variety of desultory Circumstances discussed in Parliament

[75] The close of the campaign in Virginia, in the year one thousand seven hundred and eighty-one, was an era interesting to the empire of Britain, and indeed to the European world, as well as to the United States of America. The period was beheld by the latter with a mixture of pleasure and astonishment, more easily imagined than described; and by some of the former, especially Great Britain, with chagrin and mortification, equal to their designs of conquest and subjugation. The relief of the southern colonies, and the capture of lord Cornwallis and his army, was not less unexpected than humiliating, to the king, the minister, and the British nation at large; yet from their deportment there did not appear any immediate prospect of peace.

[76] From the situation of American affairs at home, from the expected accession of new allies, and the general disposition of the European powers, to acknowledge the independence of the United States, and from their successes and their perseverance, it might rationally have been expected, that the contemplation of a general pacification among the contending powers, would at this time have originated in England: more especially when the expenses of the nation were calculated, and the misfortunes Great Britain had suffered during the war were considered.

Her national enemies abroad were accumulating; discontents and riots at home increasing; the complaints of Scotland alarming; and Ireland nearly in a state of insurrection. But the pride, the spirit, and

CHAP. XXIII the resources of the nation, appeared almost inexhaustible; and the
1 7 8 1 stake of the colonies was too great to relinquish yet, though the
ministry had hitherto played a losing game.

Thus when the British parliament met, after the confirmation of
the loss of the army in Virginia, the capture of lord Cornwallis and
his brave troops, the total defeat of the expedition to the Chesapeake,
and the declining aspect of affairs in the more southern colonies, the
speech from the throne was yet manifestly dictated by the spirit of
hostility. The king, though he [77] lamented in the preamble of his
speech, the loss of his brave officers and troops, and the unfortunate
termination of the campaign in Virginia, he still urged the most
vigorous prosecution of the war, and of measures that might extinguish
that *spirit of rebellion* that reigned in the colonies, and reduce *his*
deluded subjects to due obedience to the laws and government of
Great Britain.

"The war," he observed,

> is still unhappily prolonged by that restless ambition which first excited
> our enemies to commence it, and which still continues to disappoint my
> earnest and diligent exertions to restore the public tranquillity. But I
> should not answer the trust committed to the sovereign of a free people,
> nor make a suitable return to my subjects for their constant and zealous
> attachment to my person, family, and government, if I consented to
> sacrifice, either to my own desire of peace, or to their temporary ease and
> relief, those essential rights and permanent interests, upon the maintenance
> of which, the future strength and security of this country must ever
> principally depend.

The late accounts from America had in some measure weakened
the influence of the ministry, and in proportion, strengthened the
party who had always execrated the American war. [78] But administration, too much agitated by the desire of revenge, and too haughty
and powerful to bend to terms of pacification, flattered themselves,
that events had not yet fully ripened a general disposition for peace.
Of course, the usual compliment of an address of thanks for the
speech from the throne, was brought forward; but it was opposed
with unusual acrimony.

It was boldly asserted, that the speech breathed nothing but "rancor,
vengeance, misery, and bloodshed." The war was directly charged,
by the advocates for peace, to the wild systems of government adopted
early in the present reign. They alleged, that it was ineffectual,
delusory, and ruinous; that it was founded, not in the restless *ambition*

of the *Americans*, but that it ought to be charged on a ministry who
were "a curse to their country; who had cut up the British possessions
in the colonies, and separated England from their fellow subjects in
America;" who had drawn them to the point of losing their settlements
both in the East and the West Indies; who had distressed their
commerce, robbed them of the once undisputed sovereignty of the
seas, and rendered the nation the ridicule of Europe.*

[79] This was the language of Mr. Fox. Sentiments and opinions
nearly similar, were expressed by Burke, Barre, and the son of the
celebrated Pitt; by the lords Saville, Shelburne, Conway, and others,
in the house of commons. The same temper and opinions appeared
in the house of lords: the duke of Richmond, the lords Rockingham,
Fitzwilliam, Maitland, and many others on the list of nobility, varied
little in opinion or expression from the minority in the house of
commons. They with equal warmth opposed an address to the king;
they freely discussed the principles held up in the speech, and as
severely censured the measures it tended to enforce.

The dissenting lords observed, that

> by an address of thanks, their honor might be pledged to support a war,
> that from near seven years' experience, a determination to pursue it,
> appeared in the highest degree frantic, desperate, and ruinous; that the
> principles of the present war could never be justified; that the delusions
> by which parliament had been led on from year to year to pursue it, were
> criminal; that the abuse and mismanagement of the marine department
> had occasioned the loss in Virginia; that the minister at the head of the
> board of admiralty might be justly charged with negligence, incapacity,
> and guilt.

[80] The character of Sandwich, first lord of the admiralty, was
justly portrayed on this occasion, and exhibited in those glaring colors
merited by his private life, as well as his political blunders. In short,
every motion for a further coercion of the colonies, was reprobated
by a large and respectable party in both departments of the great
assembly of the nation. The opponents of administration in both
houses of parliament, observed, that they were actuated by the same
principles, and urged by the same motives, that had induced them

---

* See Mr. Fox's speech in the house of commons; also, several speeches in the house
of lords at this period. [See *Cobbett*, XXII: 878 ff. Also see, *Annual Register* (1782),
"History of Europe," pp. 151–153. Fox moved for an inquiry into the causes of the
navy's want of success, January 24, 1782.]

to oppose for several years, the pernicious, destructive, and ruinous system of government, that had involved the nation in irretrievable difficulties.

It was even proposed in the house of commons, that the representatives of the nation should withhold all farther supplies of monies to the crown, until a redress of grievances should take place; and thus by a legal compulsion, oblige their sovereign and his ministers to act with more moderation and justice.

The son and the nephew of the late lord Chatham distinguished themselves in this debate. They seemed at that time to have the national interest at heart, and to inherit the graces of oratory and the fire of eloquence, that had through all his life been displayed by their admired and illustrious ancestor.

[81] Sir Thomas Pitt called for a division of the house, on the question of withholding supplies. He declared at once,

> that if he retired to the doors of the house alone, he should withhold his assent to entrusting any more public monies in the hands of ministers, who had already dissipated so much wealth, and wasted such streams of human blood, in wild and fruitless projects, and who had yet shewn no contrition for the peril and disgrace in which they had involved their country.

On the other hand, many powerful reasons were urged against a step that would tend to disunite, and stain with dishonor, a nation which had been renowned for their unconquerable spirit. Lord North observed, that a generous grant of supplies to the crown, would convince their enemies, that no calamities could sink them into despair. He added,

> that he always considered the American war as a matter of cruel necessity, but that it was founded on a truly British basis; that he regretted it as peculiarly unfortunate for himself, and that he would willingly make any personal sacrifices for the restoration of peace; but that the refusal of supplies to the crown, in the midst of a war raging like the present, must inevitably lead to irretrievable calamity and disgrace, while it gave strength, animation, [82] and triumph, to France, Spain, Holland, and America.

But the party in opposition, not appalled by his reasoning, stood firm and immoveable. They claimed a right coeval with the institution of parliament, and essential to a free government, to withhold supplies from the crown, when measures were adopted that threatened to involve the empire in endless calamities.

It is undoubtedly true, that the most effectual check on an arbitrary

executive is, for the representatives of the people to hold their hand
on the string of the purse. This privilege once relinquished to the
will of a sovereign of whatever name, his power is without control,
and his projects and his extortions may lead to poverty, misery, and
slavery, beyond redemption, before a nation is apprised of its danger.
"Honest and generous nations perish oftener through confidence than
distrust."

To return to the question in debate: it terminated according to the
expectations of the observers of political operations. The rhetoric or
the reasonings of a member of the British parliament, seldom do more
than display the brilliancy of his genius, and the graces of elocution;
his arguments on the one side or the other, have little influence on
the pre-determinations of party; their opinions are generally [83] made
up before the public discussion of the subject. All parties are so
sensible of this, that they mutually consent, when weary of their
places by protracted debate, and agree to what they call *pairing off*;
that is, when one chooses to retire, a member of the opposite party
retires with him. Thus the equilibrium or the balance continues the
same at the conclusion of the most pathetic, interesting, and energetic
debate, that it was in the beginning; the minister holds his dependents,
and the popular speakers retain their adherents.

The numbers and the names of each are generally known, before
they enter the dome that rings with the beauty, the harmony, the
sublimity of their language, and the musical elegance of their finished
periods. Thus the decision of the question is usually calculated, both
within and without doors, previous to entering on debates on which
depend the honor, the interest, and the fate of the nation.

This mode of conduct may be consistent enough with the present
state of society in Europe. It is a fair deduction, that the result of
human action is owing more to the existing state or stage of society,
than to any deviations in the nature or general disposition of mankind.
All political transactions were now systematized: reasoning on the
principles of [84] equity and truth lost all its efficiency, if it clashed
with the measures of a minister, preconcerted in the cabinet of his
prince.

A very sensible writer has observed,

> that in the state of society which had taken place in America, the foundations
> of her freedom were laid long before the nations of Europe had any ideas
> of what was taking place in the minds of men. Conquest, religion, law,
> custom, habits, and manners, confirmed by military power, had established
> a state of society in Europe, in which the rights of men were obliterated

and excluded. The property and power of a nation had passed into the hands of the sovereign, nobility, and church.

The body of the people were without property, or any chance of securing any, and without education or knowledge to form them to any rational principles and sentiments: without property and without principle, they were of little or no consequence in the view of government: nothing was to be seen but one general degradation of the people, and an unnatural and excessive exaltation of those who had acquired power. This every where tended to corrupt both, and to give the most unfavorable idea of the capacity of the former, and of the dispositions of the latter.

[85] Thus, (he observes) the ministers of Britain at the time of the American contest, were men of great eminence and ability in managing business upon the European system; but they had no ideas of the state of things in America, or of a system in which nature and society had combined to preserve freedom. What they called *rebellion* was only the tendency of nature and society to preserve *freedom*, made more active by their opposition.*

Thus when the motion was made by sir Grey Cooper for the decision of a question that held out a signal for peace, or the continuance of an absurd and luckless war, the vote in favor of the latter, and of generous supplies to the crown for its support, was carried by a large majority; one hundred and seventy-two appeared in support of administration, while only seventy-seven were counted in the minority.

It would be unjust to pass over in silence the behavior of general Burgoyne at this period. He had recovered his seat in parliament, his health, and in some measure his military reputation: and no one more warmly advocated every measure for the immediate restoration of peace. He supported the motion for the recal [86] of all British troops from America; he pressed an immediate exchange of prisoners both in England and America; and strenuously urged every pacific advance that might comport with the honor, the equity, and the dignity of the British nation. He even justified the principles of American opposition to the measures of administration, and parliamentary decrees. He acknowledged, that when he engaged in the service against the United States he thought differently; but that he had been brought to conviction by the uniform conduct of the American states.

He added, that it was presumption to allege, that they were not in

---

* Dr. Williams's History of Vermont. [Samuel Williams, *The Natural and Civil History of Vermont* (Walpole, N.H., 1794), pp. 369, 370, 373.]

the right to resist. He observed, that it was reason, and the finger of CHAP. XXIII
God alone, that had implanted the same sentiments in the breasts of 1 7 8 1
three millions of people: and that comparing the conduct of the
ministry, as time had developed their system, he was convinced, that
the American war was formed on a part of the general design against
the constitution of Britain, and the unalienable rights of man.

Thus had the experience of severity from the cabinet, of ingratitude
from his king and country, and of adversity in the wilds of *Saratoga*,
taught this veteran officer, once armed for the destruction of her
rights, and the desolation of America, to stand forth a champion for
her invaded [87] liberties, a defender of the principles of her resistance
to the crown of Great Britain, and an advocate for the restoration of
peace, which equity required, and humanity claimed.

It is true, the principles of Americans were so fixed, and the
opposition to the encroachments of parliament had been so long
sustained by the united colonies, with such cool intrepidity, such a
spirit of perseverance, and such a defiance of danger, as had brought
almost all England to wish for the restoration of peace, even on the
humiliating idea of a dismemberment of the empire, and an explicit
acknowledgment of American independence. Though their affection
was too generally alienated from the inhabitants beyond the Atlantic,
they saw the ruin of their trade and manufactures, and felt the miseries
of a war protracted from year to year, without any nearer prospect of
obtaining its object.

Yet, notwithstanding the disposition of the people, neither the
king, the ministry, or the majority in parliament, were at all softened
by the wishes or sufferings of the nation. Nothing that could touch
the passions, or operate on national interest or pride, was left unessayed
by the orators in favor of reconciliation and peace. A retrospect was
taken of every important transaction in the course of the war; the
conduct and manoeuvres of the principal actors revised, scrutinized,
and censured; yet [88] this interesting session ended without any
conciliatory prospects.

Among the variety of affairs that were brought forward relative to
America, and that were discussed with masterly precision and dignity,
the cruelties exhibited at St. Eustatia, which will be immediately
related, were not forgotten. The injustice exercised toward the
sufferers of that unhappy island, was criminated in the most pointed
language.

The treatment Mr. Laurens had received, while a prisoner in the

CHAP. XXIII tower of London, was recollected and reprobated with equal severity.

1 7 8 1 The situation of other prisoners in their jails and prison ships, was painted in colors that could not fail to excite compassion. The defeat of British armies, the degradation of their best officers, the disgrace brought on the nation by the rank given to, and the confidence placed in, the infamous Arnold, were brought into the scale of accusation. Indeed, every ministerial measure was in this session censured in the house of commons, with the acrimony of resentment, and the boldness of truth, without being softened by the delicacy of the courtier.

We have seen above, that immediately after general Arnold had forfeited his honor, betrayed his trust, and endeavoured to sell his country, [89] he received his pecuniary reward from general Clinton, and was appointed to a distinguished military command in the Chesapeake. He was in a few months recalled from Virginia by sir Henry Clinton, ostensibly to assist in the defence of New York, but more probably to quiet the murmurs of men of more virtue, talents, and merit, than himself. They could not brook the insolence with which this dignified traitor sustained the caresses of his employers, nor the degradation felt by many officers of high rank and superior genius, to see one placed over their heads, whom all acknowledged deserved no elevation but by a *halter*.

The British commander in chief at New York, contrary to the old adage, appeared not to hate, but to love the traitor as well as the treason. Immediately on his recal from the Chesapeake, general Clinton had vested him with a new commission, and licensed him to ravage the borders of the state of Connecticut, and to pillage and burn the fair towns that spread along the margin of the Sound. This was a business very congenial to the character and genius of Arnold. He was accompanied by a detachment under the command of colonel Eyre. This excursion was attended with much slaughter and devastation: the inhabitants of several defenceless towns were shamefully [90] plundered and abused, without distinction of age or sex.

New London was more seriously attacked; and after a short and brave resistance, plundered and burnt. As soon as the town had surrendered, a number of soldiers entered the garrison: the officer who headed the party inquired who commanded it? the valiant colonel Ledyard stepped forward, and replied with ease and gallantry, "I did, sir, but you do now;" at the same moment he delivered his sword to a British officer. The barbarous ruffian, instead of receiving his submission like the generous victor, immediately stabbed the brave

American. Nor was his death the only sacrifice made in that place, to CHAP. XXIII
the wanton vengeance of the foes of America: several other officers 1 7 8 1
of merit were assassinated, after the surrender of the town; while
their more helpless connexions experienced the usual cruel fate of
cities captured by inhuman conquerors.

Some members in parliament endeavoured to extenuate the guilt,
and defend the promotion of general Arnold, and the confidence
placed in him by sir Henry Clinton. But after a recapitulation of the
above transactions, and some similar events, Mr. Fox observed, that
Arnold

> had dispersed his panegyrics, and scattered abuse on the characters of
> British officers; but that he shuddered at the predicament [91] in which
> his gallant countrymen were placed, when in their military capacity they
> were marked with so infamous a degradation, as to have any thing to
> apprehend, either from the reproaches or the applauses of general Arnold:
> that in the character of an American officer, he had treacherously abandoned
> his command; and now rewarded with an active military promotion in
> British service, he might probably proceed hereafter to similar transactions,
> and sacrifice for lucre the troops of Britain.

Mr. Burke was equally severe on the character of this perfidious
traitor. He observed,

> that such a person could not be held by any laws, to serve with strict
> fidelity, the people and the sovereign against whom he was before in arms,
> and to whom he had fled in the very midst of acts of treachery to the
> states whose cause he had deserted. A man whose conduct had been
> marked by glaring strokes of cruelty and perfidiousness, and which had
> furnished an indubitable proof, that he who on one side would have
> sacrificed an army, was too dangerous to be trusted with the command of
> troops belonging to the opposing party.

He lamented that the honors of high office were thus scattered on
the worthless, and frequently on men who had no inconsiderable
share in the measures that tended to the disgrace and ruin of their
country.

[92] Mr. Burke indeed, had always appeared to have a thorough
detestation of corrupt men and measures. He advocated the cause of
liberty, not only with the ability of an orator, but with an enthusiasm
for the establishment of freedom in all countries. He was an advocate
for the distressed Irish; and stretched his genius to the eastern world,
to survey the abuses, and to criminate the cruelties perpetrated there

CHAP. XXIII   by his own countrymen; and, with a pathos peculiar to himself,
1 7 8 1   brought before the tribunal of the public eye, the criminal laden with
the rich spoils, the diamonds and jewels of the princely widows, and
the immense treasures of the distant nabobs.

He ever appeared opposed to the powerful oppressors of the people,
and attached to the defenders of freedom in every nation; was the
friend of Franklin and Laurens; corresponded with the first on
American affairs, and made great exertions to mitigate the sufferings
of the last, while in rigorous imprisonment. But this unfortunate
gentleman, notwithstanding the influence of many powerful friends,
which he had in the house of commons, was refused his liberty, and
detained in the tower until near the close of the war.

However, Mr. Laurens survived his persecutions in England,
returned to his native country, and spent the remainder of his days
in private [93] life. After several years of virtuous preparation for his
exit, his only surviving son closed his eyes. His fond affection for his
father led him to deviate from the usual customs of his countrymen,
in the manner of interring their friends. He reared an altar on which
he burnt the body of the patriarch, and carefully gathered the ashes
from the hearth, deposited them in a silver urn, and placed them in
his bed-chamber, with reverence and veneration, where they remained
to the day of his death. This circumstance is mentioned as a peculiar
instance of filial affection, and at once a mark of the respect due to
the memory both of the patriot and the parent.

The celebrity of Mr. Burke for his general conduct, and his spirited
speeches in favor of the rights of man, during the revolutionary war,
were justly appreciated throughout America. He was admired for his
oratorical talents, and beloved for the part he took in the cause of
suffering individuals, either American prisoners or the oppressed in
his own country. His feelings of humanity extended to the Ganges;
and by his lively descriptions of the miseries of the wretched inhabitants
of India, he has expanded the human heart, and drawn a tear from
every compassionate eye. Certainly, to such a man, the tribute of a
tear is equally due, when he shall be beheld in the decline of [94]
life, deviating from his own principles, and drawing his energetic pen
to censure and suppress the struggles for liberty in a sister kingdom.*

When we retrace the powers of the human mind, and view the

---

* Philippic against France. [Edmund Burke, *Reflections on the Revolution in France, and
on the Proceedings in Certain Societies in London Relative to that Event* (London, 1791).]

gradations of the faculties, or the decline of genius, it is a humiliating chap. xxiii
reflection, that a more advanced period of life so often subtracts from 1 7 8 1
the character of the man, as it shone in full lustre in the meridian of
his days. Perhaps in the instance before us, a deviation from former
principles might be more owing to a decline in correct political
sentiment, than to any physical debility that was yet apparent.

It is an anticipation which many reasons render excuseable, to bring
forward in this place, the subsequent declension of this gentleman's
zeal in favor of the general liberties of mankind, when his flowery
epithets, argumentative elocution, and flowing periods, were often
equally entertaining with the best theatrical exhibitions. But, without
further apology it is proper to observe, that before he finished his
political drama, the world was astonished to behold Mr. Burke,
fulminating his anathemas against a neighbouring nation, who were
struggling [95] with every nerve for the recovery of the freedom and
the natural rights of man, of which they had long been robbed, and
which had been trodden under foot, if not annihilated, by despotic
kings, unprincipled nobles, and a corrupt clergy. It was surprising to
hear a man, who had so often expressed the most humane feelings
for the depression of his fellow beings of every class, afterwards
regretting, in the most pathetic strains, only the sorrows of royalty,
without a momentary pang for the miseries of a nation.*

* A political writer has observed, that

> "the late opinions of Mr. Burke, furnished more matter of astonishment to
> those who had distantly observed, than to those who had correctly examined
> the system of his former political life. An abhorrence for abstract politics, a
> predilection for aristocracy, and a dread of innovation, have ever been among
> the most sacred articles of his public creed. It was not likely that at his age, he
> should abandon to the invasion of audacious novelties, opinions which he had
> received so early and maintained so long, which had been fortified by the
> applause of the great and the assent of the wise, which he had dictated to so
> many illustrious pupils, and supported against so many distinguished opponents.
> Men who early attain eminence, repose in their first creed. They neglect the
> progress of the human mind subsequent to its adoption; and when, as in the
> present case, it has burst forth into action, they regard it as a transient madness,
> worthy only of pity or derision. They mistake it for a mountain torrent, that
> will pass away with the storm that gave it birth. They know not that it is the
> stream of human opinion, *in omne volubilis aevum*, which the accession of every
> day will swell, which is destined to sweep into the same oblivion, the resistance
> of learned sophistry and of powerful oppression.

> *Mackintosh's Vindiciae Galliciae, on Mr. Burke's Philippic against the French*

CHAP. XXIII   If a just portrait has been drawn below, and Mr. Burke was never
1 7 8 1   at heart, a genuine friend to the liberties of mankind, we will sigh
over [96] the versatility of human conduct, and leave him to reflect
on his own inconsistency; while the florid diction of his oratory is
admired by his contemporaries, and the generations that succeed him
will be delighted with the brilliant periods that adorned his eloquence
on every occasion.

The admiration of the finished rhetoric and fascinating talents by
which the speeches of Fox, Burke, and many other British orators,
were embellished, has occasioned the above digression, which we
now wave, and observe, that the agents who had brought on a ruinous
war with the colonies, and defection, alienation, and hostility, with
surrounding nations, had not sufficient talent, subtilty, or sophistry,
to quiet the people of England under the ideas of a longer continuance
of the war. They had long amused them by the musical powers of
language, [97] which they also possessed; but they could no longer
counteract the arguments and efforts of men of abilities, equal to any
in the ministerial interest, and possessed of more humanity, who
wished to put a period to the destructive calamities that had now for
seven years embarrassed and distressed the nation.

The most gloomy prospect pervaded every mind on the contemplation of a further protraction of war, at the same time that the
termination of the campaign in Virginia, had nearly defeated the
flattering hopes of those who had labored with so much zeal and
fervor, to subjugate the united colonies of America. It was said in
parliament, that

> the immense expense, the great accumulation of public debt, by the ever
> to be lamented contest with America, the effusion of human blood which
> it had occasioned, the diminution of trade, and the increase of taxes, were
> evils of such magnitude, as could scarcely be overlooked even by the most
> insensible and inattentive.

It was the unanimous opinion of those who had ever been favorers
of more lenient measures, that any further efforts to reduce the
revolted colonies to obedience by force, under the present circumstances, would only increase the mutual enmity, so fatal to the
interests of Great [98] Britain and America, and forever prevent a

---

Revolution. [James Mackintosh, *Vindiciae Galliciae. Defence of the French Revolution Against the Accusations of the Right Hon. Edmund Burke.* . . . (London,
1791), pp. i–ii. Mackintosh refers to Burke's *Reflections* as a "philippic."]

reconciliation; and that it would weaken the efforts of Great Britain against the house of Bourbon, and other European enemies.

It is true, that the standard of respectability on which Great Britain had long been placed, was already shaken; that she had in a degree lost her political influence with, and was viewed by, surrounding nations through a less terrific medium, than at any period since the immense increase of power acquired by her formidable navy.

The colonies alienated, Ireland in a state of desperation, Scotland little less discontented, a considerable part of the West Indies lost to Great Britain, the affairs of the kingdom in the East Indies in the most deranged and perturbed state, by the mismanagement and avarice of their officers vested with unlimited powers wantonly abused; it was impossible, under the load of calumny, opposition, and perplexity, for the old ministry, the ostensible agents of these complicated evils, longer to resist the national will.

Many plausible arguments were urged in vindication of the measures of administration, at the same time that the fatal consequences were acknowledged by their defenders; but acknowledged only as the common events which have been [99] experienced by other nations, who have failed in their best concerted enterprises, and been humbled before the enemies whose destruction had too sanguinely been calculated. But the minister was implicated by the increasing opposition, as the author of all the calamities a just Providence had seen fit to inflict on a nation, who at the close of the preceding reign had considered all the world at their feet.

The parliamentary debates indeed, were at this time very interesting. Lord John Cavendish observed, that above an hundred millions sterling had been expended within five years on the army and navy, and backed his assertion by several resolves, criminating the ministry as totally deficient in point of ability, to retrieve the wretched state of the nation, after they had thrown away the thirteen colonies and other appendages of the empire. However, had their talents been sufficient to have retrieved the public misfortunes, in which their pernicious councils had involved their country, there did not appear the smallest disposition in the present ministry to make the attempt, or to resign their places.

A detail of the expenses of the fruitless war with America, was laid before the house of commons in a very impressive style; and though many arguments were used in favor of the ministry, no subterfuge could screen them, nor [100] any reluctance they felt, retard the

CHAP. XXIII necessity of their resignation. This was called for from every quarter,
1 7 8 1   in terms severe and sarcastic. One gentleman requested, that

> whenever the prime minister, to the unspeakable joy of the nation, should
> really go to his sovereign to resign his employments, as he had once
> promised to do when parliament should withdraw its confidence from him,
> he hoped now that period was come, he would not forget to lay before
> the king, a fair representation of the flourishing state in which he found
> his majesty's empire when the government of it was entrusted to his hands,
> and the ruinous condition in which he was about to leave all that remained
> of it.

Some thought that the party in opposition were too ready to draw degrading pictures of the calamitous state of the nation, and the blunders of its officers: it was their opinion, that thus by exposing the national weakness, they might strengthen the hands of their enemies, now triumphant at the misfortunes that had already befallen them. But the irresistible force of truth, combined with imperious necessity, wrought conviction on some, and softened the obstinacy of others, by which a majority was obtained, and the late measures decidedly condemned.

The old ministry were soon after obliged to relinquish their places, and a new line of public [101] measures adopted. The hollow murmur of discontent at last penetrated the ear of royalty, and impelled the pride of majesty to listen to the general voice in favor of the immediate restoration of tranquillity; and however sanguine the king of England had long been, in favor of coercing his American subjects to unconstitutional and unconditional obedience, he could not much longer withstand the torrent of opposition to the cruel system.

Events were now nearly ripened, which soon produced a truce to the scourge of war, which had so long desolated families, villages, and cities. The energetic arguments and perspicuous reasonings, which do not always apply in their full force on the minds of those prepossessed by partial affection and esteem, covered with the veil of prejudice in favor of political opinions similar to their own, were necessarily laid aside, and the opposition to peace daily drawn into a narrower compass. Reason, humanity, policy, and justice, urged so forcibly by men of the best abilities, could not longer be withstood. Among these were many who shed the tears of sorrow over the ashes of their friends, who had fallen in the "tented fields" of America. In others, the feelings of indignation arose from a survey of the profuse expenditure, and the wanton waste of public money. Besides these,

not a few persons were mortified at the eclipse of military glory, which CHAP. XXIII
had formerly emblazoned [102] the laurels, and illumined the char- 1 7 8 1
acters of British chieftains.

Indeed, America at this period was not a theatre on which generous
Britons could expect, or wish to acquire glory. They were sensible
that their success must eradicate the noble principles of liberty, for
which their ancestors had reasoned, struggled, and fought, against the
invasions of their arbitrary kings, from the days of William the Norman
to the Tudors, and from the last of the Tudor line, their adored
queen Elizabeth, through the race of the Stuarts, no less contemptible
than arbitrary, until the necessity of equal exertion was revived in the
reign of George the third. At the same time, it was too evident to all,
that repeated defeat had already tarnished the lustre of British arms.
The celebrity of some of their most renowned commanders was
shrouded in disappointment; their minds enveloped in chagrin doubly
mortifying, as it was the result of exertion from enemies they had
viewed with contempt, as too deficient in talents, courage, discipline,
and resources, to combat the prowess and imagined superiority of
British veterans. From these circumstances it had been calculated,
that Americans might be reduced even by the terror of their approach,
and the fame of that military glory long attached to the character and
valor of British soldiers.

[103] But He who ordains the destiny of man, conceals his purposes
till the completion of the designs of divine government. This should
teach mankind the lessons of humility and candor, instead of an
indulgence of that fierce, vindictive spirit, that aims at the destruction
of its own species, under the imposing authority of obtrusive despotism.

C H A P T E R   X X I V

Naval Transactions • Rupture between England and France opened in the Bay of Biscay • Admiral Keppel • Serapis and Countess of Scarborough captured by Paul Jones—The Protection given him by the States-General resented by the British Court • Transactions in the West Indies • Sir George Bridges Rodney returns to England after the Capture of St. Eustatia—Sent out again the succeeding Year—Engages and defeats the French Squadron under the Command of the Count de Grasse—Capture of the Ville de Paris—The Count de Grasse sent to England • Admiral Rodney created a Peer of the Realm on his Return to England

CHAP. XXIV [104] To prevent breaking in upon and interrupting the thread of
1 7 8 1 narration, through a detail of the important and interesting scenes acting on the American theatre, many great naval operations have been passed over in silence, and others but slightly noticed. A particular description of nautical war was never designed by the writer of these pages; yet a retrospect may here be proper, and a cursory survey necessary, of some of the most capital transactions on the ocean, which were closely connected with American affairs, and the interests of her allies.

The beginning of naval hostilities between Great Britain and France, took place in the [105] Bay of Biscay in June, one thousand seven hundred and seventy-eight. A fleet commanded by admiral Keppel, a gentleman in whom the nation had the highest confidence, from his bravery, his prudence, and long experience in naval transactions, was at this critical period directed to sail with discretionary orders. A member of parliament of eminence observed, "that all descriptions of men seemed pleased with the choice, and to feel their own security included in the appointment" of such an able commander, at so anxious a moment. He met a squadron of thirty-two ships of the line,

and a large number of frigates, commanded by the count D'Orvilliers,
before he was in reality prepared for an interview with such a formidable
force on the part of France: this was indeed before any formal
declaration of war had taken place between the rival nations.

Two frigates from the squadron of D'Orvilliers were very soon
discovered near enough to prove evidently, that they were on a survey
of the British fleet. They were pursued, and a civil message delivered
to the captain of the Licorne, from the English admiral; but it was
not so civilly returned; some shot were exchanged, and in a short
time the frigate surrendered.

[106] The other French frigate, called the Belle-Poule, was of
heavier metal, and appearing disposed for a rencounter, captain
Marshal, who commanded the Arethusa, pursued her till out of sight
of the fleet. When near enough to announce his orders, he informed
the captain of the Belle-Poule, that he was directed to conduct him
to the British admiral. A peremptory refusal of compliance on the part
of the French captain, induced captain Marshal to fire a shot across
the Belle-Poule: this was returned by the discharge of a whole
broadside from the Belle-Poule into the Arethusa.

A severe action ensued, which continued near two hours. Both
frigates suffered much: the Arethusa was so far disabled, that she was
conducted off the French coast by two British ships that accompanied
the chase, and arrived in time to tow her back to the fleet: the Belle-
Poule escaped only by running into a small bay on the coast of France.
The resolute deportment of the French captain, in this beginning of
naval hostilities between the two nations, was much applauded by
his countrymen, and munificently rewarded by the king of France.

For some time after this action, a mutual display of the strength of
the two fleets was kept up: chasing, re-chasing, manoeuvring, and
gasconade, continued for several days, with little effective action, and
no decision. During [107] the cruise, admiral Keppel, discovered by
the officer of a frigate taken after the action of the Belle-Poule and
the Arethusa, that D'Orvilliers was in daily expectation of reinforcements of strength, while there was yet no formal declaration of war,
while the French admiral played off, as unwilling to begin hostilities,
and while, from many circumstances, Keppel himself was in no
situation for a general engagement. Thus, to the unspeakable mortification of this meritorious officer, he found it convenient to turn his
back on the French squadron, and repair to England.

His own inadequate force and equipment to meet the powerful

CHAP. XXIV
1 7 8 1

squadrons of France, which had been prepared with diligence and system for the execution of great designs, was viewed by him with the deepest regret, both for his own share in the disappointment, and the disgrace brought on his nation by such unpardonable negligence. He had however, from the discoveries he had made from the officers of the captured frigates, and the causes which had induced his immediate return, kept his opinions very much within his own breast, disposed to think candidly of men in high office, great responsibility, and some of them endowed with superior talents. He hoped, from the necessities of the moment, the honor of the nation, and the hazard of their own characters, they [108] would adopt and adhere to more decisive and efficient measures in future.

The motives of the admiral unknown to the people at large, occasioned much censure from the lips of those who were unacquainted with the circumstances. The superiority of the French fleet under D'Orvilliers, and the additional strength he expected from several other armaments prepared to join him, rendered it impossible for admiral Keppel, with only twenty ships of the line, to make any effectual resistance, if a declaration of war should warrant an attack from the French commander, who had a fleet of between thirty and forty sail of the line, besides a great number of frigates, ready for action.

Admiral Keppel very judiciously apprehended, that the most cautious and prudent steps were necessary, not only to prevent the loss of his own fleet, but other inseparable evils to his nation, which might have been the consequence of defeat. He had certain information of the meditated designs of France, unexpectedly to strike at the trade of the nation, by interrupting their convoys, and giving a wound to the honor of the English navy, which would redound much to their own advantage in the outset of a war; while his own fleet, deficient in almost every thing necessary for any effectual [109] resistance, was incapable of maintaining its station.

Conscious that his conduct needed no apology, that the failure of the hopes of the English was owing to the neglect or want of judgment in the ministry, the admiralty, and other departments, he silently bore the censure of his enemies, the clamors of the multitude, and the opprobrium that often lights on character from the tacit demeanor of false friends, and prepared with the utmost dispatch again to sail, and meet the commander of the French squadron.

New exertions were made by the directors of naval affairs; and within a few days, the brave admiral was enabled again to sail with CHAP. XXIV better prospects of success, in pursuit of the Brest fleet, which was 1 7 8 1 also reinforced by some of the heaviest ships and most distinguished commanders in the French service. The two fleets met, manoeuvred, fought, retreated, chased, bid mutual defiance, and fought again; but neither of them had a right to claim the palm of victory, from any circumstances of the interview.

The failure of this second expedition might have been owing, in part, to a misunderstanding between admiral Keppel and some of his principal officers. Other causes might co-operate. There is a delicacy of feeling in the [110] mind of man, or rather a moral sense, that forbids aggression, and excites a reluctance to striking the first blow, that must involve the human species in carnage and murder. But, when war has been denounced by regal authority, and the usual sanction of public proclamation, licensed by the common formalities of such occasions, and hardened by repeated irritation and violence, the crash of burning or sinking ships, swallowed in the yawning deep, ceases to excite due compassion in the sanguine bosom, inured to behold the miseries of his fellow-men.

This disappointment in the beginning of a war with France, occasioned much party bitterness through the English nation. The odium of ill success was bandied for some time between the partisans of sir Hugh Palliser, rear admiral of the blue, and those of the brave Keppel. Both admirals were tried by court-martial; and after long investigation, the business finally terminated in the honorable acquittal of admiral Keppel, from the charge of negligence, want of ability, or misconduct in any respect;* and his reputation completely restored, his calm dignity and cool deportment, [111] through many trying circumstances, more strongly attached his old friends, and procured him many new ones. He was afterwards appointed first lord of the admiralty. He received the thanks of both houses of parliament for his many and essential services to his country. Public rejoicings on his acquittal testified the general esteem of the people, while the ratio of disgrace that fell on admiral Palliser, led him to resign all his public employments.

There had, previous to the late engagement, been the appearance

---

* For a particular detail of this interesting affair, the trials of the two admirals, and the virulence of party on the occasion, the reader may be referred to their trials and to other British authorities. [See *Annual Register* (1781), "History of Europe," pp. 173–175.]

of the strictest friendship between admiral Keppel and sir Hugh Palliser, rear admiral of the blue. It is uncertain what interrupted this amity: it might have arisen from a spirit of rivalry, or the pride of a subordinate officer, who persecuted the aged commander with unceasing bitterness, and divided the opinion of the public for a time, relative to the appropriate merits of each; but the balance continued in favor of lord Keppel to the end of his life.

A naval rencounter took place the next year, which, though of less magnitude than many others, is worthy of notice, from the valor of the transaction, and some circumstances that attended it which were interwoven with the political conduct of the Dutch nation.

[112] Captain *John Paul Jones* had sailed from L'Orient in the summer of one thousand seven hundred and seventy-nine, in order to cruise in the North Sea. The Bon-homme Richard, which he commanded, was accompanied by the Alliance, a well built American ship, and two or three other smaller frigates.

About the beginning of September, they fell in with the Serapis, an English ship of superior force, commanded by captain Pierson; she was accompanied by a smaller ship, the countess of Scarborough. They soon engaged: the action was valorous and desperate, severe and bloody; and taken in all its circumstances, perhaps one of the bravest marine battles that took place during the war. Both the English ships were taken by the Americans. The Bon-homme Richard and the Serapis were several times on fire, at the same moment. The Bon-homme Richard was reduced to a wreck, and sunk soon after the action, which continued long enough for the Baltic fleet of British homeward-bound ships, which had been under the convoy of the Serapis and countess of Scarborough, to make their escape, and get safe to England. After this tremendous blaze of horror and destruction, the little American squadron repaired to the Texel to refit, carrying with them their prisoners and their prizes.

[113] Captain Pierson acquitted himself with the gallantry of a British commander, zealous for the honor of his nation: but he was not permitted by the American officers to go on shore in Holland, and pay his respects to sir Joseph Yorke, the British ambassador resident at the Hague. This he reported in the close of his account of the engagement, received at the admiralty office. It was circumstance grievous to himself, and highly resented by the British ambassador. He demanded of the states-general, that the Alliance and the other ships commanded by the rebel and pirate, John Paul Jones, should with their crews be stopped and delivered up.

Their high mightinesses replied to the demand of sir Joseph Yorke,
that they should not take upon themselves to judge of the legality or
illegality of those who had taken vessels on the open seas, belonging
to other countries: that their ports were open to shelter from storms
and disasters: that they should not suffer the Americans to unlade
their cargoes, but should permit them to go to sea again after refitting;
without taking upon themselves to judge, as they did not think they
were authorised to pass an opinion on the prizes, or the person of
Paul Jones.

[114] The naval rencounters between the nations were too numerous
to particularise. Those who are acquainted with maritime affairs, the
phrases of navigation, and are fond of the exhibition of sea-fights,
may dwell longer on the description of single actions; while the
curiosity of every inquirer may be sufficiently gratified, by the proud
boasters who insolently describe the British flag as controlling the
nations, and defying the universe to attack their fleets.

We shall pass over the more minute transactions, and again recur
to the general expectation relating to the siege of Gibraltar, which
was long kept awake before a final decision. It is however necessary,
previous to the relinquishment of the conquest of that contested spot,
to observe on several intervening transactions of moment. It has been
related in a former chapter, that this fortress was relieved for a time
by sir George Bridges Rodney, on his way to the West Indies, in one
thousand seven hundred and eighty.

He had been remarkably successful in the interception of convoys,
the interruption of the trade of the enemies of Britain, and the capture
of the homeward-bound ships of France and Spain. He fell in with
fifteen sail of merchantmen, under the convoy of a sixty-four gun ship
and several frigates, bound from St. Sebastian's to Cadiz. He captured
the whole fleet, [115] which belonged to the royal company of the
Caraccas. The principal part of their cargoes was wheat and other
provisions much wanted at Gibraltar, where the admiral immediately
sent them. A large quantity of bale goods and naval stores, equally
necessary for the use of his countrymen, he sent forward to England.

He soon after fell in with a Spanish squadron of eleven ships of
the line, under the command of don Juan Langara, who declined an
engagement, from the inequality of his force. But admiral Rodney,
determined to pursue his success, gave chase until the enemy were
nearly involved among the shoals of St. Lucar; and night approaching,
the brave Spaniard was compelled to the conflict. Early in the
engagement, the Spanish ship San Domingo, of seventy guns and six

hundred men, blew up, and all on board perished. The English man of war with which she was engaged, narrowly escaped a similar fate.

The action was severe, and conducted on both sides with the greatest intrepidity, until the Spanish admiral was dangerously wounded, and most of his ships had surrendered; he then struck his flag, surrendered his own ship, reduced to a wreck, and submitted to the valiant English. This action continued nearly through the night; and many singular instances of valor and generosity were displayed on both sides, [116] before the palm of victory was insured to the gallant Rodney.

His good fortune followed him to the tropical seas; and his rencounters with the admiral de Guichen, and other brave commanders of the Bourbon fleets, always terminated in his favor. Indeed, his successes were sometimes a little variant, and his squadron frequently suffered much loss and damage, in his severe conflicts with French and Spanish fleets; yet he was always victorious. On his way to the West Indies, nothing stood before him: many of the enemies of Great Britain, both in the commercial and military line, fell into his hands.

A plan had been meditated by the combined fleets of France and Spain, to seize the rich island of Jamaica: the interference of Rodney more than once prevented the loss of this valuable spot. This was a favorite object with the French; nor was it relinquished, until fortune had frowned repeatedly on the lillies of France, and humbled the Gallican flag beneath her victorious rival, who waved her proud banners around her insular possessions, to the terror of France and the mortification of America.

From the capture of Dominica by the marquis de Bouille, in one thousand seven hundred [117] and seventy-eight, the West India islands had been alternately agitated by the various successes of contending fleets, until the seizure of St. Eustatia by sir George Bridges Rodney, in February, one thousand seven hundred and eighty-one.

In the autumn of one thousand seven hundred and eighty, tempest, hurricane, and earthquake, had raged through all the islands, in a degree unparalleled in those latitudes, though always subject to the most violent tornadoes. Several of the best of the islands had been nearly ruined by those recent devastations of nature, and others rendered too weak for defence against less potent foes than those who waved the flag of Britain.

The winter after the accumulated misfortunes occasioned by those

convulsions, admiral Rodney arrived in the West Indies with a strong CHAP. XXIV
and potent fleet and army. The army was commanded by general 1 7 8 1
Vaughan. Rodney and Vaughan in conjunction, took advantage of the
weak, dismantled state to which St. Vincent's was reduced, and
attempted the reduction of the island. But unexpectedly repulsed by
the bravery of the French, commanded by the marquis de Bouille,
the next enterprise of sir George Bridges Rodney was against the rich,
but defenceless island of St. Eustatia.

[118] This unexpected attack on the Dutch island, was in consequence of secret orders, received before they left England, from the
board of admiralty. The arrival of the British armament in the West
Indies was accompanied by intelligence, not suspected by the islanders, that hostilities were denounced against the republic of Holland
by a manifesto of the king of England.

The United Netherlands had not yet ratified any formal treaty with
the American states, though, as has been observed, a plan for that
purpose had been found among the papers of Mr. Laurens. It is true,
the design of a close connexion with congress and the colonies was
avowed by the principal citizens of Amsterdam: it also appeared from
strong circumstances, that many of the most respectable inhabitants
in other parts of the Batavian circles, were equally disposed to unite
with the Americans: but it was some time after this period, before
the independence of the United States of America was acknowledged
by the stadtholder and their high mightinesses at the Hague.

Yet the assistance given by the merchants of some of the capital
provinces, their negociations with the agents of congress, and their
temporising with regard to receiving a minister, sent on after the
misfortune of Mr. Laurens, to complete the terms of amity and
commerce with the *rebellious subjects* of America, as they [119] were
termed, were steps too bold and affrontive to the sovereign of Britain,
and to the English nation, then the ancient ally of the Batavians, to
be passed over with impunity.

The Dutch court, as observed, did not openly countenance these
proceedings; yet, we have seen above, that when repeatedly called
upon by sir Joseph Yorke, in the name of his sovereign, publicly to
disavow them, and to punish by inhibitions, penalties, and other
severities, all who held any correspondence with congress, or encouraged and supported the revolted colonies; yet no explicit declaration
for that purpose could be obtained. Vexed at the equivocal conduct
of the states-general, and there being no prospect of the minister's

succeeding to his wishes, he was recalled from the Hague, and reasons were soon after assigned by manifesto, for the commencement of hostilities against the Batavian provinces, in the usual style of regal apology for the waste of human life.

Thus the storm burst upon the Dutch West India islands, before they were apprehensive of the smallest danger from a state of war. St. Eustatia had long been considered, both by Europeans and Americans, as the most advantageous mart of any of the tropical islands: consequently, their trade and their wealth had increased beyond all calculation. The inhabitants were generally absorbed in their own private [120] business, the bulk of the merchants affluent and secure, the magistrates at ease, and the Dutch officers totally unapprehensive of an attack from any *foreign foe*. The fortresses in a state of ruin, and the island weakened by the late hurricanes, they were in no condition for defence, nor did they attempt the smallest resistance, on the approach of a powerful British fleet and army.

The surprise and astonishment of both the governor and the people, on the summons to surrender themselves and their island, cannot be described. Their deliberations were short: Mr. de Graaf, the Dutch governor, with the consent of the magistrates and the principal inhabitants, returned a laconic answer to the summons of the British commander. He concisely observed,

> that confident of the lenity of sir George Bridges Rodney and general Vaughan, the whole island and its dependencies surrendered: firmly relying on their honor and humanity, they only recommended the town and the inhabitants to their mercy.

This submission proved the consignment of themselves and families to immediate poverty, desolation, and every species of misery: all descriptions of persons were at once involved in the same common ruin. Not only the officers of government, and the independent sojourner in this devoted island, but the merchant, the [121] factor, the planter, and the innocent individual of every class, whether Dutch or British, Americans or Jews, were all overwhelmed in one promiscuous, unexampled insult, outrage, and plunder. Slaves were bribed to betray their masters, and inveigled to discover the smallest pittance of property, that might have been secreted by the opulent or the aged, to preserve a wretched existence after the loss of connexions, fortune, and prospects.

When obstinate resistance and high-toned language irritates the

passions of men, it may be thought by some an apology, for the
extreme rigor too frequently exercised by the illiberal mind, toward
a conquered enemy. But when full confidence has been placed in the
generosity, urbanity, and equity of the victor, and submission made
without a blow, the cruel inflictions imposed on the unfortunate by
the successful assailant, are violations of the feelings of humanity,
and a departure from the nobler principles of the soul, that can never
be justified by the laws of policy, or even the hostile usages of war.
Nor can the dignity of rank, or the glittering badges of ancestral
honor, prevent the indignation that must ever arise in the bosom of
humanity, on a survey of the rapacity, insolence, and atrocity of
conduct in the conquerors of St. Eustatia.

[122] Submission undoubtedly entitles to protection, and the
vanquished have ever a claim, both for compassion and support, from
the victor. Instead of this just and generous line of action, all safety
was precluded, by indiscriminate abuse and plunder. After the
surrender of this opulent island, one general pillage, confiscation,
banishment, or death, succeeded; and, as observed afterwards by Mr.
Burke in the house of commons, "the Dutch were robbed and
banished, because they were Dutch; the Americans, because they
were the king's enemies; the Jews, because their religion was different
from that of the conquerors."

Some gentlemen of the most capital commercial characters, were
confined as criminals of a peculiar cast, and punished in a two-fold
sense. An extraordinary instance of this nature was exhibited in the
treatment of Messrs. Courzen and Governier, two of the first merchants
on the island: as Dutchmen, their property was confiscated; as
Englishmen, they were sent to England as traitors to the king, charged
with corresponding with American agents, imprisoned and tried for
high treason.

Mr. Hohen, an eminent Jewish merchant, a native of Amsterdam,
who had resided at St. Eustatia twenty-five years, received notice,
without any crime alleged, that he must quit [123] the island without
a day's delay. Ignorant of the place of his destination, while on his
way to embark, he experienced very severe usage; his trunk was
rifled, his clothes ripped open, and a small sum of money he had
secreted to preserve him from famine, taken from him, even to his
last penny. Thus, suddenly robbed, and reduced from high fortune
to absolute want, when he arrived in England he petitioned the house
of commons for redress, and his cause was supported by the brilliant

elocution of Mr. Burke and others; yet the injured Israelite found no relief from the justice or compassion of the nation.

Such was the rapacity of the plunderers of this unfortunate island, that in many other instances, the garments of the aged and respectable were rent open in search of a bit of gold, that might possibly have been concealed for the purchase of a morsel of bread for their innocent and helpless families. Thus, from the pinnacle of affluence, many were reduced in a day to the extreme of penury and despair. All the Jews on the island received similar treatment to that above related: their sufferings had no amelioration: they were informed, that they were all to be transported, and only one day was allowed to any of them for preparation, before they were robbed of their treasures, and sent away pennyless among strangers.

[124] Indeed, there was little discrimination among the miserable inhabitants of this once wealthy spot. The whole property of the island, collected by every undue method, was exposed to public sale: and admiral Rodney, the commander of a British fleet of upwards of thirty ships of the line, and the *renowned* general Vaughan, at the head of three or four thousand troops, were engaged from the beginning of February until the May following, in the little arts of auctioneering and traffic, in a manner that would have disgraced the petty merchant, who had not renounced all pretences to honor.

The islands of Saba, St. Martin's, and others, had surrendered to some detachments from the British fleet and army, on the same easy terms; and, with similar hopes of security and protection, they suffered nearly the same merciless fate from the hands of British conquerors, that had been recently experienced by the inhabitants of St. Eustatia.

Meantime, the marquis de Bouille improved the favorable opportunity, while the British commanders were engaged in securing the plunder of the conquered isles, to reduce Tobago to the arms of the French monarch. This required a little more military prowess than had yet been called into action, by his competitors for the possession of the West India islands.

[125] Governor Ferguson, who commanded at Tobago, made a manly defence for eight or ten days; but receiving no succors from admiral Rodney, though within twenty-four hours' sail, and too weak to hold out longer without assistance, he was obliged to capitulate.

The terms granted by the noble Frenchman were honorable and lenient. The officers and troops in garrison were permitted to march out with the honors of war; after which, the soldiers were to lay down

their arms, but the officers had liberty to retain their's. The inhabitants CHAP. XXIV
were allowed to preserve their own civil government, laws, and 1 7 8 1
customs; to enjoy their estates, rights, privileges, honors, and exemp-
tions, with a promise of protection in the free exercise of their religion,
until peace should take place. No other engagement was required on
their part, than an oath of fidelity to the king of France, to observe a
strict neutrality until that happy event should be accomplished. They
were left at full liberty to dispose of their property at leisure, and to
proceed in their commercial affairs as usual; with this farther indulgence, that no merchant ships, the property of the inhabitants of the
island or its dependencies, that might arrive from England within six
months, should be liable to confiscation or seizure.

[126] It is observable, that the distinguished traits of generosity in
the demeanor of the marquis de Bouille, were not forgotten by those
who witnessed and experienced his clemency. Some time after the
transactions above related, a large number of gentlemen in England,
belonging to the several islands, met and unanimously passed a vote,
expressive of their high sense of gratitude for his humanity, justice,
and generosity, exemplified and displayed in his treatment of the
conquered isles: and as a testimony of their veneration and esteem,
they ordered a piece of plate, with an inscription of their thanks, to
be presented him by sir William Young, chairman of the committee.*

After this short narration of the capture of the island of Tobago,
and the moderation shewn to the inhabitants by the victor, a further
detail is not necessary, to contrast the behavior of the British and
French commanders in the West Indies, at this period of the war.

Many particulars through the busy scene kept up in the tropical
seas, through this and the succeeding year, need not here be related;
though it is proper to observe, that it was but a few months after the
surrender of these islands, and the sufferings they experienced from
the [127] severity of the British conquerors, before St. Martin's, Saba,
and St. Eustatia, were surprised and recovered by the marquis de
Bouille.

It may be anticipating time, yet, to prevent the interruption of the
story of other events, it will not be deemed improper to continue the
narration of the insular war, that raged with unabating fury in the
West Indies through the succeeding year.

* Analytical Register. [See *Annual Register* (1781), "History of Europe," pp. 101–106;
"State Papers," pp. 308–310; (1782), "History of Europe," pp. 136–141; *Cobbett*,
XXII: 1023–1025.]

CHAP. XXIV   From the arrival of the count de Grasse in these seas, with his
1 7 8 1 brave, victorious fleet from the Chesapeake, at the close of the year
one thousand seven hundred and eighty-one, not the smallest mitigation of the horrors of war took place, until after the defeat of the
squadron commanded by him, an event which did not happen until
the twelfth of April, one thousand seven hundred and eighty-two.

Soon after the entire ruin of the inhabitants of St. Eustatia, sir
George B. Rodney had returned to England with his disgraceful
booty, the indiscriminate spoils of the aged, the innocent, and the
affluent. He was graciously received by his majesty and the ministry:
but, his laurels stained by his avarice and cruelty, it was impossible,
either by address, deception, or effrontery, to parry the severe
reprehensions he received from some of the first nobility in the house
of lords, as well as from many members [128] of distinction and talent
in the house of commons. A particular inquiry into his conduct, and
that of general Vaughan, was urged in the most strenuous and pathetic
manner, but with little effect. Notwithstanding the general sense of
mankind criminated the inhumanity of their proceedings, yet the
favoritism that generally prevails in courts overruled, as usual, the
dictates of justice, and all investigation was postponed.

Admiral Rodney was again immediately sent out in full force, with
design to prevent the valuable island of Jamaica from falling under
the arms of France. Indeed, the apprehensions of the ministry on this
point were sufficiently grounded. Barbadoes, Antigua, and Jamaica,
were all the possessions of consequence that the English still retained
in the West Indies; the others, as observed, had most of them been
recaptured by the French; who were pursuing victory with vigilance
and success, and in sanguine expectations of wresting all the wealthy
islands from the crown of Britain.

When sir George Bridges Rodney returned to the command in that
quarter, where he arrived about the middle of February, one thousand
seven hundred and eighty-two, he found the French inspirited by
repeated successes, ready for any enterprise, and a formidable fleet
in the highest preparation for attack or defence.

[129] Jamaica was indeed the prime object of expectation, but the
first important step taken by the count de Grasse, after his arrival in
the West Indies, was the capture of the little island of Nevis, where
he lost no time, but immediately hastened on and set down before
St. Christopher's. There he found a large armament had been landed
some days before his arrival, by the brave marquis de Bouille.

Sir Samuel Hood, with twenty sail of the British line, attempted

the relief of that island: this brought on several rencounters between
him and the count de Grasse, with various success, but with little
decision.

St. Christopher's had been vigorously defended five weeks by
general Frazer, a brave British officer: he acquired much honor by his
gallant behavior through the whole siege. Shirley, governor of Antigua,
brought forward three or four hundred militia, and fought, hazarded,
and suffered, equally with his friend general Frazer, until necessity
compelled them at last to yield. The island was surrendered by
capitulation to the crown of France, on the twelfth of February, one
thousand seven hundred and eighty-two.

[130] The same lenient and generous terms were admitted by the
conqueror, as had before been granted by him to the inhabitants of
Tobago, Demerara, Essequibo, and several other places of less
consequence than St. Christopher's or St. Eustatia, who had repeatedly, as well as those, changed their masters in the struggle, and were
now again the subjects of France. But the inhabitants of St. Christopher's, by the moderate terms of capitulation, were scarcely sensible
of a change of sovereignty. The garrison was permitted the honors of
war in the strictest sense; the troops were transported to England,
until an exchange of prisoners should take place.

By a particular article, the marquis de Bouille, as an acknowledgment
of their intrepidity and valor, discharged brigadier general Frazer and
governor Shirley, who had aided in the defence of the island, from
the condition of being considered as prisoners of war. To Mr. Shirley
he gave liberty to return to his government in Antigua, and to general
Frazer the permission of continuing in the service of his country, in
whatever place he chose.

The generosity of the marquis merited and received a large share
of applause, both from friends and foes; and the name of *Bouille* was
every where respected, for his equitable, humane, and honorable
deportment, toward all [131] the captured islands that fell into his
hands. But, notwithstanding the valor, the virtue, the magnanimity,
and the repeated successes of the marquis de Bouille, over the best
and bravest troops and officers that had been employed in any part
of the world; notwithstanding the fame and the valor of the count de
Grasse, and the strength of the French navy; fortune soon changed
her face, frowned on the flag of France, caused her lillies again to
droop beneath the showers of fire poured upon them by the hand of
the intrepid Rodney, and, as usual, placed her laurels on his brow.

On his second arrival in the West Indies, where the Bourbon flag had waved for some months under the most favorable aspect, he found both his reinforcements and his vigilance necessary, to impede the blow meditated against Jamaica. A powerful Spanish fleet had arrived at Hispaniola, also a large number of land forces, amply supplied with every thing necessary, to join the count de Grasse in the designed expedition: besides these, there was a body of troops at Cuba for the same purpose.

Though the island of Jamaica still belonged to the British crown, it was in no respect prepared for an invasion. The island was naturally strong and defensible, but there were few troops in garrison, and the inhabitants, more [132] attentive to their wealth and pleasure, than tenaciously attached to a foreign sovereign of their island, security was their object, under whatever authority they held their immense estates; and conquest would have been easy to any power that should guarantee the enjoyment of fortune, luxury, and idleness.

When admiral Rodney arrived they had little to fear. He was joined by the squadron under the command of sir Samuel Hood, and another commanded by admiral Drake. Thus the British flag among the islands appeared in a capacity to challenge, not only the naval forces of France, but all the maritime powers of Europe.

Sir George B. Rodney very early and very judiciously endeavoured, by various manoeuvres, to draw the French admiral into immediate action. This the count de Grasse was equally industrious to avoid: he was aware that it might defeat the important objects before him, and prevent the capture of the most valuable of the British possessions, yet remaining under their jurisdiction. But however reluctant, he was, much against his wishes, obliged first to come to a partial, and within a few days, to a general engagement. This ruined the expectations, the enterprise, and the hopes of the house of Bourbon in this quarter, saved Jamaica [133] from its impending fate, and destroyed a considerable part of the French fleet.

The conflict was long, severe, and bloody indeed. The count de Grasse, the marquis Vaudreuil, the renowned Bougainville, and many other characters among the Gallic commanders, had never before experienced the mortification of defeat. They fought with the impulse of the brave soldier, the enthusiasm of chivalry, the pride of nobility, and the dignity of the hero, confident of success.

The order of their line was however broken by the experienced and indefatigable Englishmen, and several of the best of the French ships were either captured, sunk, or blown up. This decisive action

began early in the morning, and lasted until the evening: the carnage CHAP. XXIV
on this occasion, on both sides, was sufficient to shock the boldest 1 7 8 1
heart. The surrender of the admiral's own ship, the *Ville de Paris*, of
one hundred and ten guns, completed the triumph of the day. Before
the count de Grasse struck his colors, he had four hundred men slain,
and scarcely any one left on deck without a wound. This ship, aimed
at as the point of victory by all the British whose thunder could reach
her, was reduced to a wreck, and on the point of sinking, when the
admiral surrendered to sir Samuel Hood at the close of the day of
action.

[134] The commanders of the other ships in the French navy
conducted with equal gallantry, and suffered in equal proportion, with
the Ville de Paris. The captains of the Centaur, the Glorieux, and
the Caesar, did themselves immortal honor in the eye of military
glory. They kept their stations until most of their men were killed or
wounded, their canvas shot away, and their ships reduced to splinters,
before they submitted: and the lives of many valiant seamen, with
some of their bravest officers, was the price of victory to their enemies.

On the other side, the loss of many valiant men and distinguished
officers, spread a temporary gloom over the face of success. Among
the number of gallant Englishmen who fell on this awful day of
carnage, no one was more lamented than the commander of the
Resolution, lord Robert Manners, the only son of the marquis of
Granby, whose gallant and noble military exploits have perpetuated
his fame; nor did his son fall short of his merit, or in any respect
disgrace the memory of his heroic father.

After the surrender of the count de Grasse, which terminated the
action, he was received on board a British ship with the highest marks
of respect, and uniformly treated with every attention due to his
distinguished character. The commanders Bougainville and Vaudreuil
conducted [135] the remainder of the fleet which escaped capture or
sinking, to Cape Francois; and admiral Rodney, with his wounded
ships and numerous prizes, repaired to Jamaica to refit, and to secure
that island from any further danger of attack, either from France or
Spain.

The count de Grasse was immediately conveyed to England in the
Sandwich, of ninety guns, commanded by sir Peter Parker, who had
the honor of delivering this noble prisoner on the shores which had
long dreaded his prowess.

The reception of the unfortunate French commander at the court

CHAP. XXIV
1 7 8 1

of Great Britain, by his majesty, by the royal family, and by all ranks, was in the highest degree respectful. His own sword, which, according to form, had been delivered to sir George Bridges Rodney, was returned to his hand by the king himself. Apartments were provided for him in the royal hotel; and during his short residence in England, nothing was neglected that could in any degree ameliorate the mortification of a mind inured to victory, and amidst expectations of conquest reduced to a state of captivity.

All that a most sumptuous elegance and hospitality could invent was displayed, to express the general esteem of the first characters in the nation, and the high sense entertained by every class of people, of the magnanimity, merits, [136] and misfortunes, of the brave and noble commanders of the French navy. He indeed needed consolations superior to the efforts of politeness and humanity: he was sensible that his court was disgusted, and his nation chagrined beyond description, at the disappointment of their projects, the loss of the Ville de Paris, and the destruction of other capital ships. The wound given to national pride appeared in the countenance of every Frenchman, on this unexpected degradation of the Bourbon flag. *"The Ville de Paris in the Thames,"* was mentioned with a shrug of contempt by every one; and a subscription was set on foot among the Parisians, for another ship of the same name, size, and weight of metal, to be immediately built.

Public opinion had its usual operation on military character, which seldom escapes untarnished when not accompanied by success. Thus, while the count de Grasse was oppressed by public considerations, and the odium mankind are prone to attach to misfortune, his feelings were hurt by the personal sufferings of himself and his family, and the imagined depreciation of fame; and in addition to the fear of a sinking reputation, the death of a favorite son completed the climax of his afflictions.

This amiable and promising young gentleman, unable to bear the reverse of fortune, the reproaches, however unjust, which he feared [137] might fall upon his father, and the incalculable consequences to his family that might take place in a despotic court, from the present misfortune,—put a period to his own existence by a pistol ball, soon after the tidings of his father's defeat.*

---

* The writer had the above account verbally, of the death of the son of the count de Grasse, from a gentleman then in Paris.

Thus merit languished in captivity, assailed by private sorrows,
apprehensive of public censure, and uncertain of the duration of his
confinement, or the grade of punishment that might be inflicted by
his king: he very well knew, that in an arbitrary court, death or the
Bastile might cover his head forever, for the failure of achievements
impracticable by the valor of man. Meanwhile, the rival of his glory,
or rather the conqueror of the noble count, might justly be deemed
one of the favorite sons of fortune.

Sir George B. Rodney was undoubtedly a brave officer, and his
repeated successes in the West Indies greatly augmented his military
fame; but for his cruelty and his avarice the preceding year, he was
justly and severely censured [138] by every virtuous man in the nation.
His accumulation of property in the plunder of the Dutch and French
islands, was thought abundantly sufficient to have satisfied the grasping
hand of avarice, without the extreme of rapacity exercised toward
every individual of the conquered plantations.

Though in the midst of inquiry into his conduct he had again been
sent out on the most honorable command, his cruelty on the capture
of St. Eustatia was not forgotten in his absence. His injustice toward
Messrs. Hohen, Courzen, Governier, and others, was brought forward
and criminated in the most pointed language. A scrutiny was again
called for in the house of commons; his reputation impeached; and a
supersedure of his command directed.

But at the critical moment when his destruction was ripening, the
news of his splendid and decided victory over so respectable a part
of the French navy, hushed at once the voice of clamor, and even of
justice. The suffering islanders were forgotten in the exultation of
national glory; his friends were emboldened, his enemies silenced,
his interest re-established; and instead of a rigid censure for former
transactions, he received the thanks of parliament for his services.
This was accompanied by the acclamations of the people, and the
applause of the nation, for his victory over their hereditary [139]
enemies; a victory that secured to Great Britain her insular possessions,
checked the pride of the house of Bourbon, and was felt with no
small degree of mortification by the American states. The smiles of
the court and favor of the king lifted him to rank, and on his return,
he was by his sovereign created a peer of the realm of England. To
this dignity was added a pension of two thousand pounds sterling per
annum, during his own life, and the lives of the two next successors
to the title of lord Rodney.

CHAP. XXIV   The maritime spirit of Britain has always been encouraged and kept
1 7 8 1 up by the munificent rewards of royal bounty, to all who signalize
themselves by their naval prowess. This encourages the nobility to
place their sons in the navy at an early period of life, as the road to
preferment. The service was always deemed honorable; and the
interests and the feelings of the first families in the nation, were
engaged to support the respectability of marine employ. This, with
many other combining circumstances, has contributed to the strength,
glory, and terror of the British navy, and raised it to a pitch of elevation
and fame, scarcely paralleled in any nation, either ancient or modern.

But the time may arrive, when the haughty superiority of her fleets
may be checked, and their power and aggressions be restrained, by a
[140] combination formed on principles of justice and humanity,
among all the nations that Britain has insulted and invaded, under
the domination of her proud flag. She may feel an irresistible
opposition; an opposition that may redound to the advantage of
commerce, the peace of mankind, and the prevention of that wanton
waste of human life, that has cemented her strength, and at once
rendered Great Britain respected and dreaded, envied, and perhaps
in a degree, hated, by all the nations; who were sometimes ready to
apprehend, that the axiom formed in Greece about three thousand
years ago, that—*The nation that is master at sea will become master on the
continent*—might be realized in modern Europe.

CHAPTER XXV

Continuation of Naval Rencounters • Affair of Count Byland—Sir Hyde Parker and Admiral Zeutman • Commodore Johnstone ordered to the Cape of Good Hope • Admiral Kempenfelt • Loss of the Royal George • Baron de Rullincort's Expedition to the Isle of Jersey • Capture of Minorca • Gibraltar again besieged, defended, and relieved • Mr. Adams's Negociation with the Dutch Provinces

[141] While the active and interesting scenes in the West Indies, related in the preceding pages, commanded the attention of America, and deranged the systems of France, other objects of importance, by sea as well as by land, equally occupied the arms, the industry, and the energies of the European powers, and equally affected the great cause of freedom, and the entire independence of the United States. The French navy had indeed suffered much in the West Indies, and the Batavians there were nearly ruined by the unexpected operations of war; yet the Dutch flag still waved with honor over the ocean, and in several instances maintained the courage, the character, and the glory, won by their Van Trumps, de Ruyters, and other naval heroes distinguished in their history.

[142] They had been called out to try their strength on the ocean, by the open hostilities of Britain in consequence of a declaration by the king, which relieved them from a state of suspense. This declaration, dated April the seventeenth, one thousand seven hundred and eighty, annihilated all former treaties of neutrality, friendship, or connexion, and suspended all stipulations respecting the freedom of navigation and commerce in time of war, with the subjects of the states-general.

A few weeks previous to the date of this declaration of war, the government of Great Britain had exercised its assumed right of searching the vessels of all nations for contraband goods. This presumptuous right they had for many years arrogated to themselves,

CHAP. XXV though no other nation had acceded to the claim; yet it had been
1 7 8 1 submitted to, from want of power sufficient for an effectual opposition,
while all considered it an infringement of the free trade of nations,
that could not be justified by the laws of equity.

A number of Dutch merchantmen, laden with timber and naval
stores for the use of France, had taken the advantage of sailing under
the protection of count Byland, who, with a small fleet of men of war
and frigates, was to escort a convoy to the Mediterranean. In
consequence of this intelligence, the English government [143] sent
out a squadron of armed ships under the command of captain Fielding,
in pursuit of them, with a commission to search, seize, and make
prizes of any of the Dutch ships, that might have on board articles
deemed contraband goods, according to the construction of the British
laws of trade.

The Dutch refused to submit to the humiliating orders; notwithstanding which, Fielding dispatched a number of boats to execute
the business. These were fired upon by the Dutchmen; on which
captain Fielding fired a shot across the head of the Dutch admiral's
ship, who returned a broadside. This salute was answered in a manner
that might have been expected from a British naval commander, and
several shot were exchanged; but count Byland, though sensible that
he was in force sufficient for a severe action that might ensue, from
the humane idea of saving the lives of his men, thought proper to
strike his colors and surrender to the English.*

In the meantime, most of the convoy, under cover of the night,
made their escape into some of the ports of France: the remainder
were detained; and the Dutch admiral informed, that he was at liberty
to hoist his colors and pursue [144] his voyage. He refused to leave
any part of his convoy, but hoisted his colors and sailed with them to
Spithead, where he continued until he received fresh instructions
from his masters.

This affair enkindled much resentment in the bosoms of the
Hollanders, who considered an attempt to search their ships as an act
of unwarrantable insolence. This, with many other concurring circumstances which then existed, had ripened their minds for the open
rupture which soon after took place between the English and Dutch
governments.

* British Annual Register. [See *Annual Register* (1781), "History of Europe," pp. 101–
  106, 162–173.]

Many feats of maritime bravery were exhibited on the ocean, during CHAP. XXV
the existing war between the two nations. The most signal event of 1 7 8 1
the kind in the European seas the same year, was an action which
took place between admiral Zeutman, commander of the Dutch fleet,
and sir Hyde Parker, who commanded a British squadron of superior
force. They met near a place called the Dogger-Bank, as admiral
Parker was returning from Elsineur with a large convoy. An engagement
immediately took place: equal valor and prowess animated the officers
on each side, and equal fury and bravery stimulated the sailors: an
action bloody indeed, was kept up for three or four hours, but without
either allowing the honor of victory to his antagonist.

[145] After a short pause, within a little distance from each other,
they withdrew to their native shores. Admiral Zeutman was honored,
caressed, promoted, and happy in the applauses of his countrymen;
while admiral Parker returned chagrined and disgusted: he indeed
received the approbation, and was honored with a visit from the king,
and an invitation to dine with him on board the royal yacht; but he
refused the honor of knighthood his majesty was about to confer on
him, complained heavily that he had not been properly supported,
and attributed the escape of any part of the Dutch fleet to the
negligence of the admiralty.

Notwithstanding the renown of the British navy, the nation had
little to boast from the termination of several marine adventures,
through the course of the present year. Their fleets had fallen under
some disappointments and disasters, which heightened the clamor
against the admiralty officers, and increased the discontent of the
nation.

Commodore Johnstone, with an handsome squadron, had been
ordered to sail for, and take possession of, the Cape of Good Hope.
Had he succeeded, his next enterprise was designed to surprise *Buenos
Ayres*, and sweep the Spanish settlements on Rio de la Plata, in South
America. [146] But he was attacked by monsieur de Suffrein, who
intercepted him near the Cape de Verd islands. Johnstone was found
rather in an unguarded situation; a considerable number of the officers
and men were on shore at the island of St. Jago in pursuit of health
and pleasure, and many of the crews of all the ships were absent,
employed either in hunting, fishing, or plundering cattle from the
islands.

Signals for repairing on board were made, and an action immediately
ensured, but it did not redound to the honor of the British commander.

CHAP. XXV After suffering much in the engagement, and his original design totally

1 7 8 1 defeated, he returned homewards, with the small reparation of his ill
fortune by the capture of a few Dutch East India ships, which were
at anchor in the Bay of Soldana.

The brave admiral Kempenfelt was not much more fortunate in an
interview with the French fleet, which he met with in the winter,
one thousand seven hundred and eighty-one. This squadron, commanded by monsieur Guichen, was unexpectedly to him, so much
superior to his own, that admiral Kempenfelt did not think it prudent
to engage. He however captured a number of transports laden with
all the implements of war, and upwards of one thousand French
soldiers and sailors, designed for the West Indies.

[147] Success so inadequate to expectation, was the occasion of
much uneasiness and censure in the nation. The first lord of the
admiralty was charged with negligence and incapacity, in conducting
the maritime affairs of England. The magnitude of the object, and
the strength of the combined foes of Great Britain, required the first
abilities, penetration, and industry; neither of which adorned the
character of lord Sandwich, the first minister in the naval department.
But the great admiral Kempenfelt lived but a short space after his
late disappointment, either to reap the applauses, or to fear the
censures, that arose from the fortuitous or natural events of time.

His ship, the Royal George of one hundred and eight guns, required
a slight repair, before he proceeded as was designed, to join the fleet
before Gibraltar. For this purpose, the ship a little on the careen, the
weather fine, and no danger to be apprehended, a great crowd of
persons of both sexes were on board, to visit and take leave of their
husbands, brothers, and friends, when a sudden, small gust of wind
struck the ship, and carried her instantly down.

In this unfortunate moment, perished near one thousand persons;
among whom was the respected admiral himself, who had scarcely
[148] time to rise from his writing desk after the alarm, before he met
his watery grave.*

A few of the guards, and most of the men who happened to be on
the upper deck, were picked up by boats, and saved from sharing the
melancholy catastrophe of their associates.

No man could have been more justly and universally lamented than

---

* Annual Register. [See *Annual Register* (1782), "History of Europe," pp. 124–125,
151–165, 225–226.]

admiral Kempenfelt. Far advanced in years, he had retained a character
unimpeached in his professional line, nor was he less meritorious in
his deportment in private life.

The various naval rencounters among the contending powers, were too diffuse for the present design, which is meant only as a sketch of a few of the most important events, in order to give a general idea of the sources of censure or applause bestowed on the principal actors: it may also elucidate the causes of that weight of opprobrium which fell on the admiralty department in England, at the close of the war. The bravery of many of the British naval commanders was signalized, though existing circumstances so frequently combined to render abortive their valorous exertions.

[149] Amidst the many enterprises of this busy period among the nations, it would not be just to pass over the year, without recollecting the honor due to a young hero, who perished in the gallant defence of the island of Jersey.

The unsuccessful attempt made to reduce the place, by a number of troops commanded by the baron de Rullincort, in the year one thousand seven hundred and eighty, did not discourage a second enterprise. This first attempt was finally defeated by relief from admiral Arbuthnot, who was then on his way to America. He had thought proper to stop, and lend his assistance to prevent the impending fate of the island. It is true he saved it from falling into the hands of the French at that time, but a very heavy balance of disadvantage was felt in consequence of this delay: the very large reinforcement, and the prodigious number of transports and merchantmen under his convoy, thus retarded, operated among other causes, to prevent timely succors to lord Cornwallis, of which he stood in the utmost necessity in Virginia.

On the sixth of January, one thousand seven hundred and eighty-one, the baron de Rullincort made a second effort to recover the island of Jersey. The design was so secret, and the attack so sudden, that the out-guards were surprised, [150] and the avenues to the town of St. Helena seized, while the inhabitants lay in perfect security. In the morning of the seventh, in the utmost dismay, they found themselves in the hands of their enemies.

Major Corbet, the lieutenant governor, received the first intelligence that the French troops were in possession of the town, from his own servant, before he had risen from his bed. He was in a few minutes after surrounded and taken prisoner; and by the peremptory demand of the baron de Rullincort, he was so far intimidated as to sign a capitulation in behalf of the town, and issued orders, that his officers on their several stations should do the same.

A few of them obeyed: but captain Pierson, a brave young officer of only twenty-five years of age, assembled the militia of the island, and with a party of British troops withdrew to the neighbouring heights, on which the French commander, agreeably to the articles of capitulation, summoned him to surrender. Instead of a compliance, he, with the utmost intrepidity, advertised the baron de Rullincort, that unless he and his troops laid down their arms, and surrendered within *twenty-four minutes*, he should attack them in their post.

At the expiration of this short time, captain Pierson agreeably to his threat, proceeded to [151] the desperate enterprise. This was done with such vigor and success, that the French were driven to a decided action: the baron de Rullincort was mortally wounded; and within half an hour from the commencement of the engagement, the French troops were totally routed, and major Corbet, who was kept as a forlorn hope by the side of their commander, until Rullincort fell, was urged by the French troops to resume his command, and permit them to surrender as prisoners of war.

But the valiant Pierson did not live to enjoy the fruits of this splendid action, or the applauses of his country; he was unfortunately shot through the head, almost at the moment victory declared in his favor. The death of this brave young officer, who at so early a period had exhibited such proofs of military genius and capacity, was greatly and justly lamented. On the other hand, the passive Corbet was tried by court-martial, censured, and dismissed from further service; while engravings of the action, and the portraits of captain Pierson, were displayed through the nation, accompanied with the highest encomiums on his valor and merit.

It has been observed, that the Spaniards had never relinquished their design of subduing the strong fortress of Gibraltar, though obliged the last year to suspend it for a time. The reduction [152] of Minorca previous to their progress against Gibraltar, was by the Spaniards deemed an object of high importance. The island was invested by an armament under the command of the duke de Crillon, in August, one thousand seven hundred and eighty-one; but the conquest was not completed until the fourth of February, one thousand seven hundred and eighty-two.

Many circumstances peculiarly affecting, accompanied the siege and surrender of fort St. Philip. Shut up by a large armament,

surrounded by a heavy train of artillery, commanded by the most able CHAP. XXV
and experienced officers, the garrison was totally unable to make any 1 7 8 1
effectual resistance. They were reduced by an inveterate scurvy that
had long prevailed, infested with a pestilential fever, dysentery, and
other disorders, without medicine for the sick or food for the healthy:
no extreme of misery could exceed theirs before they yielded to the
arms of Spain.

Yet in this condition of wretchedness, they displayed every mark
of valor and fortitude, until the combined circumstances of distress
obliged the remnant of British troops, reduced to about six hundred,
old, worn-out, emaciated skeletons, to lay down their arms. This they
did with tears of regret, and with an exclamation [153] extorted by
the pride of valor, that they *"submitted to God alone."*

Their appearance and their behavior equally excited the sympathy
of the conqueror, and even drew involuntary tears from the victorious
soldiers amidst the glory of success. The most compassionate attention
was shewn to those aged and unfortunate veterans, who had been
eleven years in garrison, by the noble Crillon, who directed every
thing necessary to be provided for the relief of the sick, and ample
supplies of provision and clothing were furnished by him, for the
naked troops who still retained a degree of health.

We now leave events of less observation and notoriety, to pursue
the termination of the interesting siege of Gibraltar. In the beginning
of the autumn of the present year, all the powers of invention were
called forth, to bring into action the most ingenious and fatal means
of destruction; and the most glorious display of European valor was
exhibited before the impregnable fortress of Gibraltar, that perhaps
any age had beheld.

Battering ships of formidable size, and fireworks of the most curious
construction, awakened attention in all. The fierce sons of *Ishmael,*
[154] whose hands are against every man, and every man's hand
against them, at this time held their hostile arm suspended, and only
viewed the work of carnage among the tributary nations, near their
own coasts.* As they took no part in the conflict, the barbarian shores

* It may be properly asked, whenever the mind adverts to the situation and
   circumstances of the Barbary states, how long the European world will submit to
   their lawless depredations? It is a strange phenomenon in human affairs, that the
   nations should so long have been kept in awe by their corsairs, and be compelled
   from time to time to purchase a temporary peace, by becoming tributary to a people
   so much inferior to themselves, in manners, in arts, in arms, and in every thing that
   aggrandizes the powers of the earth.

CHAP. XXV   of *Afric* were covered with spectators, to view the frightful engines,
1 7 8 1   and the awful play of the artillery of death.

The duke de Crillon was vested with the chief command of the mighty armament destined for the reduction of this proud fortress, that thundered defiance to all the neighbouring nations. Minorca reduced, and some other impediments surmounted, the duke, in conjunction with some of the first naval commanders in Europe, opened the formidable onset about the tenth of September. He was an officer equally distinguished for his politeness and his bravery. The last was conspicuously displayed from the beginning to the termination of this [155] awful enterprise; and a signal instance of the first appeared, when he sent a supply of vegetables and other delicacies for the table of general Elliot, while the garrison was almost without the smallest means of subsistence.

This present was accompanied with the highest expressions of personal regards for the British commander: the duke de Crillon assured him, "that he cherished a hope of meriting and meeting his future friendship, after he had learned to make himself worthy of that honor, by facing him as an enemy." General Elliot replied with equal gallantry, that however he felt himself obliged by those tenders of politeness and generosity, yet as long as his brave troops suffered, and patiently endured a scarcity of provisions, he should accept nothing for himself; that as he was determined to participate in common with the lowest of his fellow-soldiers, every hardship they might suffer, he must of consequence be excused from the acceptance of any future favor.

The count de Artois, a brother of the king, and many other princes of the blood of France, and the royal house of Spain, were in the action before Gibraltar; an action that surpassed the descriptive pen of the historian or the poet, to do ample justice to the display of military skill in both parties, to the magnificence of design, the intrepidity of execution, the grandeur of [156] the scene, and the valor and magnanimity of both officers and soldiers.

Six thousand cannon shot, and upwards of one thousand shells, were discharged on one side every twenty-four hours: while an equal scale of vigor was kept up by the unceasing blaze of the other, until several of the best ships of the assailants were blown up, others enwrapped in a torrent of fire, and reduced to such a scene of misery and distress, as excited not only the pity, but the boldest exertions of the valiant English, in several instances, to snatch their enemies from destruction and death.

The intrepid captain Curtis, at the head of a brigade of marines, CHAP. XXV
and at the hazard of his own life and the lives of his associates, 1 7 8 1
dragged many men on the point of perishing from the burning ships
of the combined fleet.

The Spanish admiral don Marino abandoned his ship but the
moment before she was blown up. A number of ships, both of France
and Spain, were reduced to the same distressed condition. A severe
storm increased the catastrophe of the navy: but every compassionate
mind will be willing to abridge a particular detail of such a period of
horror; a period which portrayed images that seem to require a solemn
pause, rather than a further dilation on the wretchedness of so many
of our fellow-mortals.

[157] Lord Howe's arrival toward the termination of this tremendous
scene, with a force sufficient for the entire relief of the besieged,
completely defeated the hopes of the house of Bourbon, of obtaining
the long contemplated object. Thus this strong fortress, of which the
English had been in possession from the treaty of Utrecht, in one
thousand seven hundred and thirty-one, was again left to the triumph
of the British nation. Its impregnable strength had often defied the
hostilities, and was now likely to continue the envy, of the neighbouring nations.

The memory of *Elliot* and *Boyde*, the two principal officers who
sustained this long and perilous siege, will be immortalized. They,
with unexampled fortitude, endured the miseries of fatigue and
famine, until worn down by the first, and on the point of perishing
by the last. With skill, bravery, and resolution, unparalleled in modern
story, they drove back the formidable invaders, blasted the expectations of their enemies, and obtained the most signal victory, when all
Europe had denounced the fall of Gibraltar.

It was about the middle of October when lord Howe arrived, with
every thing necessary for the relief of the distressed garrison. This
extinguished all remains of hope, that might have been indulged in
the breasts of some individuals among the commanders of the
combined [158] fleet, already too much wounded and shattered for
exertions of any kind. It is true a feint was made for an engagement
with the British fleet, by don de Cordova on the part of Spain, and
monsieur de Guichen the French admiral; but they soon discovered
themselves willing to retire, without any decisive operations. The
greatest part of the squadron took the first favorable opportunity to
sheer off, and repaired with all possible expedition to Cadiz.

Let us now rest a little from the roar of cannon, and the dread

CHAP. XXV sound of bombardment, thunder, and death, those horrid interpreters
1 7 8 2 of the hostile dispositions of man, and listen to the milder voice of
negociation. This often assimilates or unites nations, by more rational
and humane discussions, than the implements of slaughter and
destruction produce; and political altercations are frequently terminated, before decisions are announced by torrents of fire, spouted by
the invention of man, to spread frightful desolation over his own
species.

The capture of Mr. Laurens, who had been appointed to negociate
with the Dutch provinces, and the steps taken to effect a treaty of
amity and commerce between the United States of America and the
inhabitants of the Netherlands, have already been related; also, the
manner by which his packages were recovered by an adventurous
sailor. In this deposite was [159] found, when presented to the British
minister, the form of a treaty of amity and commerce between the
republic of Holland and the United States of America, containing
thirty-four articles. These were indeed, obnoxious enough to the court
of Great Britain; but it appeared that it had been a very deliberate
business. These articles had been examined and weighed by William
Lee, esquire, a commissioner from congress then resident in Europe.
This had been done by the advice of Van Berkel, counsellor and
pensionary of the city of Amsterdam, and some other judicious
Dutchmen. Thus every thing had promised the speedy completion
of a treaty between the two republics.*

In consequence of this discovery, orders were sent to the British
minister resident at the Hague, which were acted upon by him with
energy and fidelity. Sir Joseph Yorke complained and memorialized
to the states-general, on the nature and form of the designed treaty:
he also expatiated on the conduct of many of the principal characters
in the several united provinces, and on the treacherous and dangerous
nature and tendency to Great Britain, of [160] several other papers
and letters found among Mr. Laurens's dispatches.

He repeated his complaints of the countenance and protection given
by their high mightinesses to the *piratical Paul Jones*, while lying in
the Texel, and recapitulated other circumstances of their conduct
which had given offence to his nation; and intimated, that he expected
within three weeks from the date of his memorial, some decided

* See copies of these papers found in Mr. Laurens's trunk, in the British Annual
Register, one thousand seven hundred and eighty, in journals of congress, and many
other records. [See, *Annual Register* (1780), "State Papers," pp. 356–372.]

answer would be given, relative to the succors reclaimed eight months chap. xxv
before; otherwise his majesty would look upon their conduct as 1 7 8 2
breaking off the alliance on the part of their high mightinesses, and
would not in future consider the united provinces in any other light,
than on a footing with other neutral powers, unprivileged by treaty.
But the minister obtained little satisfaction from the reply of their
high mightinesses, or the deportment of the Hollanders.

The sum of their short reply was, that their high mightinesses were
very desirous to coincide with the wishes of the king of England, but
they could give no positive answer to his memorial, as it was impossible
to return an answer in the short term of three weeks: they observed,
that the memorial must be deliberated upon by the several provinces,
and their resolutions waited for: that they were persuaded his majesty
would not wish rigorously [161] to adhere to the afore mentioned
time. They waved the business by observing further,

> that their high mightinesses might be able to conclude upon an answer,
> in a manner conformable to the constitution of the republic, in which they
> had no right to make any alteration; and promised to accelerate the
> deliberations upon that head as much as possible.

The final result however was, that within a short time the vengeance
òf Britain was denounced against the Hollanders, by an explicit
declaration of war. This in some measure relieved the Batavian
provinces from the constrained attitude in which they had for some
time stood, between Great Britain and the United States of America.
But no treaty of alliance, amity, and commerce, was settled between
the two republics, until it was effected by the negociation of Mr.
Adams, who was appointed by congress, and repaired to the Hague
immediately after the unfortunate capture of Mr. Laurens; but the
business of his mission was not completed until the present year.

On Mr. Adams's arrival in Holland, he found every thing in a happy
train for negociation; the people well-disposed, and many of the most
distinguished characters zealous for a treaty with the American states,
without any farther [162] delay. Perhaps no man was better qualified
to treat with the Batavians, than Mr. Adams. His manners and habits
were much more assimilated to the Dutch than to the French nation;
he rendered himself acceptable to them, by associating much with
the common classes, by which he penetrated their views; yet he made
himself acquainted with the first literary characters among the citizens.
He took lodgings at Amsterdam, for several months, at the house of

CHAP. XXV   Mr. Dumas, a man of some mercantile interest, considerable com-
1 7 8 2   mercial knowledge, not acquainted with manners or letters, but much
attached to the Americans, from the general predilection of Dutchmen
in favor of republicanism.

Though this was the disposition of most of the inhabitants of the
united provinces, yet, as has been observed, there was a party attached
to the stadtholder, and to the measures of the British cabinet, that
hung as a dead weight on the wishes of the generality of their
countrymen, and for a time retarded the business of the American
plenipotentiary.

Vigilant himself, and urged by men of the best information in the
Batavian provinces, Mr. Adams, soon after his arrival in Holland,
presented a long memorial to the states-general. In this he sketched
some general ideas of the principles and the grounds of the declaration
[163] of independence, and the unanimity with which it was received
and supported by all the thirteen united colonies in America.*

He vindicated the American claim to independence in a very
handsome manner, and represented it as the interest of all the powers
of Europe, and more particularly of the united provinces of the
Netherlands, to support and maintain that claim. He pointed out the
natural and political grounds of a commercial connexion between
America and Holland, reminded them of the similarity of their religious
and political principles, of their long and arduous struggles to secure
their rights, of the sufferings of their ancestors to establish their
privileges on principles which their sons could never derelict. In short,
he urged in the memorial every reason for an alliance, with clearness,
precision, and strength of argument. He observed, "that principles
founded in eternal justice, and the laws of God and nature, both
dictated to them, to cut in sunder all ties which had connected them
with Great Britain."†

Before Mr. Adams presented this memorial, he had been indefatigable in his endeavors to [164] cherish the attachment already felt
by individual characters, toward the cause of America, and to strengthen
the favorable opinion that most of the Dutch provinces had adopted
before his arrival in Holland.

He had at the request of a private gentleman,‡ given him in a

---

* See Mr. Adams's memorial presented to the states-general one thousand seven
  hundred and eighty-one. [Adams, *Works*, VII: 396–404 (April 19, 1781).]
† Memorial. [Ibid.]
‡ Dr. Calkoen, an eminent civilian of the city of Amsterdam.

series of letters, a general idea of the situation of America, before and CHAP. XXV
at the present period. He drew a portrait of her temper, her manners, 1 7 8 2
her views, and her deportment: he stated the universal alienation and
aversion to Great Britain, that prevailed throughout the United States;
their ability to endure the protraction of the war; and observed on
the small proportion of people that still adhered to the royal cause:
he gave a concise statement of the public debt, the resources and
population of America; and asserted that they could boast a multitude
of characters, of equal ability to support the American cause, either
in the field or in congress, on the supposeable circumstance, that any
of the officers of the one or the other should be corrupted by British
gold.

In one of these letters he observed, that

> they considered themselves not only contending [165] for the purest
> principles of liberty, civil and religious, but against the greatest evils that
> any country ever suffered; for they knew, if they were deceived by England
> to break their union among themselves, and their faith with their allies,
> they would ever after be in the power of England, who would bring them
> into the most abject submission to the government of a parliament the
> most corrupted in the world, in which they would have no voice or
> influence, at three thousand miles distance.*

In another letter to the same gentleman he affirms,

> that nothing short of an entire alteration of sentiment in the whole body
> of the people, can make any material change in the councils or conduct of
> the United States; and that Great Britain had not power or art enough to
> change essentially, the temper, the feelings, and the opinions, of between
> three and four millions of people, at three thousand miles distance,
> supported as they are by powerful allies: that the people in America were
> too enlightened to be deceived in any great plan of policy; they understood
> the principles and nature of government too well, to [166] be imposed on
> by any proposals short of their object.†

These letters were published and put into the hands of influential
characters, and had a powerful effect on the liberal minds of the
Batavians, already pre-disposed to union and friendship with the
Americans. No ready reply was made by the states-general to the

* See letter second to Dr. Calkoen. [Adams, *Works*, VII: 269–271.]
† Their object then was a free, independent republic, without any approximation to
  regal authority, or monarchic usages: there was then no fighting for rank, titles, and
  the expensive trappings of nobility.

CHAP. XXV judicious memorial presented by Mr. Adams: in consequence of this
1 7 8 2 delay, petitions, remonstrances, and addresses, were presented to
their high mightinesses from all the Dutch provinces. In these they
urged both the propriety and the policy of receiving a public minister
in due form, from the United States of America.

The deputies to the states-general were every where instructed to
concur in the measure of receiving Mr. Adams, as ambassador from
the American congress, without farther deliberation: they insisted that
his letters of credence should be received, and that negociations
should be immediately entered on, between him and the high
authorities of the united provinces. Yet still the business lagged
heavily: the intrigues of the [167] duke of Brunswick, the favorite
and prime counsellor of the stadtholder, and the influence of the
British minister, were for a time an overbalance for the energy of
republican resolves or entreaties.

This occasioned great dissatisfaction: a general murmur was heard
through the several departments in the Dutch provinces: the measures
of the court, and the duke of Brunswick as the adviser, were attacked
from the presses, his dismission as field marshal was urged, and his
retirement from Holland insisted on. To him, in conjunction with the
designs of England and the subserviency of the stadtholder to the
cabinet of Britain, was attributed the derangement of their marine,
and the mismanagement of all their public affairs.

Previous to this, in the assembly of the states of Guelderland, in
November, one thousand seven hundred and eighty-one, Robert
Jasper Van der Capellen, in a very spirited speech, enforced with
much precision, the necessity of opposing the measures which had
created a general discordance through all the provinces of Holland.

He observed,

> that a mean condescension, a fawning compliance with the measures of
> England, ought no longer to prevent us from [168] acknowledging the
> independence of a republic, which after our own glorious example, has
> acquired its freedom by arms, and is daily striving to shake off entirely,
> the galling yoke of our common enemy.

He said it was his opinion, that a treaty of amity between the two
republics had been already too long held in suspense, and that it was
injuring both nations for their high mightinesses to postpone the
reception of the American minister, or keep back the negociation.

This was the general spirit of the most distinguished members of
the provinces, while Mr. Adams still persevered in every prudent

measure, to facilitate the object of his mission. He was every where CHAP. XXV
cordially received as an American, respected as a republican, and 1 7 8 2
considered in the light of an ambassador from a new and great nation.

Mr. Adams was not indeed honored with a reply to his first memorial,
but he was too zealous in the cause of his country to submit long to
such an evasive step. Determined to bring on a speedy decision, a
short time only elapsed, before the American minister, without waiting
for a replication to his first, presented a second address to the states-
general. In this he referred them to his former memorial, and demanded
a categorical answer, that he might be able [169] to transmit to the
authority under which he acted, an account of his negociation.*

This second memorial was more effective in promoting the wishes
of the friends of America, than any previous step. We have already
seen from a variety of circumstances, that such was the desire, not
only of the mercantile, but of most of the distinguished and patriotic
characters in Holland, to enter into a close alliance with the American
states, that it could no longer be postponed, without throwing the
united provinces into distraction and confusion, that could not easily
have been accommodated. The resolute and undaunted deportment
of Mr. Adams, concurring with their dispositions, and with the interests
and the views of the United Netherlands, at last accomplished the
object of his mission, entirely to his own, and to the satisfaction of
both republics, though it had been impeded by Great Britain, and
not encouraged by any other power in Europe.

On the twenty-second of April, one thousand seven hundred and
eighty-two, Mr. Adams was admitted at the Hague, and with the
usual ceremonies [170] on such occasions, received as minister
plenipotentiary from the United States of America.

Articles of alliance, and a treaty of amity, were signed by both
parties, and a loan of money was soon offered by the Dutch, and
accepted by Mr. Adams for the use of the United States. This treaty
of alliance and friendship between the sister republics of Holland and
America, was the subject of much triumph to the latter, and not less
to the minister who finished the negociation. Every expression of
satisfaction and joy appeared in all classes of inhabitants through the
Batavian provinces, on the confirmation of their union and alliance
with a sister republic.

The treaty between their high mightinesses the states-general, and

* See Mr. Adams's address presented to Van der Sandheuvel, president of the states-
general, January 9, 1782. [Probably Adams, *Works*, VII: 396–404.]

CHAP. XXV the United States of America, contained twenty-nine articles. These
1 7 8 2 were in substance, first, that there should be a firm, indissoluble, and
general peace, between the *United Provinces of the Netherlands* and the
United States of America, and the citizens, inhabitants of their respective
states. The second and third articles stipulated mutually the duties
to be paid, and the freedom of trade and navigation, without
interruption by either nation, to whatever part of the universe their
trade might be extended.

[171] The fourth article was principally relative to the rights of
commerce, the enjoyment of their own religion, and the rites of
decent sepulture to the persons who might die in the territories of
their allies. A number of other articles were inserted, which discovered, even in their treaties, the peculiar taste, genius, and
apprehensions of republicans. They were in language and expression,
in several instances, very different from the usual style and manner
observed between monarchic powers, more tenacious of the obedience
of their subjects, while living, than attentive to the preservation of
their lives, or to the decent deposite of their ashes, when dead.

The other articles contained in this treaty, principally related to
commercial intercourse between contending powers. These were of
great importance to the Dutch, whose energies were remarkable as a
trading nation; nor were they of less consideration to the Americans,
whose advantages promised that they might become one of the first
commercial powers in the world.

The British minister, sir Joseph Yorke, sent on for the purpose,
still zealously endeavoured, as he had done before, to shake the
engagements of the republic of Holland, and draw them off from the
interests of the American [172] states. Though the court of Great
Britain had been irritated until they had proceeded to the most
vigorous and severe measures against the Dutch, yet on the successes
of America, and the prospect of new acquisitions of strength and
dignity from foreign alliances, they had condescended so far, as to
permit their minister to make proposals of a separate peace with the
United States of Holland.

These overtures for a separate peace, which England had recently
made, might probably quicken the measures of the United States of
Holland, and hasten the completion of the wishes of the Americans.
They were rejected with disdain by the honest republicans: and at
this period of amity between the two republics, the American minister
boasted in a letter to the author, that he "should look down with

pleasure from the other world, on the American flag-staff planted in CHAP. XXV
Holland." 1 7 8 2

The exultation and joy exhibited in the Batavian provinces, on
signing the treaty between the two republics, was more than usually
animated, and rose to an exhilaration of spirits seldom discovered in
such a phlegmatic nation. Among many other instances of the general
approbation of the measure, a society of citizens established at *Leon
Warden*, under the motto of *Liberty and Zeal*, presented a medal to
the states of Friesland, as the first public body that had [173] explicitly
proposed a connexion and alliance with the American states.

No people on earth were more passionately enamoured with liberty,
or more obstinate in the defence of freedom, than the inhabitants of
Friesland: this is known from their ancient history. They enjoyed
their liberty, and retained a greater degree of independence than their
neighbours, through a long course of years, even from Drusus to
Charlemagne, and from Charlemagne down to the present time.*
They have always been distinguished for their free, independent
spirit; for their valor, magnanimity, and bold defence of the liberties
of their province.

Though a general uneasiness had long prevailed through every part
of Holland, the deputies of Friesland had been more explicit than
any of the provinces, with regard to the pernicious influence of the
duke of Brunswick. They had strongly expressed their discontent in
general, with respect to public measures, and particularly with those
relative to the navy department: they had written to the stadtholder,
and strongly expressed the universal distrust and discontent, respecting
the manner in which the affairs of the nation had been conducted,
[174] and the consequences they apprehended, which could not fail
to be highly prejudicial to public tranquillity. They attributed these
disorders to the mal-administration of the duke of Brunswick, requested that he might no longer be permitted to continue either as
an actor or adviser in the affairs of Holland, but that his serene
highness the stadtholder, would cause him to be removed from court
immediately.

This however was not done, nor was there any reason to suppose,
notwithstanding he had acceded thereto, that the stadtholder and
such as were attached to his family interest, and to the schemes and
projects of the duke of Brunswick, were well pleased with the alliance

* See Universal History. [*Modern Universal History*, XXXI: 27.]

between the United States of America and the Batavian provinces. Subsequent transactions evinced this, to the conviction of every one. But notwithstanding the secret chagrin which might pervade his, or the mind of any other individual, the great body of a nation, that had for near a century discovered an enthusiastic attachment to liberty, and who had surmounted inexpressible sufferings to maintain it, did not suppress the most lively demonstrations of general satisfaction on the happy event.

The medal above mentioned, presented by the society of *Leon Warden* to the states of Friesland, was expressive of the general sentiment of the nation, as well as of their own [175] alienation from England, and their attachment to America. On one side of it, dedicated by the society of *Liberty and Zeal*, was represented a Friesian, dressed according to their ancient characteristic custom, holding out his right hand to a North American, in token of friendship and brotherly love, while with the left he rejects a separate peace which England offers him.

There had been dissensions in Holland, which had existed a number of years previous to the present period. The people had been divided between an aristocratic and a republican party: the one influenced by their attachment to the stadtholder, the other had co-operated with the interests of France. In the midst of the animosities occasioned by the dissensions of these two parties, a third arose of a still more important nature, which embraced a system more free than yet existed in the republic of Holland.

This gave rise to the observations in a work of celebrity, that

> Animated by the example of North America, and by that spirit of liberty and independence which has lately diffused itself in the world, in favor of democracy, the language of pure republicanism has been held by its citizens. They have publicly talked of choosing delegates, and asserting the rights of nature: their merchants and manufacturers have taken to the use of arms, and are daily [176] improving themselves in military discipline. To judge from the auspicious contagion that has been caught from the revolution in America, we should be almost ready to say,—*One more such revolution* would give freedom to the world!

The prevalence of this spirit in the Batavian provinces, rendered the work of negociation less arduous for the American ambassador. Yet while in Holland, Mr. Adams was in no point deficient in vigilance, nor did he neglect to fan the republican zeal, by every argument in

favor of civil liberty, of the equal rights of man, and of a republican CHAP. XXV
form of government, during his residence in the low countries. 1 7 8 2

His satisfaction at the successful termination of his mission, was
evinced both in his public conduct, and in the private effusions of
his pen. In his diplomatic character, Mr. Adams had never enjoyed
himself so well, as while residing in the Dutch republic. Regular in
his morals, and reserved in his temper, he appeared rather gloomy in
a circle; but he was sensible, shrewd, and sarcastic, among private
friends. His genius was not altogether calculated for a court life,
amidst the conviviality and gaiety of Parisian taste. In France he was
never happy: not beloved by his venerable colleague, doctor Franklin;
thwarted by the minister, the count de Vergennes, and ridiculed [177]
by the fashionable and polite, as deficient in the *je ne scai quoi*, so
necessary in highly polished society; viewed with jealousy by the
court, and hated by courtiers, for the perseverance, frigidity, and
warmth, blended in his deportment; he there did little of consequence,
until the important period when, in conjunction with Dr. Franklin
and Mr. Jay, a treaty of peace was negociated between Great Britain
and the United States of America.

Soon after the present period, Mr. Adams was summoned from the
Hague by order of the American congress, directed to repair to Paris,
and assist in the important work of negociating a peace between Great
Britain and her former colonies, now a confederated and independent
nation. In this business he acquitted himself with equal firmness, and
equally to the satisfaction and approbation of his country, as he had
before done in Holland. His reputation was enhanced among his
countrymen, and his popularity kept up for a number of years, after
the honorable part he had acted as a diplomatic character, in his treaty
with Holland, and as a firm and zealous friend to the interests of his
country, through the negociations for peace with his colleagues in
France.

The loan of money obtained from Holland by the address of Mr.
Adams, was a great relief [178] to the United States. This was at a
crisis when their resources were drained by a long expensive war, and
a paper substitute for specie had ceased to be of any farther utility.
He had so handsomely anticipated the future resources of America,
and contrasted the immense public debt of Great Britain with the
comparatively small expenditures for national purposes in America,
that not only the Dutch government conceded willingly to the propriety
of assisting the United States, by the advance of monies, but the

affluent merchants, and others in possession of vast private property in that rich, commercial country, offered, with the utmost alacrity, some handsome loans, to assist and facilitate the freedom and growth of a young sister republic, from whom they expected to derive the greatest commercial advantages, when war should cease, and her independence was universally acknowledged.

Mr. Adams's opinion, at this early period, seemed to favor the idea, that America would be capable of bearing taxes to an immense amount in future, though this was a burden of which they had had, comparatively, little experience. He observed, that

> the people in America had not yet been disciplined to such enormous taxation as in England, but that they were capable of bearing as great taxes in proportion as the English; and if the English [179] force them to it by continuing the war, they will reconcile themselves to it.*

But it might have been observed, that it would require a great number of years, and many contingent events, to reconcile the inhabitants of the United States to the taxing of houses, lands, hearths, window-lights, and all the conveniences of life, as in England. Not the necessity of extricating themselves from old foreign debts, or newly-contracted expenses for exigencies or projects, which they considered unnecessary in a republican government, could suddenly lead a people generally to acquiesce in measures, to which they had heretofore been strangers. The artificial creation of expenses by those who deem a *public debt a public blessing*, will easily suggest plausible pretences for taxation, until every class is burdened to the utmost stretch of forbearance, and the great body of the people reduced to penury and slavery.

It does not always redound to the benefit of younger states and less affluent nations, to become indebted to foreigners for large sums of money; but without this assistance from several of the European powers, it would have been impossible for the United States, under their complicated inconveniences and embarrassments, to have resisted so long the opulent and powerful [180] nation of Britain. America was necessitated to borrow money abroad to support her credit at home; and had not the Dutch loan been obtained, it is impossible to calculate what would have been the consequences to the United States, who had not at this period, even the weak support of an artificial medium, while their armies were unpaid, and their soldiers on the point of

---

* See letter eleventh to Mr. Calkoen. [Adams, *Works*, VII: 291–295.]

mutiny, for the want of immediate subsistence. His countrymen CHAP. XXV
thought themselves highly indebted to Mr. Adams, for procuring this 1 7 8 2
timely supply of cash, as well as for so ably negociating a treaty of
amity and commerce. It gave a new spring to all their exertions, which
had for some time lagged heavily, for want of the necessary sinews
for the protraction of war, or for enterprise in any other line of
business.

CHAPTER XXVI

General Uneasiness with Ministerial Measures in England, Scotland, and Ireland • Loud Complaints against the Board of Admiralty • Sir Hyde Parker resigns his Commission • Motion for an Address for Peace, by General Conway • Resignation of Lord George Germaine—Created a Peer of the Realm • Lord North resigns—Some traits of his Character • Petition of the City of London for Peace • Coalition of Parties—A new Ministry • Death and Character of the Marquis of Rockingham • Lord Shelburne's Administration • Negociations for Peace—Provisional Articles signed • Temper of the Loyalists • Execution of Captain Huddy—Consequent Imprisonment of Captain Asgill—Asgill's Release

[181] While new alliances were negociating between the Americans and several European powers, and the importance of the United States was appreciating in the scale of nations, the councils of Britain were confused, and the parliament and the nation split into parties.

The American war was become very unpopular in England, and discontents prevailed in all parts of the empire. Many of the favorites of the present reign had been taken from beyond [182] the wall of Adrian,* yet there was a growing dissatisfaction with all the measures of administration, and a prevailing discontent and uneasiness, through the Scotch nation; but this was owing more to some religious

---

* No national reflection is here designed. It is very immaterial, as observed by the great lord Chatham, whether a man was rocked in his cradle on one side of the Tweed or the other. The writer of these pages has the highest respect for the distinguished literary characters that adorn the Scotch nation. Their strength of genius, and profound investigations in philosophic, political, theological, and historic compositions, are at least on an equal scale of ability, with any of the learned luminaries of the law, or any other science, nearer the splendid beams of monarchy; and when called to distinguished office, they have perhaps, with some few exceptions, discharged their public functions with equal honor, capacity, and integrity.

dissensions, than from any liberal or enlarged views of political liberty,
among the class of people loudest in complaint.

Yet much less was to be apprehended from the discontents in Scotland, than from those of the oppressed Irish, driven nearly to the point of revolt. They had long and justly murmured at the high-handed measures of the parliament of England, and the degraded and inferior rank in which they were viewed at the court of St. James. The late restrictions on their commerce, a recent embargo for three years on their staple export, the inhibitions, the [183] disqualifications, and frequent severe penalties, laid on the great body of the Roman Catholic inhabitants, with a long list of other grievances that might be enumerated, they considered as marks of national contempt, and a sacrifice of the interest of Ireland, to favor the avarice of British contractors, speculators, and pensioners. They were sensible that no means were neglected to rivet the chains in which they were held by the prejudices of Englishmen, with regard to their commerce, their police, and their religious opinions.

Their resentment did not evaporate in unmeaning and inactive complaint: they entered into combinations against the use and purchase of British manufactures, and prohibited their importation into Ireland, under very heavy penalties: measures for defence, and military associations, were every where adopted: this they justified from the apprehension of foreign invasion, and the extraordinary weakness of the state, in consequence of drawing off the troops for active service in America, which had usually been stationed in Ireland for the defence of that kingdom.

The Irish volunteers who assembled in arms on this occasion, soon amounted to near sixty thousand men, and daily increased in number and strength. These were not composed merely [184] of the middling or lower classes of people; men of fortune and character were seen in the ranks, and even many of the nobility appeared to encourage these associations.

This armament was very alarming to Great Britain, but it could not be suppressed: the inhabitants of Ireland were bold and undaunted; and, encouraged by the example of America, they strenuously supported their rights, and made use of the same arguments against a standing army in time of peace, which had been urged in the assemblies and congresses of the colonies. They resolutely refused to submit longer to such unconstitutional and dangerous measures, resisted the mutiny act, denied its validity, and opposed and prevented the

CHAP. XXVI   magistrates in making provision for the remnant of the king's troops
1 7 8 2   still left in the country.

One of their patriots* of name and ability, asserted that the act was dangerous and unconstitutional; that

> the mutiny bill, or martial law methodized, was not only different from, but directly opposite to, the common law of the land; it set aside trial by jury, departed from her principles of evidence, declined her ordinary tribunals of justice, and in their place established a summary proceeding, arbitrary [185] crimes, arbitrary punishments, a secret sentence, and a sudden execution.

The determinations of the Irish to recover their freedom, and maintain their native rights, were represented in the most eloquent strains of rhetoric: the strong and pointed language was dictated by the heart, approved by the judgment, and expressed in the periods of the best orators. The names of many well-informed Irish gentlemen were distinguished, and will be handed down on the conspicuous list, both for the brilliancy of their epithets, and their strength of reasoning. Among these, the celebrated Mr. Grattan was marked for his superior eloquence, learning, patriotism, and other virtues. The talents of Mr. Flood and others were called forth; and by the energies and exertions of those patriotic leaders, they obtained some amelioration of the burdens complained of. Thus by the decided spirit of many eminent characters in the nation, the British parliament was induced to take some steps that produced a temporary quiet in Ireland: more lenity was shewn toward the Roman Catholics, and some other small indulgencies granted, but nothing sufficient to restore lasting tranquillity to the country.

While the sister kingdoms were thus restless and dissatisfied, a general uneasiness discovered [186] itself throughout England, on the disappointment of their naval operations. After the affair on the Dogger-Bank, sir Hyde Parker thought he had been so far unsupported, that his honor impelled him to resign. The neglect of proper support to the worthy Kempenfelt, and other brave naval commanders, was highly censured throughout the kingdom.

Mr. Fox brought a number of direct and explicit charges against the board of admiralty; first, in suffering the count de Grasse to sail to the West Indies, without an effort to intercept him; secondly, the loss of the St. Eustatia convoy, when near sixty sail of British ships,

* Mr. Grattan.

with much property and many prisoners, were sent into Cadiz by don CHAP. XXVI
Lewis de Cordova, who commanded the combined fleet of France 1 7 8 2
and Spain at the time.

The engagement with admiral Zeutman, the failure of admiral
Kempenfelt to cut off the count de Guichen, and several other
disappointments in the naval line, were all attributed to the same
cause, negligence and incapacity in the first lord of the admiralty. An
address to the king was proposed, that the earl of Sandwich should
be removed from his majesty's councils forever: his character was
universally vilified in England: a writer in that country may have
delineated it more exactly than can be expected from any one at a
distance.

[187] He observes,

> that future historians may do justice to his moral character, but that in so
> barren a wilderness, it would be happy if one solitary virtue could enliven
> the prospect. But, as destitute of feeling as of principle, amidst the copious
> crop of vices which overwhelmed his whole character, not even that of
> cowardice was wanting, to move contempt as well as detestation; and
> strange it is, that though his sentiments with regard to both natural and
> revealed religion were well known, yet so timid was his nature, that he
> never dared to be alone.
>
> After these general traits, we cannot wonder, that he was in his political
> life the decided enemy of his country, and the devoted instrument of a
> corrupt cabinet. His name, indeed, was never mentioned, without exciting
> sentiments of contempt. If nature had endowed him with talents, the
> course of dissipation in which he was engaged, must have disqualified him
> for their exercise. He possessed an active, but not a strong mind: practised
> in the intrigues of a court, and the habits of parliament, he could speak
> with facility, but his ideas never took an extensive range: the paltry maxims
> of court intrigue finished the outlines of his character.*

[188] Mr. Fox's address for the removal of the earl of Sandwich,
was supported by lord Howe and admiral Keppel: they censured his
mismanagement and prodigality, exposed his blunders and want of
capacity, and painted in glowing colors his misconduct, and the fatal
consequences to the navy and to the nation, by his having been thus

---

* See History of the Reign of George the Third, by Wenderburne. [Gebhard Friedrich
August Wendeborn, *A View of England Towards the Close of the Eighteenth Century*
(2 vols.; London, 1791). The statement quoted does not appear. Nor does it appear
in Belsham, *Memoirs of the Reign of George III. To the Session of Parliament Ending
A.D. 1793* (4 vols.; London, 1795), the title of which Warren may have confused
with Wendeborn's.]

CHAP. XXVI long continued in an office of such high trust and responsibility: but
1 7 8 2 he had his friends and defenders; and after long and warm debates,
the motion for his removal was lost by a small majority.

After many desultory grounds and circumstances of uneasiness were
discussed, a motion of high importance was made in the house of
commons, by general Conway; this was for an address to the king,
requesting him to put an immediate period to the destructive war in
America. This motion was lost only by a single vote—one hundred
and ninety-three were in favor of, and one hundred and ninety-four
against it. But the object of peace was not relinquished; the address
was again brought forward, and finally carried.

After various expedients had been proposed, which were reprobated
in strong terms, lord Cavendish moved, that the house should resolve,
that the enormous expenses of the nation, the loss of the colonies, a
war with France, Spain, Holland, and America, without a single ally,
[189] was occasioned by a want of foresight and ability in his majesty's
ministers, and that they were unworthy of further confidence.

In short, such a general reprobation of all former measures ensued,
and such a universal vilification of the heads of departments, and
such unlimited censure fell on every part of their conduct, through a
seven years' war, that the old ministry found themselves on the point
of dissolution.

Lord George Germaine, who had kept his ground beyond all
expectation, through a very tempestuous season, now found himself
obliged to resign his office as minister of the American department.
Though rewarded for his services by peculiar tokens of his majesty's
favor, and dignified by a peerage, he stood for a time in a most
humiliating predicament. Several of the house of lords thought the
nation disgraced, and themselves affronted, by the creation of a man
to that illustrious order, who had formerly been censured by a court-
martial, and dismissed from all employment in a military line, and
who had recently and obstinately pursued measures in the cabinet,
and supported a destructive system, that had brought the nation to
the brink of ruin.*

[190] His promotion was also opposed in the house of commons,
from the "impolicy of rewarding, in the present conjuncture of affairs,
a person so deeply concerned in the American war." It was observed,

---

* The marquis of Carmarthen stood at the head of opposition against the promotion
of lord George Germaine.

that it might have a tendency to defeat the purposes of a great and CHAP. XXVI
solemn inquiry, in which the conduct of that noble personage might 1 7 8 2
appear to deserve the severest punishment. But supported by royal
prerogative, his lordship retained his high rank, and enjoyed a kind
of triumph in the favor of the king, in spite of the reproaches of his
enemies; yet, neither ribbons or stars could erase the stigma that
hung on his character, both as a minister and a soldier.

Nor at this period could the puissaint nobleman at the head of the
treasury, any longer stand the torrent of reproach and complaint that
was poured out against him. On the twentieth of March, one thousand
seven hundred and eighty-two, lord *North* resigned his place, and
declared to the house of commons, that the present administration
from that day ceased to exist.

It has been observed by a British writer of ability, that

> lord North was educated in the school of corruption; naturally of an easy,
> pliant temper; that that disposition was increased by the maxims he had
> imbibed. He was rather a man of wit, than consummate [191] abilities;
> ready and adroit, rather than wise and sagacious. He considered the faculty
> of parrying the strokes levelled at him in the house of commons, as the
> first qualification of a minister. Under his administration, a regular system
> of pension and contract was adopted, more pernicious than the casual
> expedients of Walpole, to facilitate his measures.*

However he might merit the severities contained in the several

---

* See a view of the reign of George the third. Another British writer has thus sketched
the character of lord North:

> It must be remarked, that a certain confusedness and indistinctness of ideas
> unfortunately pervaded his general system of thinking: he seemed habitually
> to aim at the thing that was right, but invariably stopped short of the true and
> genuine standard of political propriety. With the reputation of meaning well,
> he acquired the imputation of indecision and instability. The general tenor of
> his administration must certainly be allowed to exhibit very few indications of
> energy, wisdom, or force of penetration. But occasionally capable of resolute
> and persevering exertions, his temper was mild, equable, and pleasant, although
> his notions of government evidently appeared of the high *tory* cast.
>
> BELSHAM

[The statement quoted in the text appears in neither Gebhard Friedrich August
Wendeborn, *A View of England Towards the Close of the Eighteenth Century* (2 vols.;
London, 1791) nor in William Belsham, *Memoirs of the Reign of George III. To the
Session of Parliament ending A.D. 1793* (4 vols.; London, 1795). The statement quoted
in the footnote is very close to Belsham, I: 215.]

sketches of his character, his lordship quitted his station with as much firmness, address, and dignity, as any man of understanding and political abilities possibly could have done, who had stood at the head [192] of administration during an unfortunate war that continued near seven years. At the same time, what had greatly enhanced his difficulties and his responsibility, all the other powers in Europe, were either in alliance with America, or stood by as unconcerned spectators of a combat, which augured a train of most important events to the political, civil, and religious state of Christendom, if not to the world.

His lordship declared, that he did not mean to shrink from trial; that he should always be prepared to meet it; that a successor might be found of better judgment, and better qualified for the high and arduous station; but none more zealously attached to the interest of his country, and the preservation of the British constitution, than himself.

It is indeed easy to believe, that his lordship was willing to retire, and happy to quit the helm of state, which he had held with such an unsuccessful hand. He had sent out his mandates, and proclaimed his recisions, until the thirteen United States of America were irretrievably lost to Great Britain; until Minorca was captured by the Spaniards . . . Dominica, St. Vincent's, Tobago, Grenada, and other islands in the West Indies, by the French; and until two British armies, commanded by some of the most distinguished officers in the nation, were prisoners in the American states.

[193] Thus after the blood of thousands of the best soldiers in England, of the best officers in the nation, had been sacrificed, and multitudes of Americans, formerly the best subjects to the crown of Britain, had been immolated on the altar of ambition, avarice, or revenge; after the nation was involved in expenses beyond calculation, her trade ruined, and the national character disgraced by the iniquitous principles of the war; it is not strange that the parliament was agitated, the ministry dismayed, and the people thrown into consternation and disgust. The murmur was universal, the public councils were divided, and the ministry and their measures were become the ridicule of foreign nations.

Through all the struggle between Great Britain and her colonies, not one of the powers of Europe had declared against America; but on the contrary, most of them had either secretly or openly, espoused her cause. Yet it is not to be supposed that the passive demeanor of

some, and the friendly deportment of others, was the result of a CHAP. XXVI
general love of liberty among potent nations, or splendid courts, where 1 7 8 2
the sceptre of royalty was swayed, at least in some of them, with a
very despotic hand. Their interests and their ambition were united;
and led them [194] to anticipate and to boast the pernicious consequences to England of this unfortunate war.

Doubtless a jealousy of the enormous power of Britain, and the
proud glory to which she had arrived in the preceding reign, operated
strongly to cherish the pacific disposition of some, and to prompt
others to lend an hostile arm to dissever the growing colonies from
the crown and authority of Great Britain. They could not but rejoice
at the dismemberment of an empire, that had long been the dread of
some, and the envy and hatred of other nations. It was too soon for
them to forget, that under the wise and energetic administration of a
Chatham, the kingdoms of the earth had trembled at the power of
England; that in conjunction with the American colonies, *Britannia*,
mounted on a triumphal car, had bid proud defiance to all the
potentates in Europe; that the thunder of her cannon was dreaded
from the eastern seas to the western extreme; and that her flag was
revered, and that her navy gave laws, from the Ganges to the Missisippi.

The insolence of this proud mistress of the seas only partially
checked, her glory shrouded, and the haughty islanders humbled. . . .
humbled by their own injudicious and overbearing measures, was a
spectacle viewed with delight by neighbouring nations, and contemplated by France with peculiar satisfaction. Yet it was [195] perhaps,
equally the policy and the interest of both the French and the British
prime ministers, at this period, to promote pacific measures. It was
the wish of both nations to be relieved from the distresses of a long
and expensive war; and the officers in the first departments were
convinced, more especially in England, that they had little other
chance to keep their places, than by a compliance with the general
will of the people.

The discontents among the inhabitants of Great Britain, ran higher
than ever. Chagrined by repeated defeat and losses, both by sea and
land; alarmed at the monstrous accumulation of the national debt,
the weight of taxes; the value of landed property daily sinking, and
the public burthens increasing; many gentlemen who had been
sanguine in favor of the American war, seemed to awaken at once
from their lethargy, and to appear sensible, that ruin stared in the
face of themselves, as well as of the nation.

CHAP. XXVI   From the present temper that discovered itself within the house of
1 7 8 2 commons, or from appearances without, the minority had no reason
to be discouraged with regard to their favorite object, which was the
restoration of peace between Great Britain and the colonies. On the
twenty-seventh of February, one thousand seven hundred and eighty-
two, general Conway made [196] a second motion for addressing the
throne, and urging that the ruinous war with America should no longer
be pursued.

Fortunately, a petition from the city of London was the same day
presented, praying that a cessation of hostilities between Great Britain
and her former provinces, might immediately take place. The motion
for peace was now carried in the house without much opposition: an
address was presented for that purpose, to the king, on the first day
of March. In this he was humbly implored to lend his sanction to
measures for a restoration of general harmony. His answer, though in
milder language than had of late been the fashion of the court, was
not sufficiently explicit, but it was not left open to retraction. The
prompt measures, the zeal and vigor of an opposition that had long
been in the minority, at last gained the ascendancy, and secured a
truce so much desired by a people weary of war, and so necessary for
the relief, the honor, and the restoration of character to a gallant
nation.

In order to facilitate this happy event, a proposal for conciliation
was made, that could scarcely have been expected to succeed. A
coalescence of parties where animosities had run so high, and the minds
of men had been so embittered by a series of disappointments and
unceasing irritation, was a circumstance not [197] within the calculation
of any one. But it was found necessary to bury, or at least to suppress,
the prejudices of party, to lay aside private resentment, and to unite
in one system for the general good. All were so convinced of this
necessity, that the proposal was conceded to; and after the resignation
of lord North, a complete change of ministry took place, composed
of active and conspicuous characters from each party; but according
to a trite saying, it proved indeed, no more than a *rope of sand.*

Sir Welbore Ellis had been appointed minister for the American
department, immediately on the removal of lord George Germaine.
But his principles and his reasonings relative to American affairs; his
general observations on the transactions of war, of the belligerent
powers, of the French nation, of the American loyalists, of the means
of harmony, and the restoration of peace; subjected him to the satirical
strokes, and the severe epithets of pointed ridicule, that have always

flowed so easy from the lip of the oratorical Burke. The chastisement
also of his opinions by Mr. Fox and others, zealous for the termination
of the contest between Great Britain and her colonies, shewed that
the friend and pupil of lord Sackville did not stand on very firm
ground.

Though it appeared to the world to be composed of motley materials,
yet all matters were [198] adjusted for the establishment of a new
administration, and the nation cherished the most sanguine hopes
from the change. The marquis of Rockingham stood at the head of
the new arrangement. No character among the nobility of Britain,
was at this time held in higher estimation than his; nor was any man
better qualified for the appointment of first lord of the treasury, as a
successor to lord North, whose character, principles, abilities, and
perseverance, have been sketched in the course of narration.

The manners of Rockingham were amiable; his temper, mild and
complacent; his rank, fortune, and personal influence, commanding;
his principles, uniform in favor of the rights of man; and his capacity,
and constant opposition to the American war, rendered him a fit
person to stand in this high station of responsibility. He was well
qualified to correct the political mistakes of his predecessor, and to
retrieve the honor of the nation on the approach of negociations for
peace. But as in human life the most important events sometimes
depend on the character of a single actor, the sudden *exit* of such a
character often blasts the hopes, clouds the minds, and defeats the
expectations of contemporaries.

This observation was fully verified in the premature death of the
noble marquis, who lived [199] only three months after his appointment
to the helm of administration. All eyes had been fixed on him as the
band of union, and the promoter and the prop of both public and
private peace; but his death, which took place on the first of July,
one thousand seven hundred and eighty-two, involved his country in
new difficulties, and created new scenes of dissension and animosity.

Many other departments in the new system of ministerial measures,
were filled by gentlemen of the first character and consideration. *Lord
John Cavendish* was appointed chancellor of the exchequer—*The Duke
of Richmond*, master of the ordnance—*Grafton*, lord privy-seal—*Admiral
Keppel*, first lord of the admiralty—*Lord Camden*, president of the
council—*General Conway*, commander in chief of all the forces in Great
Britain—*Mr. Thomas Townsend*, secretary at war—*Lord Shelburne* and
Mr. Fox, principal secretaries of state—*Colonel Barre*, treasurer of the
navy—And *Mr. Burke*, paymaster of the troops.

CHAP. XXVI   On the death of the marquis of Rockingham, lord Shelburne, to
1 7 8 2 the surprise of his associates in the ministry, had gained such an
interest as to obtain the appointment of first lord of the treasury, in
the room of a favorite of the nation and of the new ministry. To the
newly coalesced administration, the unexpected advancement of lord
Shelburne to this dignified and [200] important station, was so
disgusting, that it broke the coalition. Mr. Fox and lord Cavendish
resigned their places. This precipitant dereliction of office at such a
critical period, by gentlemen of their high consideration, was regretted
by some, severely censured by others, and was mortifying indeed to
their friends, who, though far from being pleased, continued to act
with the new lord-treasurer.

The reasons assigned by Mr. Fox for thus quitting his place, at
such a crisis, were, "that the system in which he consented to unite
in the coalition, was not likely to be pursued;" that the first principle
of this system was, an express acknowledgment of the independence
of the United States of America, instead of making it an article in the
provisional treaty, as proposed by some: to this unequivocal independence of America, he knew lord Shelburne to be opposed.

In reply to this, his lordship rose and defended his own opinions.
He declared he was not ashamed to avow, and to act upon, the ideas
of the great lord Chatham: he said it was well known, that this
distinguished statesman had asserted, that "the sun of England's glory
would set, if independence was granted to America." He added,
that he

> wished himself had been deputed to congress, that he would then have
> exerted all his talents to [201] convince them, that if their independence
> was signed, their liberties were gone forever.

He expressly declared that it was his opinion,

> that the independence of the united colonies not only threatened the
> extinction of their own liberties, but the ruin of England; and that certainly
> by *giving them independence*, they would finally be deprived of that freedom
> they had been struggling to secure and enjoy.

It was difficult, even at this late period, to convince many of the
most intelligent gentlemen in England, that *independence* was a gift
that America did not now ask; the boon was their own; obtained by
their own prowess and magnanimity, in conjunction with the armies
of their brave allies.

It may be proper to observe, that if England should in reality feel,
that the splendor of her solar rays are eclipsed by the dismemberment

of such a branch of the empire, the amputation might not yet be fatal CHAP. XXVI
to her prosperity and glory. They might yet prosper in a friendly 1 7 8 2
alliance with the colonies, if the parliament, the nation, and their
sovereign, should be in future disposed to moderation and justice,
and would shew themselves sincere in promoting friendship and
harmony with an infant republic. It is true this republic has been
forced into premature [202] existence; yet she held herself in all
diplomatic concerns, on a footing with any other nation, and was now
ready to form alliances with them and all other foreign powers, without
becoming dependent on, or tributary to any.

Affairs were now brought to a point; there was no possibility of
oscillating longer between peace and war: coercion had been long
enough unsuccessfully tried; negociation was now the only path to be
trodden, however thorny it might appear to the pride of royalty, or
to the *omnipotence* of a British parliament.

After repeated captures of the best appointed armies, composed
both of domestic and foreign troops, despair of subjugating the United
States had lowered down the spirit of the nation, and of the king of
England so far, as to become willing to treat on terms for the restoration
of amity, and to speak with some degree of temper, of the total
separation and independence of America.

Lord Shelburne's opinions had been so diametrically opposite to
those of the gentlemen who had seceded from the administration,
that they thought themselves fully justified in withdrawing from public
service, even while the important business was in agitation, and every
thing ripening for new negociations, replete [203] with events beyond
the calculations of the wisest statesmen and politicians. In their self
approbation they were confirmed, when they thought they discovered
a degree of duplicity in the business. Notwithstanding lord Shelburne
had explicitly avowed, that his own wishes were of a different nature,
it appeared he had directed general Carleton and admiral Digby, to
acquaint the commander in chief of the American army, and to request
him to inform congress, that the king of Great Britain desirous of
peace, had commanded his ministers about to negociate, to insure
the independence of the thirteen provinces, instead of making it a
condition of a general treaty.*

But when Mr. Oswald, who had been appointed to act as the

---

* This sentiment had been communicated, by order of the minister, in a joint letter
from general Carleton and lord Digby to general Washington, dated New York,
August 2, 1782. [See, *Annual Register* (1783), "Appendix to the Chronicle," pp. 264–
266.]

commissioner of peace in behalf of Great Britain, and to arrange the provisional articles for that purpose, arrived at Paris, in the autumn of one thousand seven hundred and eighty-two, it appeared that his instructions were not sufficiently explicit. They did not satisfy the American agents, deputed by congress to negociate the terms of reconciliation among the contending powers. These [204] were doctor Franklin, John Jay, and John Adams, esquires: Mr. Adams was still at the Hague; but he had been directed by congress to repair to France, to assist his colleagues in their negociations for peace.

The ambiguity of Mr. Oswald's commission, occasioned much altercation between the count de Vergennes and Mr. Jay, on the subject of the provisional articles. Their disputes were not easily adjusted; and the Spanish minister, the count de Aranda, rather inclined to an acquiescence in the proposals of the British commissioner. Mr. Jay however resisted with firmness; and was supported in his opinions by Mr. Adams, who soon after arrived in Paris. But before his arrival, Mr. Reyneval, the secretary and confidential friend of the French minister, repaired rather privately to England. It was suspected, and not without sufficient grounds, that this visit was decidedly intended to procure a conference with lord Shelburne.

It was undoubtedly the wish of both France and England, to exclude America from the right of fishing on the Banks of Newfoundland; an advantage claimed by Americans as a right of nature, from their contiguous situation, and as their right by prescription. The American commissioners insisted, that their claims were equally just with any exclusive pretensions, either of Great Britain or France. The navigation [205] of the Mississippi, British debts, and the American loyalists, were matters of dissension, debate, and difficulty.

The American ministers were not disposed to relinquish any claims of honor, equity, or interest, either to the haughty demands of Great Britain, the intrigues of France, or even to the condescending instructions, in some instances, of their own national congress. This body had, in the enthusiasm of their gratitude for the assistance lent in their distress by France, instructed their agents to take no step of importance, without the advice and counsel of the marquis de la Fayette, which would have given great advantage to the French ministry.*

---

* See journals of congress. [JCC, vols. XXIII, XXIV, and XXV, are filled with discussions of the peace negotiations eventuating in the Treaty of Paris. The ratified Treaty is in XXIV.]

The limits of the *eastern* boundaries of the United States, were a CHAP. XXVI
subject of dispute, thought by some of them of less consequence; but 1 7 8 2
with regard to the *western* territorial rights, the American commissioners
were tenacious indeed. The American territory has been parcelled
out, and patenteed by the sovereigns of Europe, from the Atlantic to
the Pacific Ocean, and by existing treaties, the United States have
no inconsiderable claim in the distribution. Their claims were undoubtedly founded on as equitable a basis as those of Great Britain
and France. The negociating ministers of congress were unwilling
[206] to relinquish any part of their claim; they supported their
independent attitude with manly dignity, nor did they yield in the
smallest degree to the encroaching spirit of Britain.

The American claims to a vast uncultivated tract of wilderness,
which neither Great Britain, France, or America, had any right to
invade, may ultimately prove a most unfortunate circumstance to the
Atlantic states, unless the primary object of the American government
should be, to civilize and soften the habits of savage life. But if the
lust of domination, which takes hold of the ambitious and the powerful
in all ages and nations, should be indulged by the authority of the
United States, and those simple tribes of men, contented with the
gifts of nature, that had filled their forests with game sufficient for
their subsistence, should be invaded, it will probably be a source of
most cruel warfare and bloodshed, until the extermination of the
original possessors. In such a result, the mountains and the plains will
perhaps be filled with a fierce, independent race of European and
American emigrants, too hostile to the borderers on the seas to submit
willingly to their laws and government, and perhaps too distant,
numerous, and powerful, to subdue by arms.*

[207] It was the opinion of some of the American commissioners
for negociating the treaty of peace, that the count de Vergennes was
opposed to the claims of the United States in every stage of the
business; not because, in equity, he thought they had no right to the
fisheries, or the western lands, but from a general unfriendly disposition
to America, and a reluctance to her being declared by Great Britain,

---

* The reader will observe, that the author of this work has been in the habit of making
appropriate observations on events as they passed, and has often hazarded conjectures
on probable results. The work was written a number of years before publication,
but she did not think proper either to erase them, or alter the manner, on revision.
Some of those conjectures have already taken place; others probably may, at some
subsequent period.

CHAP. XXVI   an independent nation. But it is more probable that his cold, equivocal
1 7 8 2   demeanor arose not so much from any personal disaffection to the
people or to individuals, as from a desire to hold the Americans forever
dependent on France. It was suggested by some, to be the policy of
that nation, to endeavour to keep the United States as long as possible
dependent on her aid and protection.

The political creed of monsieur de Vergennes is said to have been,
that

> it was absolutely necessary to hate the English . . . to cajole the Spaniards
> . . . not to hurt the Emperor . . . to live on good terms with Prussia . . .
> to gain over the Dutch . . . to protect the Turks . . . to respect [208]
> Rome . . . to support the infant republic of America . . . to subsidize
> Switzerland . . . and to inspect the conduct of the Colonies.

The French were indeed generally sensible, that most of the citizens
of America spurned at all ideas of a dependence on any foreign power,
after her emancipation from Britain. Yet they were jealous that many
others felt so warmly prejudiced in favor of a nation from whom they
derived their origin, that they little doubted of a renewal of the
connexion with, or even a *dependence* again on, Great Britain, when
the noise of war should cease, and the old habits of intercourse, so
natural from consanguinity, language, and manners, should be re-
assumed. This jealousy was disseminated, and these apprehensions
were expressed, by gentlemen of judgment and penetration throughout
the kingdom of France, both in public and in private circles. Indeed
it was the general opinion there, that a predilection in favor of England
would supersede, in the American mind, a connexion with any other
European power, as soon as recent injuries were forgotten, and the
passions of men had subsided.

Time and opportunities afterwards evinced, that the most liberal
sentiments toward America governed the French nation in general: it
appeared by their conduct in many subsequent transactions, that there
was very little to justify [209] the opinion, that the design of the
nation was to hold the American colonies dependent on France, or
even to continue the alliance but on terms of reciprocity and mutual
advantage.

No national contracts ever yet bound mankind so firmly, as to not
be shaken when they militate with personal or national interests:
much less does a religious observance of treaties prevent their
abandoning former obligations, when the balance of advantage is
likely to be thrown into the hands of their foes.

From the jealousy of the French of the power and rivalry of the CHAP. XXVI
English nation, they might rationally infer, that if the old and natural 1 7 8 2
connexion with the parent state should again be revived, it would cut
off the many advantages they had promised themselves, from an
irreparable breach between Great Britain and the colonies. Thus,
some of the politicians in France judged this a reason sufficient for
the most strenuous efforts in the ancient, hereditary enemy of Great
Britain, to hold, and if possible to bind America by treaties, to
conditions that might in some measure make her dependent on
themselves; at least, these are reasons of policy: reasons of equity,
when inconsistent with interest, are seldom to be found among
statesmen [210] and politicians deputed to transact national affairs.

Among the many difficulties that occurred in the negociations for
peace, the demands made in favor of the *American loyalists*, both by
the British and the French ministry, were not the most easily
accommodated of any of the impediments thrown in the way of
conciliation. But on Mr. Oswald's receiving a new commission from
his court, soon after the count de Reyneval's visit to England,
negociations went forward, all difficulties were surmounted, and
provisional articles of peace between Great Britain and America, were
signed by both parties on the thirtieth of November, one thousand
seven hundred and eighty-two.

In the mean time, the pacific dispositions of the British cabinet
were (as observed) announced to the commanders of their armies and
fleets in America, and through them to congress, and the commander
in chief of the troops of the United States. But though the ideas of
peace were congenial to their wishes, and flattering to their hopes,
they still considered that they had much to apprehend, before they
could quietly sit down in the enjoyment of domestic felicity. The
Americans on this intelligence, lost no part of their vigilance: they
thought it more than ever necessary to be guarded at all points against
the machinations and intrigues [211] of their enemies, the emissaries
of Britain, and the rancor and violence of American refugees and
loyalists. This description of persons were now, more than ever,
embittered by the idea, that England was about to be reconciled to
the colonies on their own terms, absolute and unconditional independence.

Their situation at that time, indeed, appeared to be hapless enough.
The corps of provincial troops that had been exposed in the service
of Britain, and had risked every thing during the war, expected now
to be disbanded on the peace, when both officers and privates had

CHAP. XXVI little to hope from government, according to the provisional articles,
1 7 8 2   and still less from their country.

According to the stipulations of the British negociators, the whole
body of loyalists were left unprovided for any further, than by an
engagement from the American commissioners, to suggest to congress
and to urge in their behalf, a recommendation to the several legislatures
of the United States. The purport of this recommendation was, a
proposal that they would suffer such as had property, to return for a
limited time, to endeavour to recover or re-purchase their confiscated
estates. Twelve months was the time agreed upon by the commissioners, for the residence of the *tories* in their native provinces after
the ratification of peace.

[212] Thus, abandoned by their friends, and cast on the mercy of
their country, they had little lenity to expect from their countrymen,
after a war of seven years, in which many of them had perpetrated
every treacherous and cruel deed, to facilitate the subjugation of their
native land, and to consign succeeding generations to the shackles of
foreign domination. No prospect now appeared before them, but to
decamp in hopeless poverty, and seek some unexplored asylum, far
from the pleasant borders of their natal shores.

Instigated by despair and revenge, some of this class of people had
recently given new proofs of their vindictive feelings, and new
provocations to their countrymen. The most unjustifiable rigor, and
the most outrageous cruelties, had been practiced on those who were
so unfortunate as to fall into their hands. The story of one hapless
victim will be a sufficient specimen of the atrocious length of villany,
to which man may be prompted by disappointment and party rage.

The *Associated Board of Loyalists* at New York, impatient for the
laurels they had expected to reap from the ruin of their neighbours,
their country, and the cause of freedom; provoked at the desertion
of their British patrons, and despairing of the triumph they had
promised themselves in the complete success of the ministerial [213]
troops, and the conquest of America by the arms of Britain; adopted
the unjust and dangerous resolution, of avenging on individuals any
thing which they deemed injurious to their partisans.

They said in their own vindication, and perhaps they had too much
reason to allege, that the troops of congress, in many instances, had
not been less sanguine than themselves, in the inflictions of summary
punishment. Doubtless, both parties were far from exercising that
lenity and forbearance toward their enemies, that both humanity and

equity require. This was often made a pretext to justify enormities,
and even private executions, at which compassion and virtue shudder.

Nothing of the kind had recently occasioned so much public observation, as the wanton murder of a captain Huddy, who, with some others, had been captured by a party of loyalists. He had been some time their prisoner, without any singular marks of resentment; but on the death of a man while a prisoner, killed by the guards from whom he was endeavouring to escape, Huddy was brought out of his cell, deliberately conveyed to the Jersey shore, and without a trial, or any crime alleged against him, he was in the most ludicrous manner hanged, amidst the shouts of his enemies, who exclaimed [214] at the solemn period of execution,—*"Up goes Huddy, for Philip White."*

General Washington considered this transaction as too insolent and cruel to be passed over with impunity: it drew him into the painful resolution, by the advice of the principal officers of the army, to retaliate, by selecting some British prisoner of equal rank to suffer death, unless *Lippencot*, one of the associated loyalists, who commanded the execution of Huddy, was given up to justice. The designation of an innocent victim, to suffer death for the crime of an unprincipled murderer, is a circumstance from which the mind turns with horror; but according to the laws of war there was no receding from the determination, however severe might be the fate of him who was selected as the hapless victim.

General Washington previously demanded justice on the guilty perpetrators of the crime; but sir Henry Clinton and other officers to whom he represented the business, waved a compliance for some time, and appeared in some measure to justify the deed, by asserting that it was done only by way of example, to prevent similar enormities, which their partisans, the loyalists, *said* they had frequently experienced.

Several British officers of the same rank with Huddy, were prisoners in the American camp; [215] and, according to the denunciation made by the American to the British commander in chief, they were brought forward with great solemnity, and a lot cast for the sacrifice to be made to justice. This was done with much tenderness, sympathy, and delicacy; when the lot fell on captain *Asgill* of the guards, a young gentleman of education, accomplishments, and family expectations, who was only nineteen years of age. He was immediately ordered into close custody, until the trial and punishment of captain Lippencot should take place. But his trial was conducted with so much partiality

CHAP. XXVI and party acrimony, that Lippencot was acquitted. After this, sir
1782 Henry Clinton demanded the release of Asgill, as on a legal trial no
guilt was affixed to the transaction of Lippencot.

This occasioned much uneasiness to general Washington and to
others, who though fully convinced of the iniquity of the murderous
party that procured the death of Huddy, yet they wished for the
release of captain Asgill. Every humane bosom revolted at the idea
of seeing a youth, whose character was in all respects fair and amiable,
condemned to die instead of a wretch, whose hands stained with
blood, and his heart hardened by repeated murder and crime, might
have had an earlier claim to a halter.

[216] Great interest was made by many British officers, and by sir
Guy Carleton himself, for the life and release of captain Asgill, but
without effect. He remained a prisoner under the sentence of death,
although execution was delayed, until every compassionate heart was
relieved by the interference of maternal tenderness. The address of
lady Asgill his mother, whose heart was wrung with agonizing fears
for the fate of an only son, procured his release.

After the first pangs of grief and agitation, on the news of his critical
and hazardous situation, had subsided, she wrote in the most pathetic
terms to the count de Vergennes; urging that his influence with
general Washington and the American congress might be exerted, to
save an innocent and virtuous youth from an ignominious death, and
restore the destined victim to the bosom of his mother. This letter,
fraught with sentiments that discovered a delicate mind, an improved
understanding, and a sensibility of heart, under the diction of polished
style, and replete with strong epithets of affection, the French minister
shewed to the king and queen of France, as a piece of elegant
composition.

Though on a despotic throne, where the sovereign disposes of the
subject by his *fiat*, and cuts off life at pleasure, without regret or
hesitation, [217] the king of France and his royal partner were touched
by the distress of this unhappy mother, and lent their interest for the
liberation of her son. The count de Vergennes was directed to send
the letter to general Washington; which he did, accompanied with
the observations of the king and queen, and combined with his own
request in favor of young Asgill.

The commander in chief was happy to transmit to congress, the
several requests and observations, which he had reason to expect
would relieve him from an affair that had embarrassed his mind, both

as a man of humanity and the commander of an army. Congress CHAP. XXVI
immediately directed that captain Asgill should be liberated from 1 7 8 2
imprisonment, and left at his own option to choose his future residence:
on which, he took leave of the army and of America, and repaired to
his friends in England.

The reply of general Washington, and the resolutions of congress,
relative to granting a passport to Mr. Morgan, secretary to general
Carleton, to go to Philadelphia, was not equally condescending. On
his arrival at New York, sir Guy Carleton had requested, that he
might be permitted to send on some letters of compliment [218] to
congress. General Washington forwarded the request, which drew out
a resolve of congress,—"That the commander in chief be hereby
directed to refuse a compliance with the request of general Carleton,
to grant a pass to Mr. Morgan to bring dispatches to Philadelphia."
It was also resolved, that no intercourse should be opened, or that
any of the subjects of Great Britain should be permitted to pass or
repass from the British to the American posts, while the provisional
articles of peace were held in suspense.

This was not only a judicious, but a necessary precaution in the
congress of the United States. At this period, a small circumstance of
intelligence or information might have given a pretext to defeat a
pending negociation for peace. The fleets and armies of Britain still
kept their station in America; while the clashing interests of foreign
nations, with regard to American claims, were not yet adjusted; and
while the loyalists were clamorous and vindictive, watching the
opportunity of impeding the present measures, which, if ratified,
must leave them in a hopeless state of despondency: at the same
time, it set their countrymen on a point of elevation, contrary to their
predictions, their wishes, and their interests, which had prompted
them to opposition, and for which they had hazarded their ease, their
lives, and the friendship [219] and esteem of their former associates
and friends. These people certainly had high claims of gratitude from
the British government, for their unshaken loyalty, through the sharp
conflict that severed the colonies from the dominion of Britain, and
themselves from their native country forever.

CHAPTER XXVII

Discontents with the Provisional Articles • Mr. Hartley sent to Paris • The Definitive Treaty agreed to, and signed by all the Parties • *A General Pacification among the Nations at War* • Mr. Pitt, Prime Minister in England—His Attention to East India Affairs • Some subsequent Observations

CHAP. XXVII [220] After provisional articles for peace had been agreed on at Paris, 1 7 8 2 between the British and American commissioners, the impatient curiosity of the British nation for a full communication of their contents, was inexpressible. The ultimate determinations with regard to the unconditional independence of America, were among the most interesting of their inquiries. But the necessity of concealing affairs of such national moment for a time, within a veil of secrecy, was urged by the ministry, as it would bring on discussions and objections, which might embarrass the work of peace. All ambiguity was opposed in the house of commons by several members, with no small degree of warmth; they insisted that no disguise ought to be used, but that the whole business should be laid open, before irretrievable stipulations should bind the nation to disadvantageous or dishonorary terms. [221] But when the general tenor of the provisional articles was made known, it was far from restoring tranquillity or harmonizing the several parties.

The general dissatisfaction expressed by persons of high rank and consideration, against both the provisional articles with America and the preliminary articles for peace with France, Spain, and Holland, which now lay under consideration, was so great, that many began to be alarmed, lest all pacific measures should be set afloat, and the hope of tranquillity which had dawned upon the nations might yet finally be defeated.

Some of the first characters in the cabinet, the parliament, and the nation, discovered the most singular disgust and uneasiness at the

proposed articles of accommodation, and debate and contention ran
high in both houses of parliament. The lords Walsingham, Stormont,
Sackville, Carlisle, and others, were violent in their opposition to the
whole system of peace comprised in the provisional articles: they
thought the character of the nation tarnished, in the concession made
by the negociators on the part of Britain, in favor of the revolted
colonies; whose obstinacy had involved the crown and the kingdom
in distresses incalculable, but that the nation was not yet so reduced
as to submit to a mean dereliction of their [222] rights: they asserted
that they had yet an army, a navy, and resources sufficient to chastise
the insolence of the house of Bourbon. It was observed, that though
the councils of France had upheld the revolted colonies, in opposition
to the power of Britain, and now justified their bold demands, that
the combined fleets of France and Spain had recently felt the
superiority, and fled from the power, of the British flag.

It was not passed over in silence, that all hearts had lately been
warmed by their gallant conduct, and every tongue loud in the
applauses of the magnanimous officers who had defended Gibraltar:
that the house of commons had expressed their gratitude by a vote
of thanks to governor Elliot and general Boyde, for the astonishing
example of courage, patriotism, and patient suffering, which they had
displayed, in the vigorous defence of a fortress devoted to destruction
by a most formidable foe; that the navy had contributed its full share
in this glorious success, and that the just thanks of the nation had
been offered to lords Howe, Rodney, and others, who were still ready
for the most gallant defence of all the claims of England, against the
combined fleets of France, Spain, and the world.

In short, the sum of their declamations were, that the proud glory
of conquest, which had so [223] often perched on the helmet of
British officers, was not, by the dash of an inexperienced pen,* to be
meanly prostrated to obtain a peace, either from old hereditary
enemies, or the pertinacity and refractory conduct of their own offspring
in the colonies.

Little delicacy was observed. Mr. Oswald's abilities for the business
of a negociator were highly ridiculed: many objections were made,
and copiously dwelt on by the orators in the British parliament, with
regard to the pending articles; particularly, on the right to the fisheries,

---

* Mr. Oswald's. [Richard Oswald, one of the commissioners who negotiated for peace
with John Adams, Benjamin Franklin, John Jay, and Henry Laurens. See, in general,
Annual Register (1783), "History of Europe," pp. 134–167.]

CHAP. XXVII on the boundaries of the United States, the free navigation of the
1 7 8 2 Mississippi, and the forlorn condition of those Americans who had
been attached to the crown from the beginning of the contest. Their
friends asserted, that the abandoning the loyalists, and consigning
them over to the cold recommendation of the American congress,
only on the promise of their commissioners that their situation should
be considered by the several legislatures, and that the legislative
powers should advise to a placable spirit, and urge the people to
forgiveness, was a fallacious security on which no reliance could be
placed. It was observed, that the commissioners themselves could not
expect that such a measure would succeed; they knew too [224] well,
that this class of men were considered in America, as a ten-fold more
inveterate foe than any of the native sons of Britain.

The proposal of their return to and residence in the United States
for a limited term, was viewed by gentlemen of the first penetration
as a chimerical project: they were too well acquainted with human
nature to imagine, that this description of persons would be received
by them, when they knew, that "the Americans in general would
consider it as taking a *viper* into their bosoms, whose nature could
not be altered, and however well fed, its benefactor could not be
secured from its sting."

The neglect of stipulations in favor of a class of people who had
forsaken their country, lost their property, and risked their lives in
the field, from their attachment to the British crown, and their
fondness for the government of England, was styled criminal in every
view; it was asserted that it was marked with cruelty, injustice, and
ingratitude.

Doubtless, many of the advocates of the loyalists in the British
parliament, argued from what they thought the principles of rectitude,
rather than from the prejudices of party; and could those principles
alone have had their full operation in the minds of men, notwithstanding past provocations, it might have been the [225] policy of the
Americans at this period, to have laid aside their prejudices. At the
same time, it would have exemplified their benevolence to have
forgiven, cherished, and secured the friendship of a large body of
people, instead of perpetuating an alienation, and transmitting it from
sire to son, through successive generations. But it was the indispensable
duty of the British government, to protect and to compensate. This
they afterwards did in some instances, in a very ample manner; but
many of this unfortunate class were exposed to sufferings which they

had never contemplated, when they forsook their neighbours, their relations, and their families, for the precarious hope of better fortune from the oppressors of their country.

These and other circumstances shook the minister in his place; he felt he did not stand on very firm ground, however recently encircled by favoritism, though at the summit of power, and still the bubble of popularity; the gale was about to pass off, and leave him in private life, the sport of change, but not in the quietude of retirement. The rivals of lord Shelburne were powerful, his enemies subtil and sagacious; and the inconsistency which appeared in his principles relative to the independence of America, gave them a fair occasion to [226] discuss his opinions, and to displace him from office.

Desirous as was Mr. Fox and some other gentlemen, for a happy accommodation with America, and a happy termination of war with all the nations, they spurned at several of the proposed articles of peace: and singular as it may appear, the consequence of the present fermentation was a second coalition, composed of still more jarring atoms than the first . . . the *leopard* was indeed *to lie down with the lamb.*

Notwithstanding their former disagreement in opinion, their rancor and bitterness on many occasions; antipodes in political sentiment, with regard to the prerogative of the crown, the majesty of the people, and the American war; a strange connexion took place, viewed by the nation as a kind of political phenomenon. Lord North and Mr. Fox were seen acting together in administration, in conjunction with the lords Cavendish and Stormont, Keppel and Carlisle. The duke of Portland was appointed first lord of the treasury in the room of lord Shelburne, who had enjoyed little tranquillity in that elevated station. The reputation of neither party was much enhanced by the coalition; it created a general suspicion of the patriotism of both; and both were considered as acting a part for the gratification of their own [227] interests and passions, rather than from a regard to the public welfare.

Mr. Fox was reproached with forsaking his former friends, and assimilating his character and his attachment, as conveniency required, to the politics of the day. To this he replied, that "for the painful losses he had experienced in his friendships, he must find a consolation in the purity and consistency of his intentions, and that rectitude of design which had ever been his guide in his political career."

While the general expectation of re-sheathing the sword had spread a humane satisfaction over the countenances of many in Europe and

CHAP. XXVII in America, the minds of the contemplative and sagacious characters
1 7 8 2 in the United States were filled with anxiety, on the variety of
difficulties which lay before them. They anticipated the impractica-
bility of disbanding an army become discontented from deficiencies
in payment: they saw the impossibility of a speedy discharge of the
public debt: of defraying the expenses of a long war, and paying up
the arrearages due to the soldiery, who had bravely borne the toils of
the field, amidst poverty, hunger, danger, and death. They were too
well acquainted with human nature to expect, that a people who had
been so long in such a perturbed state should sit down in tranquillity
and order, until some necessary arrangements [228] for the operations
of a free, yet energetic government, should be established. This they
considered, in the situation of their country, a work that required the
talents of the most able statesmen, and the virtues of the most
disinterested patriots, to digest. The jarring interests of the states and
of individuals, and their dissonant opinions of forms and modes of
government, might prevent the adoption of the best that could be
suggested, and create jealousies and ferments that might terminate
in domestic confusion and war, until anarchy or despotism should
succeed.

In addition to all other difficulties apprehended by speculative and
judicious Americans, previous to the provisional articles terminating
in a definitive treaty of peace, they dreaded the idea of a large body
of loyalists left by Great Britain, to make terms of reconciliation with
their offended countrymen.

It was a very precarious hope on which these refugees had to build:
they had little reason (as observed) to expect the resentment of a
whole people would be annihilated, merely by the recommendation
of the American agents: they could not but be sensible, that if the
governing powers were mollified, and should recommend moderation
and forbearance, yet the mutual injuries and affronts between individuals and families, in consequence of political dissonance, [229]
would not be likely to lie dormant, but would be brought back to
recollection on every trivial occasion. It was to be expected that old
animosities would be raked open, that would forever disturb the peace
of society, when they took their stand beside their injured neighbours,
weeping the loss of a father, a husband, or a son, who had perished
in the dreadful conflict, many of them by the hands of a class of men
now thrown back on their wounded feelings.

In the mean time the business of negociation went forward among

the belligerent powers: some new arrangements were made: Mr.
Hartley was sent to Paris, whose commission superseded that of Mr.
Oswald. We have seen that Mr. John Adams had left Holland, and
joined the plenipotentiaries of the United States, previous to the
agreement on provisional articles for peace, signed November, one
thousand seven hundred and eighty-two. He was no favorite of the
officers and administrators of affairs at the Gallican court; his manners
were not adapted to render him acceptable in that refined and polished
nation; nor did he appear to have much partiality for, or confidence
in them. But firm to the interests of his country, and tenacious of its
claims, he advocated and defended them with ability; and by his
determined spirit, was essentially serviceable [230] in maintaining the
stipulations required in behalf of the United States.

Nor was Mr. Jay less strenuous or indefatigable, to counteract every
thing he thought might militate with the interest of America. He
invalidated difficulties as they arose, with the accuracy of the statesman, and obviated every objection to just and equal advantages, in
the treaty which his countrymen required. Dr. Franklin's known
attachment to the interest of the United States, and his conspicuous
talents as a negociator, preclude the necessity of any observations on
his abilities, his character, or his conduct.

It has been before observed, that congress had inadvertently
endeavoured to fetter their agents, by directing them to be under the
councils of France, rather too much for a free and independent nation.
These gentlemen considered such restrictions dishonorary to themselves and their country; and by their vigor, zeal, and address, acted,
through every stage of the business, as the agents of a free nation,
not to be influenced by foreign considerations or councils.

Near ten months elapsed, after signing the provisional articles,
before the definitive treaty was completed. Previous to the adjustment
of all the articles contained in this treaty, much [231] address,
altercation, intrigue, and finesse, among the parties, as is usual on
similar occasions, was intermixed with fair negociation. All prelimi-
naries at length agreed to, this important instrument was signed at
Paris on the third of September, one thousand seven hundred and
eighty-three.

David Hartley, esquire, on the part of Great Britain, and Benjamin
Franklin, John Jay, and John Adams, esquires, in behalf of America,
affixed their names and their seals to the treaty for the restoration of
harmony between Britain, the ancient potent parent, and the eman-

cipated colonies, and sent it forward for the ratification of congress,
and of the British parliament.

The definitive treaty between Great Britain and the United States contained only nine articles. The first of these was a full and complete acknowledgment of the independence of America. *His Britannic Majesty*, in article first,

> acknowledges the United States, *viz.* New Hampshire, Massachusetts Bay, Rhode Island and Providence Plantations, Connecticut, New York, New Jersey, Pennsylvania, Delaware, Maryland, Virginia, North Carolina, South Carolina, and Georgia, to be *Free, Sovereign, and Independent States*; that he treats with them as such; and for himself, his heirs, and successors, relinquishes all claim [232] to the government, property, and territorial rights of the same, and every part thereof.*

On the same day, the third of September, the definitive treaty between Great Britain and France was signed at Versailles, by the duke of Manchester in behalf of the king of England, and on the part of France by the count de Vergennes.

The count de Aranda and the duke of Manchester mutually exchanged their seals for the happy event of peace between England and Spain. The definitive treaty of peace and friendship between his Britannic majesty and the king of Spain, was also signed at Versailles the third day of September, one thousand seven hundred and eighty-three.

All impediments that barred the accommodation between England and Holland had been removed, and peace and harmony restored between his Britannic majesty and the states-general of the United Provinces. Preliminary articles for this purpose were adjusted and signed at Paris by the ministers of the respective courts, on the second of September, one thousand seven hundred and eighty-three.

[233] The king of Sweden had invited a treaty of amity and commerce with America, in a very handsome, complimentary manner. He observed, that he was "desirous of forming a connexion with a people who had so well established their independence, and who, by their wisdom and bravery, so well deserved it." This treaty had been signed the third of April, one thousand seven hundred and eighty-three, and a stipulation made for its continuance for the term of fifteen years, before any revision or renewal should take place.

Denmark ordered the American flag to be treated like that of

---

* See Appendix, Note No. III.

republics of the first order. Indeed, after the independence of the
United States was explicitly acknowledged by the king of Great
Britain, most of the European nations were, or appeared to be, fond
of forming connexions with a young, growing republic. The independent rank of America was now viewed in connexion with her
prolific soil, abundant resources, commercial genius, and political
principles, which indicated her rising into eminence and consideration,
that would set her on a footing with any nation on earth, if she did
not become corrupted by foreign vices, or sunk by the indulgence of
her own foolish passions.

The Batavian republic was the first nation beyond the Atlantic,
after the French, who sent [234] an envoy in form to the congress of
America. On the thirty-first of October, one thousand seven hundred
and eighty-three, Peter John Van Berkel was received by them, as
minister plenipotentiary from the states-general of the United Netherlands. By the president and members of congress, every mark of
respect, cordiality, and friendship, was shewn; and on the other side
it was amply returned, by the address and politeness of the Dutch
minister; who, with manly eloquence and grace, addressed that
venerable body, and expressed his own regard and the esteem of his
constituents, for the citizens of the United States. In the president's
reply, he acknowledged the high sense Americans had of the importance of the alliance, and the gratitude they all felt for the services
rendered the United States by individuals of his nation, and particularly
by himself and family, previous to the completion of the late treaty.

Thus, after the horrors of war had shed their baneful influence over
the nations, without cessation, for seven or eight years; and after the
havoc of human life had, as usual, displayed the absurdity of mankind,
in the delight they seem to discover in the destruction of their own
species; a truce to the miseries of the inhabitants of the earth, on one
side of the globe, was promised for a season. Though the nations had
been long engaged in war, peace seemed now to lift up her declined
head, and promise a [235] general tranquillity. Her advances were
made across the Atlantic; yet no official accounts were received by
congress, that a definitive treaty had been signed by the ministers of
the several belligerent powers, until the conclusion of the year one
thousand seven hundred and eighty-three.

It has already been observed, that the provisional and preliminary
articles for a general pacification among the contending powers, had
been signed at Paris, November the twenty-ninth, one thousand

seven hundred and eighty-two; but the completion of the definitive
treaty, productive of a general peace, was not agreed to until the
succeeding autumn; when, as related above, the signatures and seals
of the commissioners on all sides, were affixed to the several stipulated
articles, and the world relieved from a long constrained situation of
mind, between hope, expectation, and fear.

Yet the intelligence of the spring of one thousand seven hundred
and eighty-three, had been equally impressive in the American army,
as if peace had actually been proclaimed by sound of trumpet. Nor
was it strange that the military departments, nor indeed that all the
inhabitants of the United States, should feel the same impression.
The intelligence of the present prospects of a complete accommodation
of existing differences, was accompanied with [236] private as well as
public letters from Mr. Adams, Mr. Jay, and other distinguished
Americans, replete with the strongest assurances, that hostilities would
not be recommenced; and that the fleets and armies of Great Britain
would, in a few months, be withdrawn from the ports and cities of
the United States.

But there was yet much to be done on both sides of the water. It
could not be expected, that after a convulsion of such magnitude,
that the American officers and soldiers could at once retire, and sit
down quietly, each under his own vine and fig-tree; or that the
turbulent spirit of hostile nations could in a moment be tranquillized;
much less, that the pride of the British ministry and parliament should
suffer them to settle down in tranquil repose among themselves, after
the long series of mortification, discontent, and disunion, that had
embittered every department, and almost every individual against the
political opinions of his neighbour, and the civil and political administration of the affairs of his country.

The preliminary and provisional articles had terminated in a definitive treaty of peace: in this, the general sense of the nation, and the
wishes of the people were gratified. Yet there were still sources of
discontent sufficient to indicate, that the present ministry stood on
slippery ground.

[237] Lord North had been long unpopular: Mr. Fox had many and
potent enemies; but, "naturally of a comprehensive mind, and
constitutionally fraught with good humor and general kindness, the
field of popular applause seemed to be perfectly congenial to him."
But he had a powerful rival in a son of the late favorite of the nation,
lord Chatham. This young gentleman had in a remarkable manner,
won the favor of his sovereign and the hearts of the people: on many

interesting questions he had argued on the popular side, and had
gained an ascendency that promised eminence, celebrity, and station,
in the first grade of office and influence.

He was among the most strenuous advocates for a reform in
parliament: he was zealous for a commercial treaty with the United
States, and ridiculed the language, the conduct, and the impediments
thrown in the way; and condemned the regulations and restrictions
on the American trade, which, he observed, must forever keep open
the door of animosity between the two countries.

Nor did he less oppose and ridicule the India bill, so much the
subject of investigation and discussion, introduced by Mr. Fox, and
rejected by a majority of the house of lords. But the confusions and
distractions in the East Indies, required that some energetic and wise
measures [238] should be immediately adopted, to reform abuses,
and to restore justice and peace in that oppressed country. This
produced a second India bill, brought forward by Mr. Pitt himself,
which was also rejected, and the door still left open for much contention
and debate, relative to the affairs of India, and the distresses of the
unhappy inhabitants.

Thus animosities were kindled among the first characters in the
nation, and discontents fomented until every thing verged to the
extreme of disunion. "It was impossible for Mr. Fox to do any thing
in a cold, uninterested, or indifferent manner; he therefore always
went considerable lengths for the attainment of his object." But he
finally lost ground, and left his rival to wave his laurels triumphantly
in the field of party, and the favor of his king.

The fluctuation of office, and the changes in administration, had
been so frequent in the present reign, that it was viewed as a thing
of course, on every dispute or variation of opinion on great political
questions. From the accession of George the third, in one thousand
seven hundred and sixty-one, to one thousand seven hundred and
eighty-three, when lord Shelburne came in, there had been many
different hands who had taken the helm at the head of the [239]
ministry, and set the political bark afloat in a tempest, without the
ability to recover and moor it in the haven of peace.

In these circumstances, and at this critical period, Mr. *William Pitt*,
in the fire of youth, in the pride of brilliant talents, and with the
ambition, if not the hereditary capacity, of the aged statesman, was
appointed chancellor of the exchequer. Tenacious of his own character,
he held the high office in spite of opposition or flattery; and so
perseveringly stood his ground, and held the reins of power so long,

CHAP. XXVII
1 7 8 3

that his friends ceased to fear his removal, and his enemies at last despaired of carrying any point against a minister, that was become at once a favorite both of the prince and the people.

Notwithstanding the abilities of the new minister, and the exertions of some of his predecessors, now out of place; notwithstanding a pacification had recently taken place among the European powers; Great Britain was still tottering under the enormous expenses of the late war, and her own internal dissensions on subjects of magnitude and importance. Men of the first abilities and information, were wide in opinion, and divided on every political point; the spirit of party was heightened, and produced continual altercation in parliament, on the conduct, projects, and character, of the young minister. [240] Supported by royal favor, and sufficiently conscious of his own talents, he was not borne down by any opposition. It was soon perceptible, that the embarrassments of government, the derangement in political, commercial, domestic, and foreign affairs, still required much energy and decision, and perhaps the capacity of older and more experienced statesmen.

The cruel mismanagement in the East Indies interested the whole nation. The derangement and distraction of their affairs there, the enormities committed, and the tragical scenes of barbarity perpetrated, under the presidency of Warren Hastings, governor general of Bengal, which reduced the country to the extreme of penury and misery, were afterwards copiously displayed and amply detailed, in his long protracted trial. This finally terminated without decision on delinquency, or satisfaction to the public.

The dreadful famine in Calcutta, in one thousand seven hundred and seventy-nine, is well known: that which succeeded it in one thousand seven hundred and eighty-one was still more deplorable, when 14,000 persons died weekly, of hunger, at Madras; while the provinces of Oude and Benares suffered in equal degree, under the same calamity, brought on by means which will never be blotted from [241] the memory of man.* These were too complicated and diffuse

---

* Read the story of the nabob of Oude—† of Cheit-Sing—of the widow of Sujah Dowla—of the conquest of the Benares—the treatment of the nabobs of Bengal; and indeed of all who fell under the power of the English government, in their wars with the unfortunate Indians. These are to be found in a variety of authentic accounts of the conduct and intercourse of the English with the oriental nations.

† See a part of a speech made by Mr. Sheridan on this subject, Appendix, Note No. IV.

for a place here, but some cursory observations on the conduct of
British officers in that country, may be admitted.

A specimen of the tragedy acted by general Matthews at Onore, where he directed no quarter should be given, but every man be put to the sword, will be impressive from an extract of a letter from one of his own officers. He observed, that

> The carnage was great; we trampled thick on the dead bodies that were strewed in the way: it was rather shocking to humanity, but such are only secondary considerations; and to a soldier whose bosom glows with heroic glory, they are thought accidents of course: his zeal makes him aspire after further victory.

[242] What a perversion of just ideas! The true glory of man is benignity and kindness to his fellow-mortals; nor can even military glory be enhanced by the triumphant butchery of mankind. But the same cruel apathy expressed by one of them, seemed to pervade most of the officers on this expedition: the riches and splendor of the peninsula, and the extermination of the inhabitants that they might possess their wealth, seemed to be the only object.

From Onore, general Matthews proceeded to Hydernagur, the capital of Canara. It is true, by astonishing feats of valor, he reached the metropolis, where the wealth of the inhabitants was immense. The place was surrendered by capitulation; the general possessed of the treasure, and no distribution made. The avarice of the officers to obtain their full share of the plunder, raised murmur and mutiny that were not easily quieted; nor was it ever ascertained, in whose coffers the whole was finally deposited.

Before general Matthews returned to Bombay, he sent a detachment from Hydernagur to Annanpour, under the command of major Campbell; the orders were for a *storm* and *no quarter*. The cruel mandates were received with alacrity, and put in execution without delay: every man in the place was put to the sword, except one horseman, who escaped after being wounded in three different places. The [243] women, unwilling to be separated from their relations, or exposed to the brutal licentiousness of the soldiery, threw themselves in multitudes into the moats with which the fort was surrounded. Four hundred beautiful young women, pierced with the bayonet, and expiring in each other's arms, were in this situation treated by the British with every kind of outrage. The avenging hand of justice soon overtook the barbarous, butchering Matthews; he fell into the hands of Tippoo Saib, after that victorious commander had re-captured

CHAP. XXVII   Hydernagur, was loaded with chains, imprisoned, and soon after put
1 7 8 3   to death by his orders.*

For a further detail of the enormities committed by the servants of
Britain, and the sufferings of the inhabitants of India for a number of
years, without mitigation, the reader is referred to the history of that
unfortunate country. There he will find a description of a great part
of this garden of nature, whose prolific shoots have expanded over
the four quarters of the globe, few of whose inhabitants have yet
arrived to a perfect knowledge of the arts, the ingenuity, the sciences,
contained in their Shanscript and other languages.

[244] Indeed, new discoveries have been recently brought to light,
by the investigation of learned and virtuous Englishmen; who, while
pursuing their inquiries, weep to behold so fair a spot of creation†
bathed in the blood of its native sons, by the hands of a nation who
boast higher degrees of civilization, without possessing their simplicity,
urbanity, and perhaps their knowledge. But their progress in the arts,
their histories of the first progenitors of mankind, their astronomical
discoveries, and their knowledge of nature and its operations, must
now lay buried with the wreck of their fortunes, and many of them
enveloped in the rubbish of complete ruin, brought on them by
European avarice and ambition.

But a correction of some abuses in India, took place early in the
administration of Mr. Pitt: new regulations were adopted; and critical
inquiry made into the conduct of the East India [245] company, and
their officers: several of the old officers of government were removed,
and men of more humanity sent forward in their places. Among them,
sir William Jones was appointed one of the judges of the supreme
court of judicature. The character of this gentleman deserves every
encomium: from his writings and the testimony of contemporaries,
he was an honor to his country, a benefactor to mankind, and an
ornament to the world. His elegant manners, profound erudition,

---

* It has been said, that the manner of his death was that of pouring melted gold down
his throat: a strong expression of the ideas the natives had of his avarice.

† BENGAL has been described as exhibiting the most charming and picturesque
scenery, opening into extensive glades, covered with a fine turf, and interspersed
with woods filled with a variety of birds of beautiful colors; amongst others, peacocks
in abundance, sitting on the vast horizontal branches, displayed their dazzling
plumes to the sun; the Ganges winding its mighty waters through the adjacent
plains, adding to the prospect inexpressible grandeur: while the artist at his loom,
under the immense shade of the banyan-tree, softened his labor by the tender
strains of music.

pure morals, and strict justice, were conspicuous in all the transactions
of his life. The deep researches of sir William Jones in ancient oriental
history, have thrown great light on the customs, manners, habits, and
the various religions among the Indians, both ancient and modern.
His learned labor must undoubtedly tend to improvements in science,
and the culture of virtue and true religion, through the enlightened
parts of the world; and perhaps to soften and humanize the hearts of
his own countrymen, in their future unwarrantable invasions of the
inhabitants of the East.

The *English* are, indeed, an astonishing nation. Though frequently
involved in hostilities with half the world; confounded by the immensity of their own national debt, accumulating almost beyond
calculation; plunged in luxury and venality; their manners and their
constitution [246] corrupted; yet, by their extensive commerce, the
strength of their navy, their valor, their genius, and their industry,
they surmount all embarrassments with address and facility, and rise
superior to evils that would augur the downfal of any other nation on
earth.

No country has produced men more learned and liberal, of more
comprehensive genius, virtue, and real excellence, than England; yet
the contrast may as justly be exhibited there, as in any part of the
world. But the balance of real merit, both individual and national,
must be left to the all-pervading eye, which, with a single glance,
surveys the moral and intellectual system of creation. We now leave
them to the rotations of time, and the re-action of human events, to
the period which shall be pointed by the providential government of
HIM, to whom a thousand years are as one day; when they also may
be viewed a spectacle of wo, by the remnant of nations, annihilated
by their rapacity, ambition, and victorious arms.

Let us hasten to turn our eyes from the miserable Mahrattas, the
desolated tribes of Indostan, and the naked Carnatic,* divested of
every thing that had breathed, by the ravages of a [247] relentless
foe. A dead and dreary silence reigns over an extent of five or six
hundred miles of these once full peopled plains. Nor will we dwell
longer on any of the proud projects of conquest in the cabinet of
Great Britain, either in the East or the West; but carry the mind
forward, and indulge a pleasing anticipation of peace and independence
to the *United States of America.*

---

* See Mr. Burke's speech in the house of commons, relative to the desolation in the
  Carnatic. [See *Cobbett*, XXII: 126–131 (April 30, 1781).]

CHAPTER XXVIII

Peace proclaimed in America • General Carleton delays the Withdraw of the Troops from New York • Situation of the Loyalists—Efforts in their Favor by some Gentlemen in Parliament—Their final Destination—Their Dissatisfaction, and subsequent Conduct

[248] The discordant sounds of war that had long grated the ears of the children of America, were now suspended, and the benign and heavenly voice of harmony soothed their wounded feelings, and they flattered themselves the dread summons to slaughter and death would not again resound on their shores. The independence of America acknowledged by the first powers in Europe, and even Great Britain willing to re-sheathe the sword on the same honorable terms for the United States, every prospect of tranquillity appeared.

These were events for which the statesman had sighed in the arduous exertions of the cabinet; for which the hero had bared his breast, and the blood of the citizens had flowed in copious streams on the borders of the Atlantic, from the river St. Mary's to the St. Croix, on the eastern extreme of the American territory. Peace was proclaimed in the American army, [249] by order of the commander in chief, on the nineteenth of April, one thousand seven hundred eighty-three. This was just EIGHT YEARS from the memorable day, when the first blood was drawn in the contest between the American colonies and the parent state, in the fields of *Concord* and *Lexington*.

The operation and consequences of the restoration of peace, were now the subject of contemplation. This opened objects of magnitude indeed, to a young republic, which had rapidly passed through the grades of youth and puberty, and was fast arriving to the age of maturity: a republic consisting of a number of confederated states, which by this time had received many as inhabitants, who were not originally from the stock of England. Some of them, indeed, were from more free governments, but others had fled from the slavery of despotic courts; from their numbers and abilities they had become respectable, and their opinions weighty in the political scale. From these and other circumstances it might be expected, that in time, the general enthusiasm for a republican system of government in America, might languish, and new theories be adopted, or old ones modified under different names and terms, until the darling system of [250] the inhabitants of the United States, might be lost or forgotten in a growing rabiosity for monarchy.

Symptoms of this nature, already began to appear in the language of some interested and ambitious men, who endeavoured to confound ideas, and darken opinion, by asserting that *republicanism* was an indefinite term. In social circles they frequently insinuated, that no precise meaning could be affixed to a word, by which the people were often deceived and led to pursue a shadow instead of an object of any real stability. This was indeed, more the language of art than principle, and seemed to augur the decline of public virtue in a free state.

It required the utmost vigilance to guard against, and counteract designs thus secretly covered. It was not unexpected by the judicious observers of human conduct, that many contingencies might arise, to defeat or to render fruitless the efforts that had been made on the practicability of erecting and maintaining a pure, unadulterated, republican government.

Time must unfold the futility of such an expectation, or establish the system on a basis, that will lead mankind to rejoice in the success of an experiment that has been too often tried in vain. Those who have been nurtured in [251] the dark regions of despotism, who have witnessed the sale of the peasantry with the glebe they have cultivated from infancy, and who have seen the fire and the son, transferred with the stables and the cattle, from master to master, cannot realize the success of a theory that has a tendency to exalt the species, and elevate the lower grades of mankind to a condition nearer to an equality with adventitious superiority. It is not wonderful, that a people of this description and education, should be incredulous of the utility of more free modes of government. They are naturally tenacious of old customs, habits, and their own fortuitous advantages; they are unable to form an idea of general freedom among mankind, without distinction of ranks that elevate one class of men to the summit of pride and insolence, and sink another to the lowest grade of servility and debasement.

But Americans born under no feudal tenure, nurtured in the bosom of mediocrity, educated in the schools of freedom; who have never been used to look up to any lord of the soil, as having a right by prescription, habit, or hereditary claim, to the property of their flocks, their herds, and their pastures, may easily have been supposed to have grown to maturity with very different ideas, and with a disposition to [252] defend their allodial inheritance to the last moment of their lives.

The United States of America, however, had yet many matters of the highest importance to adjust. They had many descriptions of persons to quiet, and many circumstances connected with foreign nations that required diplomatic discussion, particularly with regard to the laws of trade and the regulation of commerce, both at home and abroad, before a stable form of government could either be adopted or organized. The army was not yet disbanded, and a powerful body of loyalists were retarding the completion of some of the articles in the treaty of peace, and embarrassing the commander in chief of the British army, by their murmurs and discontents.

When sir Henry Clinton was recalled from the command of the king's forces in America, he was succeeded by sir Guy Carleton, who was vested with a very extensive commission. He had the direction and government of all military affairs in Canada, New-York, and wherever else the crown of England claimed any stand in the United States.

According to the articles of the definitive treaty, all the posts held by the troops of his Britannic majesty within the territories of the [253] United States, were to be immediately evacuated; and on the certitude of a general accommodation, every British and Hessian soldier was to be drawn off and retire from the continent. But a delay took place, which, in some instances, we shall see was fatal to the peace of the United States.

The British troops still occupied New-York, though by treaty it was to have been relinquished on the declaration of peace. It is true, however, that general Carleton had usually conducted with great politeness both towards Congress and the commander in chief of the armies of the United States; but he was himself embarrassed between his duty and his honour.

The reasons for staying longer at New-York than was stipulated by treaty, were not grounded on mere plausible pretence. The principal argument offered by him for a non-compliance with orders, and

delaying the expectations of the Americans, was the obligation he CHAP. XXVIII
thought Great Britain under, to protect the loyalists. At the same 1 7 8 3
time, his own mind was impressed with the necessity and justice of
aid and support to a body of hapless men, "who ought not be thrown
by as an useless garment, when administration no longer needed the
[254] assistance of disaffected Americans and refugees."

Whether wholly influenced by compassion towards the loyalists, or
whether stimulated by political reasons in the cabinet of his court,
general Carleton did not appear to shew any extraordinary degree of
moderation, in consequence of the delay. Several months after the
proclamation for peace, general Carleton wrote the president* of the
congress of the United States, that he wished to accelerate his orders
to evacuate New York; and that "he should lose no time, as far as
depended upon him, to fulfil his majesty's commands, but that the
difficulty of assigning the precise period for this event, is of late
greatly increased."

He complained in this letter, that the violence of the Americans,
which broke out soon after the cessation of hostilities, increased the
number of their countrymen who looked to him, for escape from
threatened destruction: and that these terrors had of late been so
considerably augmented, that almost all within the lines, conceived
the safety, both of their property and their lives, depended upon
being removed by him, which rendered it impossible to say, when
the evacuation could be completed. He said,

> whether [255] they had just grounds to assert, that there was either no
> government within the limits of the American territory, for common
> protection, or that it secretly favoured the committees, in the sovereignty
> they assume and are actually exercising, he should not pretend to determine.

He observed, that

> as the public papers furnished repeated proofs, not only of a disregard to
> the articles of peace, but contained barbarous menaces from committees
> formed in various towns, cities, and districts, and even at Philadelphia,
> the very place which the congress had chosen for their residence; that he
> should show an indifference to the feelings of humanity, as well as to the
> honour and interest of the nation whom he served, to leave any of the
> loyalists, that are desirous to quit the country, a prey to the violence, they
> conceive they have so much cause to apprehend.

* See general Carleton's letter to Mr. Boudinot, then president. [*Annual Register*
(1783), "State Papers," pp. 265–266.]

He intimated that congress might learn from his letter, how much depended upon themselves and the subordinate legislatures, to facilitate the service he was commanded to perform; that they might abate the fears and lessen the number of the emigrants. But should these fears continue, and compel such multitudes to remove, he should hold himself acquitted [256] from every delay in fulfilling his orders, and the consequences which may result therefrom. He also added, that

> it made no small part of his concern, that the congress had thought proper to suspend, to so late an hour, recommendations stipulated by the treaty, and in the punctual performance of which, the king and his ministers had expressed such entire confidence.

This letter was considered by congress, the officers of the army, and the people in general, as evasive, if not affrontive; and taught them the necessity of standing on their guard, and holding their arms in their hands, until the removal of all hostile appearances, the entire evacuation of New-York, and until the fleets of his Britannic majesty were withdrawn from the American seas.

The loyalists were still very numerous in the city, though some of them had dispersed themselves in despair, to seek an asylum without much dependence on government. Their situation was indeed truly deplorable; they had every thing to fear if the British troops withdrew and left them to the clemency of their countrymen now elated by success, and more hardened against the feelings of humanity, by the cruel scenes of war they had witnessed.

[257] The conduct of the American refugees had been such from the commencement of hostilities, that they could not but be conscious, as expressed by a celebrated American patriot,* that "they were responsible for all the additional blood that had been spilt by the addition of their weight in the scale of the enemy." He observed,

> they were sensible they could never regain the confidence of their late fellow-subjects, whose very looks must confound and abash men, who in defiance of nature and education, have not only by a reversed ambition, chosen *bondage* before *freedom*, but waged an infernal war against their nearest connexions, for not making the like abhorred election.

Every one will readily conceive, that these people at this time, were really in a distressed situation. Their own ideas of the improb-

---

* Governor Livingston. [Source not identified.]

ability of harmony and quiet, even if permitted to return to the bosom
of their country, comported with the above observations. These were
strongly expressed in a memorial to the British secretary of state,
forwarded by them soon after the definitive treaty.

In this memorial they observe,

> that the personal animosities that arose from civil dissensions, had been
> heightened by the blood [258] that had been shed, to such a degree that
> the two parties could never be reconciled. They therefore prayed, that
> they might have an assignment of lands, and assistance from the crown,
> to make settlements for themselves and families.

The experiment of this intermixture and reunion of heterogeneous
characters, had not yet been tried; but from the temper of the people
throughout the continent, there did not appear to be any great
probability, that the recommendation of congress to the legislative
bodies, would disarm the resentment, or eradicate the painful ideas
that the presence of American refugees would revive. The minds of
many had suffered too much in their persons or connexions, from
such as they thought ought to have assisted in the struggle for the
independence of their country, to be healed in a moment.

It is beyond a doubt that there was little conciliatory feeling on
either side; so far from it, the vanquished in New-York were threatened
with severe vengeance by one party, while the other poured out the
most bitter expressions of resentment against the congress and the
people of America, now rejoicing in the success of their own arms.
This temper was far from justifiable: it was neither acting as [259]
wise politicians, or real christians; but it was the natural ebullition of
injured and provoked human nature, which too seldom pays the
strictest regard to national faith, honor, or moral precept, when passion
has been wrought up beyond a certain degree of forbearance.

It is matter of wonder, that the whole class of loyalists, though
disarmed of power, were so imprudent as not to discover any disposition
to harmonize with, or a wish to conciliate the affections of their former
friends and associates. They expressed their rancor on all occasions,
and when assured that the definitive treaty was actually signed, they
broke out into the most violent paroxysms of rage and disappointment.
Epithets of the most indecent and vindictive nature often fell from
their lips, and increased the general disgust planted in the bosoms of
their countrymen from their first defection from the American cause.

The recent outrages that had been committed, sanctioned by orders from the *Associated Board of Loyalists,* as they styled themselves, had given reason to apprehend that a spirit of revenge would be excited, that might preclude all lenity and forbearance in the minds of those citizens who had been pillaged, insulted, and abused. It was justly apprehended, that the unhoused mourners for fathers, brothers, or [260] beloved sons, betrayed into the hands of pitiless enemies by this description of persons, could not readily forgive.

In order to check this rancorous spirit, or rather to lessen the influence of such an invidious temper, and prevent the fatal effects that might on both sides arise from its indulgence, general Carleton soon after his arrival at New York, had directed the dissolution of the society, and forbidden any more meetings as an associated body, under any name or form. But he considered the situation of this class, more particularly those who had been active members of the Board of Associated Loyalists, as too hazardous to desert at the present moment. It has been observed, that he thought it his indispensable duty to reside in the city, and to retain the British troops for a time, for the protection of all the unhappy people under the description of *tories* or *loyalists*. He therefore waited until some arrangements and proper provisions could be made for their subsistence.

Notwithstanding the British negociators had been obliged to leave them in a very indeterminate situation, or recede from the negociations for peace, great attention had been paid to this description of persons in the debates of the British parliament. Sir Adam Ferguson had [261] suggested, some time before the peace, in the course of debate, that they ought to be divided into three classes;

> first, those who had early taken arms in the cause of Britain; secondly, those who had fled to England with their families; lastly, those who had continued at home, and did not act, or style themselves *loyalists* until the king's troops called them out to express their opinions, by personally acting against the Americans.

He said, that "a discrimination ought to be made, and that they should be rewarded according to their merits and sufferings."

This discrimination was attended with difficulty; but every one thought that government was under obligations to each of these classes that could not be winked out of sight; but they all had claims of consideration and compensation, for their efforts to support the measures of parliament, if not for any essential services rendered to the crown.

Many noblemen were zealous that suitable provision should be

made for the American loyalists of all descriptions, and no one CHAP. XXVIII
appeared more interested in their favor than lord Shelburne. In 1 7 8 3
consequence of this, some arrangements were made for their establishment, and an apportionment of lands assigned them in the province
of Nova Scotia. They were there assisted [262] by the British
government, to erect a town, which was incorporated by the name of
Shelburne, and patronized by his lordship. But it was a sterile spot,
and many of them took better ground for themselves at New
Brunswick, St. John's, and other parts of Nova Scotia, Canada, and
within the limits of any part of the American territory yet claimed by
Great-Britain.

The officers of the provincial corps were allowed half pay for life,
but notwithstanding any partial compensations made to the loyalists
by the British government, their situation in every view was truly
pitiable. Many of them had been long separated from their families
and tenderest connexions; they had flattered themselves with the
hope of returning in very different circumstances at the conclusion of
a war, which they had expected would much sooner have terminated,
and have terminated in a manner, equal to their sanguine ideas of
the irresistible arm of Britain.

The most exalted opinion of the strength and power of that nation,
a reverential attachment to the monarch, and the fond influence of
old habits of government, and obedience to parliamentary regulations,
had all co-operated with their ideas of the complete subjugation of
the American colonies. They naturally calculated [263] that they
should then be restored to their former residences, and become the
favorite subjects of royal patronage. They had reason to expect, that
their unshaken loyalty, and uniform exertions to facilitate the designs
of the court of St. James, justly deserved a higher tribute of gratitude
from the crown than they had received. Their banishment to an iron
shore, with a cold recommendation to the state legislatures to permit
them to revisit those friends, that might yet have survived the hand
of time and misfortune; and to make an effort to recover their scattered
property that had frequently shifted hands, as is usual in the confusion
of revolutionary struggles, could not be viewed by them as very high
marks of consideration.

Yet many of them submitted afterwards to their condition, with a
spirit of enterprize and resolution, and endeavoured to establish their
new settlements on a respectable footing. But their embarrassments
in a situation so new, the soil unprolific, the climate frigid, and the
natural propensity of the human mind to sigh after a return to its

CHAP. XXVIII natal spot, to finish the career of present existence, all co-operated to

1 7 8 3 defeat their success. *Shelburne*, the pride of their hopes, was in a few years nearly depopulated, and many expensive and elegant buildings left without an inhabitant.

[264] As we shall not again have any further occasion to recur to the subject of the loyalists, a few observations, the result of their subsequent conduct, may be here introduced with propriety, though it is rather an anticipation.

Those who fixed themselves on the more fertile borders of the Bay of Fundy and St. John's river, succeeded better than those at Shelburne; but though few of them felt themselves greatly obligated to the justice or the generosity of the British government, they continued their fealty and attachment to the crown of England, with the same zeal and fervor which formerly glowed in the bosoms of the inhabitants of all the American colonies.

The planting a new settlement is an unpleasant task to those who have been used to foster habits, from the industry, fatigue, and self-denial, necessary to promote its success. Nor does the laborious exercise of felling trees and erecting log-huts for themselves, yield much satisfaction to those of a rougher class, but in the anticipation of better prospects in future. The hand of time, which generally ameliorates the miseries of man, or reconciles the mind to its misfortunes, was not sufficiently lenient, to make happy these once voluntary emigrants, either in Canada, Nova Scotia, or even in England. Impatient under the sentence of exile from [265] their native land, some of them returned to America as aliens, and availed themselves of the benefit of the act of naturalization, afterwards passed by the American government, in favour of those who wished to become citizens of the United States. But under the influence of their old prejudices in favour of monarchy, and their minds lowered down by habit, to succumb to the doctrine of passive obedience, some of them were restless and uneasy in the society of men, who had recently suffered so much to procure liberty and independence to themselves and posterity. They fomented divisions, disseminated party opinions, ridiculed the principles of the revolution, and vilified many of the first characters who had exerted themselves to secure the liberties of their country. These, combined with other circumstances that took place, seemed to throw a temporary veil over the republican system.

All those who returned to the bosom of their country after the peace, ought not to be implicated as inheriting such vindictive dispositions. Whenever the loyalists are mentioned in a collective body, it is but just to make a reservation of some exceptions in favor of such as fled, from the terrors awakened in their bosoms by the convulsive sounds of war. [266] These only wished to return to their native soil, and enjoy a quiet residence in the land which gave them birth. Persons of this description were to be found in every state in the union, after they were permitted by treaty to return. These were objects of commiseration rather than blame. They had lost their property, their friends, and their felicity, from a mistaken apprehension of the power of the hostile arm that had been stretched out for the invasion of America, before their emigration.

Whatever testimony truth may require from an historian, when investigating the motives of action in public bodies, or scrutinizing individual character, the proneness of man to err, should always admonish him that it is an indispensable duty, "to be candid where he can."

It is to be lamented, when political opinion is the only bond of attachment, when merit, however conspicuous, is not acknowledged, but by the party in which it is enlisted, the web of prejudice is then so thickly interwoven, that no ray of brotherly kindness can penetrate, and that charity which covers a multitude of sins is totally annihilated.

Though the anticipation in the preceding short chapter, may not exactly accord with the rules of historic writing, no other apology [267] is necessary, than that the awakened curiosity of the reader, as well as his compassion, will naturally excite a wish to trace the destiny of a body of men, who had set their faces against the liberties of mankind and the exertions of their countrymen. This class had hazarded their own fortune and liberty, which were staked against the independence of America, and the freedom of future generations.

This cursory review of the situation of those unhappy emigrants, the treatment which they received from the British government, their destination and compensation in consequence of their attachment to the monarch of England, will doubtless be permitted, though not in due order of time, as it was the natural result of a survey of their character, their condition, their fate at the close of the war, and their subsequent deportment.

CHAPTER XXIX

Conduct of the American Army on the News of Peace • Mutiny and Insurrection • Congress surrounded by a Part of the American Army • Mutineers disperse • Congress removes to Princeton • Order of Cincinnati • Observations thereon

[268] Before we close the curtain on the scenes that have empurpled the plains of America, with the blood of some of the best of her citizens, or before we congratulate the European world on the opportunity of closing the temple of *Janus,* for a season, it is proper to retrospect and mark some of the intermediate transactions of the American troops, from the capture of lord Cornwallis and his army to the proclamation for peace, and the disbanding the troops of the United States.

We have seen through the narration of events during the war, the armies of the American states suffering hunger and cold, nakedness, fatigue, and danger, with unparalleled patience and valor. A due sense of the importance of the contest in which they were engaged, and the certain ruin and disgrace in which themselves and their children would be involved on the defeat of their object, was a strong stimulus [269] to patient suffering. An attachment to their commanding officers, a confidence in the faith of congress, and the sober principles of independence, equity, and equality, in which the most of them had been nurtured, all united to quiet any temporary murmurs that might arise from present feelings, and to command the fidelity of soldiers contending for personal freedom, and the liberties of their country.

The deranged state of the American finances from a depreciating currency, the difficulty of obtaining loans of monies, and various other causes, had sufficiently impressed them with the danger that threatened the great object, the independence of the United States of America. These circumstances had led the army to submit to a delay

of payment of their equitable dues, notwithstanding their personal CHAP. XXIX
sufferings, and to wait the effects of more efficient stipulations for 1 7 8 3
adequate rewards in some future day.

But on the certain intelligence that peace was at hand, that it had
been proposed to disband the army by furloughs, and that there was
no appearance of a speedy liquidation of the public debts, many of
both officers and soldiers grew loud in their complaints, and bold in
their demands. They required an immediate payment of all arrearages;
and insisted on the security of the commutation engaged by congress
some time before, on the recommendation of general [270] Washington: he had requested, that the officers of the army might be assured
of receiving seven years' whole pay, instead of half pay for life, which
had been stipulated before: this, after reducing the term to five years,
congress had engaged.

They also demanded a settlement for rations, clothing, and proper
consideration for the delay of payment of just debts, which had long
been due, and an obligation from congress for *compensation*, or
immediate payment. They chose general M'Dougal, colonel Brooks,
and colonel Ogden, a committee from the army to wait on congress,
to represent the general uneasiness, and to lay the complaints of the
army before them, and to enforce the requests of the officers, most
of whom were supposed to have been concerned in the business.
Anonymous addresses were scattered among the troops; poisonous
suggestions whispered, and the most inflammatory resolutions drawn
up, and disseminated through the army: these were written with
ingenuity and spirit, but the authors were not discovered.

Reports were every where circulated, that the military department
would do itself justice; that the army would not disband until congress
had acceded to all their demands; and that they would keep their
arms in their hands, until they had compelled the delinquent states
to [271] a settlement, and congress to a compliance with all the claims
of the public creditors.

These alarming appearances were conducted with much art and
intrigue. It was said, and doubtless it was true, that some persons not
belonging to the army, and who were very *adroit* in fiscal management,
had their full share in ripening the rupture.

Deeply involved in public contracts, some of the largest public
creditors on the continent were particularly suspected of fomenting a
spirit, and encouraging views, inconsistent with the principles and
professions of the friends to the revolution. These were disgusted at

CHAP. XXIX
1 7 8 3

the rejection of the late five per cent. impost, which had been contemplated: they were thought to have been busy in ripening projects, which might bring forward measures for the speedy liquidation of the public demands. The private embarrassments and expenses of some of this class, had frequently prompted them to ill-digested systems for relief to themselves, in which the public were also involved, from the confidence placed in them by men of the first consideration: but their expedients and their adventures ended in the complete ruin of some individuals.

Those gentlemen, however, most particularly implicated in the public opinion, sustained a character pure, and morals correct, when viewed [272] in comparison with others who were looking forward to projects of extensive speculation, to the establishment of banks and funding systems, and to the erecting a government for the United States, in which should be introduced ranks, privileged orders, and arbitrary powers. Several of these were deep, designing instruments of mischief; characters able, artful, and insinuating; who were undoubtedly engaged in the manoeuvres of the army; and though their designs were not fully comprehended, it was generally believed, that they secretly encouraged the discontents and the attempts of the disaffected soldiery.

In answer to the address of the officers of the army, congress endeavoured to quiet by palliatives, and by expressions of kindness, encouragement, and hope. Several months passed in this uneasy situation: the people anxious, the officers restless, the army instigated by them, and by ambitious and interested men in other departments, proceeded to the most pernicious resolutions, and to measures of a very dangerous nature.

In the mean time, general Washington, both as commander in chief, and as a man who had the peace of his country at heart, did every thing in his power to quiet complaint, to urge to patience, and to dissipate the mutinous spirit that prevailed in the army. By his assiduity, [273] prudence, and judgment, the embers were slightly covered, but the fire was not extinguished: the secret murmurs that had rankled for several months, and had alternately been smothered in the sullen bosom, or blazed high in the sanguine, now broke out into open insurrection.

On the twentieth of June, one thousand seven hundred and eighty-three, a part of the Pennsylvania line, with some others belonging to the different corps of several of the United States, in defiance of all

order and military discipline, and in contempt of the advice and even
importunity of such as were better disposed, marched from Lancaster
to Philadelphia. There they were joined by some discontented soldiers
in the barracks within the city, who had recently returned poor,
emaciated, and miserable, from the southern service.

This seditious host surrounded the state house where congress was
sitting, placed guards at the doors, and threatened immediate outrage,
unless their demands were complied with in the short space of twenty-
four minutes.

Prompt requisitions and immediate decision, all well-disciplined
armies are used to, but this is no apology for the precipitation of their
present [274] measures. However, from the pride and success of
military manoeuvres, to which they had been accustomed, they
felt themselves superior to all civil subordination or control. This is
usually the case with all armies or detachments from them, in all
countries, after they have stood their ground long enough, to feel
their strength sufficient to indulge that military tyranny which grows
by habit, and makes a standing army a fit instrument for the support
of the most cruel despotism.

It was indeed very alarming to see the general congress of the
United States held in a kind of *duress*, by a part of their own army:
but though extremely clamorous and insolent, the mutineers did not
proceed to personal abuse; and, as if struck by a consciousness of the
impropriety of their own conduct, or overawed by the appearance of
that honorable body in a state of imprisonment by those whom they
ought to command, the members were soon permitted to separate.
Indeed, they did not meet with any personal insult from the rude
and disorderly soldiers, though their demands were not complied
with, nor any new concessions made in favor of men, who threatened
to become the military masters of the country.

Congress thus rudely assaulted, resented the public affront as they
ought, and judged it improper for themselves to continue longer in a
[275] city where they could not be sure of protection. The president
and the members of congress agreed to leave Philadelphia immediately,
and to meet on the twenty-sixth at Princeton, to proceed on the
business of the United States.

General Washington, very far from countenancing any of the
measures of these disturbers of order and tranquillity, and very unhappy
at the discontents that had appeared among many of his officers, lost
not a moment after he was informed of the riotous proceedings of a

part of his army in Philadelphia: he ordered general Robert Howe to march without delay, with a body of fifteen hundred men, to quell the mutineers. Aided by the prudent conduct of the magistrates of the city, things were not carried to the extremities apprehended; the refractory soldiers were soon reduced to obedience, tranquillity restored, and no blood spilt.

Some of the ringleaders of sedition were taken into custody, but soon after received a pardon from congress. The most decided steps were immediately taken, not only to quell the clamors of the rioters, but to do justice to the armies of the United States. The commutation, which had labored in congress for some time, was finally agreed on: five years' full pay was acceded to, instead of half pay during the lives of the officers of the army. To this was [276] added, a promise of a large proportion of uncultivated land in the western territory, to be distributed among them according to their rank in the army. Yet they were not satisfied;—their complaints were loud, the grievances and the merits of the army recapitulated, and their demands high, even to the alarm of all who had the interest of their country at heart, lest the consequences of this mutinous spirit might be fatal to its future tranquillity.

The disbanding of an army, and throwing a number of idle people at once on the community, always requires the most guarded, cautious, and judicious steps. Congress sensible of this, had immediately on the news of peace, recommended to general Washington the measure of furloughing a number of commissioned and non-commissioned officers. They were of the opinion, that if a considerable part of the soldiery who had enlisted for three years, were sent from the army in this way, it would be the most prudent method of separating a body of men, usually dangerous to the liberties and morals of their own country, when no foreign foe obliges them to unite in the general defence.

But it was a measure not pleasing to the army, and had fomented the uneasiness and increased the clamor among the officers, previous to the audacious step of investing the congressional [277] assembly, and obliging them, under the threats of an armed force, to disperse for their own personal safety. Yet this mutinous disposition did not appear to have infected the whole army: many of the soldiers were the substantial yeomanry of the country; many of the officers had stood in the same grade of life, and were far from wishing to involve

the inhabitants of their native country in scenes of new confusion and
distress, for the redress of their complaints, or the payment of their
arrearages.

At the same time, the people at large generally thought, that the
compensations engaged by congress were equal to the services and
sufferings of the army, however meritorious: it was judged, that if
held up in a comparative view with the exertions, the sufferings, and
dangers of men in other departments, that gratitude was not exclusively
due to the military line; but that others, who had with vigilance and
energy opposed the common enemy, were entitled to some consideration in the public eye. Every sober and judicious man considered
patience and moderation requisites that ought to adorn every public
character, and censured in strong terms, the indulgence of that restless
and turbulent spirit that had recently appeared to prevail in the army
of the United States.

[278] The public in general were soon confirmed in the opinion,
that the intrigues of some of the officers were deep, ambitious,
designing, and pernicious. In the outset of the American revolution,
the institution of ranks, the creation of nobles, the rearing a monarchy,
or the aggrandizement of a monarch, and the factitious ideas of
aristocratic birth, had no existence in the minds of a rising republic
or their army, organized to oppose the encroachments of kings. These
were ideas afterwards suggested by aspiring individuals, who had no
prescriptive rights by any superiority of birth, wealth, or education,
to assume dignified names or ennobled orders. By degrees, these
views were nurtured by certain designing characters, and matured by
circumstances to which the inhabitants of the states had hitherto been
strangers.

But a connexion with European powers, formed from necessity,
kept open by negociation, and the intercourse strengthened by
speculators and men of pleasure, tainted the purity and simplicity of
American manners, long before the conclusion of the war. The
friendships formed in the field with a foreign army, had their influence,
and the habits and opinions of military men, who had long been the
servants of monarchy or despotism, were adopted by a considerable
part of the army of the United States. Nor were some men of other
descriptions [279] less fascinated with the splendor of courts, and the
baubles of ambitious spirits, sceptres, diadems, and crowns. Doubtless,
some of these had lent their co-operating influence to undermine the

beautiful fabric of *republicanism,* which Americans had erected with enthusiastic fondness, and for which they had risked ease, property, and life.

It may be observed, that pure republicanism is cherished by the philosopher in his closet, and admired by the statesman in his theories of government; yet when called into operation, the combinations of interest, ambition, or party prejudice, too generally destroy the principle, though the name and the form may be preserved.

There is a change of manners, of sentiments, of principles, and of pursuits, which perhaps similar circumstances will in time produce, in all ages and countries. But from the equality of condition to which they had been used, from the first emigration of their ancestors; from their modes of life, and from the character and professions of its inhabitants; such a change in America was not contemplated, nor could have been expected to approach, at so early a period of her independence. But new ideas, from a rivalry of power and a thirst for wealth, had prepared the way to corruption, and the awakened passions were hurried to new images of [280] happiness. The simpler paths which they had trodden in pursuit of competence and felicity, were left to follow the fantastic fopperies of foreign nations, and to sigh for the distinctions acquired by titles, instead of that real honor which is ever the result of virtue.

A writer of celebrity has observed, that "military commanders acquiring fame, and accustomed to receive the obedience of armies, are in their hearts generally enemies to the popular equality of republics." Thus, the first step taken in the United States for the aggrandizement of particular families by distinguished orders, and assumed nobility, appeared to originate in the army; some of whom, as observed of the ancient barons of England, "soon forgot the *cause* and the patriotism of their ancestors, and insensibly became the servants of luxury and of government."

By the articles of confederation unanimously acceded to by each legislature on the continent, the great American republic admitted no titles of honor, no ennobled or privileged orders. But willing to make the experiment, and reap the first fruits of exclusive dignity, a *self-created rank* was contemplated by some officers of the army, and an order of military knighthood projected, before the disturbances at Philadelphia, but not publicly avowed until after the insurrection was subdued.

[281] This institution embraced the whole body of officers belonging

to the army and navy, both French and Americans. The right of CHAP. XXIX
admitting as honorary members persons of eminence of any nation, 1 7 8 3
was also assumed. This adoption of honorary members gave the right
only of partaking present munificence, and the enjoyment of the
honor during their own lives, however they might have been distinguished in name or character. An hereditary claim to the peerage of
the *Order of Cincinnati*, and the privileges annexed thereto, was
confined solely to the military line.

The count de Rochambeau, the duke de Noailles, and many of
the principal officers of the French army, and several other foreign
officers, whose term of service had been too short to admit a claim
according to the rules of the order, were however adopted on its first
institution. The French ambassador and many other gentlemen, bred
in the schools of monarchy in various parts of Europe, and even some
princes and crowned heads, were invited to dignify the order by
becoming honorary members.

This was a deep laid plan, which discovered sagacity to look forward,
genius to take advantage, and art to appropriate to themselves the
opening prospects of dignity and rank, which [282] had fired the
minds of ambitious men. The ostensible design of this novel institution, was striking to the compassionate mind, and flattering to the
lovers of freedom among the American officers. Many of them knew
not enough of the world, and of the history and character of man, to
suspect any latent mischief or any concealed object that must not yet
be divulged, for fear of disgusting the public ear. Others had
comprehensive ideas of the system, and with great complacency of
mind anticipated the honor of hereditary knighthood, entailed on
their posterity.

The members were invited to embody as a society of friends, to
perpetuate the memory of the revolution, and to engage to be vigilant
in preserving inviolate, the exalted rights and liberties of human
nature, for which they had fought and bled. On his initiation into the
society, each member was to advance a month's pay, in order to begin
a fund for the relief of any unfortunate family or distressed individual,
who did himself, or whose father had belonged to the order.

They mutually engaged that this union should not be dissolved but
with their lives; and that their attachment and their honors should
descend to the eldest of their male posterity, and in failure thereof,
to the collateral branches.

[283] They were to be furnished with a diploma, and to appropriate

CHAP. XXIX to themselves as a badge of their order, a golden medal, with a bald
1 7 8 3   eagle spread on the one side, and on the other a symbol and a motto
indicative of the dignity of their order. The medal was to be suspended
on a broad blue ribbon edged with white, designed to intimate the
union between America and France; this was to be hung to a buttonhole
of their vest.

As the officers of the American army had styled themselves of the
order, and assumed the name of *CINCINNATUS*, it might have been
expected that they would have imitated the humble and disinterested
virtues of the ancient Roman; that they would have retired satisfied
with their own efforts to save their country, and the competent rewards
it was ready to bestow, instead of ostentatiously assuming hereditary
distinctions, and the *insignia* of nobility. But the eagle and the ribbon
dangled at the button-hole of every youth who had for three years
borne an office in the army, and taught him to look down with proud
contempt on the patriot grown grey in the service of his country.

Arduous indeed was the task of raising, regulating, and maintaining
an army, to secure the freedom, the mediocrity, and the independent
spirit, as well as the name of Americans. Those [284] who had been
long engaged in this laborious work had never imagined, that any
class of the citizens of the United States would pant for peerages in
the shade of retirement, instead of practising in their primeval state,
the humble virtues, and imitating the laudable manners of their
ancestors.

The benevolent principles avowed in the declarations of the society,
allured many to unite with them who had no ideas of establishing an
hereditary rank of nobility in America. Their views were too circum-
scribed, and perhaps too virtuous, to wish for any thing more than
independence, retirement, and peace, and to return to the plough,
or to the humbler occupations of their former life, with the conscious
disposition of doing good to their old associates, if affliction should
assail, or misfortunes render them, in any future day, the objects of
commiseration and beneficence. But America had nurtured sons of
boundless ambition, who thus early contemplated stars, garters, and
diadems, crowns, sceptres, and the regalia of kings, in the yet simple
bosom of their country.

General Washington was looked up to as the head of the society,
though for a time he prudently declined the style of president or
grand master of the order, and chose to be considered only as an
honorary member. This might have [285] been from an apprehension

that it would give a stab to his popularity, but more probably it was CHAP. XXIX
from a sense of the impropriety of an assumption so incompatible 1 7 8 3
with the principles of a young republic. The commander of the armies
of the United States, however, after the baron de Steuben had acted
as grand master of the order until October, one thousand seven
hundred and eighty-three, publicly acknowledged and subscribed
himself the president of the Society of the Cincinnati.

It was observed by a writer in England, that "this was the only blot
hitherto discovered in the character of this venerable hero." The same
writer adds

> It is impossible however to exculpate him: if he understood the tendency
> of his conduct, his ideas of liberty must have been less pure and elevated
> than they have been represented; and if he rushed into the measure
> blindfold, he must still be considered as wanting in some degree, that
> penetration and presence of mind so necessary to complete his character.

He was censured by several opposed to such an institution, who wrote
on the subject both in Europe and America: it was considered as a
blameable deviation in him from the principles of the revolution,
which he had defended by his sword, and appeared now ready to
relinquish by his example.

[286] The name of Washington was alone sufficient to render the
institution popular in the army; but neither his or any other name
could sanction the design in the eye of the sober republican, and
other men of moderate views in the common grades of life. These
were tenacious of the principles and the articles of the confederation,
which expressly forbade any rank or dignity to be conferred on the
citizens of the United States, either by princes abroad or self-created
societies at home.*

Much less satisfied were many high-spirited individuals in the higher
classes of life. Ambassadors abroad, who had adopted a fondness for
nominal distinctions, members of congress and of state legislatures,
and many others who had acquired a taste for the external superiority
that wealth and titles bestow, could not be pleased to see themselves
and their children thus excluded from hereditary claim to the honors,
privileges, and emoluments, of the first order of American nobility.
These asserted without hesitation, that this self-created peerage of
military origin, would throw an undue weight into the scale of the
army; while the sincere votaries to freedom, and the natural equality

* Confederation, article sixth.

CHAP. XXIX   of man, apprehended that this institution would give a fatal wound
1 7 8 3   to the liberties of America.

[287] Many judicious observers of the story of mankind thought, that the United States had now, at the conclusion of the war, an opportunity to make a fair experiment between the advantages of a republican form of government and more despotic modes.

It is true, America had obtained her independence, and spurned at every idea of kingly power: yet at this period it was difficult to conjecture, into what form of government the United States would finally settle. Republicanism had been the order of the day: the theory was beautiful, and the system warmly advocated by many of the best political writers: but the manners and the opinions of many discovered, that they had not entirely shaken off their prejudices in favor of monarchy, under which their ancestors had suffered enough to lead them to impress the wisest lessons on their posterity.

Some circumstances augured symptoms, that Americans, like most other nations, would succumb to the will of assumed superiority, and by their servility justify the attempt to establish inequalities of rank; and that they would relinquish with their rights, the spirit that ought to support them: that the dignity of republican principles would, in some not very distant day, be lost in the adulation of the sycophant, trembling under the frown of a despotic master.

[288] This was consistent with the ideas of a sensible American writer, on the subject of the institution of the *Cincinnati.* He observes,

> that this order was a deep laid plan, to beget and perpetuate family grandeur in an aristocratic nobility, which might terminate at last in monarchical tyranny. But (adds the same writer) never let so foul a stain be fastened on the human character, as that the very men who, with unfading honor, rescued their country from the galling yoke of foreigners, should lay the corner stone for erecting a tyranny themselves. Let not their example prove, that all that Plato, Sidney, and Locke, have said, and others have bequeathed to posterity on the subject of political happiness, was no more than ideal pictures of a fine imagination.*

The baron de Steuben and many other foreign officers, were very active and zealous in promoting this new institution. It was however generally thought it originated more in the ambition of some American, than in the influence of any European officers: and perhaps the society was not more indebted to any individual, who was a native son of

---

* Edanus Burke, esquire, chief justice of the state of South Carolina.

America, for this dignified innovation, than to major general [289] *Knox*, a man of extensive ambition, who had imbibed ideas of distinction too extravagant for a genuine republican.

Mr. Knox had not had the advantages of a literary education; but his natural inquisitive disposition and attention to books, rendered him a well-informed, agreeable man, with ingratiating accomplishments. His love of military parade, and the affability of his manners, brought him forward to the command of a cadet company in Boston, before the commencement of the American war. Naturally of a complacent disposition, his jovial humor and easy deportment rendered him acceptable in all companies, and made him a favorite with the commander in chief, even before his talents as a soldier were called into exercise. With an assemblage of pleasing qualities, it is not strange that he rose rapidly in the military line. He commanded the artillery department for several years before the conclusion of the war; and performed his duty in this line with courage and vigilance, which did honor to his military character.

Towards the close of the war, many gentlemen had indulged the most expensive modes of life, without resources sufficient to support the pernicious habits, which they had adopted from a wild fondness for novel ideas of rank, titles, and privileged orders, little short of men of [290] princely education, birth, and expectations. These probably might think, that some badge of hereditary nobility might give consequence to certain characters and families; while they might have sagacity to see that new exigencies might arise, that would open new sources of wealth to favored individuals, sufficient to maintain the pageantry assumed by self-originated titles and distinguished orders.

Friendship and brotherly kindness, patriotism and charity, were held up as the basis of the institution: and however the pride of man might be flattered by the ideas of a frivolous honorary title, attached to his family forever, doubtless the urbanity of Mr. Knox, as well as many other gentlemen, members of the society, was gratified more by the expectation, that much utility would redound to a very large class in the community, who might be benefitted by the donations of the society, though they reaped none of the honors of the institution.

But it was not long before the people were generally aroused from their supineness, by the alarming aspect of these pretensions of the officers of the army. Instead of an affectionate respect to them, which had been generally felt, or any new veneration awakened toward the new military nobles, a universal disgust was intermingled with the apprehensions of danger. This innovation was considered as striking at [291] once at the equality, liberty, simplicity, and interest, of the nation at large. The legislatures of several states announced their disapprobation of the institution, in strong and pointed language: they declared it an unjustifiable, dangerous, and bold presumption; and threatened, if persisted in, to manifest stronger tokens of their displeasure against the officers of the army, for separating themselves from their fellow-citizens, and erecting a pedestal on which they might be elevated to distinguished rank, and grades of honor inhibited by the confederacy of the states, and the principles of the revolution.

The state of Rhode Island carried their resentment still farther; they cut them off from the usual privileges which had been enjoyed by the subjects of the state, and annulled their claims to the common rights of citizenship by declaring, that any who were members of the Cincinnati should be considered as incapable of holding any office under the government. In short, so general was the dissatisfaction expressed, at the appearance of a deep laid foundation for building up a strong aristocracy, if not a monarchy, on the ruins of the American republic, that at the meeting of the Order of Cincinnati in May, one thousand seven hundred and eighty-four, they withdrew, or rather drew a veil over, some of their former pretensions; they apparently renounced the idea of hereditary [292] distinctions, and several other obnoxious claims, but in reality they relinquished nothing.

They afterwards continued the general and state meetings, the former once in three years, and the latter annually, retained their badges of honor, invited the eldest sons of deceased officers to accept the diploma, and to wear the eagle of their fathers, to associate with them on all public occasions, and to keep up the ancestral claim, in spite of the disapprobation of most of their countrymen. Their funds increased rapidly: according to their articles, the yearly interest only was to be annually appropriated to charitable purposes; this was much more than was expended: thus the wealth of the society was continually enhancing; and by their riches and their numbers they were indeed a formidable body, capable of becoming a preponderating weight in the political scale of their country, in whatever exigencies it might hereafter be involved.

There was undoubtedly much merit in the conduct of the American officers and soldiers through the war; there was also much to apprehend from them, by the existing circumstances at the close of hostilities:

various combinations and circumstances rendered it improbable, that such a corps of ambitious spirits, hardened in the field of valor and enterprise, should at once return to their former occupations, [293] and sit down as quiet citizens, without intriguing or intermeddling too much, and claiming a kind of prescriptive right to dictate in the civil administration of government.

The distressed state of American finances was alarming: congress was without revenue, resource, or fiscal arrangements that promised to be sufficiently productive; without power or energy to enforce any effectual measure, until the consent of each individual state was obtained. There had been a violent opposition to a proposal for raising a revenue, by an impost of five per cent. on all goods imported from foreign countries. As this was an experiment, it was limited to twenty-five years. Had the expedient been adopted, it might have prevented many subsequent difficulties and embarrassments that took place, previous to, as well as after, the adoption of a permanent constitution for the United States of America.

It was said, however, by some very wise and judicious statesmen, that this imperceptible mode of drawing money from the pockets of the people, was better suited to more despotic forms of government, than to the free and independent spirit that had produced the confederacy of the American states; that more open measures, and even direct taxes, were more consistent with republican opinions and manners, than the secret drains of imposts and excises, [294] which might bankrupt a nation, amidst the delusory dreams of wealth and independence.

Though this opinion was not universal, yet it had its influence so far as to retard the measure. Rhode Island rejected it entirely; Massachusetts and some other states threw impediments in the way; and finally, no effectual step was yet taken to restore public credit, or to quiet the murmurs of the army, just on the point of dissolution. The state, thus incapable of satisfying their just demands, had every thing to fear from that "peremptory and untemporising spirit, which is usually the fruit of a series of military service."

America now beheld an existing clamorous army, on the point of dissolution, or about to assume military domination. There now appeared a large body of proud, ambitious officers, unsatisfied with the honor of victory, and impatient under the promise of pecuniary compensation, as soon as the exigencies of public affairs would admit: many of them were needy from the delay of payment for meritorious,

CHAP. XXIX military services and sufferings. They were now (as observed) fighting
1 7 8 3 for distinction, aiming to establish hereditary rank among themselves, and eager for wealth sufficient to support the taste and style of nobility; a taste newly adopted by an intercourse with foreigners of [295] high rank, and habits of expense and dissipation under monarchic governments.

It was obvious to every one, that dignified ranks, ostentatious titles, splendid governments, and supernumerary expensive offices, to be supported by the labor of the poor, or the taxation of all the conveniences of the more wealthy, for the aggrandizement of a few, were not the objects of the patriot in the cabinet: nor was this the contemplation of the soldier in the field, when the veins of the children of America were first opened, and the streams of life poured out, both on the borders and the interior of the United States, against the combinations of civilized and savage warriors. The views of the virtuous of every class in those exertions, were for the purchase of freedom, independence, and competence, to themselves and their posterity.

At the same time, the congress of the United States was without sufficient powers by the old confederation, either to restrain the most dangerous irregularities, or to command public justice: they were also deprived by absence, ineligibility, or death,* of the abilities of many [296] of the members who first composed that honorable body. Some men had been introduced in their stead, whose ideas of public liberty were very different; who had neither the capacity, the comprehension, nor even the wishes, to establish the freedom of their country on the basis of equal liberty, and the renunciation of monarchic principles. Some of them had always been men of doubtful character, others had decidedly favored the claims of the British king and parliament.

The several governments involved in a weight of public debt; the people embarrassed in their private resources, from the expensive exigencies of an eight years' war; and every difficulty enhanced by being long without a medium of stability, without confidence in the faith of public bodies, or securities that could be relied on in private contracts,—the public mind was now agitated like a forest shaken in a tempest, and stood trembling at the magnitude of opening prospects, and the retrospect of past events.

---

* Three of the most distinguished and upright members of congress, who early fell under the hand of this dread conqueror of all men, were, PEYTON RANDOLPH, esquire, of *Virginia*, Mr. LYNCH, of *South Carolina*, and governor WARD, of *Rhode Island*.

We have seen the seeds of animosity and dissension were sown among themselves before the American army was disbanded; danger- ous symptoms indeed in a young republic, just setting out for itself, with the command and entire jurisdiction of an immense territory, while yet no digested system was formed, or seriously [297] contemplated but by few, for governing a newborn nation, still in its pupilage with regard to the ends, the origin, and the most perfect mode of civil government.

America was a country remarkable for its rapid population, not yet so much from the ingress of foreigners, as in consequence of the operations of nature, where a people are not corrupted by habits of effeminacy, where subsistence for a family was easily acquired, and where few factitious wants had yet cankered the minds of the great mass of the people, and dislodged that complacency which results from competence and content. Many indeed, at the present period, seemed to have lost sight of their primeval ideas and obligations; yet they were not eradicated from the intelligent, the virtuous, and well-informed mind: the genial flame of freedom and independence blazed in its original lustre, in the breasts of many, long after the termination of the revolutionary war.

After this period, the American continent was viewed by all nations as a theatre just erected, where the drama was but begun: while the actors of the old world having run through every species of pride, luxury, venality, and vice, their characters are become less interesting than those of the new. America may stand as a [298] monument of observation, and an asylum of freedom. The eyes of all Europe were upon her: she was placed in a rank that subjected her to the inspection of mankind abroad, to the jealousy of monarchs, and the envy of nations, all watching for her halting, to avail themselves of her mistakes, and to reap advantages from her difficulties, her embarrassments, her inexperience, or her follies.

Perhaps at no period of her existence, was America viewed with an eye of higher veneration, than at the present, both by statesmen and princes: at the same time, the philosopher in his retirement contemplates, and the lovers of mankind of every description behold, the shackles of ancestral pride annihilated, in a respectable portion of the globe. Yet, it may be observed, that it will require all the wisdom and firmness of the most sagacious heads, united with the most upright hearts, to establish a form of government for an extensive nation, whose independence has been recently acknowledged by

Great Britain. This must be done on a just medium, that may control the licentiousness of liberty, and the daring encroachments of arbitrary power; a medium that may check the two extremes of democracy, and the overbearing influence of a young aristocracy, that may start up from a sudden acquisition of wealth, where it had never before been tasted.

[299] But after all the speculative opinions with regard to government, that have occupied the minds and the pens of men, before many years roll over, some aspiring genius, without establishing the criterion or waiting the reward of real merit, may avail himself of the weakness, the divisions, and perhaps the distresses, of America, to make himself the designator and the fountain of honor and expectation. Such a sovereign without a crown, or the title of *king,* with his favorites and his instigators about him, may not be a less dangerous animal, than the *monarch* whose brow is decorated by the splendor of a diadem.

These are, however, ideas that may evanish with time; or if realized, it must be to the grief of the genuine patriot and the misery of thousands, who now dream only of freedom, wealth, and happiness, beneath the protection of just, equal, and lenient governments of their own, without any commixture of foreign influence or domination.

CHAPTER XXX

A Survey of the Situation of America on the Conclusion of the War with Britain • Observations on the Declaration of Independence • Withdraw of the British Troops from New York—A few Observations on the Detention of the Western Posts • The American Army disbanded, after the Commander in Chief had addressed the Public, and taken Leave of his Fellow-Soldiers—General Washington resigns his Commission to Congress

[300] We have seen the banners of Albion displayed, and the pendants of her proud navy waving over the waters of the western world, and threatening terror, servitude, or desolation, to resisting millions. We have seen through the tragic tale of war, all political connexion with Great Britain broken off, the authority of the parent state renounced, and the independence of the American states sealed by the definitive treaty. The mind now willingly draws a veil over the unpleasing part of the drama, and indulges the imagination in future prospects of peace and felicity; when the soldier shall retreat from the field, lay by the sword, and resume the implements of husbandry—the mechanic return to his former occupation, and the merchant rejoice in the prosperous view of commerce; when trade shall not be restricted [301] by the unjust or partial regulations of foreigners; and when the ports of America shall be thrown open to all the world, and an intercourse kept free, to reap the advantages of commerce extended to all nations.

The young government of this newly established nation had, by the recent articles of peace, a claim to a jurisdiction over a vast territory, reaching from the St. Mary's on the south, to the river St. Croix, the extreme boundary of the east, containing a line of postroads of eighteen hundred miles, exclusive of the northern and western wilds, but partially settled, and whose limits have not yet been explored. Not the Lycian league, nor any of the combinations of the Grecian states, encircled such an extent of territory; nor does modern history furnish any example of a confederacy of equal magnitude and respectability with that of the United States of America.

We look back with astonishment when we reflect, that it was only in the beginning of the seventeenth century, that the first Europeans landed in Virginia, and that nearly at the same time, a few wandering strangers coasted about the unknown bay of Massachusetts, until they found a footing in Plymouth. Only a century and an half had elapsed, before their numbers and their strength accumulated, until they bade defiance to foreign oppression, and stood ready [302] to meet the power of Britain, with courage and magnanimity scarcely paralleled by the progeny of nations, who had been used to every degree of subordination and obedience.

The most vivid imagination cannot realize the contrast, when it surveys the vast surface of America now enrobed with fruitful fields, and the rich herbage of the pastures, which had been so recently covered with a thick mattress of woods; when it beholds the cultivated vista, the orchards and the beautiful gardens which have arisen within the limits of the Atlantic states, where the deep embrowned, melancholy forest, had from time immemorial sheltered only the wandering savage; where the sweet notes of the feathered race, that follow the track of cultivation, had never chanted their melodious songs: the wild waste had been a haunt only for the hoarse birds of prey, and the prowling quadrupeds that filled the forest.

In a country like America, including a vast variety of soil and climate, producing every thing necessary for convenience and pleasure, every man might be lord of his own acquisition. It was a country where the standard of freedom had recently been erected, to allure the liberal minded to her shores, and to receive and to protect the persecuted subjects of arbitrary power, who might there seek an asylum from the chains of servitude to which they had [303] been subjected in any part of the globe. Here it might rationally be expected, that beside the natural increase, the emigration to a land of such fair promise of the blessings of plenty, liberty, and peace, to which multitudes would probably resort, there would be exhibited in a few years, a population almost beyond the calculation of figures.

The extensive tract of territory above described, on the borders of the Atlantic, had, as we have seen, been divided into several distinct governments, under the control of the crown of Great Britain; these governments were now united in a strong confederacy, absolutely independent of all foreign domination: the several states retained

their own legislative powers; they were proud of their individual CHAP. XXX
independence, tenacious of their republican principles, and newly 1 7 8 3
emancipated from the degrading ideas of foreign control, and the
sceptred hand of monarchy. With all these distinguished privileges,
deeply impressed with the ideas of internal happiness, we shall see
they grew jealous of each other, and soon after the peace, even of
the powers of the several governments erected by themselves: they
were eager for the acquisition of wealth, and the possession of the
new advantages dawning on their country, from their friendly connexions abroad, and their abundant resources at home.

[304] At the same time that these wayward appearances began early
to threaten their internal felicity, the inhabitants of America were in
general sensible, that the freedom of the people, the virtue of society,
and the stability of their commonwealth, could only be preserved by
the strictest union; and that the independence of the United States
must be secured by an undeviating adherence to the principles that
produced the revolution.

These principles were grounded on the natural equality of man,
their right of adopting their own modes of government, the dignity
of the people, and that sovereignty which cannot be ceded either to
representatives or to kings. But, as a certain writer has expressed it,

> Powers may be delegated for particular purposes; but the omnipotence of
> society, if any where, is in itself. Princes, senates, or parliaments, are not
> proprietors or masters; they are subject to the people, who form and
> support that society, by an eternal law of nature, which has ever subjected
> a part to the whole.*

These were opinions congenial to the feelings, and were disseminated by the pens, of political writers; of Otis, Dickinson, [305]
Quincy,† and many others, who with pathos and energy had defended
the liberties of America, previous to the commencement of hostilities.

---

* See Lessons to a Prince, by an anonymous writer. [David Williams, *Lessons to a
Young Prince on the Present Disposition in Europe to a General Revolution: with an Addition
of a Lesson on the Mode of Studying and Profiting by the Reflections on the French Revolution
by . . . Edmund Burke, by an old Statesman* (6th. ed. New York, 1791).]

† The characters of Dickenson and Otis are well known, but the early death of Mr.
Quincy prevented his name from being conspicuous in the history of American
worthies. He was a gentleman of abilities and principles which qualified him to be
eminently useful, in the great contest to obtain and support the freedom of his
country. He had exerted his eloquence and splendid talents for his purpose, until
the premature hand of death deprived society of a man, whose genius so well

On these principles, a due respect must ever be paid to the general will; to the right in the people to dispose of their own monies by a representative voice; and to liberty of conscience without religious tests: on these principles, frequent elections, and rotations of office, were generally thought necessary, without precluding the indispensable subordination and obedience due to rulers of their own choice. From [306] the principles, manners, habits, and education of the Americans, they expected from their rulers, economy in expenditure, (both public and private,) simplicity of manners, pure morals, and undeviating probity. These they considered as the emanations of virtue, grounded on a sense of duty, and a veneration for the Supreme Governor of the universe, to whom the dictates of nature teach all mankind to pay homage, and whom they had been taught to worship according to revelation, and the divine precepts of the gospel. Their ancestors had rejected and fled from the impositions and restrictions of men, vested either with princely or priestly authority: they equally claimed the exercise of private judgment, and the rights of conscience, unfettered by religious establishments in favor of particular denominations.

They expected a simplification of law; clearly defined distinctions between executive, legislative, and judiciary powers: the right of trial by jury, and a sacred regard to personal liberty and the protection of private property, were opinions embraced by all who had any just ideas of government, law, equity, or morals.

These were the rights of men, the privileges of Englishmen, and the claim of Americans: these were the principles of the Saxon ancestry of the British empire, and of all the free nations [307] of Europe, previous to the corrupt systems introduced by intriguing and ambitious individuals.

These were the opinions of Ludlow and Sydney, of Milton and Harrington: these were principles defended by the pen of the learned, enlightened, and renowned Locke; and even judge Blackstone, in his excellent commentaries on the laws of England, has observed, "that trial by jury and the liberties of the people went out together." Indeed, most of the learned and virtuous writers that have adorned

---

qualified him for the investigation of the claims, and the defence of the rights of mankind. He died on his return from a voyage to Europe, a short time before war was actually commenced between Great Britain and the colonies.

The writings of the above named gentlemen, previous to the commencement of the war, are still in the hands of many.

the pages of literature from generation to generation, in an island
celebrated for the erudite and comprehensive genius of its inhabitants,
have enforced these rational and liberal opinions.

These were the principles which the ancestors of the inhabitants of the United States brought with them from the polished shores of Europe, to the dark wilds of America: these opinions were deeply infixed in the bosoms of their posterity, and nurtured with zeal, until necessity obligated them to announce the declaration of the independence of the United States. We have seen that the instrument which announced the final separation of the American colonies from Great Britain, was drawn by the elegant and energetic pen of Jefferson, with that [308] correct judgment, precision, and dignity, which have ever marked his character.

The declaration of independence, which has done so much honor to the then existing congress, to the inhabitants of the United States, and to the genius and heart of the gentleman who drew it, in the belief, and under the awe, of the Divine Providence, ought to be frequently read by the rising youth of the American states, as a palladium of which they should never lose sight, so long as they wish to continue a free and independent people.

This celebrated paper, which will be admired in the annals of every historian, begins with an assertion, that all men are created equal, and endowed by their Creator with certain unalienable rights, which nature and nature's God entitle them to claim; and, after appealing to the Supreme Judge of the world for the rectitude of their intentions, it concludes in the name of the *good people* of the *colonies*, by their representatives assembled in congress, they publish and declare, that they are, and of right ought to be, Free and Independent States: in the *name* of the *people*, the fountain of all just authority, relying on the protection of Divine Providence, they mutually pledged themselves to maintain these rights, with their lives, fortunes, and honor.

[309] These principles the *Sons of Columbia* had supported by argument, defended by the sword, and have now secured by negotiation, as far as the pledges of national faith and honor will bind society to a strict adherence to equity. This however is seldom longer than it appears to be the interest of nations, or designing individuals of influence and power. Virtue in the sublimest sense, operates only on the minds of a chosen few: in their breasts it will ever find its own reward.

In all ages, mankind are governed less by reason and justice, than

CHAP. XXX by interest and passion: the caprice of a day, or the impulse of a
1 7 8 3 moment, will blow them about as with a whirlwind, and bear them
down the current of folly, until awakened by their misery: by these
they are often led to breaches of the most solemn engagements, the
consequences of which may involve whole nations in wretchedness.
It is devoutly to be hoped, that the conduct of America will never
stand upon record as a striking example of the truth of this observation.
She has fought for her liberties; she has purchased them by the most
costly sacrifices: we have seen her embark in the enterprise, with a
spirit that gained her the applause of mankind. The United States
have procured their own emancipation from foreign thraldom, by the
sacrifice of their heroes and their friends: they are now ushered on to
the temple of peace, who holds [310] out her wand, and beckons
them to make the wisest improvement of the advantages they had
acquired, by their patience, perseverance, and valor.

They had now only to close the scenes of war by a quiet dispersion
of their own armies, and to witness the last act of hostile parade, the
decampment of the battalions of Britain, and the retirement of the
potent fleets that had long infested their coasts. This was to have
been done at an earlier day: it was expected that on the ratification
of the definitive treaty, there would have been an immediate evacuation of all the posts which had been held by the British, within the
limits of the United States.

The seventh article of the treaty expressly stipulated, that

His Britannic Majesty shall, with all convenient speed, and without causing
any destruction, or carrying away any negroes or other property of the
American inhabitants, withdraw all his armies, garrisons, and fleets, from
the said United States, and from every post, place, and harbor, within the
same; leaving in all fortifications the American artillery that may be therein:
and shall also order and cause all archives, records, deeds, and papers,
belonging to any of the said states, or their citizens, which in the course
of the war may have fallen into the hands of his officers, to be forthwith
restored [311] and delivered to the proper states and persons to whom
they belong.

General Carleton had assigned his reasons for delay relative to the
evacuation of New York, in his correspondence with the president of
congress and general Washington. Some satisfactory arrangements
were however soon after made, relative to the loyalists, the exchange
of prisoners, and several other points, for which the reader is referred
to the journals of congress. When this was done, a detachment from

the American army, under the command of general Knox, was directed
to enter New York, in order to prevent any irregularities, confusion,
or insult, among the citizens, on the important movement now about
to take place.

On the twenty-fifth of November, one thousand seven hundred
and eighty-three, all the British, Hessian, and other foreign troops in
the pay of his Britannic majesty, were drawn off from the city of New
York: general Carleton embarked the same day; and admiral Digby
sailed for England with the remainder of the British fleet, that had
for many years invaded the sea-coasts of America. Thus the shores of
the Atlantic states, that had so long been alarmed by the terrific
thunders of the British navy, and ravaged by hostile squadrons, were
left in repose. In consequence of this much desired event, a general
joy pervaded the borders, [312] from Georgia to the extreme boundaries
of the New England states.

No sufficient apology was however yet made for the detention of
the western posts: they were long retained; and this breach of faith
was afterwards attended with very important consequences. Under
various frivolous pretences of non-compliance on the part of the United
States, with some articles stipulated in the definitive treaty of peace,
a long line of posts in the western territory were not relinquished.

We have seen by the seventh article of the treaty, that the king of
England was to have immediately withdrawn not only his fleets and
armies from the sea-coasts, but all the garrisons, forts, and places of
arms, within the United States, should at the same time have been
evacuated. But the British interest and trade with the natives of the
wilderness, in the extensive territories from the Mississippi to the
Alleghany Mountains on the river Ohio, could not easily be relinquished by their government. The forts of Michillimackinak and
Detroit, the posts on Lake Erie, Niagara, Oswego, and several others,
were held by British officers and troops, and a jurisdiction long
exercised over all the country in the vicinity, under the direction of
colonel Simcoe, afterwards governor of Upper Canada.

[313] The disposition of this man toward the United States, was
no less cruel and savage, than that of the fierce uncultivated natives
beyond the lakes: this we have seen him display when a marauding
partisan in the Jersies, Virginia, and other places. He was now left at
full liberty to indulge this disposition among savages, whose ferocity
and cruelty seemed to be perfectly congenial to the feelings of his
own heart, when, while in command there, he instigated the fierce

and blood-thirsty warriors to make incursions on the frontier settlements.

The hostile character of governor Simcoe, the licentiousness and barbarity of the borderers, both European and American, united with the interests of Britain and the weakness of an infant government in America, some time after the present period, produced a horrid Indian war, in which, assisted by British soldiers in disguise, many brave officers of the old army, and some of the flower of the American youth, perished in the wilderness.

Those subsequent circumstances in American story which have been cursorily mentioned above, suggest the reflection, that it might have been happy for the United States, and happier for the individual "who weeps alone its lot of wo," if, instead of extending their views [314] over the boundless desert, *a Chinese wall* had been stretched along the Apalachian ridges, that might have kept the nations within the boundaries of nature. This would have prevented the incalculable loss of life and property, and have checked the lust of territory, wealth, and that ambition which has poured out streams of innocent blood on the forlorn mountains. The lives of our young heroes were too rich a price for the purchase of the acres of the savages, even could the nations be extinguished, who certainly have a prior right to the inheritance: this is a theme on which some future historians may more copiously descant.

The acquisition and possession of territory seems to be a passion inwove in the bosom of man: we see it from the peasant who owns but a single acre, to the prince who commands kingdoms, and wishes to extend his domains over half the globe. This is thought necessary at some times to distance troublesome neighbours, at others to preserve their own independence; but if the spring of action is traced, it may generally be found in the inordinate thirst for the possession of power and wealth.

A writer of celebrity has observed,

The enlargement of territory by conquest, is not only not a just object of war, but, in the greater part of the instances in which it is attempted, not even desirable. It is certainly [315] not desirable, where it adds nothing to the numbers, the enjoyments, or the security of the conquerors. What, commonly, is gained to a nation by the annexing of new dependencies, or the subjugation of other countries to its dominions, but a wider frontier to defend, more interfering claims to vindicate, more quarrels, more enemies, more rebellions to encounter, a greater force to keep up by sea and land,

more services to provide for, and more establishments to pay? Were it true CHAP. XXX
that the grandeur of the prince is magnified by those exploits, the glory 1 7 8 3
which is purchased, and the ambition which is gratified, by the distress of
one country, without adding to the happiness of another, which at the
same time enslaves the new and impoverishes the ancient part of the
empire, by whatever names it may be known or flattered, ought to be an
object of universal execration.*

These are the reflections of a philosopher; princes and statesmen
view things in a very different light. The expense of either treasure
or blood, the waste of human life, the anguish of the afflicted bosom,
or the tears wrung from the eye of sorrow, have little weight in the
scale of ambition, whose object is the extension of territory and power
to the utmost of their [316] limits, however contrary to the laws of
nature and benevolence.

Perhaps neither reason nor policy could justify the American
government in offensive war, on the natives of the interior of the
western territory; but the detention of the posts on the borders by
the British, obliged them after peace took place, to make some military
defence against the incursions of the savages on the frontiers, the
consequences of which will be seen hereafter.

We have already observed, that New York was relinquished and
the British forces withdrawn from the Atlantic states only, and the
further adjustment relative to the out-posts left to the decision of a
future day.†

Immediately after the British armament was withdrawn from New
York, all hostile arrangements disappeared, and the clarion of war
ceased to grate the ear of humanity; and notwithstanding [317] the
obstacles that had arisen, and the dangers feared from the face of
general discontent among the officers and soldiers, the American army
was disbanded with far less difficulty than was apprehended. The
commander in chief, and many of the officers, conducted the business
of conciliation and obedience, after the late mutiny and insurrection,
with the most consummate judgment and prudence; and the whole

* Paley's Moral Philosophy. [William Paley, *The Principles of Moral and Political
Philosophy* (London, 1785), p. 645 (Book VI, Ch. XII).]
† The defence made by the British for the breach of treaty in the detention of the
western posts, may be seen at large in a correspondence since published between
Mr. Jefferson, the American secretary of state, and Mr. Hammond, the British
plenipotentiary to the United States; on which a British writer observed to his
countrymen—"Your diplomatists have shrunk before the reasonings of Jefferson."

CHAP. XXX American army was dismissed in partial detachments, without tumult
1 7 8 3 or disorder.

The merits of the commander in chief of the united armies of
America, have been duly noticed through the preceding pages of this
work, in their order of time; and ample justice has been done to the
integrity and valor, to the moderation and humanity, of this distinguished character. The virtues and talents which he really possessed,
have been appreciated in a measure consistent with a sacred regard
to truth. Imputed genius and lustre of abilities ascribed beyond the
common ratio of human capacity and perfection, were the result of
his commanding good fortune, which attached to his person and
character, the partiality of all ranks and classes of men.

An exclusive claim to the summit of human excellence, had been
yielded as a kind of prescriptive right, to this worthy and justly
venerated citizen, from affection, from gratitude, [318] and from the
real services rendered his country, under existing circumstances that
had never before, and perhaps never will again, take place. His
remarkable retention of popular favor and good-will, carried him
through a long and perilous war without a change in public opinion,
or the loss of confidence in the commander first appointed by the
congress of America, to meet the veterans of Britain and other European
powers, on hostile ground.

Thus, the renowned WASHINGTON, without arrogating any undue
power to himself, which success and popularity offered, and which
might have swayed many more designing and interested men, to have
gratified their own ambition at the expense of the liberties of America,
finished his career of military glory, with decided magnanimity, unimpeached integrity, and the most judicious steps to promote the tranquillity of his country. He had previously published a circular letter
to each governor of the individual states: this was an elegant address,
replete with useful observations and excellent advice to the inhabitants
of the United States, in their social, civil, and military capacities. Nor
did he neglect on all occasions, after the approach of peace, to inculcate
on the soldiery, and to impress on the minds of the people, the
necessity of union, subordination, economy, and justice, in the
punctual discharge of all contracts, both public and private.

[319] In full possession of the confidence of the people, the applause
of his country, the love of the army, the esteem of foreigners, and
the warm friendship and respect of the Gallican nation whose armies
and treasures had aided him to glory and victory, general Washington

disbanded the troops without noise, inconvenience, or any apparent CHAP. XXX
murmur at his measures. By order of the commander in chief, the 1 7 8 3
peace was celebrated at New York on the first day of December, one
thousand seven hundred and eighty-three, with high demonstrations
of satisfaction and joy; and on the twenty-third of the same month,
general Washington resigned his commission to congress, and, after
acting so conspicuous a part on the theatre of war, retired from public
scenes and public men, with a philosophic dignity honorary to himself
and to human nature.

Before the separation of the army, the general took a very affectionate
leave of his brave and faithful soldiers, and of each of the officers
singly. His farewell to his brave associates through the perilous scenes
of danger and war, was attended with singular circumstances of
affection and attachment. His address to the army was warm, energetic,
and impressive. While the sensibility of the commander in chief
appeared in his countenance, it was reciprocated in the faces of both
officers and soldiers; and in the course of this solemn *adieu*, [320] the
big tear stole down the cheeks of men of courage and hardihood, long
inured to scenes of slaughter and distress, which too generally deaden
the best feelings of the human heart.*

The mutual recollection of past dangers and fatigue which they
had endured together, and the contemplation of a retreat that would
probably prevent their ever meeting again, rendered this period of
separation, between this band of veteran chieftains and valiant soldiers,
a moment of extreme sensibility. Many of them had left their pruning-
hooks from principle, and had girded on the sword in defence of civil
and religious liberty; they were now returning to the plough, uncertain
what kind of masters would in future reap the reward of their labors:
they had left many of their brethren on the field of death, the voluntary
sacrifices to the independence of their country: they had freed
themselves from the fetters of kings, and by their prowess and their
perseverance, they had obtained a national independence.

General Washington was attended to the margin of the river, (where
he embarked on his way to Annapolis,) by crowds of spectators of
every sex and age; while the procession of [321] officers and gentlemen
who followed, with solemn steps and mournful visage, was indicative
of a last adieu to their most beloved and respected friend.

* General Washington's farewell orders to the army of the United States, may be seen
in Appendix, Note No. V.

Congress was then sitting at Annapolis, where they received the resignation of the magnanimous and disinterested commander of the army of the United States, with the same emotions of veneration and affection that had agitated the breast of the soldier. He had refused all pecuniary compensation for his services, except what was sufficient for his necessary expenditures, and laid his accounts before the congress: he then hastened with all possible celerity, to his peaceful mansion in the state of Virginia: there his return was hailed by the joyous acclamations of his friends, his neighbours, his servants, and the crown of his domestic felicity, his amiable partner. Mrs. Washington had long sighed for the return of her hero, whom she adored as the saviour of her country, and loved as the husband of her fond affection. In this lady's character was blended that sweetness of manners, that at once engaged the partiality of the stranger, soothed the sorrows of the afflicted, and relieved the anguish of poverty, even in the manner of extending her charitable hand to the sufferer.

[322] Thus possessed of all the virtues that adorn her sex, Mrs. Washington now contemplated the completion of her happiness; and observed afterwards in a letter to the author, that she

> little thought when the war was finished, that any circumstance could possibly happen to call the general into public life again; that she anticipated that from that moment they should have grown old together, in solitude and tranquillity:—this, my dear madam, was the first and fondest wish of my heart.*

But general Washington had yet much to do on the theatre of public action; much for his own fame, and much for the extrication of his country from difficulties apprehended by some, but not yet realized.

America has fought for the boon of liberty; she has successfully and honorably obtained it: she has now a rank among the nations: it was now the duty of the wise and patriotic characters who had by inconceivable labor and exertion obtained the prize, to guard on every side that it might not be sported away by the folly of the people, or the intrigue or deception of their rulers. They had to watch at all points, that her dignity was not endangered, nor her independence renounced, by too servilely copying [323] either the fashionable vices or the political errors of those countries, where the inhabitants are become unfit for any character but that of master and slave.

* Mrs. Washington's letter to Mrs. Warren, 1789. [Source not identified. See MOW to Martha Washington, (October?) 1789, MOWLB, pp. 127–128.]

Thus, after the dissolution of the American army, the withdrawing CHAP. XXX
of the French troops, the retirement of general Washington, and the 1 7 8 3
retreat of the fleets and armies of the king of Great Britain, a solemnity
and stillness appeared, which was like the general pause of nature
before the concussion of an earthquake. The state of men's minds
seemed for a short time to be palsied by the retrospect of dangers
encountered to break off the fetters, and the hazards surmounted to
sweep away the claims, and cut the leading strings in which they had
been held by the crown of Britain.

But though the connexion was now dissolved, and the gordian knot
of union between Great Britain and America cut in sunder; though
the independence of the United States was, by the treaty, clearly
established on the broad basis of liberty; yet the Americans felt
themselves in such a state of infancy, that as a child just learning to
walk, they were afraid of their own movements. Their debts were
unpaid, their governments unsettled, and the people out of breath
by their long struggle for the freedom and independence of their
country. They [324] were become poor from the loss of trade, the
neglect of their usual occupations, and the drains from every quarter
for the support of a long and expensive war.

From the versatility of human affairs, and the encroaching spirit of
man, it was yet uncertain when and how the states would be
tranquillized, and the union consolidated, under wise, energetic, and
free modes of government; or whether such, if established, would be
administered agreeable to laws founded on the beautiful theory of
republicanism, depictured in the closets of philosophers, and idolized
in the imagination of most of the inhabitants of America.

It is indeed true, that from a general attention to early education,
the people of the United States were better informed in many branches
of literature, than the common classes of men in most other countries.
Yet many of them had but a superficial knowledge of mankind; they
were ignorant of the intrigues of courts, and though convinced of the
necessity of government, did not fully understand its nature or origin;
they had generally supposed there was little to do, but to shake off
the yoke of foreign domination, and annihilate the name of *king*.

[325] They were not generally sensible, that most established modes
of strong government are usually the consequences of fraud or violence,
against the systems of democratic theorists. They were not sensible,
that from age to age the people are flattered, deceived, or threatened,
until the hood-winked multitude set their own seals to a renunciation

CHAP. XXX of their privileges, and with their own hands rivet the chains of
1 7 8 3 servitude on their posterity. They were totally fearless of the intrigues
or the ambition of their own countrymen, which might in time render
fruitless the expense of their blood and their treasures. These they
had freely lavished to secure their equality of condition, their easy
modes of subsistence, and their exemption from public burdens
beyond the necessary demands for the support of a free and equal
government. But it was not long before they were awakened to new
energies, by convulsions both at home and abroad.

New created exigencies, or more splendid modes of government
that might hereafter be adopted, had not yet come within the reach
of their calculations. Of these, few had yet formed any adequate
ideas, and fewer indeed were sensible, that though the name of *liberty*
delights the ear, and tickles the fond pride of man, it is a jewel much
oftener the play-thing of his imagination, than a possession of real
stability: it may be acquired to-day in all the triumph of [326]
independent feelings, but perhaps to-morrow the world may be
convinced, that mankind know not how to make a proper use of the
prize, generally bartered in a short time, as a useless bauble, to the
first officious master that will take the burden from the mind, by
laying another on the shoulders of ten-fold weight.

This is the usual course of human conduct, however painful the
reflection may be to the patriot in retirement, and to the philosopher
absorbed in theoretic disquisitions on human liberty, or the portion
of natural and political freedom to which man has a claim. The game
of deception is played over and over to mislead the judgment of men,
and work on their enthusiasm, until by their own consent, hereditary
crowns and distinctions are fixed, and some scion of royal descent is
entailed upon them forever. Thus by habit they are ready to believe,
that mankind in general are incapable of the enjoyment of that liberty
which nature seems to prescribe, and that the mass of the people
have not the capacity nor the right to choose their own masters.

The generous and disinterested of all nations must, however, wish
to see the American republic fixed on such a stable basis, as to become
the admiration of the world. Future generations will then look back
with gratitude, on the era which wafted their ancestors from the
European [327] shores: they will never forget the energetic struggles
of their fathers, to secure the natural rights of men. These are
improved in society, and strengthened by civil compacts: these have
been established in the United States by a race of independent spirits,

who have freed their posterity from the feudal vassalage of hereditary
lords. It is to be hoped, that the grim shades of despotic kings will
never hover in the clouds of the American hemisphere, to bedizzen
the heads of the sons of Columbia, by imaginary ideas of the splendid
beams of royalty.

Let it never be said of such a favored nation as America has been,
as was observed by an ancient historian, on the rise, the glory, and
the fall of the republic of Athens, that "the inconstancy of the people
was the most striking characteristic of its history." We have, with the
historian who depictured the Athenian character, viewed with equal
astonishment, the valor of our soldiers and the penetration of the
statesmen of America. We wish for the duration of her virtue; we sigh
at every appearance of decline; and perhaps, from a dread of deviations,
we may be suspicious of their approach when none are designed.

It is a more agreeable anticipation to every humane mind, to
contemplate the glory, the happiness, the freedom, and peace, which
may for ages to come pervade this new-born nation, [328] emancipated
by the uncommon vigor, valor, fortitude, and patriotism of her soldiers
and statesmen. They seemed to have been remarkably directed by
the finger of Divine Providence, and led on from step to step beyond
their own expectations, to exhibit to the view of distant nations,
millions freed from the bondage of a foreign yoke, by that spirit of
freedom, virtue, and perseverance, which they had generally displayed
from their first emigrations to the wilderness, to the present day.

Let us here pause a few moments, and survey the vast continent
of America, where the reflecting mind retrospects and realizes the
beautiful description of the wide wilderness, before it became a fruitful
field; before "the rivers were open in high places, and fountains in
the midst of the vallies;" when He who created them pronounced,

I will plant the cedar, the myrtle, and the oil-tree; I will set in the desart
the fir-tree, and the pine, and the box-tree together; that all may see, and
know, and consider, and understand together, that the hand of the Lord
hath done this, and the Holy One of Israel hath created it.*

Let the striking contrast, since the forest has been made to blossom
as the rose, be viewed in [329] such an impressive light, as to operate
on the mind of every son and daughter of America, and lead to the
uniform practice of public and private virtue.

From the education, the habits, and the general law of kindness,

* Isaiah, 41st chap.

which has been nurtured among the children of those pious worthies who first left the pleasant and prolific shores of Europe, and took up their residence in the bosom of a wilderness, to secure the peaceful enjoyment of civil and religious liberty, it may reasonably be expected, that such a unanimity may long be preserved among their posterity, as to prevent the fatal havoc which dissension and war have brought on most nations found in the records of time.

The mind now rejoices to return from the scenes of war in which it has been immersed, and feels itself sufficiently collected to take an abstracted view of the condition of human nature. Here we might, before we leave the local circumstances of America, survey the contrasts exhibited in their conduct, by a world of beings who boast their rationality: we might indulge some moments of reflection and calm contemplation, on the infinite variety of combinations in the powers of the human mind, as well as the contrarieties that make up the character [330] of man. But amidst the various images which present, in viewing the complex state of man, we will only add in this place, a few observations on their hostile dispositions toward each other.

It must appear among the wonders of Divine Providence, that a creature endowed with reason should, through all ages and generations, be permitted the wanton destruction of his own species. The barbarous butchery of his fellow-mortals, exhibits man an absurd and ferocious, instead of a rational and humane being. May it not be among the proofs of some general lapse from the original law of rectitude, that no age or nation since the death of Abel, has been exempt from the havoc of war? Pride, avarice, injustice, and ambition, have set every political wheel in motion, to hurry out of existence one half the species by the hands of the other.

The folly of mankind in making war on each other, is strongly delineated on the conclusion of almost every hostile dispute; and perhaps this folly was never more clearly exhibited than in that between Great Britain and her former colonies. Each circumstance will in future be weighed, when the world will judge of the great balance of advantage to the one country or the other, on the termination of the struggle.

[331] A full detail of the sufferings of the English nation, in consequence of the absurd war upon their colonies, may be left to more voluminous writers; while we only observe, that Great Britain lost an extensive territory containing millions of subjects, the fruits of whose genius and industry she might have reaped for ages, had

she not been avaricious of a revenue by methods, which neither the
much boasted constitution of Englishmen, or the laws of prudence or
equity, could justify. . . . She lost the extensive commerce of a
country growing in arts and population, to an astonishing degree. . . . She lost the friendship of thousands, and created the
alienation of millions, that may last forever. . . . She lost a nursery
for seamen, that had replenished her navy from the first settlement
of America. . . . She lost, by the best British calculations, an hundred
thousand of her best soldiers, either by sickness or the sword, and a
proportionate number of most gallant officers*. . . . She sunk an
immensity of her treasures for the support of her armies and navies,
for the execution of the chimerical project of subduing the colonies
by arms, which by justice, protection, friendship, and a reciprocity of
kind offices, would have been her's for ages.

And what has she gained by the contest?—surely not an increase
of honor or reputation. [332] Corroborative evidence of these truths
may be drawn from the testimony of British writers. A very sensible
man† of this class has observed, that

> Thus ended the most unfortunate war in which England has ever been
> engaged; a war commenced in the very wantonness of pride and folly,
> which had for its object to deprive America of the rights for which our
> ancestors have contended; a war, the professed object of which was, to
> levy a tax that would not have paid the collectors; a war conducted with
> the same weakness and incapacity on the part of the British ministry, with
> which it was commenced; which might in the early stages of the dispute
> have been avoided by the smallest concession; and which might have been
> terminated with honor, but for the incorrigible obstinacy and unparalleled
> folly of the worst administration that ever disgraced the country. This
> deplorable war has ended in the dismemberment of a considerable part of
> the British empire, cost the nation more money than the ever memorable
> campaigns of Marlborough, and the still more glorious war of lord Chatham;
> more indeed than all the wars in which Great Britain has been engaged
> since the revolution, to the peace of Aix la Chapelle.

* See British Encyclopaedia, published 1792. [Warren might be referring to the
Encyclopaedia Britannica, the first edition of which appeared 1768–1771, the second
1777–1784, and the third 1788–1797.]

† See View of the Reign of George the Third. [The quoted statement appears in
neither Gebhard Friedrich August Wendeborn, *A View of England Towards the Close
of the Eighteenth Century* (2 vols.; London, 1791) nor William Belsham, *Memoirs of the
Reign of George III. To the Session of Parliament ending A.D. 1793* (4 vols.; London,
1795).]

CHAP. XXX   On the other hand, it may be proper here to take a survey of the
1 7 8 3 United States, and to view [333] them on every ground. They have
struggled with astonishing success for the rights of mankind, and have
emancipated themselves from the shackles of foreign power. America
has indeed obtained incalculable advantages by the revolution; but in
the innumerable list of evils attendant on a state of war, she, as well
as Great Britain, has lost her thousands of brave soldiers, veteran
officers, hardy seamen, and meritorious citizens, that perished in the
field, or in captivity, in prison-ships, and in the wilderness, since the
beginning of the conflict. She has lost an immense property by the
conflagration of her cities, and the waste of wealth by various other
means. She has in a great measure lost her simplicity of manners, and
those ideas of mediocrity which are generally the parent of content;
the Americans are already in too many instances hankering after the
sudden accumulation of wealth, and the proud distinctions of fortune
and title. They have too far lost that general sense of moral obligation,
formerly felt by all classes in America. The people have not indeed
generally lost their veneration for religion, but it is to be regretted,
that in the unlicensed liberality of opinion there have been some
instances, where the fundamental principles of truth have been
obscured. This may in some measure have arisen from their late
connexions with other nations; and this circumstance may account for
the readiness of many, to engraft [334] foreign follies and crimes with
their own weak propensities to imitation, and to adopt their errors
and fierce ambition, instead of making themselves a national character,
marked with moderation, justice, benignity, and all the mild virtues
of humanity.

But when the seeds of revolution are planted, and the shoots have
expanded, the various causes which contribute to their growth, and
to the introduction of a change of manners, are too many to recount.
The effervescence of party rage sets open the flood-gates of animosity,
and renders it impossible to calculate with any degree of accuracy, on
subsequent events. Not the most perspicacious human eye can foresee,
amidst the imperious spirit of disunion, and the annihilation of former
habits and connexions, the benefits that may result from the exertions
of virtue, or the evils that may arise from problematic characters which
come forward, the new-born offspring of confusion, and assume merit
from the novelty of their projects, and the inscrutability of their
designs. These are like hot-bed plants, started from extraneous causes;
prematurely forced into existence, they are incapable of living but in

the sunshine of meridian day. Such characters often hurry into
irretrievable mischief, before time has ripened the systems of men of
more principle and judgment.

[335] Thus, after the conclusion of peace, and the acknowledgment of the independence of the United States by Great Britain, the situation of America appeared similar to that of a young heir, who had prematurely become possessed of a rich inheritance, while his inexperience and his new felt independence had intoxicated him so far, as to render him incapable of weighing the intrinsic value of his estate, and had left him without discretion or judgment to improve it to the best advantage of his family.

The inhabitants of the United States had much to experiment in the new rank they had taken, and the untrodden ground which they were now to explore, replete with difficulties not yet digested or apprehended by the most sagacious statesmen. They had obtained their independence by a long and perilous struggle against a powerful nation: we now view them just emancipated from a foreign yoke, the blessings of peace restored upon honorable terms, with the liberty of forming their own governments, enacting their own laws, choosing their own magistrates, and adopting manners the most favorable to freedom and happiness. Yet it is possible that their virtue is not sufficiently stedfast, to avail themselves of those superior advantages.

The restless nature of man is forever kindling a fire, and collecting fuel to keep the [336] flame alive, that consumes one half the globe, without the smallest advantage to the other, either in a moral or in a political view. Men profit little by the observations, the sufferings, or the opinions of others: it is with nations as with individuals, they must try their own projects, and frequently learn wisdom only by their own mistakes. It is undoubtedly true, that all mankind learn more from experience than from intuitive wisdom: their foolish passions too generally predominate over their virtues; this civil liberty, political and private happiness, are frequently bartered away for the gratification of vanity, or the aggrandizement of a few individuals, who have art enough to fascinate the undistinguishing multitude.

If the conduct of the United States should stand upon record, as a striking example of the truth of this observation, it must be remembered that this is not a trait peculiar to the character of America, it is the story of man; past ages bear testimony to its authenticity, and future events will convince the unbelieving.

It is an unpleasing part of history, when "corruption begins to

CHAP. XXX prevail, when degeneracy marks the manners of the people, and
1 7 8 3 weakens the sinews of the state." If this should ever become the
deplorable situation of the United States, let some unborn historian,
[337] in a far distant day, detail the lapse, and hold up the contrast
between a simple, virtuous, and free people, and a degenerate, servile
race of beings, corrupted by wealth, effeminated by luxury, impov-
erished by licentiousness, and become the *automatons* of intoxicated
ambition.

C H A P T E R   X X X I

Supplementary Observations on succeeding Events, after the Termination of the American Revolution • Insurrection in the Massachusetts • A general Convention of the States • A new Constitution adopted—General Washington chosen President • British Treaty negotiated by Mr. Jay • General Washington's second Retreat from public Life • General Observations

[338] The narration of the revolutionary war between Great Britain and her former colonies, brought down to its termination, leaves the mind at leisure for more general observations on the subsequent consequences, without confining it to time or place.

At the conclusion of the war between Great Britain and America, after the rejection of the claims of a potent foreign nation, the dissevering of old bands of governmental arrangement, and new ones were adopted, the proud feelings of personal independence warmed every bosom, and general ideas of civil and religious liberty were disseminated far and wide.

On the restoration of peace, the soldier had returned to the bosom of his family, and the artisan and the husbandman were stimulated to new improvements; genius was prompted [339] to exertion, by the wide field opened by the revolution, and encouraged by the spirit of inquiry to climb the heights of literature, until it might stand conspicuous on the summit of fame.

Under such circumstances, every free mind should be tenacious of supporting the honor of a national character, and the dignity of independence. This claim must be supported by their own sobriety, economy, industry, and perseverance in every virtue. It must be nurtured by that firmness and principle that induced their ancestors to fly from the hostile arm of tyranny, and to explore and begin a new nation in the forlorn and darksome bosom of a distant wilderness. The social compacts, the religion, the manners, and the habits of

CHAP. XXXI these wandering strangers, and their immediate successors, taught their sons the noble example of fortitude and love of freedom, that has led them to resist the encroachments of kings and nobles, and to dissipate the cloud that threatened to envelope the mind in darkness, and spread the veil of ignorance over the bright hemisphere that encircles the children of Columbia.

Indeed America was at this period possessed of a prize, replete with advantages seldom thrown into the hand of any people. Divided by nature from three parts of the globe, which [340] have groaned under tyrants of various descriptions, from time immemorial, who have slaughtered their millions to feed the ambition of princes, she was possessed of an immense territory, the soil fertile and productive, her population increasing, her commerce unfettered, her resources ample. She was now uncontrolled by foreign laws; and her domestic manufactures might be encouraged, without any fear of check from abroad: and under the influence of a spirit of enterprise, very advantageous in a young country, she was looking forward with expectations of extending her commerce to every part of the globe.

Nothing seemed to be wanting to the United States but a continuance of their union and virtue. It was their interest to cherish true, genuine republican virtue, in politics; and in religion, a strict adherence to a sublime code of morals, which has never been equalled by the sages of ancient time, nor can ever be abolished by the sophistical reasonings of modern philosophers. Possessed of this palladium, America might bid defiance both to foreign and domestic intrigue, and stand on an eminence that would command the veneration of nations, and the respect of their monarchs: but a defalcation from these principles may leave the sapless vine of liberty to droop, or to be rooted out by the hand that had been stretched out to nourish it.

[341] If, instead of the independent feelings of ancient republics, whose prime object was the welfare and happiness of their country, we should see a dereliction of those principles, and the Americans ready to renounce their great advantages, by the imitation of European systems in politics and manners, it would be a melancholy trait in the story of man: yet they, like other nations, may in time, by their servility to men in power, or by a chimerical pursuit of the golden fleece of the poets, become involved in a mist ascending from the pit of avarice. This may lead to peculation, to usurious contracts, to illegal and dishonest projects, and to every private vice, to support the factitious appearances of grandeur and wealth, which can never

maintain the claim to that rich inheritance which they so bravely CHAP. XXXI defended.

Thus it was but a short time after the restoration of peace, and the exhilarating view of the innumerable benefits obtained by the general acknowledgment among foreign nations of the independence of America, before the brightened prospect, which had recently shone with so much splendor, was beclouded by the face of general discontent. New difficulties arose, and embarrassments thickened, which called for the exercise of new energies, activity, and wisdom.

[342] The sudden sinking of the value of landed, and indeed of all other real property, immediately on the peace, involved the honest and industrious farmer in innumerable difficulties. The produce of a few acres had been far from sufficient for the support of a family, and at the same time to supply the necessary demands for the use of the army, when from the scarcity of provisions every article thereof bore an enhanced price, while their resources were exhausted, and their spirits wasted under an accumulated load of debt.

The general congress was yet without any compulsory powers, to enforce the liquidation of public demands; and the state legislatures totally at a loss how to devise any just and ready expedient for the relief of private debtors. It was thought necessary by some to advert again to a paper medium, and by others this was viewed with the utmost abhorrence: indeed the iniquitous consequences of a depreciating currency had been recently felt too severely, by all classes, to induce any to embrace a second time with cordiality such a dangerous expedient. Thus, from various circumstances, the state of both public and private affairs presented a very serious and alarming aspect.

The patriotic feelings of the yeomanry of the country, had prompted them to the utmost [343] exertions for the public service. Unwilling to withhold their quota of the tax of beef, blankets, and other necessaries indispensable for the soldiery, exposed to cold and hunger, many of them had been induced to contract debts which could not be easily liquidated, and which it was impossible to discharge by the products from the usual occupations of husbandry. While at the same time, the rage for privateering and traffic, by which some had suddenly grown rich, had induced others to look with indifference on the ideas of a more moderate accumulation of wealth. They sold their patrimonial inheritance for trifling considerations, in order to raise ready specie for adventure in some speculative project. This, with many other causes, reduced the price of land to so low a rate, that the most

CHAP. XXXI valuable farms, and the best accommodated situations, were depreciated to such a degree, that those who were obliged to alienate real property were bankrupted by the sales.

The state of trade, and the derangement of commercial affairs, were equally intricate and distressing at the close of the war. The natural eagerness of the mercantile body to take every advantage that presented in that line, induced many, immediately on the peace, to send forward for large quantities of goods from England, France, and Holland, and wherever else they could gain a credit. Thus the markets [344] loaded with every article of luxury, as well as necessaries, and the growing scarcity of specie united with the reduced circumstances of many who had formerly been wealthy, the enormous importations either lay upon hand, or obliged the possessor to sell without any advance, and in many instances much under the prime cost. In addition to these embarrassments on the mercantile interest, the whole country, from north to south, was filled with British factors, with their cargoes of goods directly from the manufacturers, who drew customers to their stores from all classes that were able to purchase. Every capital was crowded with British agents, sent over to collect debts contracted long before the war, who took advantage of the times, oppressed the debtor, and purchased the public securities from all persons whose necessities obliged them to sell, at the monstrous discount of seventeen shillings and six pence on the pound. At the same time, the continent swarmed with British emissaries, who sowed discord among the people, infused jealousies, and weakened their reliance on the public faith, and destroyed all confidence between man and man.

Nor did religion or morals appreciate amidst the confusion of a long war, which is ever unfavorable to virtue, and to all those generous principles which ennoble the human character, much more than ribbons, stars, and other playthings [345] of a distempered imagination. These soon sink to the level of their own insignificance, and leave the sanguine admirer sickened by the chace of ideal felicity.

The wide field of more minute observation on these great and important subjects, shall at present be waved. Agriculture may be left to the philosophic theorist, who may speculate on the real value and product of the lands, in a country in such an improveable state as that of America; while the advance in the profits of the husbandman must be estimated by the ratio of future experiment. The statesman versed in the commerce and politics of Europe, and the commercial treaties

which may be, or have already been formed, has a labyrinth to trace, CHAP. XXXI
and investigations to unfold, before every thing can be fixed on the
principles of equity and reciprocity, that will give complete satisfaction
to all nations. Religious discussions we leave to the observation of
the theologian, who, however human nature may be vilified by some
and exalted by others, traces the moral causes and effects that operate
on the soul of man. The effects only are level to the common eye,
which weeps that the result is more frequently productive of misery
than felicity to his fellow beings.

Besides the circumstances already hinted, various other combinations caused a cloud of chagrin [346] to sit on almost every brow, and
a general uneasiness to pervade the bosoms of most of the inhabitants
of America. This was discoverable on every occasion; they complained
of the governments of their own instituting, and of congress, whose
powers were too feeble for the redress of private wrongs, or the more
public and general purposes of government. They murmured at the
commutation which congress had agreed to, for the compensation of
the army. They felt themselves under the pressure of burdens, for
which they had not calculated; the pressure of debts and taxes beyond
their ability to pay. These discontents artificially wrought up, by men
who wished for a more strong and splendid government, broke out
into commotion in many parts of the country, and finally terminated
in open insurrection in some of the states.

This general uneasy and refractory spirit had for some time shewn
itself in the states of New Hampshire, Rhode Island, Connecticut,
and some other portions of the union; but the Massachusetts seemed
to be the seat of sedition. Bristol, Middlesex, and the western counties,
Worcester, Hampshire, and Berkshire, were more particularly culpable. The people met in county conventions, drew up addresses to
the general assembly, to which were annexed long lists of grievances,
some of them real, others imaginary. They drew up many resolves,
some of [347] which were rational, others unjust, and most of them
absurd in the extreme. They censured the conduct of the officers of
government, called for a revision of the constitution, voted the senate
and judicial courts to be grievances, and proceeded in a most daring
and insolent manner to prevent the sitting of the courts of justice, in
the several counties.

The ignorance* of this incendiary and turbulent set of people,

---

* Some of them indeed were artful and shrewd, but most of them were deluded and
  persuaded to attempt, by resistance to government, to relieve themselves from debts

CHAP. XXXI might lead them to a justification of their own measures, from a recurrence to transactions in some degree similar in the early opposition to British government. They had neither the information, nor the sagacity to discern the different grounds of complaint. Nor could they make proper distinctions with regard to the oppressions complained of under the crown of Britain, and the temporary burdens they now felt, which are ever the concomitants and consequences of war. They knew that a successful opposition had been made to the authority of Britain, while they were under the dominion of the king of England; but they were too ignorant to distinguish between an [348] opposition to regal despotism, and a resistance to a government recently established by themselves.

County meetings and conventions, and the opposition of the body of the people to submit to judiciary proceedings, in direct violation of their charter, and the stipulated indulgencies which they claimed in common with their fellow subjects in Great Britain, wore a very different aspect from those of the clamorous and tumultuary proceedings of the Massachusetts' insurgents. These were violating the constitutions of their own forming, and endeavouring to prostrate all legal institutions, before they were cemented on the strong basis of a firm and well established government.

Those disturbances were for a time truly alarming, and gave cause for serious apprehensions that civil convulsions might spread through the country within the short term of three or four years after independence had been established, and peace restored to the United States of America. Under existing circumstances, the high-handed and threatening proceedings of the insurgents wore a very formidable aspect. There were among them very many men hardy, bold and veteran, who had been very serviceable in the field during the late revolutionary war. They had assembled in great numbers, in various places, and at different times, [349] and seemed to bid defiance to all law, order, and government.

In the winter of one thousand seven hundred and eighty-six, several thousands of those disorderly persons armed and embodied, and appeared in the environs of Springfield. They chose for their leader a man who had been a subaltern officer* in the revolutionary war,

---

which they could not pay, and from the hand of tax-gatherers, who had distrained in some instances to the last article of their property.
* Daniel Shays.

threatened to march to Boston, and by compulsory measures oblige CHAP. XXXI
the governor and general assembly to redress the grievances of the
people, which they alleged were brought upon them by enormous
taxation, and other severities from their own government: they however
thought proper to send forward a petition, instead of marching sword
in hand to the capital.

In the mean time, the exertions and the resolves of the legislative
body, with a view of relieving the public distresses, only increased
the discontents of the people. They were much divided in opinion,
relative to the best modes of quieting the disturbances. Tender laws
and sumptuary regulations were superficial expedients, that like paper
money eventually would increase, rather than eradicate the evils
complained of; while the temper of the people of various descriptions,
and from various [350] motives, augured an approaching crisis that
might produce convulsions too extensive for calculation.

In this situation of affairs, the governor was empowered by the
legislature to order a military force to be in readiness to march, under
the command of general Lincoln. The temerity of the insurgents had
emboldened them to move forward in hostile array, which made it
necessary to direct general Lincoln to give a check to their insolence,
and to restore peace and order to the state. But before the troops
from the lower counties had collected at Worcester, great numbers of
the insurgents had embodied, and moved forward to Springfield, with
a design to attack the continental arsenal: this was defended by
general Shepard, who took every precaution to prevent the shedding
of blood. He expostulated with their leaders, and warned them against
the fatal consequences of perseverance in their rebellious and hostile
proceedings: they however neglected the warning, and rushed on in
the face of danger; this obliged general Shepard to fire upon them,
which so disconcerted them that they immediately retreated. General
Lincoln reached Springfield about the same time, which entirely
defeated this project; the field was left with dismay, and with the
loss only of two or three of their party. The next movement of any
importance was their again collecting from all [351] quarters, and
taking a position on the heights of Pelham.

General Lincoln, unwilling to see his countrymen involved in a war
among themselves, passed on to Hadley without proceeding to
extremities. There he received letters from some of the leaders of
the insurgent parties, and with his usual mildness and humanity
endeavoured to persuade them to quit their hostile parade, and by

their peaceable demeanor to render themselves worthy of the lenity of government, which was ready, on their return to proper submission, to extend a general pardon, and throw a veil of oblivion over past transactions: but there appeared no signs of repentance, or of a relinquishment of their atrocious projects; and though without system, or any determinate object, and without men of talents to direct, or even to countenance, their disorderly conduct, in any stage of the business, they soon moved from Pelham in a strong body, entered and halted in the town of Petersham.

General Lincoln heard of the decampment of Shays and his followers from Pelham, at twelve o'clock, and had certain intelligence by the hour of six that they had moved on to Petersham. Convinced of the necessity of a quick march, he ordered his troops to be ready at a moment's morning. By eight o'clock they [352] began their route. Notwithstanding the intrepidity of general Lincoln, when immediate hazard required enterprise, he would not have exposed his troops to a march of thirty miles, in one of the severest nights of a remarkably severe winter, had not the entrance of the evening been mild and serene. The sky unclouded, and the moon in full splendor, they began their march under the promise of a more easy termination; but after a few hours the wind rose, the clouds gathered blackness, and the cold was so intense that it was scarcely supportable by the hardiest of his followers: nothing but the quickness of their motion prevented many of his men from falling victims to the severity of the season. The difficulty of their march was increased by a deep snow that had previously fallen, and lain so uncemented that the gusts drove it in the faces of the army with the violence of a rapid snow storm. They however reached Petersham before nine o'clock the next morning, but so miserably fatigued and frost bitten, that few of them were fit for service; and had not a general panic seized the insurgents, on the first alarm of the approach of the government troops, they might have met them with great slaughter, if not with total defeat; but though in warm quarters, well supplied with arms and provisions, they left this advantageous post with the greatest precipitation, and fled in all directions.

[353] General Lincoln was not in a capacity for immediate pursuit; it was necessary to halt and refresh his men: besides, his known humanity was such, that he might be willing they should scatter and disappear, without being pushed to submission by the point of the sword. The insurgents never again appeared in a collective body, but

spread themselves over the several parts of the western counties, and CHAP. XXXI
even into the neighbouring states, plundering, harassing, and terrifying
the inhabitants, and nourishing the seeds of discontent and sedition,
that had before been scattered amongst them. It was not long before
general Lincoln pursued and captured many of them, who implored
and experienced the clemency of the commander, and only a few
were taken into custody for future trial. Thus those internal com-
motions, which had threatened a general convulsion, were so far
quelled, that most of the troops returned to Boston early in the spring.
Before his return, general Lincoln marched to the borders of the state,
and found many in the counties of Hampshire and Berkshire, ready
to take the oath of allegiance, with all the marks of contrition for their
late guilty conduct. Commissioners were afterwards sent forward, with
powers to pardon, after due inquiry into the present temper and
conduct of individuals: to administer the oath of allegiance to the
penitent, and to restore to the confidence of their country all such as
[354] were not stigmatized by flagitious and murderous conduct.

Perhaps no man could have acted with more firmness, precision,
and judgment, than did governor Bowdoin, through the turbulent
period of two years, in which he presided in the Massachusetts: yet
notwithstanding his conspicuous talents, and the public and private
virtues which adorned his character, the popular current set strongly
against him on the approaching annual election; and governor Hancock,
who had once resigned the chair, was again requested to resume his
former dignified station, and was brought forward and chosen with
eclat and expectation. He did not however contravene the wise
measures of his predecessor. He was equally vigilant to quiet the
perturbed spirits of the people, and to restore general tranquillity:
this he did by coercive or lenient measures, as circumstances required;
and by his disinterested conduct, and masterly address, he was very
influential in overcoming the remains of a factious and seditious spirit
that had prevailed. Thus he did himself much honor, and acquired
the applause of his constituents.

The governor was authorised by the legislature to keep in pay any
number of troops that might be thought necessary to preserve the
public peace. Eight hundred men were stationed [355] on the western
borders of the state, but before the summer elapsed the insurgents
were so generally subdued that the troops were recalled and dismissed.

The governors of all the neighbouring states had been requested
not to receive or protect any of the guilty party, who had fled for

CHAP. XXXI security within their limits. These were all so sensibly impressed with the danger of disunion and anarchy, which had threatened the whole, that they readily gave assurances of detection, if any should flatter themselves with impunity, by flying without the jurisdiction of their own government. Several of the most notorious offenders were secured, and tried by the supreme judicial court, and received sentence of death; but the compassion of the people, coinciding with the humane disposition of the governor, induced him to grant reprieves from time to time, and finally prevented the loss of life by the hand of civil justice, in a single instance.

Thus, by well-timed lenity, and decided energy, as the exigencies of the moment required, was terminated an insurrection, that, by its dangerous example, threatened the United States with a general rupture, that might have been more fatal than foreign war, to their freedom, virtue, and prosperity. But though the late disturbances were quelled, and the turbulent [356] spirit, which had been so alarming, was subdued by a small military force, yet it awakened all to a full view of the necessity of concert and union in measures that might preserve their internal peace. This required the regulation of commerce on some stable principles, and some steps for the liquidation of both public and private debts. They also saw it necessary to invest congress with sufficient powers for the execution of their own laws, for all general purposes relative to the union.

A convention was appointed by the several states, to meet at Annapolis, in the state of Maryland, in the year one thousand seven hundred and eighty-six, for these salutary purposes; but the work was too complicated: the delegates separated without doing any thing, and a new convention was called the next year, to meet at Philadelphia, with the same design, but without any enlargement of their powers; they however framed a new constitution of government, and sent it for the consideration and adoption of the several states: and though it was thought by many to be too strongly marked with the features of monarchy, it was, after much discussion, adopted by a majority of the states.

We must consult the human heart, says the marquis Beccaria, for the foundation of the rights of both sovereign and people.

> If we [357] look into history, we shall find, that laws which are or ought to be conventions between men in a state of freedom, have been, for the most part, the work of the passions of a few, or the consequences of a fortuitous, temporary necessity, not dictated by a cool examiner of human

nature, who knew how to collect in one point the actions of a multi- CHAP. XXXI
tude, and had this only end in view, *the greatest happiness of the greatest
number.*

It was thought by some, who had been recently informed of the
secret transactions of the convention at Philadelphia, that the greatest
happiness of the greatest number was not the principal object of their
contemplations, when they ordered their doors to be locked, their
members inhibited from all communications abroad, and when proposals were made that their journals should be burnt, lest their
consultations and debates should be viewed by the scrutinizing eye
of a free people.* These extraordinary [358] movements appeared to
them the result of the passions of a few. It is certain, that truth,
whether moral, philosophical, or political, shrinks not from the eye
of investigation.

The ideas of royalty, or any thing that wore the appearance of regal
forms and institutions, were generally disgusting to Americans, and
particularly so to many characters who early came forward, and
continued to the end of the conflict, stedfast in opposition to the
crown of Britain. They thought that after America had encountered
the power, and obtained a release from foreign bondage, and had
recently overcome domestic difficulties and discontents, and even
quieted the spirit of insurrection in their own states; that the republican
system for which they had fought, should not be hazarded by vesting
any man or body of men with powers that might militate with the
principles, which had been cherished with fond enthusiasm, by a
large majority of the inhabitants throughout the union.

Republicanism, the idol of some men, and independence, the glory
of all, were thought by many to be in danger of dwindling into theory;
the first had been defaced for a time, by a degree of anarchy, and
fears were now awakened that the last might be annihilated by views
of private ambition.

[359] The people were generally dissatisfied with the high preten-

---

* This convention was composed of some gentlemen of the first character and abilities;
of some men of shining talents and doubtful character: some of them were uniform
republicans, others decided monarchists, with a few neutrals, ready to join the
strongest party. It was not strange there was much clashing and debate, where such
dissentient opinions existed: but after some modification and concession, a constitution was formed, which when the amendments took place immediately on its
adoption, the government of the United States stood on a basis which rendered the
people respectable abroad and safe at home.

CHAP. XXXI sions of the officers of the army, whose equality of condition previous to the war, was, with few exceptions, on the same grade with themselves. The assumption of an appropriate rank was disgusting, in a set of men, who had most of them been taken from mechanic employments, or the sober occupations of agriculture. Thus jealousies were diffused, with regard to the officers of the old army, the Cincinnati, and several other classes of men, whom they suspected as cherishing hopes and expectations of erecting a government too splendid for the taste and professions of Americans. They saw a number of young gentlemen coming forward, ardent and sanguine in the support of the principles of monarchy and aristocracy. They saw a number of professional characters too ready to relinquish former opinions, and adopt new ones more congenial to the policy of courts, than to the maxims of a free people. They saw some apostate whigs in public employments, and symptoms of declension in others, which threatened the annihilation of the darling opinion, that the whole sovereignty in the republican system is in the people: "that the people have a right to amend and alter, or annul their constitution and frame a new one, whenever they shall think it will better promote their own welfare and happiness to do it."*

[360] This brought forward objections to the proposed constitution of government, then under consideration. These objections were not the result of ignorance; they were made by men of the first abilities in every state; men who were sensible of the necessity of strong and energetic institutions, and a strict subordination and obedience to law. These judicious men were solicitous that every thing should be clearly defined; they were jealous of each ambiguity in law or government, or the smallest circumstance that might have a tendency to curtail the republican system, or render ineffectual the sacrifices they had made, for the security of civil and religious liberty to themselves; they also wished for the transmission of the enjoyment of the equal rights of man to their latest posterity. They were of opinion, that every article that admitted of double confusion, should

* Lessons to a Prince. [David Williams, *Lessons to a Young Prince on the Present Disposition in Europe to a General Revolution: With an Addition of a Lesson on the Mode of Studying and Profiting by the Reflections on the French Revolution by . . . Edmund Burke, by an Old Statesman* (6th. ed.; New York, 1791). The words quoted actually come from the Massachusetts Constitution, Bill of Rights, Art. VII, though they are consistent with Williams's views. See Herbert J. Storing, ed., *The Complete Anti-Federalist* (7 vols.; Chicago, 1981), 6: 248 n.5.]

be amended, before it became the supreme law of the land. They CHAP. XXXI were now apprehensive of being precipitated, without due consideration, into the adoption of a system that might bind them and their posterity in the chains of despotism, while they held up the ideas of a free and equal participation of the privileges of pure and genuine republicanism.

Warm debates in favor of further consideration, and much energetic argument took place, between gentlemen of the first abilities, in several of the state conventions. The system was [361] ratified in haste by a sufficient number of states to carry it into operation, and amendments left to the wisdom, justice, and decision of future generations, according as exigencies might require.* This was not sufficient to dissipate the apprehensions of gentlemen who had been uniform and upright in their intentions, and immoveably fixed in the principles of the revolution, and had never turned their eyes from the point in pursuit, until the independence of America was acknowledged by the principal monarchs in Europe.

But while the system was under discussion, strong objections were brought forward in the conventions of the several states. Those gentlemen who were opposed to the adoption of the new constitution *in toto*, observed, that there was no bill of rights to guard against future innovations. They complained that the trial by jury in civil causes was not secured; they observed, that some of the warmest partisans, who had been disposed to adopt without examination, had started at the discovery, that this essential right was curtailed; that the powers of the executive and judiciary were dangerously blended: that the appellate jurisdiction [362] of the supreme federal court, subjected the inhabitants of the United States, by a litigious process that militated with the rights formerly claimed by the individual states, to be drawn from one end of the continent to the other, for trial. They wished for a rotation in office, or some sufficient bar against the perpetuity of it, in the same hands for life; they thought it necessary there should be this check to the overbearing influence of office, and that every man should be rendered ineligible at certain periods, to keep the mind in equilibrio, and teach him the feelings of the governed, and better qualify him to govern in his turn. It was also observed by them, that all sources of revenue formerly possessed by the individual states were now under the control of congress.

---

* Many amendments were made soon after the adoption of the constitution.

CHAP. XXXI   Subsequent measures were not yet realized; banks, monopolies, and a funding system, were projects that had never been thought of, in the early stages of an infant republic, and had they been suggested before the present period, would have startled both the soldier and the peasant. The sober principled statesmen, and the judicious band of worthies, who organized the system of freedom, digested it in the cabinet, and conducted the public councils, which led to the independence of America, with a firm, disinterested magnanimity, and an energy seldom found in the courts of princes would have revolted at those ideas. Nor were they [363] less alarmed at the contemplation of a president with princely powers, a sextennial senate, biennial elections of representatives, and a federal city, "whose cloud-capt towers" might screen the state culprit from the hand of justice, while its exclusive jurisdiction might, in some future day, protect the riot of standing armies encamped within its limits. These were prospects viewed by them with the utmost abhorrence.

Indeed the opinions of the gentlemen who formed the general convention, differed very widely, on many of the articles of the new constitution, before it was sent abroad for the discussion of the people at large. Some of them seceded, and retired without signing at all, others complied from a conviction of the necessity of accommodation and concession, lest they should be obliged to separate without any efficient measures, that would produce the salutary purposes for which many characters of the first abilities had been convened. The philosophic doctor Franklin observed, when he sent his signature to the adoption of the new constitution, "that its complexion was doubtful; that it might last for ages, involve one quarter of the globe, and probably terminate in despotism."* He signed the instrument for the [364] consolidation of the government of the United States with tears, and apologized for doing it at all, from the doubts and apprehensions he felt, that his countrymen might not be able to do better, even if they called a new convention.

---

* See doctor Franklin's speech, on his signing the articles of the new constitution of government, which was to be laid before the people. [Franklin's "Speech in the Convention, At the Conclusion of its Deliberations," in Albert Henry Smyth, ed., *The Writings of Benjamin Franklin* (10 vols.; New York, 1905–1907), 9: 607–609. Warren's version of Franklin's speech is inaccurate. Herbert J. Storing suggests that Warren relied on a distorted rendition of the speech reported in the *Massachusetts Gazette*, December 14, 1787. Storing, ed., *The Complete Anti-Federalist* (7 vols.; Chicago, 1981), 6: 248 n.6.]

Many of the intelligent yeomanry and of the great bulk of inde- CHAP. XXXI
pendent landholders, who had tasted the sweets of mediocrity,
equality, and liberty, read every unconditional ratification of the new
system in silent anguish, folded the solemn page with a sigh, and
wept over the manes of the native sons of America, who had sold
their lives to leave the legacy of freedom to their children. On this
appearance of a consolidated government, which they thought required
such important amendments, they feared that a dereliction of some
of their choicest privileges might be sealed, without duly considering
the fatal consequences of too much precipitation. "The right of
taxation, and the command of the military," says an ingenious writer,
"is the completion of despotism." The last of these was consigned to
the hands of the president, and the first they feared would be too
much under his influence. The observers of human conduct were not
insensible, that too much power vested in the hands of any individual,
was liable to abuses, either from his own passions, or the suggestions
of others, of less upright and immaculate intentions than himself.

[365] Of thirteen state conventions, to which the constitution was
submitted, those of Connecticut, New Jersey, Pennsylvania, Delaware, Maryland, and Georgia, ratified it unconditionally, and those
of New Hampshire, Massachusetts, New York, Virginia, and South
Carolina, in full confidence of amendments, which they thought
necessary, and proposed to the first congress; the other two, of Rhode
Island and North Carolina, rejected it. Thus, it is evident that a
majority of the states were convinced that the constitution, as at first
proposed, endangered their liberties; that to the opposition in the
federal and state conventions, are the public indebted for the amendments and amelioration of the constitution, which have united all
parties in the vigorous support of it; and that in a land of freedom,
sovereignty, and independence, the great and important affairs of
state will be finally subject to reason, justice, and sound policy.

Thus, notwithstanding the many dark appearances, that for a time
spread a cloud over the United States; notwithstanding the apprehensions and prejudices against the new constitution, which had pervaded
the minds of many; though strong parties had arisen, and acrimonious
divisions were fomented, on the great and important question of
ratification; yet, by the mode adopted by five states, of proposing
amendments at the time of ratifying [366] it, the fears of the people
in general evaporated by degrees. The new constitution was adopted
with applause and success, and the promise and the expectations of

CHAP. XXXI amendments, flattered all classes with every advantage that could be rationally expected.

The new system of government was ushered into existence under peculiar advantages; and no circumstance tended more rapidly to dissipate every unfavorable impression, than the unanimous choice of a gentleman to the presidential chair, at once meritorious, popular, and beloved, beyond any man. Washington, the favorite of every class of people, was placed at the head of a government of experiment and expectation. Had any character of less popularity and celebrity been designated to this high trust, it might at this period have endangered, if not have proved fatal to the peace of the union. Though some thought the executive vested with too great powers to be entrusted to the hand of any individual, Washington was an individual in whom they had the most unlimited confidence.

After the dissolution of the American army, and the retirement of the commander in chief from the conspicuous station in which he had been placed, the celebrity of his life and manners, associated with the circumstances of a remarkable revolution, in which he always [367] stood on the fore-ground, naturally turned the eyes of all toward him. The hearts of the whole continent were united, to give him their approbatory voice, as the most suitable character in the United States, to preside at the head of civil government.

The splendid *insignia* of military command laid aside, the voluntary retirement of general Washington had raised his reputation to the zenith of human glory. Had he persevered in his resolution, never again to engage in the thorny path of public life, his repose might have been forever insured, in the delightful walks of rural occupation. He might, in his retirement on Mount Vernon, have cherished those principles of republicanism which he always professed, as well as the patriotism which he exhibited in the field; and by his disinterested example he might have checked the aspiring ambition of some of his former associates, and handed down his own name to posterity with redoubled lustre:* but man, after long habits of activity, in the meridian of applause, is generally restless in retirement. The difficulty of entirely quitting the luminous scenes on the great stage of public action, is often exemplified in the most exalted characters: thus, even the dignified Washington [368] could not, amidst the bustle of the

---

* This was the opinion of some of his most intimate associates at the time; yet doubtless general Washington thought it his duty to aid his country at so critical an era.

world, become a calm, disinterested spectator of the transactions of CHAP. XXXI statesmen and politicians. His most judicious friends were confident he had no fame to acquire, and wished him to remain on the pinnacle he had already reached; but, urged by the strong voice of his native state, and looked up to by every state in the union, the call was strong and impressive, and he again came forward in public life, though it appeared to be in counteraction of his former determinations.

Thus the former commander of the armies of America had been chosen one of the delegates for a general convention of the states, and lent his hand to the formation of a new constitution of civil government. This instrument, as above observed, appeared to the public eye to lie open to many objections: it was viewed as doubtful in its origin, dangerous in its aspect, and for a time very alarming to the feelings of men, who were *tremblingly alive* on the smallest encroachment of rights and privileges, for which they had sacrificed their fortunes, immolated their friends, and risked their own lives. General Washington himself observed, when he signed the new constitution, that "it was an experiment on which the destiny of the republican model of government was staked." But the system was adopted with expectations of amendment, and the experiment [369] proved salutary, and has ultimately redounded as much to the honor and interest of America, as any mode or form of government that could have been devised by the wisdom of man.

It is beyond a doubt, that no man in the union had it so much in his power to assimilate the parties, conciliate the affections, and obtain a general sanction to the new constitution, as a gentleman who commanded their obedience in the field, and had won the veneration, respect, and affections of the people, in the most distant parts of the union. Yet, soon after the organization of the new constitution of government, a struggle began to take place between monarchists and republicans, the consequences of which some future period must disclose. From a variety of new sources; of new objects of magnificence opening before them; of new prospects of wealth anticipated, the spirit of intrigue was matured even among the politicians of yesterday. Some of them were sighing for more liberty, without discretion or judgment to make a proper use of what they already possessed; others were grasping at powers, which neither reason or law, constitutions of their own forming, nor the feelings of nature could justify.

[370] Thus it appeared, convulsions might ensue, great conflicts be sustained, and great spirits be subdued, before the minds of every

CHAP. XXXI class could be perfectly tranquillized, even under the wisest system of human government. But such a people as the Americans cannot suddenly be reduced to a state of slavery; it is a work of time to obliterate old opinions, founded in reason, and fanned by enthusiasm, till they had become a part of the religious creed of a nation. Notwithstanding the apprehensions which have pervaded the minds of many, America will probably long retain a greater share of freedom than can perhaps be found in any other part of the civilized world. This may be more the result of her local situation, than from her superior policy or moderation. From the general equality of fortune which had formerly reigned among them, it may be modestly asserted, that most of the inhabitants of America were too proud for monarchy, yet too poor for nobility, and it is to be feared, too selfish and avaricious for a virtuous republic.

The people of America however were not yet prepared, like the ungrateful Israelites to ask a king, nor were their spirits sufficiently broken, to yield the "best of their olive-grounds to his servants, or to see their sons appointed to run before his chariots." Yet it was to be regretted, that there soon appeared [371] a class of men, who, though taken from the bar, the shop, or the more simple occupations of life to command armies, and to negociate with foreign nations, had imbibed ideas of distinguished rank and ostentatious titles, incompatible with republican principles, and totally repugnant to the views of the zealous advocates of American freedom. Indeed many of these had been swept off by the hand of time and death; those who still lived in the shade of retirement, observed with regret, that unless counteracted with firmness, the fiat of an individual might become more respected than the general will of the people.

There yet remained a considerable class of these firm adherents to the principles of the revolution; they were strongly impressed with the necessity of an energetic government, and the weakness of the old confederation. They were also sensible of the many difficulties that must arise in the fiscal arrangements of a people, who had been long without a stable medium of trade, while agriculture, commerce, and every other pursuit, wore a new face, in consequence of a long war. But they had not contemplated the introduction of new projects, which were thought designed to enrich and ennoble some of the officers of the army, to create a splendid government, and to support the dignity of new orders in the state. These were articles that had made no part of their creed.

[372] The spirit of finance, which, a sensible writer observes, CHAP. XXXI "accumulates woes on the head of a people, by stripping them of the means of subsistence, and what is infinitely more to be regretted, saps the foundations of morality," had heretofore been only the dream of some overgrown public creditor. A funding system afterwards introduced, attended with all the intricacies of more aged financiers, which never could be understood, and a public debt thereby enhanced, which was probably never intended to be paid, was impregnated in the brain of a young officer* of foreign extraction, an adventurer of a bold genius, active talents, and fortunate combinations, from his birth to the exalted station to which he was listed by the spirit of favoritism in American arrangements. Yet when the system appeared, it was embraced with warmth by a considerable class, as the legitimate child of speculation. But it appeared a monster in the eye of a very large part of the community, who viewed it as the parent of a national debt that would hang on the neck of America to the latest generations.

Hence, a train of restless passions were awakened, that excited to activity, and created a rage for project, speculation, and various artifices, to support a factitious dignity, which finally ruined multitudes of unsuspecting citizens [373]. Hence a spirit of public gambling, speculation in paper, in lands, in every thing else, to a degree unparalleled in any nation. Many other contingencies were felt too severely to require a particular specification.

When general Washington was placed in the presidential chair, he doubtless felt all the solicitude for the discharge of his duty, which such a sacred deposite entrusted to his integrity would naturally awaken. His own reputation was blended with the administration of government on those principles of republicanism, which he had always professed, and which he had supported by his sword; while time, circumstances and interests had changed the opinions of many influential characters.

Thus, the favored and beloved Washington, called from his first retirement to act as chief magistrate in the administration of civil government, whatever measures he sanctioned, were considered as the best, the wisest, and most just, by a great majority of the people. In most instances, it is true, he presided with wisdom, dignity, and moderation, but complete perfection is not to be attributed to man. Undue prejudices and partialities often imperceptibly creep into the

---

* Alexander Hamilton.

CHAP. XXXI best of hearts; and with all the veneration due to so meritorious a character, there were many who thought him too much under the influence of military favorites.

[374] A very judicious gentleman well acquainted with ancient history, and with modern politics,* observed, during the administration of general Washington, that

> the president of the United States held the hearts of all America in his hand, from the moment of his elevation to the command of her armies, to his honorable retirement to private life, and from his dignified retreat to his inauguration at New York. Placed in the executive chair by the united voice of all parties, it was expected the chief magistrate, whom flattery endows with all perfection, and to whom justice attributes many excellent qualities, would have felt himself above the partialities that usually hang about the human heart; and that, divesting himself of the little prejudices that obtrude and frequently sully the greatest characters, he would have been of no party in his appointments, and that real merit, whether *federal* or *anti-federal*, would have been equally noticed.
>
> It was not expected, that those gentlemen who wished for a more perfect system of government, or some amendments to the present, would have been cut off from every social and political claim; and that only the officers of the late army, and the devotees to unconditional ratification, would have [375] been thought worthy of confidence or place under a government that has yet the minds of a considerable part of the people to soothe, and the affections of a judicious and discerning party to conciliate.†
>
> True policy should have dictated the most impartial distribution of office in the new arrangement. It is a new and untried experiment, into which many of the people think they have been precipitated, without time for due consideration. They begin to feel the weight of taxes and imposts to which they have been accustomed. They begin to inquire whether all the late energetic exertions, were designed only to subserve the interests of a certain party, and to furnish salaries, sinecures, and extravagant compensations for the favorites of the army and the sycophants of power, to the exclusion of all who had not adopted the creed of passive obedience.

A cool examiner, who may hereafter retrospect the period, from the establishment of the American constitution to the close of the administration of the first president, will judge, on the detail of facts, whether there was or was not just reason for the above observations. [376] Future historic writers may scrutinize and survey past transactions

---

* Letter to the author. [Source not identified.]

† This letter was written before several important amendments were made.

with due criticism and candor, when, whatever may have been CHAP. XXXI observed on any other subject, all will allow that no steps, during the civil functions of president Washington, were so unpopular as the Indian war, sanctioned by the president soon after the operation of the measures of the new government, and his ratification of a treaty with Great Britain, negociated by John Jay, Esq. The appointment of this gentleman to a diplomatic character, while chief justice of the supreme court of the union, was thought very objectionable, and very sensible protests were entered in the senate, against the blending of office. It was thought very incompatible with the principles of the constitution, to act in the double capacity of a negociator abroad and the first officer of justice at home.

Notwithstanding these objections, Mr. Jay was commissioned, and repaired to England, ostensibly to require the surrender of the western posts, the retention of which had brought on the war with the savages, as observed above, and to demand satisfaction for the depredations and spoliations that had for several years been made on American commerce, in defiance of the late treaty of peace. The war in which England was then engaged against France had given a pretext for those spoliations. The happiness and tranquillity of the English nation [377] had not appeared to have been much enhanced, either by the struggle or the termination of the war with their former colonies. After the pacification of the nations at war, and the conclusion of peace between Great Britain and America, such feuds arose in England from various sources and causes of discontent, as discovered that the nation were for a time far from being more tranquillized than the United States, previous to their adoption of the present constitution.

Indeed the English nation had few causes of triumph; their systems of policy had been every where deranged, and their fatal mistakes exemplified in the distresses of their eastern dominions, as well as those in the west. The confusion in the East Indies, and the misconduct of their officers there, called aloud for inquiry and reform: and amidst the complicated difficulties which embarrassed the measures of administration, their king became insane, the royal family were at variance, and the heir apparent had many causes of discontent, besides the alienation of his parents, which had been some time increasing. The parliament and the ministry were intriguing for power, and various parties claimed their right to assume the reins of government during the king's disability, and the recollections of all were embittered, by a retrospect [378] of the misfortunes they had experienced during the

CHAP. XXXI late war. Their losses had been incalculable, nor could the wisest of their statesmen devise methods for the payment of even the interest of the enormous national debt, and the recovery of the nation to that scale of honour, prosperity and grandeur they had formerly enjoyed.

In this summary view of the state of the British nation for the last ten years, a treaty with England was not a very desirable object in the eyes of many of the most judicious statesmen in America. Perhaps no man was better qualified than Mr. Jay to undertake to negociate a business of so much delicacy and responsibility. He was a gentleman of strict integrity, amiable manners, and complacent disposition; whose talents for negociation had been evinced by his firmness, in conjunction with his colleagues, when they effected a treaty of peace at Paris, in one thousand seven hundred and eighty-three. But while in England, whether from the influence of the court of St. James, or from any predetermined system, with regard to England or France, or from the yielding softness of a mind, naturally urbane and polite, is uncertain. Yet whatever might have been the principal operative cause, it is beyond a doubt, that Mr. Jay fell from the dignified, manly, independent spirit which ought to have marked an American negociator. He was led to succumb [279] too far to the dictations of lord Grenville; this condescension undoubtedly arose, more from an apprehension that he could not do better, than from any inclination to swerve from the interests of his country. The consequence was, he agreed to a treaty highly advantageous to Great Britain, degrading to the United States, very offensive to France, the ally of America in the days of her tribulation, and who was now herself at war with Great Britain, in conjunction with most of the European potentates, combined* to overthrow the newly established government in France.

This government they had erected, through civil convulsions that distorted every thing from its ancient form and order. Monarchy was overthrown, their king decapitated, hierarchy abolished, and a super-stitious priesthood annihilated, amidst the destruction of the lives of thousands of all classes, and a series of such bloody deeds of horror as freeze the soul of humanity on the recollection. These revolutionary scenes in every nation, are generally attended with circumstances shocking to the feelings of compassion; yet undoubtedly all nations have a right to establish such modes and forms of government as a

---

* See treaty of Pilnitz. [The Declaration of Pilnitz, August 27, 1791, was the response of Leopold II and King Friedrich William II of Prussia to the flight and eventual arrest of Louis XVI of France. The agreement pledged armed intervention against the revolutionary regime, and war with France followed within a year.]

majority of the people shall think most conducive to the general CHAP. XXXI
interest. The various causes which contributed to more [380] distressful
scenes of barbarity than are usually exhibited in so short a period,
may be left to the discussion of those who have written, or may write
the history of the late revolution in France, and the character and
conduct of that *wonderful people.*

It was with apparent reluctance that president Washington signed
the treaty negociated by Mr. Jay: he hesitated, and observed, "that
it was pregnant with events." Many gentlemen of the first penetration
foresaw and dreaded the consequences of this diplomatic transaction;
some scrupled not to declare, that it was not only "pregnant with
events," but "with evils." But, notwithstanding it wore so disgusting
an aspect to more than one half the citizens of the United States, it
was ratified by a majority in the senate, signed by the president, and
became the supreme law of the land.

This ratification created a division of sentiment, which was artfully
wrought up, until a disseveration of opinion appeared throughout the
union. In congress, the parties on every great question seemed nearly
equally divided; each had their partisans: the spirits of the people
were agitated and embittered to an alarming degree, by the extreme
point of opposition in which the instrument was viewed. The whole
body of the people were designated under traits of distinction which
never ought [381] to exist in the United States; and a struggle took
place, the consequences of which some future period must disclose.

It is disgraceful indeed to Americans, who had just broken the
shackles of foreign domination, to submit to the unhappy distinction
of British or French partisans. But the attachment of many of their
old allies, to whom they felt themselves obliged, of many others to
the British nation, its modes of government and its commerce,
occasioned such a stigma to mark them for a time.

America should indeed forever have maintained a character of her
own, that should have set her on high ground, whence she might
have looked down from the pinnacle of independence and peace, and
only have pitied the squabbles, the confusion, and the miseries of
the European world. A quarter of the globe blessed with all the
productions of nature, increasing astonishingly in population, improv-
ing rapidly in erudition, arts, and all the sciences necessary to the
happiness of man; bounded by a vast ocean, by rivers, by mountains,
that have been the wonder of ages, ought forever to hold herself
independent on any power on earth.

Imagination may indulge a pleasing reverie, and suppose for a

CHAP. XXXI moment, that if the government [382] of the United States had reared a defence around her sea-board, that might have reached to the heavens, by her bold inhibitions against all foreign connexions, or commercial and political intercourse with distant nations, it might have been the best barrier to her peace, liberty, and happiness. But there are no mounds of separation, either natural or artificial, and perhaps had it been practicable there should have been, they might have been penetrated by a thirst for wealth; commerce might have shaken them to the foundation, or ambition might have broken down the battlements.

Instead of guarding round the infant republic of America, by a total detachment from foreign connexions, affection, or influence, we have already seen the inhabitants of the United States, interesting themselves beyond the common feelings of humanity, in the operations of European wars, dissensions, politics, and government.

It is not strange that the astonishing revolution in France should be beheld with very extraordinary emotions. The world had viewed the excision of a king, queen, and the royal family of the house of Bourbon. The existing generation had witnessed the extinction of the claims of a long line of ancestral dignitaries, that had been supported from Charlemagne to Lewis the sixteenth, under all the appendages of despotism that had oppressed its millions, [383] until they had reached that point of degradation and servility, beyond which the elastic mind of man can bend no farther. This yoke was broken, and the bars burst in sunder by the strong hand of the people, and by the operations of a resentment which discovered more than the imaginary reactions of nature, among the inhabitants of a vast domain. This people had been too long viewed as a nation of slaves, and their struggles for freedom and the equal rights of man ought to have been cherished by Americans, who had just obtained their own independence, by a resistance that had cost them much of the best blood of their citizens.

But the Gallican nation at this period was not viewed with that cordiality by some classes in America, which might have been expected. The government of the United States manifestly discovered a coolness to a nation which had so essentially aided the great American cause, in the darkest of its days; a nation with whom the United States had formed treaties, and become the allies, from interest, necessity and gratitude, and to whom they yet felt obligations that could not be easily cancelled.

The president had indeed published a proclamation of neutrality, CHAP. XXXI and made great professions of friendship to the republic of France. He also sent an envoy to reside there, while the government of France was in the hands of the [384] directory: but it was thought the appointment was not the most judicious.

A character eccentric from youth to declining age; a man of pleasure, pride, and extravagance, fond of the trappings of monarchy, and implicated by a considerable portion of the citizens of America, as deficient in principle, was not a suitable person for a resident minister in France at so important a crisis. The Gallican nation was in the utmost confusion: the effervescence of opposition to their revolution boiling high in most parts of Europe. Dissensions were heightening in America, and existing treaties in danger of being shaken. These circumstances required a man of stable principles, and respectability of character, rather than a dexterous agent of political mischief, whose abilities and address were well adapted either for private or court intrigue.

The exigencies of affairs, both at home and abroad, required an American negociator of different habits and manners. A supersedure took place. Mr. Munroe, a gentleman of unimpeachable integrity, much knowledge and information, united with distinguished abilities, great strength of mind, and a strong attachment to the republican system, was appointed and sent forward by president Washington.

A full detail of the state and situation of France, on the arrival of Mr. Munroe in a diplomatic [385] character, the impressions that had been made on the directory, relative to American affairs, the conduct of his predecessor,* and his own negociations, may be seen at large in a general view afterwards given by him of existing prejudices which had arisen from misrepresentation, neglect or design, from the excision of the king of France, until the recal and return of Mr. Munroe to his native country. It was generally believed that America derived no advantage from the former minister's repairing to England, after his mission was ended in France. He there continued for some time, fomenting by his letters the jealousies which had already arisen between the United States of America and the republic of France.

These jealousies were increased by a variety of causes, and the dissensions of party in America arose to such a height, as to threaten the dissolution of that strong cement, which ought to bind the colonies

---

* Gouverneur Morris.

CHAP. XXXI together forever. These differences of opinion, with the assuming demeanor of some of his officers, who often urged to measures that he neither approved nor wished for, rendered the president of the United States less happy than he was before he sanctioned by his name a treaty, which was disgusting to almost every state in the Union, and which perhaps he never would have signed, but [386] from the impressive influence of heads of departments, and other favorites about his person. This was a class of men who had been implicated by a considerable portion of the people, as prompting the president of the United States to call out a body of militia, consisting of fifteen thousand men, ostensibly to subdue a trivial insurrection at the westward, which it was asserted by many judicious persons, acquainted with the circumstances, might have been subdued by five hundred only.* They attributed this effort to a wish to try the experiment of the promptitude with which an army might be called forth to subserve the purposes of government, to enhance the dignity of office, and the supreme power of the first magistrate.† There was certainly a class who aimed not so much to promote the honor of the national character, as to establish the basis of a standing army, and other projects approaching to despotic sway, which cannot be supported in America, without the aid of that dangerous engine.

It is dangerous indeed for the ear of the chief magistrate to be open to favorites of such a complexion. Such an one will probably neglect his old associates, and confer places upon [387] men of not the first abilities in the Union. These are selected only in times of imminent danger; after which their services, integrity and zeal, are too frequently repaid by the ingratitude of the people, which joins the cry of the artful, who have never labored in the vineyard, to send them into oblivion.

The men most opposed to the British treaty, negociated in one thousand seven hundred and ninety-four, and who stated their objections on the most rational grounds, were generally those who had been distinguished for their patriotism, firmness and abilities. They had been very influential in a variety of departments, previous to the year one thousand seven hundred and seventy-five. Nor had

---

* See Findley's history of the disturbances in the back parts of Pennsylvania. [William Findley, *History of the Insurrection in the Four Western Counties of Pennsylvania: in the Year MDCCXCIV* (Philadelphia, 1796).]

† General Hamilton was believed to be the prime mover and conductor of this extraordinary business.

they ever relaxed in their energies during the course of the war, to effect the emancipation of their country from the tyranny of the crown of Britain, and to obtain the independence of the United States.

These circumstances, with the approach of a period when nature requires rest, rendered the weight of government oppressive to declining age. The man who had long commanded, in a remarkable manner, the affection, the esteem, and the confidence of his country, again abdicated his power, took leave of the cares of state, and retired a second time from all public occupations, to the delightful retreats of private [388] life, on his highly cultivated farm, on the banks of the Patowmack.

Previous to general Washington's second return to his rural amusements, he published a farewel address to the inhabitants of the United States, fraught with advice worthy of the statesman, the hero, and the citizen. He exhorted them to union among themselves, economy in public expenditure, sobriety, temperance, and industry in private life. He solemnly warned them against the danger of foreign influence, exhorted them to observe good faith and justice toward all nations, to cultivate peace and harmony with all, to indulge no inveterate antipathies against any, or passionate attachments for particular nations, but to be constantly awake against the insidious wiles of foreign influence, observing, that "this was one of the most baneful foes of republican government." This was indeed, after they were split into factions; after an exotic taste had been introduced into America, which had a tendency to enhance their public and to accumulate their private debts; and after the poison of foreign influence had crept into their councils, and created a passion to assimilate the politics and the government of the United States nearer to the model of European monarchies than the letter of the constitution, by any fair construction, would admit. It was also, after luxury had spread over every class, while the *stimulus* to [389] private industry was in a degree cut off by the capture of their shipping by the belligerent powers, under various pretences of the breach of neutrality.

After this period new contingencies arose, and new discussions were required with regard to foreign relations and connexions, that had no pacific operation, or any tendency to conciliate the minds, or to quiet the perturbed spirits of existing parties.

The operations and the consequences of the civil administration of the first president of the United States, notwithstanding the many excellent qualities of his heart, and the virtues which adorned his

CHAP. XXXI life, have since been viewed at such opposite points, that further strictures on his character and conduct shall be left to future historians, after time has mollified the passions and prejudices of the present generation. A new constitution, and an extensive government, in which he acted eight years as chief magistrate, open a new field of observation, for future pens to descant on the merits or demerits of a man, admired abroad, beloved at home, and celebrated through half the globe: this will be done according to the variety of opinions which will ever exist among mankind, when character is surveyed in the cool moments of calm philosophy, which contemplates the nature and passions of man, and the contingent [390] circumstances, that lift him to the skies, or leave him in the shade of doubtful opinion.

Public opinion is generally grounded on truth; but the enthusiasm to which the greatest part of mankind are liable, often urges the passions to such a degree of extravagance, as to confound the just ratio of praise or reproach: but the services and merits of general Washington, are so deeply engraven on the hearts of his countrymen, that no time or circumstance will or ought ever to efface the lustre of his well earned reputation.

We have already seen, that after the peace, the infant confederated states exhibited scenes and disclosed projects that open too wide a field for discussion, to bring down a regular historical work, farther than the moment which winds up the drama of the military, political, and civil administration of a man, whose name will have a conspicuous place in all future historical records.

History may not furnish an example of a person so generally admired, and possessed of equal opportunities for making himself the despotic master of the liberties of his country, who had the moderation repeatedly to divest himself of all authority, and retire to private life with the sentiments expressed by himself in the close of his farewel address: he there observed

> I [391] anticipate with pleasing expectation that retreat, in which I promise myself to realize, without alloy, the sweet enjoyment of partaking, in the midst of my fellow citizens, the benign influence of good laws under a free government—the ever favorite object of my heart, and the happy reward, as I trust, of our mutual cares, labor, and dangers.

The commander of the armies of the United States, has been conducted from the field of war, and from the zenith of civil command, to the delicious retreats of peaceful solitude. We now leave him in

the shade of retirement, with fervent wishes that he may wind up CHAP. XXX.
the career of human life in that tranquillity which becomes the hero
and the Christian.

The administration of his immediate successor we shall also leave,
after some general observations on the character of a man who long
acted in the most conspicuous departments of American affairs. The
veracity of an historian requires, that all those who have been
distinguished, either by their abilities or their elevated rank, should
be exhibited through every period of public life with impartiality and
truth. But the heart of the annalist may sometimes be hurt by political
deviations which the pen of the historian is obliged to record.

[392] Mr. Adams was undoubtedly a statesman of penetration and
ability; but his prejudices and his passions were sometimes too strong
for his sagacity and judgment.

After Great Britain had acknowledged the independence of the
dismembered colonies, Mr. Adams was sent to England, with a view
of negociating a treaty of commerce; but the government too sore
from the loss of the colonies, and the nation too much soured by the
breach, nothing was done. He however resided there four or five
years; and unfortunately for himself and his country, he became so
enamoured with the British constitution, and the government, manners, and laws of the nation, that a partiality for monarchy appeared,
which was inconsistent with his former professions of republicanism.
Time and circumstances often lead so imperfect a creature as man to
view the same thing in a very different point of light.

After Mr. Adams's return from England, he was implicated by a
large portion of his countrymen, as having relinquished the republican
system, and forgotten the principles of the American revolution, which
he had advocated for near twenty years.

The political errors of men of talents, sometimes spring from their
own passions; often [393] from their prejudices imbibed by local or
incidental circumstances; and not unfrequently from the versatile
condition of man, which renders it difficult, at one period, to decide
on the best system of civil government; or at another, on the most
effectual means of promoting the general happiness of mankind. This
may lead the candid mind to cast a veil over that ambiguity which
confounds opinion, and that counteraction of former principles, which
often sets a man in opposition to himself, and prevents that uniformity
of conduct which dignifies, and that consistency which adorns the
character.

Pride of talents and much ambition, were undoubtedly combined the character of the president who immediately succeeded general Washington, and the existing circumstances of his country, with his own capacity for business, gave him an opportunity for the full gratification of the most prominent features of his character.

Endowed with a comprehensive genius, well acquainted with the history of men and nations; and having long appeared to be actuated by the principles of integrity, by a zeal for the rights of men, and an honest indignation at the ideas of despotism, it was viewed as a kind of political phenomenon, when discovered that [394] Mr. Adams's former opinions were beclouded by a partiality for monarchy. It may however be charitably presumed, that by living long near the splendor of courts and courtiers, with other concurring circumstances, he might become so biassed in his judgment as to think that an hereditary monarchy was the best government for his native country.* From his knowledge of men, he was sensible it was easy to turn the tide of public opinion in favor of any system supported by plausible argumentation. Thus he drew a doleful picture of the confusion and dissolution of all republics, and presented it to the eyes of his countrymen, under the title of a "Defence of their constitutions." This had a powerful tendency to shake the republican system through the United States. Yet the predilection of Americans in general, in favor of a republican form of government was so strong, that few had the hardiness to counteract it, until several years after the United States had become an independent nation.

On Mr. Adams's return from England, he undoubtedly discovered a partiality in favor of [395] monarchic government, and few scrupled to assert for a time, that he exerted his abilities to encourage the operation of those principles in America. But any further strictures are unnecessary in this place on the character of a gentleman, whose official stations, abilities and services, amidst the revolutionary conflict, may probably excite some future historian to investigate the causes of his lapse from former republican principles, and to observe with due propriety on his administration and its consequences while president of the United States.

---

* Circumstances may in some future day render it necessary to adopt this mode of government in the United States. Rome had not a master until the people had become prepared for the yoke by their dissensions and follies. These, more than the arm of Caesar, rivetted their chains, and sunk them to a level with the most abject and servile nations.

It is with more pleasure the writer records, that notwithstanding CHAP. XXXI
any mistakes or changes in political opinion, or errors in public
conduct, Mr. Adams, in private life, supported an unimpeachable
character; his habits of morality, decency and religion, rendered him
amiable in his family, and beloved by his neighbours. The opinions
of a man of such sobriety of manners, political experience, and general
knowledge of morals, law and government, will ever have a powerful
effect on society, and must naturally influence the people, more
especially the rising generation, the young men, who have not had
the opportunity of acquainting themselves with the character, police,
and jurisprudence of nations, or with the history of their own country,
much less with the principles on which the American revolution was
grounded.

[396] There is a propensity in mankind, to enlist themselves under
the authority of names, and to adopt the opinions of men of celebrity,
more from the fashion of the times, than from the convictions of
reason. Thus with the borrowed language of their chieftain, they
impose upon themselves, until they think his opinions are their own,
and are often wrought up to such a fierce spirit of contention, that
they appear ready to defend them in all the cruel modes of the savage,
who is seldom actuated by motives of candor and forgiveness of
injuries.

Both history and experience have proved, that when party feuds
have thus divided a nation, urbanity and benevolence are laid aside;
and, influenced by the most malignant and corrupt passions, they lose
sight of the sacred obligations of virtue, until there appears little
difference in the ferocious spirits of men in the most refined and
civilized society, or among the rude and barbarous hordes of the
wilderness. Though some symptoms of this degradation of the human
character have appeared in America, we hope the cloud is fast
dissipating, and that no vicissitudes in human affairs, no intrigues of
the interested, nor any mistakes of upright men will ever damp the
prospect of the establishment and continuance of a republican system,
which appears to be best adapted to the genius of Americans. This
form of government has the voice of the majority; the [397] energies
and sacrifices of the sons of Columbia, have been exerted to leave a
republican form, defined, modified and digested, as a model to
promote the happiness of posterity.

Yet there is still a division of parties, and a variety of sentiment,
relative to a subject that has heated the imaginations, and divided

CHAP. XXXI the opinions of mankind, from the rise of the Roman republic to the destruction of her splendid empire; and from that day to the present, when the divisions of the literati of every age, have called the attention of genius and ability to speculate and to dissent in their ideas of the best modes and forms of government.

It may be a subject of wonder and inquiry, that though so many ages have elapsed, and so great a part of the world been civilized and improved, that the science of politics is still darkened by the variety of opinions that prevail among mankind. It may be beyond the reach of human genius, to construct a fabric so free as to release from subordination, nor in the present condition of mankind ought it ever to be wished. Authority and obedience are necessary to preserve social order, and to continue the prosperity or even the existence of nations. But it may be observed, that despotism is not always the certain consequence of monarchy, nor freedom the sure result of republican theories.

[398] It would be presumption in the writer, to entangle herself on a subject of such magnitude and importance, as to decide peremptorily, whether aristocratic, monarchic, or democratic government, is best adapted to the general happiness of the people. This shall be left to bolder pens; she will indulge little farther aberration of her's, after the expression of her wishes, that amidst the heterogeneous opinions of a theoretic age, America may not trifle away her advantages by her own folly and levity, nor be robbed of any of the essential rights which have cost her so dear, by the intrigues or ambition of any class of men.

The speculative of every age have theorized on a system of perfect republicanism, but the experiment has much oftener failed in practice, among all mankind, than been crowned with success. Those that have come nearest thereto, the free states of Greece, the Achean league, the Amphyctions, and other confederacies, fell under the power of Philip, Alexander, and their successors. The republic of Athens, the most conspicuous among the ancients, corrupted by riches and luxury, was wasted and lost by the intrigues of its own ambitious citizens.

The Roman commonwealth, the proud boast, the pattern, and exemplar of the republics, fell under the despotism of a long line of Caesars, generally the most debauched and brutal race [399] of emperors that ever disgraced human nature. More modern experiments, Venice, and indeed all the Italian states, who boasted their freedom, were subjected to the tyranny of an oligarchy or aristocracy, CHAP. XXXI frequently more severe and cruel than that of monarchy. In England, the struggles of Hampden and his virtuous associates were lost, and the strong reasonings of the patriots of that day in favor of freedom were obliterated, after the death of Charles, by the artful, the hypocritical, and the arbitrary Cromwell; and the most voluptuous of kings was restored, and re-seated on the throne of Britain.

Thus, from the first of the Stuarts to the last of the line of Brunswick who have yet reigned, their republican opinions and the freedom of the nation have been in the wane, and have finally sunk into an empty name under the tyranny of George the third. Indeed the most enlightened, rational, and independent characters in Great Britain continue still to defend the principles of liberty with their pens, while they have had reason to apprehend its total extinction through the realm.

Innumerable other instances might be adduced of the defeat of republicanism, in spite of the efforts of its most zealous friends: yet this is no proof that this system of government may not be more productive of happiness to mankind than that of monarchy or aristocracy. [400] The United States of America have now a fair experiment of a republican system to make for themselves; they may perhaps be possessed of more materials that promise success than have ever fallen to the lot of any other nation. From the peculiar circumstances of the emigration of their ancestors, there is little reason to fear that a veil of darkness, tyranny, and barbarity will soon overspread the land to which they fled. These were a set of men very different in principles and manners from any that are to be found in the histories of colonization, where it may be observed, the first planters have been generally either men of enterprise for the acquisition of riches or fame, or convicted villains transported from more civilized societies.

In the outset of the American revolution, the arm of foreign power was opposed by a people uncontaminated by foreign luxury, the intricacies of foreign policies, or the theological jargon of metaphysical sceptics of foreign extract. Philosophy then conveyed honorable ideas of science, of religion, and morals: the character is since degraded by the unprincipled sarcasms of men of letters, who assume the dignity of philosophic thought. Instead of unfolding the sources of knowledge, and inculcating truth, they often confound without convincing, and by their sophistical reasonings leave the superficial [401] reader, their newly initiated disciple, on the comfortless shores of annihilation.

CHAP. XXXI   These observations are not confined to any particular nation or character; the historians of Britain, and the philosophers and poets of France, Germany, and England, are perhaps equally culpable; and it is to be regretted that America has not preserved a national character of her own, free from any symptoms of pernicious deviation from the purest principles on morals, religion, and civil liberty. She has been conducted through a revolution that will be ever memorable, both for its origin, its success, and the new prospects it has opened both at home and abroad. The consequences of this revolution have not been confined to one quarter of the globe, but the dissemination of more liberal principles in government, and more honorable opinions of the rights of man, and the melioration of his condition, have been spread over a considerable part of the world.

But men, prone to abuse the best advantages, sent by the beneficent hand of providence, sometimes sport them away, or confound causes with effects, which lead to the most erroneous conclusions. Thus it has been the recent fashion of courtiers, and of a great part of the clergy, under monarchic governments, to impute [402] the demoralization and scepticism that prevails, to the spirit of free inquiry, as it regards the rights of civil society. This fashion has been adopted by all anti-republicans in America; but it may be asked, whether the declamation and clamor against the dissemination of republican opinions on civil government, as originating the prevalence of atheistical folly, is founded on the basis of truth?

Examine the history of the ancient republics of Greece, and the splendid commonwealth of Rome; was not the strictest regard paid to the worship of their gods, and a sacred observance of their religious rites enjoined, until the Grecian republics were overthrown by ambitious individuals? It was then that sceptical disputes more generally employed the philosophers; in consequence of which the rulers and the people sunk into an indifference to all religion. The rich city of Athens particularly, was early corrupted by the influx of wealth, the influence of aristocratic nobles, and the annihilation of every principle connected with religion.

Survey the Roman commonwealth before its decline, when it was most worthy of the imitation of republicans. Was not a general regard paid to the worship of their deities, among this celebrated people, and a superstitious attention observed, relative to omens, prodigies and judgments, as denounced and executed by their [403] gods, until republicanism was extinguished, the commonwealth subverted, and

the sceptre of a single sovereign was stretched over that vast empire? CHAP. XXXI
It was then that Caligula set up his horse to be worshipped, as a
burlesque on religion, and the sycophants of the court encouraged
every caprice of their emperor. The people did not become so
universally corrupt as to throw off all regard for religion, and all
homage to the deities of their ancestors, until the libidinous conduct
of their august sovereigns, and the nobles of the court, set the
example.

Nor do we read in more sacred history, through all the story of the
Israelites, that the fool ever said in his heart, there is no God, until
under the dominion of kings.

It may be observed in the character of more modern republics, that
religion has been the grand palladium of their institutions. Through
all the free states of Italy, democracy and religion have been considered
in union; some of them have indeed been darkened by superstition
and bigotry, yet not equally hoodwinked under republican governments as are the neighbouring kingdoms of Spain and Portugal,
subjected to monarchic despotism.

By no fair deduction can it be asserted, that the scepticism and the
late appearance of a total disregard to religious observances in France,
[404] are in consequence of the democratic struggles of the nation.
The dereliction of all religious principles among the *literati* of France,
and the abominable opinions of some of their philosophers, cannot
be too much detested; but they have sprung from various causes,
remote from political freedom, and too complicated to trace their
origin, in a page of cursory observations.

The French have long been a highly civilized, refined, luxurious
nation, divided into two classes, the learned and the infidel, the
ignorant and superstitious, both equally pursuing present pleasure,
with little regard to moral principle, the laws of reason, of God, or of
nature, any further than prompted by the gratifications of the moment.
The first were patronised by the court; the rich and the noble had
been generally infidel for more than a century before the revolution.
The last were poor, depressed and degraded by monarchic and prelatic
power, until their indigence and misery produced universal murmur,
and revolution burst on a nation, too ignorant to investigate the
sources of their own wretchedness, and too volatile and impatient to
wait the operation of measures adapted for relief by men of more
information and ability than themselves.

Thus from the ignorance and imbecility of a people degraded by oppression, and long the dupes of priestly as well as monarchic tyranny, they [405] naturally followed the lead of their superiors. These had long been the infidel disciples of Voltaire, D'Alembert, and Diderot; the atheistical opinions of these men, and others of their character, had been cherished only by courtiers and academicians, until near the middle of the eighteenth century, when their numerous adherents, who had concealed their pernicious opinions under the veil of modesty, threw off the mask, came out openly, and set religion at defiance. But the shackles of superstition were not yet broken, nor were any remarkable struggles made in favor of civil liberty, until the flame was caught by their officers and soldiers, and resistance to tyranny taught them, while in union with the sober and pious Americans. They were animated by the principles of freedom while they lent their arm in aid of the energies of a people, whose character had never been impeached as favorers of atheistical opinions, and who were only exerting their abilities, both in the cabinet and the field, in supporting the civil and social rights of men.

On the return of this veteran band of officers and soldiers to their own nation, they found as they had left, a voluptuous court, a licentious and extravagant nobility, a corrupted priesthood, and an ignorant multitude spread over the face of one of the finest countries on earth. Yet the murmurs against tyranny and oppression [406] had become so general, that some ineffectual efforts for relief had been made without any digested system of means that might produce it. Previous to this period, some of their parliaments had discovered spirit and energy to resist the despotic mandates of the crown: but the arm of royalty was yet too potent to receive any check, while the whole nation was held in bondage by the strong hand of their *grand monarch.*

These combined circumstances brought forward an assembly of notables, and a national convention, neither of which were capable of quieting the universal discontent and disaffection to royalty that prevailed. Hence the destruction of the Bastile; the imprisonment and decapitation of their king and queen; the extermination of their nobility and clergy; the assassination of many of their first literary characters; and the indiscriminate murder of ladies of the fairest fame and virtue, and women of little consideration; of characters of the highest celebrity, of nobles, magistrates, and men without name or distinction.

These sudden eruptions of the passions of the multitude, spread, like the lava of a volcano, throughout all France, nor could men of CHAP. XXXI correct judgment, who aimed only at the reform of abuses, and a renovation in all the departments, check the fury of the torrent. This confusion [407] and terror within, and an army without, sent on by the combined despots of Europe, with the professed design of subjecting the nation, and re-establishing the monarchy of France, gave an opportunity to ambitious, unprincipled, corrupt, and ignorant men, to come forward, under pretence of supporting the rights and liberties of mankind, without any views but those of disorder and disorganization. Thus in the midst of tumult and confusion, was indulged every vicious propensity, peculation, revenge, and all the black passions of the soul. The guillotine was glutted with the blood of innocent victims, while the rapidity of execution, and their jealousy of each other, involved the most guilty, and cut down many of the blackest miscreants, as well as the most virtuous characters in the nation.

But from the rise and progress of this period of horror, this outrage of humanity, it is evident that it originated more from former monarchic and priestly oppression, than from the operation of infidel opinions, united with republican efforts. In consequence of this state of things, though there were very many characters of the best intentions, principles and abilities, animated and active for the promotion of civil liberty in France, they had to regret with all the humane, benevolent, and pious, that while engaged to eradicate the superstitions of their country, and the arbitrary strides of their [408] civil rulers, law was annihilated and even the government of Heaven renounced. Thus, all religious opinions were set afloat, the passions let loose, and all distinctions levelled. Decency, humanity, and every thing else re-spected in civil society, disappeared, until the outrages of cruelty and licentiousness resembled the regions of pandemonium. Thus was republicanism disgraced by the demoralization of the people, and a cloud of infidelity darkened the hemisphere of France; but there is nothing to countenance the opinion, that scepticism was the origin or the result of the struggles of the Gallican nation in favor of civil liberty.*

This people may have had their day of licentious enjoyment, of literary fame, of taste, elegance and splendor; they have abused his

---

* The above summary of the French revolution was written several years before monarchy was re-established in France.

CHAP. XXXI gifts and denied the God of nature, who, according to the usual course of his government among men, may devote them to that ruin which is the natural consequence of luxury and impiety. Yet the God of providence, when national punishment has been sufficiently inflicted, may bring them back again to a due sense of religion and order; while the seeds of liberty, which they have disseminated far and wide, may ripen in every soil, and in full maturity [409] extend the branches of general freedom, through Europe, and perhaps throughout the world. After all, we are inadequate to any calculation on future events; the ways of heaven are hidden in the depths of time, and a small circumstance frequently gives a new turn to the most probable contingencies that seem to measure the fate of men or of empires.*

We will now leave this extraordinary nation, which has furnished materials for history of the most interesting nature, as it regards the character of man; their civil, political, and religious institutions, and the moral and social ties that connect society. From them we will look over to the island of Britain, and survey the gradations of principles, manners, and science, there. We shall find that lord Herbert, one of the first and most notorious infidels in England, sprung [410] up under kingly government; and none will deny that scepticism has prevailed, and has been gathering strength both in France and England, under monarchy, even before the correspondencies of British infidels with St. Evremond, and other sceptical Frenchmen. Hobbes, Hume, and Bolingbroke, were subjects of a

* The duke D'Alencour, who visited the family of the author, in his exile under the tyranny of Robespierre, observed justly, that "the sources of disorder in France were so innumerable, that it was impossible to conjecture when tranquillity would be again restored, or what masters or what government the nation would sit down under, after their violent convulsions subsided." Through a very interesting conversation relative to the causes and consequences of the revolution, the deepest marks of grief and sensibility sat on the countenance of the noble sufferer, expressive of the pain he felt for the miseries of his country, and the misfortunes of his family. [Duc de la Rochefoucauld-Liancourt recounted his visit to the Warrens in *Voyages dans les Etats-Unis d'Amerique* (Paris, 1799), III: 150. He observed that James Warren was "now an old man, and very frail. His wife is as old as himself, but much more lively in conversation. Like the other ladies of America, she has read a great deal on a variety of subjects. She has even published one or two volumes of tales, which are much esteemed; and she has written a history of the American revolution. . . . This old lady, at the age of seventy, is truly interesting; for she has lost neither the activity of her mind, nor the graces of her person. . . ." *Travels Through the United States of North America, the Country of the Iriquois, and Upper Canada, in the Years 1795, 1796, and 1797* (London, 1799), I: 485.]

king of England; and while their disciples have been increasing, and CHAP. XXXI
their deistical opinions have poisoned the minds of youth of genius,
and shaken the faith of some even in clerical professions, yet no
democratic opinions have been generally spread over the nation.

In the zenith of British monarchy, and the golden age of nobility,
while republicanism has been quite out of fashion, has not the cause
of Christianity suffered by the fascinating pen of a Gibbon, whose
epithets charm while they shock, and whose learned eloquence leads
the believer to pause and tremble for the multitudes that may be
allured by the sophistry of his arguments, his satirical wit, the elegance
of his diction, and the beautiful antithesis of many of his periods.

The elegance of his style confers an "alarming popularity on the
licentiousness of his opinions." The rise and fall of the Roman republic
will probably be read by many who have not the inclination or the
opportunity to study the writings of Locke, Boyle, Butler, [411]
Newton, Clarke, and many others, who have by their example and
by the pen supported and defended the Christian system on principles
of reason and argument, that will forever adorn the character of
Englishmen. A writer of ingenuity has observed, that, "there are
probably more sceptics in England than in any other country"*; yet
we do not infer that the examples of infidelity that disgrace the world,
by blasting the principles of truth, though nurtured under princely
patronage, are in consequence of the cherishing influence of monarchy.
Nor is it more just to suppose that the writings of French philosophists,
or the jejune trumpery that has for years exuded from the brain of
other theorists of that nation, is the result of speculative opinions,
with regard to civil liberty.

It is neither a preference to republican systems, nor an attachment
to monarchic or aristocratic forms of government that disseminates
the wild opinions of infidelity. It is the licentious manners of courts
of every description, the unbridled luxury of wealth, and the worst
passions of men let loose on the multitude by the example of their
superiors. Bent on gratification, at the expense of every moral tie,
they have broken down the barriers of religion, and the spirit of
infidelity is nourished at the [412] fount; thence the poisonous streams
run through every grade that constitutes the mass of nations.

* Dr. F. A. Wenderburne. He gives his reason for his assertion, page 475 of his view
  of England at the close of the eighteenth century. [Gebhard Friedrich August
  Wendeborn, A View of England Towards the Close of the Eighteenth Century (2 vols.;
  London, 1791), II: 475.]

CHAP. XXXI   It may be further observed, that there is a variety of additional causes which have led to a disposition among some part of mankind, to reject the obligations of religion, and even to deny their God. This propensity in some may easily be elucidated, without casting any part of the odium on the spirit of free inquiry relative to civil and political liberty, which had been widely disseminated, and had produced two such remarkable revolutions as those of America and France. It may be imputed to the love of novelty, the pride of opinion, and an extravagant propensity to speculate and theorize on subjects beyond the comprehension of mortals, united with a desire of being released from the restraints on their appetites and passions; restraints dictated both by reason and revelation; and which, under the influence of sober reflection, forbid the indulgence of all gratifications that are injurious to man. Further elucidations, or more abstruse causes, which contribute to lead the vain inquirer, who steps over the line prescribed by the Author of nature, to deviations from, and forgetfulness of its Creator, and to involve him in a labyrinth of darkness, from which his weak reasonings can never disentangle him, may be left to those who delight in metaphysical disquisitions.

[413] The world might reasonably have expected, from the circumstances connected with the first settlement of the American colonies, which was in consequence of their attachment to the religion of their fathers, united with a spirit of independence relative to civil government, that there would have been no observable dereliction of those honorable principles, for many ages to come. From the sobriety of their manners, their simple habits, their attention to the education and moral conduct of their children, they had the highest reason to hope, that it might have been long, very long, before the faith of their religion was shaken, or their principles corrupted, either by the manners, opinions, or habits of foreigners, bred in the courts of despotism, or the schools of licentiousness.

This hope shall not yet be relinquished. There has indeed been some relaxation of manners, and the appearance of a change in public opinion not contemplated when revolutionary scenes first shook the western world. But it must be acknowledged, that the religious and moral character of Americans yet stands on a higher grade of excellence and purity, than that of most other nations. It has been observed, that "a violation of manners has destroyed more states than the infraction of laws."* It is necessary for every *American*, [414] with

* Montesquieu. [See Charles Louis de Secondat, Baron de Montesquieu, *The Spirit*

becoming energy to endeavour to stop the dissemination of principles chap. xxxi evidently destructive of the cause for which they have bled. It must be the combined virtue of the rulers and of the people to do this, and to rescue and save their civil and religious rights from the outstretched arm of tyranny, which may appear under any mode or form of government.

Let not the frivolity of the domestic taste of the children of Columbia, nor the examples of strangers of high or low degree, that may intermix among them, or the imposing attitude of distant nations, or the machinations of the bloody tyrants of Europe, who have united themselves, and to the utmost are exerting their strength to extirpate the very name of *republicanism*, rob them of their character, their morals, their religion, or their liberty.

It is true the revolution in France had not ultimately tended to strengthen the principles of republicanism in America. The confusions introduced into that unhappy nation, by their resistance to despotism, and the consequent horrors that spread dismay over every portion of their territory, have startled some in the United States, who do not distinguish between principles and events, and shaken the firmness of others, who have fallen off from their primary object, and by degrees returned back to their former adherence to monarchy. Thus, [415] through real or pretended fears of similar results, from the freedom of opinion disseminated through the United States, dissensions have originated relative to subjects not known in the constitution of the American republic. This admits no titles of honor or nobility, those powerful springs of human action; and from the rage of acquisition which has spread far and wide, it may be apprehended that the possession of wealth will in a short time be the only distinction in this young country. By this it may be feared that the spirit of avarice will be rendered justifiable in the opinion of some, as the single road to superiority.

The desire of distinction is inherent in the bosom of man, notwithstanding the equality of nature in which he was created. Few are the numbers of elevated souls, stimulated to act on the single motive of disinterested virtue; and among the less powerful incentives to great and noble actions, the pursuit of honour, rank, and titles, is undeniably as laudable as that of riches. The last too generally narrows the mind,

of the Laws (2 vols.; first Am. ed. from 5th London ed.; Worcester, 1802), I, Book XIX. The quote does not appear, but Montesquieu discusses here the reciprocal influence of laws and manners.]

CHAP. XXXI debases it by meanness, and renders it disgracefully selfish, both in the manner of hoarding and squandering superfluous wealth; but the ambitious, stimulated by a thirst for rank, consider the want of generosity a stain on the dignity of high station.

[416] It may be asked, are not those states the most likely to produce the greatest number of wise and heroic spirits, where some mark of elevation, instead of pecuniary compensation, is affixed to the name and character of such, as have outstripped their contemporaries in the field of glory or integrity? A Roman knight ennobled for his patriotism or his valour, though his patrimonial inheritance was insufficient for a modern flower-garden, was beheld with more veneration than the most wealthy and voluptuous citizen. But we shall not here decide how far honorary rewards are consistent with the principles of republicanism. Indeed some have asserted, that "nobility is the Corinthian capital of polished states;" but an ingenious writer has observed, that

> a titled nobility is the most undisputed progeny of feudal barbarism; that the august fabric of society is deformed and encumbered by such Gothic ornaments. The massy doric that sustains it is labor, and the splendid variety of arts and talents that solace and embellish life, form the decorations of its Corinthian and Ionic capitals. *

It is to be regretted that Americans are so much divided on this point as well as on many other questions; we hope the spirit of division will never be wrought up to such a height as to terminate in a disseveration of the states, or any [417] internal hostilities. Any civil convulsions would shake the fabric of government, and perhaps entirely subvert the present excellent constitution; a strict adherence to which, it may be affirmed, is the best security of the rights and liberties of a country that has bled at every vein, to purchase and transmit them to posterity. The sword now resheathed, the army dismissed, a wise, energetic government established and organized, it is to be hoped many generations will pass away in the lapse of time, before America again becomes a theatre of war.

Indeed the United States of America embrace too large a portion of the globe, to expect their isolated situation will forever secure them from the encroachments of foreign nations, and the attempts of potent Europeans to interrupt their peace. But if the education of

---

* Mackintosh's Vindiciae Galliciae, p. 77, 79. [James Mackintosh, *Vindiciae Gallicae. Defence of the French Revolution Against the Accusations of the Right Hon. Edmund Burke.* . . . (London, 1791.) Warren's quotation is substantially accurate.]

youth, both public and private, is attended to, their industrious and CHAP. XXXI economical habits maintained, their moral character and that assemblage of virtues supported, which is necessary for the happiness of individuals and of nations, there is not much danger that they will for a long time be subjugated by the arms of foreigners, or that their republican system will be subverted by the arts of domestic enemies. Yet, probably some distant day will exhibit the extensive continent of America, a portrait analogous to the other quarters of [418] the globe, which have been laid waste by ambition, until misery has spread her sable veil over the inhabitants. But this will not be done, until ignorance, servility and vice, have led them to renounce their ideas of freedom, and reduced them to that grade of baseness which renders them unfit for the enjoyment of that rational liberty which is the natural inheritance of man. The expense of blood and treasure, lavished for the purchase of freedom, should teach Americans to estimate its real worth, nor ever suffer it to be depreciated by the vices of the human mind, which are seldom single. The sons of America ought ever to bear in grateful remembrance the worthy band of patriots, who first supported an opposition to the tyrannic measures of Great Britain. Though some of them have long since been consigned to the tomb, a tribute of gratitude is ever due to their memory, while the advantages of freedom and independence are felt by their latest posterity.

The military character of the country has rung with deserved applause; many of the heroes who have been sacrificed in the field, are justly recollected with a sigh; but the laborious statesmen who with ability and precision defined the rights of men, and supported the freedom of their country; without whose efforts America never would have had an army, are many of them neglected or forgotten. [419] Private virtue may be neglected; public benefits disregarded, as they affect the individual, while at the same time society feels their cherishing beams, which like the silent rills that water the great garden of nature, pour forth their bounties, unasked, on the whole family of ungrateful man.

It has been justly said, that

there is seldom any medium between gratitude for benefits, and hatred to the authors of them; a little mind is hurt by the remembrance of obligations, begins by forgetting; and not uncommonly ends by persecution.

And that

that circle of beings, which dependence gathers around us, is almost ever unfriendly; they secretly wish the terms of this connexion more equal. Increasing the obligations which are laid upon such minds, only increases their burden; they feel themselves unable to defray the immensity of their debt.

Thus the names of many of the men, who laid the foundations of American independence, and defended the principles of the revolution, are by the efforts of the artful, depreciated, if not vilified. The ancient Persians considered ingratitude as the source of all enmities among men. They considered it "an indication of the vilest spirit, nor believed it possible for an ungrateful man to love the gods, or even his parents, friends, or country."

[420] The partiality to military honor, has a tendency to nourish a disposition for arbitrary power; and wherever there is a tyrannic disposition, servility is its concomitant: hence, pride of title and distinction, and an avarice for wealth to support it. Where these passions predominate, ingratitude is usually added; this makes a *tripodium* to lift the ambitious to the summit of their nefarious designs. Under an established despotism mankind are generally more prone to bend than to resist; losing their ideas of the value of independence, the timid, the doubtful, and the indiscreet, for the most part, determine in favor of whatever wears the appearance of established authority. This should be a lasting admonition, which should forever prevent the vesting any individual or body of men with too much power.

The people of the United States are bound together in sacred compact and a union of interests which ought never to be separated. But the confederation is recent, and their experience immatured; they are however generally sensible, that from the dictatorship of Sylla to the overthrow of Caesar, and from the ruin of the Roman tyrant to the death of the artful Cromwell, deception as well as violence have operated to the subversion of the freedom of the people. They are sensible, that by a little well-concerted intrigue, an artificial consideration may be obtained, far exceeding the degree [421] of real merit on which it is founded. They are sensible that it is not difficult for men of moderate abilities, and a little personal address, to retain their popularity to the end of their lives, without any distinguished traits of genius, wisdom, or virtue. They are sensible, that the characters of nations have been disgraced by their weak partialities, until their freedom has been irretrievably lost in that vortex of folly, which throws a lethargy over the mind, till awakened by the fatal conse-

quences which result from arbitrary power, disguised by specious CHAP. XXXI
pretexts, amidst a general relaxation of manners.

An ingenious writer has observed, that

the juvenile vigor of reason and freedom in the new world, where the
human mind was unencumbered with that vast mass of usage and prejudice,
which so many ages of ignorance had accumulated to load and deform
society in Europe,

brought forward those declarations of the rights of men, which hastened
the emancipation of their own country, and diffused light to others.

It is equally just to observe, that in the eighteenth century, the
enlightened writers of Europe had so clearly delineated the natural
rights of men, and the equal freedom of the human race, before they
by compact had yielded a part for the preservation and safety of the
[422] whole, as to have a powerful effect on public opinion. This had
manifestly, in some degree, broken the fetters that had long enthralled
and dissipated the darkness that shrouded the mind, under the
influence of superstitious bigotry, and their ideas of the divine right
of kings. The Colossus of tyranny was shaken, and the social order
meliorated by learned sages, who evinced that government, as ele-
gantly expressed by one,* is not

a scientific subtilty, but a practical expedient for general good; all recourse
to elaborate abstractions is frivolous and futile, and the grand question in
government it not its source, but its tendency; not a question of right, but
a consideration of expediency.

All the governments in the world,

the same writer adds,

have been fortuitously formed; they are the produce of chance, not the
work of art. They have been altered, impaired, improved, and destroyed
by accidental circumstances, beyond the foresight or control of wisdom.
Their parts thrown up against present emergencies, formed no systematic
whole. It was certainly not to have been presumed, that these *fortuitous
governments* should have surpassed the works of intellect, and precluded
all nearer approaches to perfection.

---

* Mackintosh. [Mackintosh, *Vindiciae Gallicae. Defence of the French Revolution Against
the Accusations of the Right Hon. Edmund Burke. . . .* (London, 1791), pp. 215, 115.
Surprisingly, Warren neglected to quote a significant part of Mackintosh's statement:
"All the Governments that now exist in the world, (except the United States of
America) have been fortuitously formed." (p. 215).]

CHAP. XXXI   [423] Perfection in government is not to be expected from so imperfect a creature as man; experience has taught, that he falls infinitely short of this point; that however industrious in pursuit of improvements in human wisdom, or however bold the inquiry that employs the human intellect, either on government, ethics, or any other science, man yet discovers a deficiency of capacity to satisfy his researches, or to announce that he has already found an unerring standard on which he may rest.

Perhaps genius has never devised a system more congenial to their wishes, or better adapted to the condition of man, than the American constitution. At the same time, it is left open to amendments whenever its imperfections are discovered by the wisdom of future generations, or when new contingencies may arise either at home or abroad, to make alterations necessary. On the principles of republicanism was this constitution founded; on these it must stand. Many corrections and amendments have already taken place, and it is at the present period* as wise, as efficient, as respectable, as free, and we hope as permanent, as any constitution existing on earth. It is a system admired by statesmen abroad, envied by distant nations, and revered [424] by Americans. They pride themselves on this palladium of safety, fabricated at a dangerous crisis, and established on the broad basis of the elective voice of the people. It now depends on their own virtue, to continue the United States of America an example of the respectability and dignity of this mode of government.

Notwithstanding the advantages that may be derived, and the safety that may be felt, under so happy a constitution, yet it is necessary to guard at every point, against the intrigues of artful or ambitious men, who may subvert the system which the inhabitants of the United States judged to be most conducive to the general happiness of society.

It is now indeed at the option of the sons of America to delegate such men for the administration of government, as will consider the designation of this trust as a sacred deposite, which binds them to the indispensable duty of aiming solely at the promotion of the civil, the economical, the religious, and political welfare of the whole community. They therefore cannot be too scrutinous on the character of their executive officers. No man should be lifted by the voice of his country to presidential rank, who may probably forget the repub-

---

* The beginning of the nineteenth century, which circumscribes the limits of the supplementary observations subjoined to the History of the Revolution.

lican designation, and sigh to wield a sceptre, instead of guarding CHAP. XXXI
sacredly the charter from the people. It is to be hoped, that no
American citizen will [425] hereafter pant for nobility. The senators
of the United States should be wise, her representatives uncorrupt,
the judiciary firm, equitable, and humane, and the bench of justice
ever adorned by men uninfluenced by little passions, and adhering
only to the principles of law and equity! The people should be
economical and sober; and the clergy should keep within their own
line, which directs them to enforce the moral obligations of society,
and to inculcate the doctrines of peace, brotherly kindness, and the
forgiveness of injuries, taught by the example of their Divine Master,
nor should they leave the appropriate duties of their profession, to
descant on political principles or characters!* [426] Such a happy
combination of propriety and dignity in each department might prevent
all apprehensions of danger to religion from the sceptical absurdities
of unprincipled men; neither the foolish, the learned, or licentious,
would be able to sap the foundations of the kingdom of Christ. In
the present state of society and general information, there is no reason
to fear the overthrow of a system, by the efforts of modern infidels,
which could not be shaken by the learned unbelievers of Greece, the
persecutions of the Caesars, nor the power of the Roman empire.

All who have just ideas of the equal claims of mankind to share the
benefits of a free and benign government, and virtue sufficient to aid
its promotion, will fervently pray, that the narrow passions of the
selfish, or the ambitious views of more elevated minds, may never
render fruitless the labors of the wise and vigilant patriot, who
sacrificed much to this noble purpose, nor defeat the severe efforts
of the soldier, who fell in the field, or stain the laurels of such as
have survived the conflict.

However literature has been improved, and knowledge diffused by

---

* It is true that this respectable order of men interested themselves on the great
subject of opposition to the aggressions of the British parliament; this was sometimes
done at the request of legislators, who thought every aid necessary to awaken the
people to a sense of their rights. But the ground on which the clergy came forward
on political subjects, was then very different from the present party disputes. There
was then, (with few exceptions) a united opposition of the whole collective body of
the people, against a foreign power aiming to deprive them of their civil and religious
privileges, and to load them with taxes, impositions and innovations, novel and
grievous. The dissentions are now wholly internal, which render the influence of
every pious clergyman necessary to soothe the passions and heal the animosities
enkindled among the people of his own particular charge.

CHAP. XXXI the pen of genius, and the industry of liberal minded and erudite instructors, there has been a conspiracy formed against the dissemination of republican opinions, by interested and aspiring characters, eager for [427] the establishment of hereditary distinctions and noble orders. This is a conspiracy formidable for the wealth and talents of its supporters in Europe, and not less so from the same description of men in America. This should stand as a beacon before the eyes of an infant republic, recently established by the suffrages of the inhabitants of the United States, who already have had to fear the *progress of opinion,* which produced the American revolution, might change its complexion, and there might be a tyranny to depose, more formidable than kings.

Public opinion, when grounded on false principles, and dictated by the breath of ambitious individuals, sometimes creates a tyranny, felt by the minority more severely, than that usually inflicted by the hand of the sceptred monarch. From this tyranny of opinion often starts a political enthusiasm, which, as expressed by the cardinal de Retz, "would at one period exalt to a throne, and at another, conduct the enthusiast to a gallows." This tyranny of opinion is spread or extinguished by factitious circumstances, sometimes combining to exalt the mind to the most sublime ideas of human freedom; at others, beclouding it with prejudices which sink it into habitual servility, when reason languishes until overwhelmed by a torpor become too general to awaken, without producing convulsions more to be dreaded than submission, [428] and too painful for the contemplation of benevolent minds.

Great revolutions ever produce excesses and miseries at which humanity revolts. In America indeed, it must be acknowledged, that when the late convulsions are viewed with a retrospective eye, the scenes of barbarity were not so universal as have been usual in other countries that have been at once shaken by foreign and domestic war. Few histories have recorded examples of equal moderation and less violation of the feelings of humanity, where general revolt and revolution had pervaded such an extensive territory. The enthusiasm of opinion previous to the year one thousand seven hundred and seventy-five, bore down opposition like a torrent, and enkindled the flame which emancipated the United States. Yet, it was not stimulated by a fierce spirit of revenge, which, in similar circumstances, too frequently urges to cruelties which can never be licensed by the principles of justice or freedom, and must ever be abhorrent to humanity and benevolence.

The United States may congratulate themselves on the success of CHAP. XXXI
a revolution which has done honor to the human character, by
exhibiting a mildness of spirit amidst the ferocity of war, that prevented
the shocking scenes of cruelty, butchery, and slaughter, which have
too often stained the actions of men, when their [429] original
intentions were the result of pure motives and justifiable resistance.
They have been hailed by distant nations in terms of respect and
applause for the glorious and successful stand made by them in favor
of the liberties of mankind. They have now to maintain their well-
earned fame, by a strict adherence to the principles of the revolution,
and the practice of every public, social and domestic virtue.

The enthusiastic zeal for freedom which had generally animated all
classes throughout the United States, was retained, with few exceptions, to the conclusion of the war, without any considerable appearance
of relaxation in any part of the union, until the sword was resheathed,
and the conflict terminated by a general peace. After this indeed,
though the spirit for freedom was not worn down, a party arose,
actuated by different principles; new designs were discovered, which
spread suspicions among the people, that the object of their exertions
was endangered, from circumstances they had never calculated as
probable to take place in their country, until some ages had elapsed.
But notwithstanding the variety of exigencies, and the new opportunities which offered to interested individuals, for the aggrandizement
of family, and the accumulation of wealth, no visible dereliction
appeared, nor any diminution of that general partiality in favor of
republicanism which had taken deep root in the minds [430] of the
inhabitants of the United States. These principles did not apparently
languish, until some time after the adoption of the new constitution;
exertions were then made to damp their ardor by holding up systems
of government asserted by some to be better adapted to their happiness,
and absolutely necessary for the strength and glory of the American
states. The illusion was however discovered, and a constitutional
ardency for general freedom revived among the people. The feelings
of native freedom among the sons of America, and their own good
sense taught them, that they did not need the appendages of royalty
and the baneful curse of a standing army to support it. They were
convinced, that rational liberty might be maintained, their favorite
system of republicanism might be revived, established, and supported,
and the prosperity of their country heightened, at a less gorgeous
expense than a resort to the usages of monarchic states, and the
introduction of hereditary crowns and the proud claims of noble

CHAP. XXXI ancestry, which usually involve the mass of the people in poverty, corruption, degradation, and servility.

Under the benediction of Divine Providence America may yet long be protected from sanguine projects, and indigested measures, that have produced the evils felt or depictured among less fortunate nations, who have not laid the foundations of their governments on the firm [431] basis of public virtue, of general freedom, and that degree of liberty most productive of the happiness of mankind in his social state. But from the accumulated blessings which are showered down on the United States, there is reason to indulge the benign hope, that America may long stand a favored nation, and be preserved from the horrors of war, instigated either by foreign combinations or domestic intrigue, which are equally to be deprecated.

Any attempt, either by secret fraud, or open violence, to shake the union, to subvert the constitution, or undermine the just principles, which wrought out the American revolution, cannot be too severely censured. It is true, there has been some agitation of spirits between existing parties; but doubtless the prudence of the inhabitants of the United States will suffer this to evaporate, as the cloud of the morning, and will guard against every point that might have the smallest tendency to break the union. If peace and unanimity are cherished, and the equalization of liberty, and the equity and energy of law, maintained by harmony and justice, the present representative government may stand for ages a luminous monument of republican wisdom, virtue, and integrity. The principles of the revolution ought ever to be the pole-star of the statesman, respected by the rising generation; and the advantages [432] bestowed by Providence should never be lost, by negligence, indiscretion, or guilt.

The people may again be reminded, that the elective franchise is in their own hands; that it ought not to be abused, either for personal gratifications, or the indulgence of partisan acrimony. This advantage should be improved, not only for the benefit of existing society, but with an eye to that fidelity which is due to posterity. This can only be done by electing such men to guide the national counsels, whose conscious probity enables them to stand like a Colossus, on the broad basis of independence, and by correct and equitable arrangements, endeavor to lighten the burdens of the people, strengthen their unanimity at home, command justice abroad, and cultivate peace with all nations, until an example may be left on record of the practicability of meliorating the condition of mankind.

The internal strength of America is respectable, and her borders CHAP. XXXI
are fenced by the barriers of nature. May the wisdom, vigour, and
ability of her native sons, teach her to surmount every difficulty that
may arise at home or abroad, without ever calling in the aid of *foreign*
relations! She wants not the interference of any other nation, to give
a model to her government, or secretly influence the administration
by bribes, flatteries, or threats. The enterprising [433] spirit of the
people seems adapted to improve their advantages, and to rival in
grandeur and fame those parts of creation which for ages have been
meliorating and refining, until the period of decay seems to have
arrived, that threatens the fall of some of the proudest nations.
Humanity recoils at a view of the wretched state of vassalage, in
which a great part of mankind are involved. Yet, America may sit
tranquil, and only extend her compassion to the European world,
which exhibits the shambles of despotism, where the purple of kings
is stained by the blood of their subjects, butchered by thousands to
glut the ambition of a weak individual, who frequently expires himself
before the cup of his intoxication is full. The vesture of royalty is
however still displayed, and the weapons of war spread death over
three fourths of the globe, without satiating the thirst that drinks up
rivers of human gore, when the proud victor wipes the stained lip
and covers the guilty visage with a smile at the incalculable carnage
of his own species, by his mandates and his myrmidons.

It will be the wisdom, and probably the future effort of the American
government, forever to maintain with unshaken magnanimity, the
present neutral position of the United [434] States.* The hand of
nature has displayed its magnificence in this quarter of the globe, in
the astonishing rivers, lakes, and mountains, replete with the richest
minerals and the most useful materials for manufactures. At the same
time, the indigenous produce of its fertile lands yields medicine,
food, and clothing, and every thing needful for man in his present
condition. America may with propriety be styled a land of promise; a
happy climate, though remarkably variegated; fruitful and populous,
independent and free, both necessity and pleasure invite the hand of
the industrious to cherish and cultivate the prolific soil, which is ready
to yield all that nature requires to satisfy the reasonable wishes of
man, as well as to contribute to the wealth, pleasure, and luxury of

---

* The limits of the present work preclude any historical record subsequent to the year
  1801.

CHAP. XXXI the inhabitants. It is a portion of the globe that appears as a fair and fertile vineyard, which requires only the industrious care of the laborers to render it for a long time productive of the finest clusters in the full harvest of prosperity and freedom, instead of yielding thorns, thistles, and sour grapes, which must be the certain fruits of animosity, disunion, venality, or vice.

Though in her infantile state, the young republic of America exhibits the happiest prospects. Her extensive population, commerce, [435] and wealth, the progress of agriculture, arts, sciences, and manufactures, have increased with a rapidity beyond example. Colleges and academies have been reared, multiplied, and endowed with the best advantages for public instruction, on the broad scale of liberality and truth. The effects of industry and enterprise appear in the numerous canals, turnpikes, elegant buildings, and well constructed bridges, over lengths and depths of water that open, and render the communication easy and agreeable, throughout a country almost without bounds. In short, arts and agriculture are pursued with avidity, civilization spreads, and science in full research is investigating all the sources of human knowledge.

Indeed the whole country wears a face of improvement, from the extreme point of the northern and western woods, through all the southern states, and to the vast Atlantic ocean, the eastern boundary of the United States. The wisdom and justice of the American governments, and the virtue of the inhabitants, may, if they are not deficient in the improvement of their own advantages, render the United States of America an enviable example to all the world, of peace, liberty, righteousness, and truth. The western wilds, which for ages have been little known, may arrive to that stage of improvement and perfection, beyond which the limits of human genius cannot reach, [436] and this last civilized quarter of the globe may exhibit those striking traits of grandeur and magnificence, which the Divine Economist may have reserved to crown the closing scene, when the angel of his presence will stand upon the sea and upon the earth, lift up his hand to heaven, and swear by Him that liveth for ever and ever, that there shall be time no longer.

END OF VOL. III.

A P P E N D I X

T O   V O L U M E   S E C O N D

[Continued]

─────────── Note No. IX. Page 410. ───────────

[411] Governor Trumbull observed thus:

The only obstacle which I foresee to the settlement of foreigners in the country, will be the taxes, which must inevitably for a time run high, for the payment of the debts contracted during the present war. These, indeed, will be much lightened by the care which has been taken, to confine these debts as much as possible among ourselves, and by emitting a paper currency in place of borrowing from abroad. But this method, though it secures the country from being drained hereafter, of immense sums of solid coin, which can never return, has exposed us to a new and very disagreeable embarrassment, by its monstrous depreciation. An evil which had its rise in, and owes all its rapid increase to the single cause of our not having provided at a sufficiently early period, for its reduction and payment by taxes. This measure was indeed rendered impracticable, at the proper time, by the radical derangement of the system of government, and consequently of revenue in many of the United States; and its [412] necessary delay till the removal of these impediments, gave time for avarice and suspicion to unite in sapping the foundations of our internal credit.

He adds,

I' am no advocate for internal or foreign loans. In my opinion, they are like cold water in a fever, which allays the disease for a moment, but soon causes it to rage with a redoubled violence; temporary alleviations, but ultimately real additions to the burden. The debts which we have already contracted, or may hereafter be necessitated to contract abroad, I have not a doubt, but will be paid with the utmost punctuality and honor; and there can be no surer foundation of credit, than we possess in the rapidly increasing value and importance of our country.

In short, it is not so much my wish that the United States should gain credit among foreign nations, for the loan of money, as that all nations, and especially your countrymen in Holland, should be made acquainted with the real state of the American war. The importance and greatness of this rising empire, the future

─────────

extensive value of our commerce, the advantages of colonization, are objects which
need only to be known, to command your attention, protection, and support.

Give me leave most sincerely to express my grief, that the efforts you have made
for the removal of oppression in your own country, and for extending the blessings
of liberty and plenty to the poor, should have met with so ungrateful a return of
persecution and insult. Unhappy state of man! where opulence and power conspire
to load the poor, the defenceless, and the innocent, with accumulated misery;
where an unworthy few join to embitter the life of half their fellow men, that they
may wallow in the excess of luxurious debauch, or shine in the splendid trappings
of folly.

A P P E N D I X
T O   V O L U M E   T H I R D

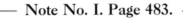 Note No. I. Page 483.

Earl Cornwallis to Sir Henry Clinton, K.B. dated York-Town, Virginia, October 21, 1781.

Sir,

[437] I have the mortification to inform your excellency, that I have been forced to give up the posts of York and Gloucester, and to surrender the troops under my command, by capitulation, on the 19th instant, as prisoners of war, to the combined forces of America and France.

I never saw this post in a very favorable light; but when I found I was to be attacked in it, in so unprepared a state, by so powerful an army and artillery, nothing but the hopes of relief would have induced me to attempt its defence; for I would either have endeavoured to go to New York, by rapid marches from the Gloucester side, immediately on the arrival of general Washington's troops at Williamsburgh, or I would, notwithstanding the disparity of numbers, have attacked them in the open field, where it might have been just possible that fortune would have favored the gallantry of the handful of troops under my command; but being assured by your excellency's letters, that every possible means would be tried by the navy and army to relieve us, I could not [438] think myself at liberty to venture upon either of those desperate attempts; therefore, after remaining for two days in a strong position, in front of the place, in hopes of being attacked, upon observing that the enemy were taking measures which could not fail of turning my left flank in a short time; and receiving, on the second evening, your letter of the 24th of September, informing that the relief would sail about the 5th of October, I withdrew within the works on the night of the 29th of September, hoping by the labor and firmness of the soldiers, to protract the defence until you could arrive. Every thing was to be expected from the spirit of the troops, but every disadvantage attended their labor, as the works were to be continued under the enemy's fire, and our stock of entrenching tools, which did not much exceed four hundred, when we began to work in the latter end of August, was now much diminished.

The enemy broke ground on the night of the 30th, and constructed on that night, and on the two following days and nights, two redoubts, which, with some works that had belonged to our outward position, occupied a gorge between two creeks or ravines, which come from the river on each side of the town. On the night of the 6th of October they made their first parallel, extending from its right on the river to a deep ravine on the left, nearly opposite to the centre of this place, and embracing our whole left, at the distance of six hundred yards. Having perfected this parallel, their batteries opened on the evening of the 9th, against our left, and other batteries fired at the same time against a redoubt advanced over the creek upon our right, and defended by about one hundred and twenty men of the twenty third regiment and marines, who maintained that post with uncommon gallantry. The fire continued incessant from heavy cannon, and from mortars and howitzers, throwing shells from eight to sixteen inches, until all our guns on the left were silenced, our work much damaged, and [439] our loss of men considerable. On the night of the 11th they began their second parallel, about three hundred yards nearer to us; the troops being much weakened by sickness, as well as by the fire of the besiegers, and observing that the enemy had not only secured their flanks, but proceeded in every respect with the utmost regularity and caution, I could not venture so large sorties as to hope from them any considerable effect; but otherwise, I did every thing in my power to interrupt this work, by opening new embrasures for guns, and keeping up a constant fire with all the howitzers, and small mortars that we could man. On the evening of the 14th, they assaulted and carried two redoubts that had been advanced about three hundred yards, for the purpose of delaying their approaches and covering our left flank, and during the night inclosed them in their second parallel, on which they continued to work with the utmost exertion. Being perfectly sensible that our work could not stand many hours after the opening of the batteries of that parallel, we not only continued a constant fire with all our mortars, and every gun that could be brought to bear upon it, but a little before day-break, on the morning of the 16th, I ordered a *sortie* of about three hundred and fifty men, under the direction of lieutenant colonel Abercrombie, to attack two batteries which appeared to be in the greatest forwardness, and to spike the guns. A detachment of guards, with the eightieth company of grenadiers, under the command of lieutenant colonel Lake, attacked the one, and one of light infantry, under the command of major Armstrong, attacked the other, and both succeeded by forcing the redoubts that covered them, spiking eleven guns, and killing or wounding about one hundred of the French troops, who had the guard of that part of the trenches, and with little loss on our side. This action, though extremely honorable to the officers and soldiers who executed it, proved of little public advantage; for the cannon, having been spiked in a hurry, were soon rendered fit for service again, and before dark [440] the whole parallel and batteries appeared to be nearly complete. At this time we knew that there was no part of the whole front attacked, on which we could shew a single gun, and our shells were nearly expended; I therefore had only to choose between preparing to surrender next day, or endeavouring to get off with the greatest part of the troops; and I determined to attempt the latter, reflecting, that though it should prove unsuccessful in its immediate object, it might at least delay the enemy in the prosecution of farther enterprises: sixteen large boats were prepared, and upon other pretexts were ordered to be in readiness to receive troops precisely at ten o'clock. With these I hoped to pass the infantry during the night, abandoning our baggage, and leaving a detachment to capitulate for the town's people, and the sick and wounded; on which subject a letter was ready to be delivered to general Washington. After making my arrangements with the utmost secrecy, the light infantry, greatest part of the guards, and part of the twenty-third regiment, landed at Gloucester; but at this critical moment, the weather, from being moderate and calm, changed to a most violent storm of wind and rain, and drove all the boats, some of which had troops on board, down the river. It was soon evident that the intended passage was impracticable, and the absence of the boats rendered it equally impossible to bring back the troops that had passed, which I had ordered about two in the morning. In this situation, with my little force divided, the enemies batteries opened at day-break; the passage between this place and Gloucester was much exposed, but the boats having now returned, they were ordered to bring back the troops that had passed during the night; and they joined us in the forenoon, without much loss. Our works were in the mean time going to ruin: and not having been able to strengthen them by *obbatis*, nor in any other manner but by a slight fraizing, which the enemy's artillery were demolishing wherever they fired, my opinion entirely coincided with that of the [441] engineer and principal officers of the army, that they were in many places assailable in the forenoon, and that by the continuance of the same fire for a few hours longer, they would be in such a state as to render it desperate with our numbers to attempt to maintain them. We at that time could not fire a single gun, only one eight inch, and little more than a hundred cohorn shells remained. A diversion by the French ships of war that lay at the mouth of York river, was to be expected. Our numbers had been diminished by the enemy's fire, but particularly by sickness, and the strength and spirits of those in the works were much exhausted, by the fatigue of constant watching and unremitting duty. Under all these circumstances, I thought that it would have been wanton and inhuman to the last degree, to sacrifice the lives of this small body of gallant soldiers, who had ever behaved with so much fidelity and courage, by exposing them to an assault, which, from the numbers and precautions of the enemy, could not fail to succeed: I therefore proposed to capitulate; and I have the honor to inclose to your excellency the copy of the correspondence between general Washington and me on that subject, and the terms of capitulation agreed upon. I sincerely lament that better could not be obtained, but I have neglected nothing in my power to alleviate the misfortunes and distresses of both officers and soldiers. The men are well clothed and provided with necessaries, and I trust will be regularly supplied by the means of the officers that are permitted to remain with them. . . .

Note No. II. Page 485.

Copy of the articles of capitulation, settled between his excellency general Washington, commander in chief of the combined forces of America and France; his [442] excellency the count de Rochambeau, lieutenant general of the armies of the king of France, great cross of the royal and military order of St. Louis, commanding the auxiliary troops of his most Christian majesty in America; and his excellency the count de Grasse, lieutenant general of the naval armies of his most Christian majesty, commander of the order of St. Louis, commander in chief of the naval army of France in the Chesapeak, on the one part; and the right honorable earl Cornwallis, lieutenant general of his Britannic majesty's forces, commanding the garrisons of York and Gloucester; and Thomas Symmonds, Esq. commanding his Britannic majesty's naval forces in York river in Virginia, on the other part.

ARTICLE I

The garrisons of York and Gloucester, including the officers and seamen of his Britannic majesty's ships, as well as other mariners, to surrender themselves prisoners of war to the combined forces of America and France; the land troops to remain prisoners to the United States; the navy to the naval army of his most Christian majesty.

Granted.

ARTICLE II

The artillery, arms, accoutrements, military chest, and public stores of every denomination, shall be delivered unimpaired to the heads of departments appointed to receive them.

Granted.

ARTICLE III

At twelve o'clock this day the two redoubts on the left flank of York to be delivered, the one to a detachment of American infantry, the other to a detachment of French grenadiers.

[443] Granted. The garrison of York will march out to a place to be appointed, in front of the posts, at two o'clock precisely, with shouldered arms, colors cased, and drums beating a British or German march; they are then to ground their arms and return to their encampments, where they will remain until they are dispatched to the places of their destination. Two works on the Gloucester side will be delivered at one o'clock, to a detachment of French and American troops appointed to possess them. The garrison will march out at three o'clock in the afternoon; the cavalry with their swords drawn, trumpets sounding, and the infantry in the manner prescribed for the garrison of York. They are likewise to return to their encampments until they can be finally marched off.

ARTICLE IV

Officers are to retain their side arms. Both officers and soldiers to keep their private property of every kind; and no part of their baggage or papers to be at any time subject to search or inspection. The baggage and papers of officers and soldiers, taken during the siege, to be likewise preserved for them.

Granted. It is understood, that any property obviously belonging to the inhabitants of these states, in the possession of the garrison, shall be subject to be reclaimed.

ARTICLE V

The soldiers to be kept in Virginia, Maryland, or Pennsylvania, and as much by regiments as possible, and supplied with the same rations of provisions as are allowed to soldiers in the service of America. A field officer from each nation, *to wit*, British, Anspach, and Hessian, and other officers on parole, in the proportion of one to fifty men, to be allowed to reside near their respective regiments, to visit them frequently, and be witnesses of their treatment, and that their officers may receive and deliver clothing and [444] other necessaries for them, for which passports are to be granted when applied for.

Granted.

ARTICLE VI

The general, staff, and other officers not employed as mentioned in the above articles, and who choose it, to be permitted to go on their parole to Europe, to New York, or to any other American maritime posts at present in the possession of the British forces, at their own option, and proper vessels to be granted by the count de Grasse to carry them under flags of truce to New York, within ten days from this date if possible, and they to reside in a district to be agreed upon hereafter, until they embark.

The officers of civil department of the army and navy to be included in this article. Passports to go by land to be granted to those to whom vessels cannot be furnished.

Granted.

ARTICLE VII

Officers to be allowed to keep soldiers as servants, according to the common practice of the service; servants not soldiers are not to be considered as prisoners, and are to be allowed to attend their masters.

Granted.

ARTICLE VIII

The Bonetta sloop of war to be equipped, and navigated by its present captain and crew, and left entirely at the disposal of lord Cornwallis, from the hour that the capitulation is signed, to receive an aid du camp to carry dispatches to sir Henry Clinton; and such soldiers as he may think proper to send to New York, to be permitted to sail without [445] examination. When his dispatches are ready, his lordship engages on his part that the ship shall be delivered to the order of the count de Grasse, if she escapes the danger of the sea; that she shall not carry off any public stores. Any part of the crew that may be deficient on her return, and the soldiers passengers, to be accounted for on her delivery.

ARTICLE IX

The traders are to preserve their property, and to be allowed three months to dispose of or remove them; and those traders are not to be considered as prisoners of war.

The traders will be allowed to dispose of their effects, the allied army having the right of pre-emption. The traders to be considered as prisoners of war upon parole.

A R T I C L E   X

Natives or inhabitants of different parts of this country, at present in York or Gloucester, are not to be punished on account of having joined the British army.

This article cannot be assented to, being altogether of civil resort.

A R T I C L E   X I

Proper hospitals to be furnished for the sick and wounded. They are to be attended by their own surgeons on parole; and they are to be furnished with medicines and stores from the American hospitals.

The hospital stores now in York and Gloucester shall be delivered for the use of the British sick and wounded. Passports will be granted, for procuring them further supplies from New York, as occasion may require; and proper hospitals will be furnished, for the reception of the sick and wounded of the two garrisons.

A R T I C L E   X I I

[446] Waggons to be furnished to carry the baggage of the officers attending the soldiers, and to surgeons when travelling on account of the sick, attending the hospitals at public expense.

They are to be furnished if possible.

A R T I C L E   X I I I

The shipping and boats in the two harbours, with all their stores, guns, tackling, and apparel, shall be delivered up in their present state to an officer of the navy appointed to take possession of them, previously unloading the private property, part of which had been put on board for security during the siege.

Granted.

A R T I C L E   X I V

No article of capitulation to be infringed on pretence of reprisals; and if there be any doubtful expressions in it, they are to be interpreted according to the common meaning and acceptation of the words.

Granted.

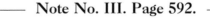

Note No. III. Page 592.

The *definitive treaty* of *peace* and *friendship* between his Britannic majesty and the United States of America, signed at Paris the 3d day of September, 1783.

In the name of the most holy and undivided Trinity.

It having pleased the Divine Providence to dispose the hearts of the most serene and most potent prince, George the third, by the grace of God king of Great Britain, [447] France, and Ireland, defender of the faith, duke of Brunswick and Lunenburg, arch treasurer and prince elector of the holy Roman empire, &c., and of the United States of America, to forget all past misunderstandings and differences that have unhappily interrupted the good correspondence and friendship which they mutually wish to restore, and to establish such a beneficial and satisfactory intercourse between the two countries, upon the ground of reciprocal advantages and mutual convenience, as may promote and secure to both perpetual peace and harmony; and having for this desirable end already laid the foundation of peace and reconciliation, by the provisional articles signed at Paris on the 30th of November, 1782, by the commissioners empowered on each part; which articles were agreed to be inserted in and to constitute the treaty of peace proposed to be concluded between the crown of Great Britain and the said United States, but which treaty was not to be concluded until terms of peace should be agreed upon between Great Britain and France, and his Britannic majesty should be ready to conclude such treaty accordingly; and the treaty between Great Britain and France having since been concluded, his Britannic majesty and the United States of America, in order to carry into full effect the provisional articles above mentioned, according to the tenor thereof, have constituted and appointed; that is to say, his Britannic majesty on his part, David Hartley, Esq. member of the parliament of Great Britain; and the said United States on their part, John Adams, Esq. late a commissioner of the United States of America at the court of Versailles, late delegate in congress from the state of Massachusetts, and chief justice of the said state, and minister plenipotentiary of the said United States to their high mightinesses the states general of the United Netherlands; Benjamin Franklin, Esq. late delegate in congress from the state of Pennsylvania, president of the convention of the said state, and minister plenipotentiary from the United States of America at the court of Versailles; and John Jay, Esq. late president of congress, and chief justice of the [448] state of New York, and minister plenipotentiary from the said United States at the court of Madrid; to be the plenipotentiaries for the concluding and signing the present definitive treaty, who, after having reciprocally communicated their respective full powers, have agreed upon and confirmed the following articles.

ARTICLE I

His Britannic majesty acknowledges the said United States, *viz.* New Hampshire, Massachusetts Bay, Rhode Island and Providence Plantations, Connecticut, New York, New Jersey, Pennsylvania, Delaware, Maryland, Virginia, North Carolina, South Carolina, and Georgia, to be free, sovereign, and independent states; that he treats with them as such, and for himself, his heirs, and successors, relinquishes all claim to the government, proprietary, and territorial rights of the same, and every part thereof.

ARTICLE II

And that all disputes which might arise in future on the subject of the boundaries of the said United States may be prevented, it is hereby agreed and declared that the following are and shall be their boundaries, *viz.* From the north-west angle of Nova Scotia, viz. that angle which is formed by a line drawn due north from the source of St. Croix river to the high lands, along the said high lands which divide those rivers that empty themselves into the river St. Lawrence, from those which fall into the Atlantic ocean, to the north-westernmost head of Connecticut river; thence drawn along the middle of that river to the forty-fifth degree of north latitude; from thence by a line due west on said latitude, until it strikes the river Iroquois or Cataraquy; thence along the middle of said river into Lake Ontario; through the middle of said lake, until it strikes the communication by water between that lake and Lake Erie; thence along the middle of the said communication into Lake Erie, through the middle of said lake, until it arrives at the water communication between that [449] lake and Lake Hurion; thence through the middle of said lake, to the water communication between that lake and Lake Superior; thence through Lake Superior northward to the isles Royal and Philipeaux, to the Long Lake; thence through the middle of said Long Lake, and the water communication between it and the Lake of the Woods, to the said Lake of the Woods; thence through the said lake to the most north-westernmost point thereof, and from thence on a due west course to the river Missisippi; thence by a line to be drawn along the middle of the said river Missisippi, until it shall intersect the northernmost part of the thirty-first degree of north latitude: south, by a line to be drawn due east from the determination of the line last mentioned, in the latitude of thirty-one degrees north of the equator, to the middle of river Apalachicola or Catahouche; thence along the middle thereof, to its junction with the Flint river; thence straight to the head of St. Mary's river, to the Atlantic ocean: east, by a line to be drawn along the middle of the river St. Croix, from its mouth in the bay of Fundy to its source, and from its source directly north to the aforesaid high lands, which divide the rivers that fall into the Atlantic ocean from those which fall into the river St. Lawrence, comprehending all islands within twenty leagues of any part of the shores of the United States, and lying between lines to be drawn due east from the points where the aforesaid boundaries between Nova Scotia on the one part and East Florida on the other, shall respectively touch the bay of Fundy and the Atlantic ocean, excepting such islands as now are or heretofore have been within the limits of the said province of Nova Scotia.

A R T I C L E   I I I

It is agreed that the people of the United States shall continue to enjoy unmolested, the right to take fish of every kind on the Great Bank, and on all the other banks of Newfoundland; also in the gulf of St. Lawrence, and at [450] all other places in the sea where the inhabitants of both countries used at any time heretofore to fish: and also that the inhabitants of the United States shall have liberty to take fish of every kind on such part of the coast of Newfoundland as British fishermen shall use, (but not to dry or cure the same on that island,) and also on the coasts, bays, and creeks, of all other of his Britannic majesty's dominions in America; and that the American fishermen shall have liberty to dry and cure fish in any of the unsettled bays, harbours, and creeks of Nova Scotia, Magdalen Islands, and Labrador, so long as the same shall remain unsettled; but so soon as the same shall be settled, it shall not be lawful for the said fishermen to dry or cure fish at such settlement, without a previous agreement for that purpose with the inhabitants, proprietors, or possessors of the ground.

A R T I C L E   I V

It is agreed, that the creditors on either side shall meet with no lawful impediment to the recovery of the full value in sterling money of all *bona fide* debts heretofore contracted.

A R T I C L E   V

It is agreed, that congress shall earnestly recommend it to the legislatures of the respective states, to provide for the restitution of all estates, rights, and properties, which have been confiscated, belonging to real British subjects; and also of the estates, rights, and properties, of persons resident in districts in the possession of his majesty's arms, and who have not borne arms against the said United States; and that persons of any other description shall have free liberty to go to any part or parts of any of the thirteen United States, and therein to remain twelve months unmolested in their endeavours to obtain the restitution of such of their estates, rights, and properties, as may have been confiscated: and that congress shall also earnestly recommend to the several states a reconsideration and revision of all acts or laws regarding the premises, so as to [451] render the said laws or acts perfectly consistent, not only with justice and equity, but with that spirit of conciliation which, on the return of the blessings of peace, should invariably prevail: and that congress shall also earnestly recommend to the several states, that the estates, rights, and properties of such last mentioned persons, shall be restored to them, they refunding to any persons who may be now in possession, the *bona fide* price, (where any has been given,) which such persons may have paid on purchasing any of the said lands, rights, or properties, since the confiscation.

And it is agreed, that all persons who have any interest in confiscated lands, either by debts, marriage settlements, or otherwise, shall meet with no lawful impediment in the prosecution of their just rights.

A R T I C L E   V I

That there shall be no future confiscations made, nor any prosecutions commenced against any person or persons, for or by reason of the part which he or they may have taken in the present war; and that no person shall on that account suffer any future loss or damage, either in his person, liberty, or property; and that those who may be in confinement on such charges, at the time of the ratification of the treaty in America, shall be immediately set at liberty, and the prosecutions so commenced be discontinued.

A R T I C L E   V I I

There shall be a firm and perpetual peace between his Britannic majesty and the said United States, and between the subjects of the one and the citizens of the other; wherefore all hostilities, both by sea and land, shall from henceforth cease; all prisoners, on both sides, shall be set at liberty; and his Britannic majesty shall, with all convenient speed, and without causing any destruction, or carrying away any negroes or other property of the American inhabitants, withdraw all his armies, garrisons, and fleets, from the said United States, and from every post, place, and harbour within the same, leaving in all fortifications [452] the American artillery that may be therein: and shall also order and cause all archives, records, deeds, and papers belonging to any of the said states, or their citizens, which in the course of the war amy have fallen into the hands of his officers, to be forthwith restored, and delivered to the proper states and persons to whom they belong.

A R T I C L E   V I I I

The navigation of the river Missisippi, from its source to the ocean, shall forever remain free and open to the subjects of Great Britain and the citizens of the United States.

ARTICLE IX

In case it should so happen, that any place or territory, belonging to Great Britain or to the United States, should have been conquered by the arms of either from the other, before the arrival of the said provisional articles in America, it is agreed that the same shall be restored without difficulty and without requiring any compensation.

ARTICLE X

The solemn ratifications of the present treaty, expedited in good and due form, shall be exchanged between the contracting parties in the space of six months, or sooner if possible, to be computed from the day of the signature of the present treaty.

In witness whereof, we, the undersigned, their ministers plenipotentiary, have in their name, and in virtue of our full powers, signed with our hands the present definitive treaty, and caused the seals of our arms to be affixed thereto.

Done at Paris, this third day of September, in the year of our Lord one thousand seven hundred and eighty-three.

DAVID HARTLEY (L. S.)

JOHN ADAMS   (L. S.)

B. FRANKLIN   (L. S.)

JOHN JAY   (L. S.)

—————————— Note No. IV. Page 596. ——————————

[453] The celebrated Mr. Sheridan observed in a speech on the ravages in India, under the government of Mr. Hastings:

Had a stranger at this time gone into the kingdom of Oude, ignorant of what had happened since the death of Sujah Dowla, that man, who with a savage heart had still great lines of character, and who, with all his ferocity in war, had with a cultivating hand preserved to his country the riches which it derived from benignant skies, and a prolific soil; if this stranger, ignorant of all that had happened in the short interval, and observing the wide and general devastation, and all the horrors of the scene; vegetation burnt up and extinguished; villages depopulated and in ruin: temples unroofed and perishing; reservoirs broken down and dry; he would naturally inquire, What war has thus laid waste the fertile fields of this once beautiful and opulent country? What civil dissensions have happened, thus to tear asunder and separate the happy societies that once possessed those villages? What disputed succession? What religious rage has with unholy violence demolished those temples, and disturbed fervent but unobtruding piety in the exercise of its duties? What merciless enemy has thus spread the horrors of fire and sword? What severe visitation of Providence has thus dried up the fountains, and taken every vestige of verdure from the earth? Or rather, What monsters have stalked over the country, tainting and poisoning with pestiferous breath, what the voracious appetite could not devour? To such questions what must be the answers? No wars have ravaged these lands, and depopulated these villages; no civil discords have been felt; no disputed succession; no religious rage; no merciless enemy; no affliction of Providence, which, while it scourged for the moment, cut off the sources of resuscitation; no voracious and poisoning monsters; no: all this has been accomplished by the friendship, generosity, [454] and kindness of the English nation; they have embraced us with their protecting arms, and lo! these are the fruits of their alliance.

Note No. V. Page 637.

General Washington's farewel orders to the army of the United States.

Rocky Hill, near Princeton, Nov. 2, 1783

The United States in congress assembled, after giving the most honorable testimony to the merits of the federal armies, and presenting them with the thanks of their country, for their long, eminent, and faithful services, having thought proper, by their proclamation, bearing date the 18th of October last, to discharge such parts of the troops as were engaged for the war, and to permit the officers on furlough to retire from service, from and after tomorrow, which proclamation having been communicated in the public papers, for the information and government of all concerned; it only remains for the commander in chief to address himself once more, and that for the last time, to the armies of the United States, (however widely dispersed individuals who composed them, may be,) and to bid them an affectionate, a long farewel.

But before the commander in chief takes his final leave of those he holds most dear, he wishes to indulge himself a few moments in calling to mind a slight review of the past; he will then take the liberty of exploring with his military friends, their future prospects; of advising the general conduct which in his opinion ought to be pursued; and he will conclude the address, by expressing the obligations he feels himself under for the spirited and able assistance he has experienced from them in the performance of an arduous office.

[455] A contemplation of the complete attainment (at a period earlier than could have been expected) of the object for which we contended, against so formidable a power, cannot but inspire us with astonishment and gratitude. The disadvantageous circumstances on our part, under which the war was undertaken, can never be forgotten. The singular interpositions of Providence in our feeble condition, were such as could scarcely escape the attention of the most unobserving; while the unparalleled perseverance of the armies of the United States, through almost every possible suffering and discouragement, for the space of eight long years, was little short of a standing miracle.

It is not the meaning, nor within the compass of this address, to detail the hardships peculiarly incident to our service, or to describe the distresses which in several instances have resulted from the extremes of hunger and nakedness, combined with the rigours of an inclement season; nor is it necessary to dwell on the dark side of our past affairs. Every American officer and soldier must now console himself for any unpleasant circumstances which may have occurred, by a recollection of the uncommon scenes in which he has been called to act no inglorious part, and the astonishing events of which he has been a witness; events which have seldom, if ever before, taken place on the stage of human action, nor can they possibly ever happen again. For who has before seen a disciplined army formed at once, from such raw materials? Who that was not a witness could imagine that the most violent local prejudices would cease so soon, and that men who came from the different parts of the continent, strongly disposed by the habits of education to despise and quarrel with each other, would immediately become but one patriotic band of brothers? Or who that was not on the spot, can trace the steps by which such a wonderful revolution has been effected, and such a glorious period put to all our warlike toils?

[456] It is universally acknowledged, that the enlarged prospects of happiness opened by the confirmation of our independence and sovereignty, almost exceed the power of description; and shall not the brave men who have contributed so essentially to these inestimable acquisitions, retiring victorious from the field of war to the field of agriculture, participate in all the blessings which have been obtained? In such a republic, who will exclude them from the rights of citizens, and the fruits of their labors? In such a country so happily circumstanced, the pursuits of commerce and the cultivation of the soil, will unfold to industry the certain road to competence. To those hardy soldiers who are actuated by the spirit of adventure, the fisheries will afford ample and profitable employment; and the extensive and fertile regions of the west will yield a most happy asylum to those, who, fond of domestic enjoyment, are seeking for personal independence. Nor is it possible to conceive, that any one of the United States will prefer a national bankruptcy, and the dissolution of the union, to a compliance with the requisitions of congress, and the payment of its just debts, so that the officers and soldiers may expect considerable assistance in recommencing their civil occupations, from the sums due to them from the public, which must and will most inevitably be paid.

In order to effect this desirable purpose, and to remove the prejudices which may have taken possession of the minds of any of the good people of the States, it is earnestly recommended to all the troops, that, with strong attachments to the union, they should carry with them into civil society the most conciliatory dispositions; and that they should prove themselves not less virtuous and useful as citizens, than they have been persevering and victorious as soldiers. What though there should be some envious individuals, who are unwilling to pay the debt the public has contracted, or to yield the tribute due to merit; yet let such unworthy treatment produce no invective, or any instance of intemperate conduct; let it [457] be remembered that the unbiassed voice of the free citizens of the United States has promised the just rewards, and given the merited applause. Let it be known and remembered, that the reputation of the federal armies is established beyond the reach of malevolence; and let a consciousness of their achievements and fame still excite the men who composed them to honorable actions, under the persuasion, that the private virtues of economy, prudence, and industry, will not be less amiable in civil life, than the more splendid qualities of valour, perseverance and enterprise were in the field; every one may rest assured, that much, very much, of the future happiness of the officers and men, will depend upon the wise and manly conduct which shall be adopted by them, when they are mingled with the great body of the community. And although the general has so frequently given it as his opinion, in the most public and explicit manner, that unless the principles of the federal government were properly supported, and the power of the union increased, the honor, dignity, and justice of the nation would be lost forever; yet he cannot help repeating on this occasion, so interesting a sentiment, and leaving it as his last injunction to every officer, and every soldier, who may view the subject in the same serious point of light, to add his best endeavours to those of his worthy fellow citizens, towards effecting those great and valuable purposes, on which our very existence as a nation so materially depends.

The commander in chief conceives little is now wanting to enable the soldier to change the military character into that of a citizen, but that steady and decent tenor of behaviour which has generally distinguished not only the army under his immediate command, but the different detachments and separate armies, through the course of the war. From their good sense and prudence, he anticipated the happiest consequences; and while he congratulates them on the glorious occasion, which renders [458] their services in the field no longer necessary, he wishes to express the strong obligations he feels himself under for the assistance he has received from every class, and in every instance. He presents his thanks, in the most serious and affectionate manner, to the general officers, as well for their counsel on many interesting occasions, as for their ardor in promoting the success of the plans he had adopted; to the commandants of regiments and corps, and to the officers, for their zeal and attention in carrying his orders promptly into execution; to the staff, for their alacrity and exactness in performing the duties of their several departments; and to the non-commissioned officers and private soldiers, for their extraordinary patience in suffering, as well as in their invincible fortitude in action. To various branches of the army, the general takes this last and solemn opportunity of professing his inviolable attachment and friendship. He wishes more than bare professions were in his power, that he was really able to be useful to them all in future life. He flatters himself, however, they will do him the justice to believe, that whatever could with propriety be attempted by him, has been done. And, being now to conclude these his last public orders, to take his ultimate leave in a short time of the military character, and to bid a final adieu to the armies he has so long had the honor to command, he can only again offer in their behalf his recommendations to their grateful country, and his prayers to the God of armies. May ample justice be done them here, and may the choicest of Heaven's favors, both here and hereafter, attend those who, under the divine auspices, have secured innumerable blessings for others! With these wishes, and this benediction, the commander in chief is about to retire from service; the curtain of separation will soon be drawn, and the military scene to him will be closed forever.

EDWARD HAND, *Adjutant General*

INDEX.

A.

H.

S.

T.

Y.

INDEX

The text of this book was set in a type called Caslon 540.
It is a modern design based on the famous fonts that
William Caslon cut more than two hundred years ago.
William Caslon, born in 1692 at Cradley in Worchester,
turned to letter-founding after being apprenticed to an engraver
of ornamental gunlocks and barrels. There was nothing
startlingly new about his designs; he took as his models
the best Dutch types of the seventeenth century, particularly
those of Van Dijck. The fact that he started a great era of
British typography was due less to his originality than to his
competence and ability at engraving and casting types at a
time when letter-founding in England was at a very low ebb.

*This book is printed on paper that is acid-free and meets
the requirements of the American National Standard
for Permanence of Paper for
Printed Library Materials, Z39.84, 1984* ∞

Book design by Herman Strohbach, New York, New York
Editorial services by Harkavy Publishing Service, New York, New york
Typography by Monotype Composition Company, Baltimore, Maryland
Printed and bound by Edwards Brothers, Inc., Ann Arbor, Michigan